T0329779

From Cotton Mill to Business Empire

THE EMERGENCE OF

REGIONAL ENTERPRISES IN

MODERN CHINA

Harvard East Asian Monographs 229

From Cotton Mill to Business Empire

THE EMERGENCE OF

REGIONAL ENTERPRISES IN

MODERN CHINA

Elisabeth Köll

Published by the Harvard University Asia Center
Distributed by Harvard University Press
Cambridge (Massachusetts) and London, 2003

Printed in the United States of America

The Harvard University Asia Center publishes a monograph series and, in coordination with the Fairbank Center for East Asian Research, the Korea Institute, the Reischauer Institute of Japanese Studies, and other faculties and institutes, administers research projects designed to further scholarly understanding of China, Japan, Vietnam, Korea, and other Asian countries. The Center also sponsors projects addressing multidisciplinary and regional issues in Asia.

Library of Congress Cataloging-in-Publication Data

Köll, Elisabeth, 1965–
From cotton mill to business empire : the emergence of regional enterprises in modern China / Elisabeth Köll.
    p. cm. -- (Harvard East Asian monographs ; 229)
Includes bibliographical references and index.
    ISBN 0-674-01394-8 (cloth edition : alk. paper)
1. Da sheng sha chang (China)--History. 2. Textile industry--China--Jiangsu Sheng--History. 3. Business enterprises--China--Jiangsu Sheng--History. 4. Industries--China--Jiangsu Sheng--History. 5. Corporations--China--Jiangsu Sheng--History. 6. Businesspeople--China--Jiangsu Sheng--History. 7. Jiangsu Sheng (China)--Economic conditions. I. Title. II. Series.
    HD9866.C54 D335 2004
    338.0951 22--dc21   2003018588

Index by the author

⊗ Printed on acid-free paper

Last figure below indicates year of this printing
13 12 11 10 09 08 07 06 05 04 03

For my parents

Ernestine and Franz Köll

Acknowledgments

This book could not have been written without the tremendous support of my teacher and advisor at Oxford, David Faure. I am deeply grateful for the time and constant intellectual stimulation he contributed to this project. Equally, I thank him for not losing patience with my Germanic prose as a beginning graduate student; I hope that this aspect of my work has improved. Michael Quirin, Regine Mathias, and Horst Albach provided role models as excellent scholars and teachers during my undergraduate years in Bonn.

Many librarians, libraries, and academic institutions have supplied the research material this book is based on. Among them I particularly thank David Helliwell and the staff at the Bodleian Library, Oxford; Tony Hyder and the staff at the Chinese Studies Institute Library, Oxford; the staff at the Nantong Municipal Archives; Liang Zhan, Zhang Guolin, and Liu Daorong at the Nantong Library; Liu Weidong at the Nantong Textile Museum; Lu Ronghua for his introduction to the Nantong Museum; the Shanghai Municipal Archives; Professor Huang Hanmin and the staff at the Business History Research Center, Shanghai Academy of Social Sciences; and Professor Wei Xiumei and the library of the Institute of Modern History, Academia Sinica, Taibei.

A long list of teachers, colleagues, and friends have provided helpful comments on this project in its various stages, among them Bian Linan, Raj Brown, David Buck, Chan Kai Yiu, Wellington Chan, Choi Chi-Cheung, Maybo Ching, Parks Coble, Du Xuncheng, Glen Dudbridge, Hamashita Takeshi, Christian Henriot, Paul Howard, Kwan Man Bun, Lai Chi-Kong, Ma Min, Andrea McElderry, Mori Tokihiku, Che Chang Ooh, Thomas Rawski, Kristin Stapleton, Xiong Yuezhi, Yang Liqiang, and Yasutomi Ayumu; I am grateful to them all. Raj Brown, Christian Henriot, Andrea

McElderry, Parks Coble, and an anonymous reviewer for the Harvard East Asian monograph series provided detailed and valuable suggestions for the manuscript revision. My colleagues in the Department of History at Case Western Reserve University have been incredibly supportive in various ways; among them, Alan Rocke deserves special thanks as mentor, friend, and tireless proofreader. Parts of Chapter 4 were previously published in David Faure and Tao Tao Liu, *Town and Country in China: Identity and Perception*, 2002, Palgrave Publishers, reproduced with permission of Palgrave Macmillan, for which I am grateful.

I thank the people of Nantong for their friendliness and hospitality, especially Lu Ronghua and his family for adopting me during my year in Nantong, Zhang Guolin and Liang Zhan for helping me with the reading of difficult handwriting, Wu Ying for arranging interviews, and Liu Ying and her family for moral support. In Shanghai I thank Professor Xiong Yuezhi for introducing me to other scholars and Zhao Nianguo and Li Yihai for looking after me and discouraging me from acquiring a Subei accent. I am grateful to Professor Lü Fangshang for his introduction to sources and interview partners at the Institute of Modern History, Academia Sinica.

My studies were generously financed through a Rhodes scholarship at Oxford and, with special thanks to Sir Anthony Kenny, a generous travel grant from the Rhodes trust for my year in Nantong. I have been further assisted by travel subsidies from the Davis Fund and St. Antony's College. A pre-doctoral fellowship from the Chiang Ching-Kuo Foundation supported me during my last year in Oxford. Two generous junior faculty grants from Case Western Reserve University allowed me to complete my field research in China.

I especially thank my closest *tongxue*, Cheung Sui-wai, for his friendship and moral support and Puk Wing-kin for his optimism and for helping me with software problems. Aniza Kraus at Case Western Reserve University displayed patience and technical expertise in touching up the illustrations and photographs. Thanks also go to Ulrike and Christian Bauch, Elizabeth Butland, Alex Chan and his family, Claire Gordon, Kimura Takeko, the Leifer family, Antonia Stiawa, and Erna Winter for the help each of them gave to this project.

Finally, the biggest thanks go to my parents, Franz and Ernestine Köll, who were willing to let me go at an early age and never complained about having to understand their daughter's life in the context of three different continents. Most important of all, they were always confident that some day this project would come to its fruition. To their love, genuine interest, and untiring support this book is dedicated.

E. K.

Contents

Maps, Figures, and Tables

Tables

From Cotton Mill to Business Empire

THE EMERGENCE OF

REGIONAL ENTERPRISES IN

MODERN CHINA

Introduction

Watching the development of business institutions and economic structures in contemporary China has never been more fascinating. The slow demise of state-owned enterprises, the transformation of collectives into shareholding cooperatives, and the creation of investment opportunities through stock markets document China's movement from a socialist state-controlled economy toward a socialist market economy. The drastic changes inaugurated by the economic reforms of the early 1980s have prompted economists, historians, political scientists, sociologists, and anthropologists to analyze and reevaluate these new business institutions and structures and their economic, social, political, and cultural impact. News media and scholarly and popular publications grapple with defining the resulting structural changes and understanding the implications for business of "socialism with Chinese characteristics." Indeed, the problems are not small.

The decentralization of economic management, increased local and regional political autonomy, and the introduction of new enterprise structures based on the concepts of shareholding or limited liability have created high expectations on all sides. Even as these new businesses are released from state control and the Chinese government transfers financial and social responsibilities to the enterprise managers, assumptions about greater transparency, accountability, and profitability have captured the imagination of managers and business investors, particularly in the foreign business community.

The problem, however, is that the corporate structures of these new enterprises do not fit Western legal and managerial definitions. The transformation of a collective enterprise into a shareholding company does not, for example, necessarily involve the transfer of property rights from the original owner, the collective; this leaves the financial and managerial control of the enterprise untouched. At the same time, personal and kinship networks in Chinese business continue to play significant roles in the control and ownership of these new enterprises. Given the different concepts, complex definitions, and flexible interpretations of property rights, corporate structures, and business practices in contemporary China, we need to understand their historical, institutional, and cultural roots, particularly if we wish to compare them with Western business models. And this is where business history can be of help.

"Business historians do business history because they are not shrewd enough to do business." This statement by a former teacher of mine contains a certain element of truth, but it was intended to encourage us to be shrewd and critical and to avoid writing conventional business history. Chinese business history has traditionally been concerned with the relationship between state and merchants, entrepreneurial personalities, or the sociocultural context of doing business in a non-Western environment. However, as interest in late imperial and Republican China and its economic development has grown, the business institution has become a subject for research. Even the most basic and thus the most complex questions concerning the institutional nature of the Chinese business enterprises that emerged in the late nineteenth century still need adequate answers: What is the best definition of "the firm" in the Chinese context? How can the hierarchical, managerial, and financial aspects of the Chinese business enterprise best be characterized? What institutional tools were used to control the functional units of the firm? Is the term *corporation* a valid institutional definition for Chinese businesses?

In the Western historical context, we often identify the American or European corporation around 1900 as the epitome of the modern business firm. Of course, Chinese business associations based on corporate principles are an invention neither of the West nor of the Republican period; organizationally and structurally they are rooted in the lineage trusts of the Ming and Qing dynasties. However, interpreting modern corporate enterprises in early twentieth-century China as a continuation of these lineage trusts would be as simplistic and deceptive as considering the imperial workshops the prototype of modern factories in China.

It is useful, even necessary, for historians of China to borrow Western theoretical models of the firm for comparison and provisional definitions.

However, we also need to develop a distinctive theoretical concept of the Chinese firm based on documentation produced by Chinese enterprises. In order to explore the application and transformation of this concept over time, it is essential to expand the research focus from external factors such as government policies, local politics, or family networks to internal aspects such as control and ownership, accounting, and management. That is a principal goal of this book.

This study examines the emergence of large industrial companies founded in late nineteenth-century China in the form of regional enterprises that grew into substantial local business empires during the Republican period. I illustrate the amalgamation of different institutional traditions—"modern" corporate structures based on Western standards with "traditional" structures rooted in Chinese family business—in the emergence of the modern Chinese firm by analyzing the Dasheng textile mills. Dasheng was the first successful private Chinese-owned business conglomerate. It was founded by the famous scholar-official Zhang Jian (1853–1926) near Nantong city in 1895, flourished as a stockholding company with limited liability in the early Republican period, and continues to exist today as a state-owned enterprise.

Neither based solely on the principles of the Chinese family firm nor organized as a full-fledged corporation, Dasheng, with its strong economic and social ties to the region, provides an excellent focus for exploring important issues in modern Chinese history such as the legal and managerial evolution of the firm, the introduction and management of industrial work, and the integration and interdependency of local, national, and international markets in Republican China. As a business institution, Dasheng was characterized by a confusion of private and public in terms of assets and managerial decisions; this resulted in a number of complications and financial difficulties for the enterprise. In the mid-1920s, the financial situation had become so disastrous that creditor banks had to intervene and make what turned out to be permanent changes in the managerial and financial set-up of the company. A detailed study of Dasheng allows us therefore to explore the eventful history of incorporation and management in China as it unfolded in large-scale industrial ventures from the late nineteenth to the mid-twentieth century.

The focus on control and accountability in the management of the enterprise is one important theme in this book, and it shapes my analysis of Dasheng as a business institution. A second leitmotiv is institutional transfer, that is, the interpretation, adaptation, and application of Western corporate structures to existing Chinese business institutions and environment. Although I stress the importance of institutional business analysis based on enterprise-related archival material, I do not neglect the impact of the general environment on the development of business enterprises. No institutional analysis of an enterprise with such complex and close ties to a region could make a compelling argument about the nature and operations of that enterprise without reference to the wider social, economic, political, and cultural conditions at the local as well as the national level. Consequently, this study combines institutional business history and social history. By merging these two approaches and embedding the analysis in the context of China's historical development between the 1890s and the early 1950s, I seek to present a comprehensive narrative and highlight changes in China's political, legal, economic, and social framework and their profound impact on the emergence and shaping of modern business institutions.

Part I begins with a theoretical discussion and comparison of the development of the concept of the corporation and business enterprise in China and the West. As we shall see, the founding of the Dasheng cotton mill as a regional enterprise in northern Jiangsu province after 1895 resulted from the implementation of national policies in a particular regional environment favorable to cotton cultivation and textile production. The general economic backwardness and agricultural orientation of the area presented specific advantages as well as disadvantages for the introduction of industrialization in the form of large cotton mills.

Part II deals with the physical entities of the business institution—the factories in the countryside north of Shanghai. It describes the founding of the Dasheng No. 1 mill, the industrial core of the Dasheng business complex, and introduces its prominent founder, Zhang Jian. As the initial support of senior government officials quickly faded, Zhang Jian came to depend mainly on support from local businessmen and dignitaries since he was an outsider to the local society and business community in Nantong. This fact sheds light on the particular nature of managerial and financial control as well as ownership of this enterprise.

In addition, I examine the Dasheng cotton mills as a concrete operation in its local context. This analysis of the factory compound, the shop floor, and the workforce illustrates the organization and hierarchy of work within the factory and the local origins of skilled and unskilled workers, united under Zhang Jian's innovative factory discipline. Since the Dasheng cotton mills introduced factory work to the Nantong area, I also explore the potential economic and social transformation of the surrounding villages and their inhabitants. Curiously, the introduction of factory work to the area was not accompanied by the simultaneous emergence of a working class.

In Part III, I turn to the hierarchical and financial aspects of the business institution by discussing Dasheng's corporate structure, its accounting system, legal status, management, and shareholding structure. This discussion also explores the role of members of the Zhang family. I argue that Zhang Jian was able to exercise complete control over Dasheng through the development of institutional tools, specifically the Shanghai accounts office, which became a centralized instrument for handling his private and business affairs.

This leads to the problem of why Dasheng almost went bankrupt in the early 1920s and had to be rescued by a consortium of Shanghai banks. I approach this problem through a detailed analysis of the enterprise's overall financial performance, based on figures extracted from annual reports and company documents. The numerical analysis provides an explanation of Dasheng's planning and investment strategies and their direction by personal, shareholder, and bank interests. I argue that it was not so much increasing costs but increasing indebtedness together with financial transfers between business and personal accounts and an unwise expansion that led to insolvency in 1922.

Part IV treats the enterprise's relation with the region and its role in the area's development. I examine, in particular, the land reclamation companies and their impact on agriculture, economy, and society. In Nantong city itself, social division instead of community building characterized the relationship between workers in the mills and the townspeople. Since the Dasheng enterprise was (and still is) identified with Nantong city and its development in the early twentieth century, I question to what extent "modernization" propagated by Zhang Jian really served the community's interest and to what extent it was a public relations strategy serving other aims.

Finally, I examine what a case study of Dasheng's development can tell us about the success of modern enterprises in their interactions with the Republican state and the challenges to its political system. The company's experiences after the founder's death and during the Japanese occupation and war say much about the viability of Chinese businesses as corporate entities.

As a private enterprise established by a first-generation entrepreneur, Dasheng's business development was compromised by unwise political alliances, succession problems, and the economic pressures of changing markets. Like most enterprises at the time, Dasheng was unable to escape the impact of the various political crises that beset Republican China, but its structural flexibility allowed it—and the Zhang family— to survive.

Like other recent studies of Republican history, this book also demonstrates that the institutional and social framework of the modern Chinese business firm exhibits historical continuities as well as discontinuities. Functions of the firm that we might identify as "modern" were supported by "traditional" formations that survived until the late 1940s. On a larger historical scale, the success and failure of regional enterprises like Dasheng illustrate the opportunities created by economic, political, and social reforms in the early twentieth century as well as the shortcomings of institutional structures in business, as they were exacerbated by various economic and political crises, locally and nationally, in Republican China.

Nevertheless, the trajectory of regional enterprises bridges the 1949 divide. In the context of China's present economic changes, this study examines Dasheng's contribution to the region's local development, which has been glorified in the official media and in the literature of the 1980s and 1990s. Regional enterprises have been resurrected in the new form of township-village enterprises during the economic reforms of the past two decades, and I seek to offer a fresh perspective on an important business institution that has historical as well as contemporary significance. My intent is to offer not so much a primer on starting a business in China as insights into how business was conducted in the past and how this understanding might be applied to contemporary business issues.

Note on Archival Sources

Like many historians, I have benefited from the opening of local archives and the easier access to research material in China in the past decade. Until recently the only primary sources available were Zhang Jian's personal writings, published posthumously by his son in Shanghai in 1931 and subsequently reprinted in Taiwan in 1980.[1] I was fortunate to have been able to work for long stretches of time in the Nantong Municipal Archives, and I hope that this book encourages other scholars interested in business, social, and economic history to pursue work in this local archive. Only a tiny fraction of the vast material concerning the history of Dasheng, Nantong city, and Nantong county has been published.[2] So far one compilation of annual company reports on the Dasheng No. 1, No. 2, No. 3, and No. 8 spinning mills between 1900 and 1926 has been published as well as a reprint of the No. 1 mill's shareholder reports, which in particular document activities during the 1930s and 1940s.[3]

In addition to working with archival documents such as account books, business and private correspondence, share certificates, or board meeting reports from the Nantong Municipal Archives, I also used material from the Nantong Municipal Library, the Nantong Textile Museum, and the Nantong Museum. The Nantong Municipal Library houses documents relevant to the area's local history such as gazetteers, newspapers from the Republican period, and private publications; the Nantong Textile Museum's collection includes archival documents such as passbooks for Dasheng shares, rent books for company housing, and material related to Zhang Jian's textile school. The material held in the local Nantong Museum found its way there almost by accident. Much of it appears to have been handed over to the museum by private donors if no other cultural institution laid a claim to it.[4] For example, among its interesting collection the copy books of the correspondence of Wu Jichen (1873–1935), the head of the Shanghai accounts office, present a unique source of information on Dasheng's internal management.[5]

I also benefited from interviews with the granddaughter of Zhang Jian, Mrs. Zhang Rouwu (1919–). These interviews were useful in fleshing out the general picture of Zhang Jian's personality and his family. Interviews with former workers or descendants of Zhang Jian's former associates provided information on the business aspects of Dasheng. Although members of the Zhang family remain prominent in Nantong politics and society, Zhang Jian's private documents are no longer in the possession of his descendants. Together with other personal objects and property, they were transferred to government institutions in Nantong before and during the Cultural Revolution when Zhang Jian was branded as capitalist and exploiter of the very people he is now said to have launched on the path to regional economic and social modernization in the twentieth century.

PART I

Setting the Scene

CHAPTER I

Regional Enterprise and the Corporation

as a Concept

Regional Enterprise Past and Present

In *Midnight* (*Ziye*), Mao Dun's famous novel about Shanghai in the 1930s, the industrialist Wu Sunfu ponders the future expansion of his business portfolio. A plan of great vision develops in his mind as he stares at a sheet of paper,

which listed only three items: first, capital of five million yuan, one third to be paid up; second, a plan for several new enterprises—textile industry, long-distance buses, mining, chemical industry; third, a relief package for several of his already existing enterprises—a silk filature, a silk-weaving factory, a steamship company etc. . . . Sun Wufu took the outline, and while looking at it again, a great, much desired scenario arose straight from the sheet of paper: tall chimneys like a forest, belching black smoke; steamships braving the wind and the waves; buses flying across the open country. He couldn't help smiling. However, his ideas were not coming out of nothing. With his rich practical experience he knew that it did not matter that his enterprises would start small, but that the scale in his plans had to be big. When he had been enthusiastic about developing his native place three to four years ago, he had also followed this strategy. At that time he had started with a power station as a base in order to build up his "[personal] empire of Shuangqiao" from there.[1]

Although a work of fiction, Mao Dun's novel accurately portrays a new type of businessman that was emerging at the time. Wu Sunfu is representative of the ambitious Chinese businessmen who, in the early twentieth century, set up enterprises in the hinterlands of large cities and created a sphere of economic and political power in their former native places while controlling these domains from their headquarters in the big financial and commercial centers. Writers like Mao Dun saw these businessmen as urban capitalists beset by foreign economic aggression, the forces of tradition, labor disputes, and political struggles.[2] In *Midnight*, Wu Sunfu owns cotton mills and speculates on the stock market in Shanghai; stewards manage his enterprises in the countryside. As substantial business ventures with a significant amount of control over local society, these enterprises developed into personal domains that buttressed the influence of the owner, his family, and his networks in his native place. Dominating the development of local economy and society, they became regional enterprises. Like most businesses in China, regional enterprises suffered from the war that began in 1937 and the transition to socialism in 1949. Those that survived the war with Japan and the civil war vanished in the 1950s when collectivization and state ownership led to the death of private enterprises in China.

Nevertheless, after fifty years under a socialist economy, China is again experiencing the renaissance of regional enterprises, now under collective management. Since the 1980s China's official media have celebrated dynamic entrepreneurs and their regional businesses in the form of township-village enterprises as a new alternative that is creating economic growth and thus promoting social stability in areas outside the main industrial centers. A passage from a local newspaper in northern Jiangsu province in 1994, quoting the director of the Nantong Yintie Hongfang Tinplate Factory, is typical:

Since the late 1980s, my factory's output has more than quadrupled. . . . Once the enterprise was thriving and developing and I had money in my hands, the first thing I did for my hometown was to set up a school and to promote education.

I took more than 300,000 yuan to set up in the village a kindergarten, an all-day primary school, and a lower middle school. I subsidize the teachers to the amount of 10 yuan per month for their living expenses. Each year I pay for a trip for them, and I offer good awards to the three students with the best outside exam results and their supervising teachers.

It has always been my long-cherished wish to bring some benefits to my elders and my people and to do something practical for my hometown! For the past seven years, each year I set aside a fixed proportion of my funds from the factory to build bridges, to repair roads, and to acquire water pumps, tractors, and other agricultural machinery. . . . In 1993 my factory donated one million yuan to the village. . . . Last year I contributed more than 500,000 yuan to provide running water for over 1,150 farm households in the village. In addition, I also set up a cooperative medical station. To date, the funds given by my factory for benefiting my elders and my people have already amounted to more than four million yuan.[3]

In describing this enterprise's charitable contributions to its hometown's education, welfare, and infrastructure, like the industrialists of the 1930s, the director of the tinplate factory, Mr. Shen Binyi, turned the community he was benefiting into a personal domain. Not only did his enterprise generate much needed employment and tax income for the government, but its profits contributed to public education, health care, and other social benefits. The enterprise has assumed community responsibilities that formerly belonged to the state and its most powerful local organ in Chinese society, the work unit (*danwei*), which, before its weakening in the market reforms, managed every aspect of personal and communal welfare.

The Nantong Yintie Hongfang Tinplate Factory is a typical example of the growth of enterprise involvement in local government responsibilities. Regional enterprises all over the country have built schools and housing for senior citizens, installed electricity, dug wells, and raised money for impoverished villages and flood victims. Their directors, praised as successful regional party officials or exemplary model workers (*laodong mofan*), occupy vital positions in community political, economic, and cultural organizations.[4] As used in this book, *regional* refers to much more than just a rural industrial enterprise: a regional enterprise is a large-scale industrial operation in a rural environment with considerable economic and social impact on at least one or more counties. Whereas the direct economic impact of an industrial enterprise on any rural setting would be expected, its social and, to a certain extent, cultural impact depends on the leadership of the enterprise's director and his personal concept and application of local development and control. This rather broad definition allows us to look for historical precedents.

At the beginning of the twentieth century the Dasheng No. 1 Cotton Mill, established in the countryside near Nantong city, was very similar to the tinplate factory of the 1990s. Dasheng's founder, Zhang Jian, a distinguished scholar-official, set up the factory in 1895 under official patronage. Although the mill started operations as a government-sponsored enterprise, Zhang Jian soon assumed total control of the firm. By founding schools, donating to charity, and making improvements in Nantong's infrastructure, Zhang Jian became a local magnate. In short, the Dasheng cotton mills became a regional enterprise and the mainstay of Nantong's economic, social, and cultural development.

The Nantong region, northwest of Shanghai, borders the Yangzi River to the south and the East China Sea to the east (see Map 1). Historically,

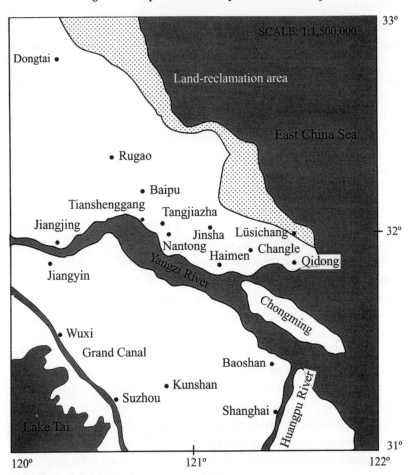

Map 1 The Nantong area in the early twentieth century

this region in central Jiangsu province was dominated by salt production and the salt trade.[5] As the salt trade declined at the beginning of the twentieth century, Zhang Jian turned the saline soil along the coastline into agricultural land through land-reclamation projects that produced the raw materials for his mills and thus brought industrialization and new agricultural production to the area.

As we shall see in the following chapter, the Nantong region has always been economically and culturally far less developed than the prosperous southern part of Jiangsu province.[6] Suffice it to say here that Nantong was certainly more than just the hinterland of Shanghai, but it never developed into an economic core dominating northern Jiangsu. Therefore, Nantong's growth under Zhang Jian received much public attention in the 1910s and 1920s.[7] An enthusiastic Western visitor to Nantong in 1922 summarized her impressions: "At every turn is to be seen the embodiment of His Excellency Chang Chien [Zhang Jian]. Everything is typical of modern thought and development. . . . Modernity in regard to industrial and economic conditions is his hobby and the scope of it is very wide, it must be admitted."[8] Even the terminology shows the continuity between the 1920s and the 1990s. Observers as well as the founders and directors were concerned with the contribution of the enterprise to the community. That, of course, is what lies behind the idea of combined economic and social "development"—in the Republican period as well as today.

   In China, Dasheng as a modern business operation and Nantong as a leading example of local business initiatives are now frequently cited in the context of contemporary regional developments. The restructuring of central-local relations, in particular fiscal decentralization, has not only intensified provincial regionalism and localism but also provided the necessary political conditions for enterprise reforms.[9] Certainly, for a comparative approach to regional enterprises in the past and present, we need to consider that township-village enterprises (*xiangzhen qiye*) such as the Yintie Hongfang Tinplate Factory are owned by the collective whereas Dasheng was organized as a shareholding company with limited liability.[10] However, despite their differences in terms of property rights, I suggest that we need to view the development of the two forms of enterprises as analogous. As I will show in my comparative analysis in the Conclusion, we should consider them analogous not only in regard to their impact on the regional society and economy but even more so in regard to the development of control without private ownership or majority shareholding. Here, in particular, recent research by political scientists, sociologists, and anthropologists on the evolution and transformation of property rights in Chinese collective enterprises and the role of local government and local elites provides useful comparative perspectives.[11] For example, just as Zhang Jian's influence through personal managerial control dominated Dasheng's fate despite its corporate structure, the creation of new shareholding rights in collective village enterprises has cemented rather than diminished the power of party secretaries over village corporations.[12] In order to understand the challenge of incorporation to Chinese enterprises past and present, we need first to reflect on the interpretation and application of the concept of the corporation in Chinese business history.

The Business Corporation in China

Enterprise, firm, corporation—we tend to think of these institutional entities as products of industrialization and the modern nation-state, which are said to have created the necessary economic, legal, and social frameworks for their formation. China's industrialization started slowly in the mid-nineteenth century. Before the Sino-Japanese war of 1894–95 and the Treaty of Shimonoseki in 1895, foreigners did not have the right to establish factories in China.[13] The state turned a blind eye to foreign-owned enterprises in the treaty ports that were either small in scale or essential, such as shipbuilding and repair, but it drew the line sharply at cotton spinning and weaving.[14]

Within the Chinese sector of the economy, new industries were state-run. Arsenals, shipyards, and mines were first established under government sponsorship.[15] The need for substantial capital for those enterprises and the government's inability to provide it led to new financial and business structures. Government supervision and merchant management (*guandu shangban*) became the form under which official patronage and private investment were joined.[16] In reality, no major factory could have been started in China without the approval and support of a senior official.

As will be discussed in Chapter 2, more active private involvement in industry came after 1895. The consequences were dramatic. Between 1895 and 1911, 35 mining enterprises were founded as private enterprises (*shangban*) in contrast to nine mining enterprises totally owned by the government (*guanban*), ten enterprises under joint government-merchant management (*guanshang heban*), and two government supervision–merchant management operations.[17] As the government withdrew from direct involvement in the enterprises under joint management, new forms of private business operations developed, now supported by structural aspects of incorporation, limited liability, and legal accreditation. The age of the modern firm in China had begun.

But what did these modern firms look like? In a discussion of the emergence of capitalism in China, David Faure has suggested that modern business operations appeared mainly in the form of three categories: as corporate enterprises through privatization of government-sponsored enterprises, as family enterprises, or as regional enterprises.[18] Well-known examples of government-sponsored enterprises are the China Merchants' Steamship Navigation Company, the Hanyeping Company, and the Hengfeng Spinning Mill.[19] According to Chi-kong Lai's research, the China Merchants' Steamship Navigation Company attempted to consolidate government-business cooperation with its new joint-stock structure between 1872 and 1884 but continued under dominant government influence in the following years.[20] When the company was privatized after 1895, the supervising director of the company appointed by the government, Sheng Xuanhuai (1849–1916), became an appointee of the board of directors. As Albert Feuerwerker has shown, it was more a change in name than in fact, since Sheng Xuanhuai, while supervising director, had already acquired a substantial number of shares in the company.[21]

Second, some modern enterprises grew out of family businesses. The organization and cultural aspects of the Chinese family firm have been the focus of many recent discussions.[22] Family businesses have a long tradition in China, but it was only with changes in business law, which came about first in the treaty ports and then by 1904 in the rest of China, that these businesses began to incorporate. Between 1904 and 1908, some 272 companies registered with the Chinese government, over half of them as joint-stock companies with limited liability.[23] For example, the Nanyang Brothers Tobacco Company registered under English law in Hong Kong in 1905 and later as a joint-stock company with the Beijing government under Chinese law in 1918.[24]

Various studies have addressed the subject of how the holding structure of the business company affects its style of management. Sherman Cochran has documented a managerial innovation in the Nanyang Brothers Tobacco Company in the 1919 appointment of a financial controller responsible for reorganizing the company's finances.[25] However, the management of the company, especially its debt and credit arrangements, was always problematic because it was never clear whether the former compradors who managed it acted as agents or principals.

The Yong'an (Wing On) company, founded by the Guo family in Hong Kong in 1907, is another example of a large family business that was registered under English law and continued to exist as a joint-stock limited liability company after 1912. The family exerted strong financial control over the company's shareholding structure.[26] As Kubo Tōru and Wellington Chan have shown, even though the company was public, the Guo brothers achieved almost a complete consolidation between ownership and control through shares held by members of their extended family, overseas and native-place networks, interlocking directorships, and intercompany loans.[27] Even those family firms that registered with the Chinese government (and most family firms in the treaty ports did not) did not necessarily give up their family business structure. However, instead of a stable hierarchy across several generations, the internal power structure in the Chinese family business was, according to Chi-cheung Choi, a simultaneous process of "continuous integration and disintegration."[28]

The third category of modern enterprises, the regional enterprise, began to emerge by the end of the nineteenth century. Originally designed as motors for industrial development, they were formed by privatization of government enterprises. However, even these incorporated enterprises exhibited many of the managerial characteristics of the family business. The subject of this study, the Dasheng enterprise—by which I mean the whole business group including all its subsidiaries and affiliated companies—is an example of such a business. Before 1895 regional enterprises were nonexistent; by the time they came to be promoted, the imperial government had already been weakened by war and social disorder. Although Dasheng was founded as a joint government-private venture, government involvement became negligible after the first five years and finally redundant when the company acquired legal status as a shareholding company in 1907.[29] The government never played a role in the management or ownership of the company, but Zhang Jian and his family did, though without ever turning Dasheng into a family business.

Although we know something about the institutional structure and development of modern enterprises rooted in government-sponsored enterprises and family businesses from various case studies, we still lack an institutional analysis of industrial corporate firms that developed from regional enterprises. Since their evolution into corporate business enterprises occurred in a context of both government sponsorship and family influence, they are crucial for exploring the history of the modern firm, especially the history of incorporation and management, in early twentieth-century China. Therefore, the aim of my book is not just to confirm or to contradict a specific typology of business but, through institutional analysis, to present a new approach to the theoretical interpretation of incorporation and management in Chinese business enterprises in general.

Unfortunately, in contrast to Western business history, where the search for a comprehensive theory of the firm has produced various methodological approaches analyzing the definition, behavior, and functional roles of firms through issues ranging from transactions costs to entrepreneurship, we still lack a specific theory of the firm in China.[30] Even in regard to the identification of structural patterns, opinions differ greatly. As Rajeswary Brown has suggested, Chinese entrepreneurs and their relationship to the state, family structure, management hierarchies and style, accounting methods, and business networks are part of the research necessary to identify the patterns of the Chinese firm.[31] However, before we can concentrate on analyzing the institutional components of the business enterprise in comparative perspective, we need to consider our point of departure.

As the reader may have noticed, in my discussion of the evolution of modern Chinese enterprise I have largely avoided the use of the term *corporation* in favor of locutions such as *corporate structure* and *corporate enterprise*. The choice is deliberate. The debate about the nature of the modern firm in China is often based on the assumption that we are dealing with an entity similar to the large corporation in the West that emerged in the late nineteenth and early twentieth centuries. However, as this book will show, *corporation* may not be the most appropriate term for Chinese businesses in general and regional enterprises such as Dasheng in particular.

According to contemporary Western definitions, the corporation is characterized by perpetual life, limited liability, free transferability of interests, and centralized management. Accountability and the separation of ownership and control are also typical of the corporate structure. As a business entity, Dasheng exhibited characteristics not only of the Western corporation but also of traditional Chinese business. Labeling these "modern" and "traditional," respectively, can be dangerous since these general terms are often pitted against each other as misleading substitutes for Western rationality and Chinese culture. For lack of a better word (and despite its unavoidable disadvantages), however, I will use the term *modern* to indicate the adoption of certain Western corporate characteristics. In contrast, "traditional" business structures refer to those that function without the prescribed characteristics of incorporation such as family firms. For example, by adopting limited liability and a centralized management, Dasheng qualifies as a modern enterprise.

Yet at the same time, the role of Dasheng's founder in the enterprise elevated him above any rule or charter, and the boundaries between his private assets and the corporate assets of the enterprise were never clear. This lack of accountability simultaneously characterizes Dasheng as a traditional business.

In the context of the evolution of business enterprises in China, Dasheng was a modern enterprise because its managerial and financial organization differed greatly from existing structures of family business and government enterprises. But the involvement of the founder's brother and son in the company arguably characterizes Dasheng to some extent as a family business. In this case, however, the family network was so small that the enterprise never developed into a family company. By being aware of the more complex structure of the modern firm in China, we can avoid equating the corporate structure of Western firms with "Western rationality" and the traditional structures of Chinese businesses with "Chinese culture." Both the corporate and the traditional structures are rational and efficient modes of business operation.

Part of the reason that regional enterprises such as Dasheng do not fit readily into the classification "corporate company" is that the history of the Chinese business company as an entity incorporated by law is comparatively short. In a study of pre-industrial capitalism, Fernand Braudel has traced the origins of the firm in the West, or, to be more precise, in the Mediterranean region, to its simplest form as a maritime venture in the twelfth century.[32] His description of the historical development of different types of firms in Europe—joint-liability family firms, limited partnerships, joint-stock companies—spans the seventeenth to the late eighteenth centuries. However, despite a clear pattern of development, Braudel concedes that the majority of firms were still small, often ill-defined, and limited in their business scope well into the nineteenth century.[33] If we search for a similar pattern of development in China, we face one major problem: commerce as a separate subject of law was undeveloped in China until 1904 (see Chapter 3).[34]

To be sure, the lack of a statutory framework for business did not preclude substantial and successful enterprises in China. In the place of statutory law, Chinese merchants sought support in other institutional arrangements such as native-place organizations or guilds.[35] To understand Chinese business, we need to examine all aspects of the institutional framework of business. Our starting point must be that the enterprise worked as one institution in interacting with society, economy, and state and as a combination of separate institutions such as workshops and accounting practices that make up the business operation. To understand the institutional basis of the business, we can turn to Max Weber.

In the seminal *Economy and Society*, Weber described capitalism not as a state of mind but as a way of working in the economy that draws on numerous institutions, such as property or the market, that is to say, on common understandings and practices.[36] Weber defined the firm in the sense of a modern capitalist enterprise in the West as a rational, profit-seeking economic organization with enforced regulations that also exists as a technical entity divided between administrators and workers.[37] Institutions may arise within a culture, or they can move from one culture to another. For example, although business had been conducted for generations under indigenous institutions in China, the decline of the imperial government and the impact of the West in the early years of the twentieth century led to new institutional arrangements for doing business. In any concrete historical case, a combination of different traditions will affect the evolution of the firm as an economic organization. In time, these different traditions might converge, but a case like Dasheng shows that substantial institutional disparities emerged in the process.

In the following chapters, I will use institutional analysis to argue that in the case of Dasheng we are not dealing with a firm but with an economic institution developing toward the model of the firm. In a firm, private and business accounts, household and office, private assets and company assets, have to be separated.[38] However, in the years covered in detail by this book, broadly from the establishment of the Dasheng Cotton Mill in 1895 to the death of the founder in 1926, private and public were not clearly distinguished, despite the outward corporate appearance of the enterprise. The lack of distinction between private and public in terms of assets and structures resulted in a number of complications and financial difficulties for the enterprise and finally required the intervention of creditor banks, which permanently changed the managerial and financial setup of the company. An analysis of the relationships of power, property, and institutionalization in the Dasheng enterprise allows us to explore the history of incorporation and management in China.

In a recent reappraisal of Weber's theory and its applicability to the Chinese economy and its institutions, Du Xuncheng addresses the issue of developing a definition of the Chinese firm. Although his detailed study makes many valuable points, Du's more general assertion that Chinese enterprises can be clearly divided into two categories, family and non-family, seems questionable.[39] Whereas he characterizes the non-family businesses as more "'Westernized" and the family businesses as more "traditional," Du nevertheless admits a certain amount of exchange and interaction between Western and traditional principles in both enterprise types. However, he defines the traditional impact on the firm more in terms of cultural and social interactions, for example, in the emphasis on native-place ties and family networks, but he fails to specify what traditional institutional structures were adopted by Chinese firms.[40]

The research presented in this book shows that corporate firms in early twentieth-century China did adopt traditional *institutional* characteristics of the Chinese family business. In the case of Dasheng, the enterprise utilized an institutional feature of the traditional family business—the central accounts office—to achieve managerial and financial control, and this sustained the implementation of other modern business structures. Thus this study introduces a new category of Chinese business firms.

By now it should be clear that modern Chinese enterprises are not imports from the West with Chinese characteristics. This is not to say that business historians working on China should ignore the work of Western business historians like Sidney Pollard and Alfred Chandler, but we must be aware of its limitations. Pollard, for example, has shown the importance of the rise of the industrial manager, the adaptation of the labor force, and accountancy as a tool of management in the Industrial Revolution.[41] In particular, his discussion of accounting as a method of control provides an important perspective on exploring the development of accounting practices and their institutionalization in modern Chinese enterprises. Chandler's definition of the modern enterprise as containing "many distinct operating units" and "managed by a hierarchy of salaried executives" offers a useful point of comparison for analyzing internal structures.[42] However, in his explanation of the initial appearance and continuing growth of modern corporations in the United States, Chandler does not regard government involvement or the legal framework as essential factors.[43] Therefore, his definitions cannot be automatically applied to the development of modern business in China, where the government wielded a dominant influence on the economic sector through control and patronage.[44]

Apart from dealing with the institutional framework of the Chinese firm as a single business unit, this study also addresses the issue of the emergence of the business group, its organizational structure, and its economic functions. Building on Ronald Coase's seminal article "The Nature of the Firm" in which he explained the existence of firms through their avoidance of transaction costs, Mark Granovetter defines the business group as "a collection of firms bound together in some formal and/or informal ways" and as characterized by an "intermediate level of binding."[45] Chinese business groups have increasingly become the object of research in terms of informal and intermediate ways of binding, since they are often strongly connected with, and even dominated by, family businesses and their networks. In particular, Chinese business groups overseas have recently attracted much attention because of their impressive successes, before the Asian economic crisis, in the local economies of such emerging markets as Indonesia, Malaysia, and Thailand.[46] Patronage, networks, and entrepreneurial culture based on different ethnic backgrounds and cultural adaptation have become popular issues. I will argue, however, that cultural analysis has to be supplemented by institutional analysis in order to explain the rationales and economic motives behind the formation of business groups.

Even with its less than perfect corporate structure, Dasheng grew into a substantial and highly diversified business group whose activities ranged from industrial to agricultural production to financial and transportation services. The analysis in this book of the Dasheng business group is concerned less with its economic performance within the national economy and the international textile industry and market of the early twentieth century and more with formal and informal structures that connected the various parts of this business group.[47] I will argue that transaction costs and their management through the central accounts office played a vital role in the management and control of the Chinese business group. To a great extent, this institution determined the structure of authority and ownership relations within the Dasheng business group and became the central instrument for decision making in terms of transaction costs for a complex, diverse group of subunits. At the same time, the institutional structure of Dasheng as a business group was also characterized by informal ties and networks. In fact, the Dasheng case confirms Granovetter's general assumption that a business group based on a particular firm developed a more vertical configuration that changed over time due to institutional influences both outside and inside the core firm.[48]

In a recent survey article on enterprise history in China, Chi-kong Lai suggests seven complex issues that require more detailed research based on company archives: the relationship between the central office and branches, the emergence of corporate structures, marketing strategies and management styles, consumer styles, legal disputes, Chinese business networks, and industrial technology.[49] This study addresses most of these issues. By focusing on the enterprise's institutional setup, I examine the corporate structure and the specific function of the central office in the enterprise. The issues of management styles, marketing strategies, and industrial technology are of particular interest in the context of Dasheng's factory production and the Chinese cotton textile market. I address legal disputes and business networks in regard to Dasheng's management, accounting, and investment structure. This institutionally oriented approach allows us to at least approximate a new theory of the firm in modern China. However, to show how this approach departs from earlier studies, particularly their highly politicized subtexts, it is necessary for us to take a look at the existing literature on Dasheng and Zhang Jian.

Zhang Jian and Dasheng in Chinese Business History

The treatment of Dasheng and Zhang Jian in the literature offers valuable insights into the relationship between Chinese politics and the historiography of Chinese business. A substantial literature in Chinese, Japanese, and English discusses the achievements of Dasheng and its founder. Most of it adopts a biographical approach, which is understandable considering the fact that Zhang Jian was one of the most colorful and versatile personalities in late nineteenth- and early twentieth-century China. Another reason for the biographical focus is the obsession of conventional Chinese historical studies on business-related topics with the relationship between morality (*daode*) and engaging in a profit-oriented business.[50] Needless to say, although the biographical approach per se is not incompatible with the analysis of business institutions, the biographical material on Zhang Jian has been of only limited use to my specific focus on the institutional aspects of the business.

Biographies of Zhang Jian were published almost immediately after his death and, to a considerable extent, propagated an image much cultivated by

Zhang in his lifetime.[51] Samuel Chu's 1965 study, which followed this tradition, was the first Western-language work to treat Zhang Jian and the Dasheng enterprises.[52] In this solid, detailed study, based mainly on Zhang Jian's collected works, Chu introduced the Dasheng cotton mill and Zhang's other business activities such as land reclamation and water control. The title *Reformer in Modern China* clearly defined Chu's point of view in evaluating Zhang Jian: he considered him "a modernizer [who] did not abandon the traditional values in which he was steeped."[53] Chu also discussed the question whether Zhang Jian succeeded or failed in his aspirations for modernizing China and concluded that the country lacked a sufficient number of persons like Zhang Jian who could have changed China's economic and political predicament in the early twentieth century.[54]

In China the political climate and ideological propaganda culminating in the Cultural Revolution led to Zhang Jian's vilification as a class enemy and capitalist who had ruthlessly exploited his workers.[55] Zhang Jian and his business activities were rehabilitated only in the late 1980s by historians such as Lin Gang, Yan Xuexi, and Wu Yiye.[56] Since state policy at the time promoted local enterprise initiatives, much of this literature praised Zhang Jian for his contributions to China's economic independence.[57] Suddenly, his business success was intrinsically linked to his superior personal morality, and the greedy industrialist of the Cultural Revolution became the benevolent patriot of the reform era.

These changes in interpretation were generally not based on newly discovered research material; rather, they reflect changes in the government's political agenda.[58] A strong ideological slant, often in favor of indigenous efforts for "development," is apparent in recent studies that eulogize Zhang Jian as "the founder of modern Chinese industry."[59] For example, one volume in the biographical fiction series *The Dream of a Powerful Nation (Qiangguo zhi meng)*, which covers patriotic reformers of the late imperial and Republican periods such as Lin Zexu (1785–1850), Kang Youwei (1858–1927), Liang Qichao (1873–1929), and Cai Yuanpei (1868–1940), is devoted to Zhang Jian and his patriotic commitment to national and local economic development.[60] Publications such as the glossy series *Shanghai Tycoon Legends (Shanghai jushang yanyi)* cater to a popular audience and stress the creativity and entrepreneurial spirit of Chinese businessmen like Zhang Jian.[61]

One weakness of the biographical approach is that it does not spell out the obstacles and limitations Zhang Jian had to confront. Zhang Kaiyuan's biography of Zhang Jian stands out as the first attempt to present a realistic picture of the man and his economic and political aspirations.[62] In a bold departure from accepted Chinese historiography, Zhang Kaiyuan concentrates on Zhang Jian's relations with his social environment, since he considers categories such as class or social stratum of little use in analyzing a person in the historical context. By "social environment," he means the various communities to which the individual belongs; he notes that an individual derives a different identity from interacting with each.[63] Thus Zhang stresses Zhang Jian's social and political networks, which were indeed vital to his many activities.

Another relevant study is Qin Shao's analysis of the political culture of Nantong. Shao focuses on Habermas's public sphere concept and argues for its partial emergence in Nantong at the beginning of the early twentieth century, and she makes the point that Zhang Jian was able to dominate and monopolize the community by introducing new Western concepts of time and space, such as modern buildings and Western clocks. Shao argues that Zhang Jian used these new concepts of time and space to construct political power and to promote himself in Nantong.[64]

True though this might be, the attempt to relate Zhang Jian to a new political culture is of limited use for the institutional history of Dasheng as a regional enterprise. Admittedly, Zhang Jian succeeded in giving Nantong a progressive image and thereby increased his control over it, but the centerpiece of his business operations and the financial and strategic anchor of his activities in the community was not public relations but the Dasheng enterprise itself. Moreover, once the enterprise is given pride of place in an analysis, the question of control dissolves because its boundaries were fluid. Qin Shao's study is the first attempt to analyze the myth of Nantong as it was portrayed in the early twentieth century. However, we still need a better understanding of what the commercialized display of power meant to the members of the community and whether they benefited from it.

A recent study by Chang Zonghu is concerned with the question of Nantong's modernization in terms of its social development.[65] Despite the author's serious attempt to address a broad variety of changes in the economic, social, and cultural structure of local society and the region, he is still primarily concerned with evaluating Zhang Jian and his thought. Consequently, in his conclusion, he pursues the unfruitful question of Zhang's success or failure in promoting China's modernization. In the same vein, Japanese scholars like Nakai Hideki have hailed Zhang Jian as one of China's most prominent entrepreneurs and introduced Dasheng rather uncritically as the most striking example of modernization in Chinese business.[66]

The most detailed study in a Western language on Dasheng and its role as a business institution in the development of the local economy is Kathy Le Mons Walker's work on the political economy of cotton textiles in Nantong, which examines the enterprise's reaction to external factors such as prices, trade, and political conditions. Her strong theoretical overtone focuses on the interactions of imperialism, semicolonialism, and local society.[67] In her own words, her book "takes the problem of the formation of particular peasants as its grounding point."[68] By analyzing modern industry and farm production in the region, she shows how Dasheng gained a monopoly over cotton through Zhang Jian's land-reclamation companies, which provided the raw material for his cotton mills to a large extent. Walker argues that because of its monopolistic position, the Dasheng enterprise became an obstacle to sustained economic growth in the area and as a consequence suffered a drastic decline.[69]

This approach has its own problems, however. Although I agree with Walker that the Dasheng mills and their affiliated enterprises did not lead to sustained growth in the area as a whole, I think that holding semicolonial politics and the overdevelopment of social inequities responsible for Nantong's and Dasheng's problems in the 1920s is too simple an explanation. It neglects internal business factors, which would have required a detailed financial and managerial analysis of the enterprise. By focusing on the impact of capitalist industry, which Walker associates with the destabilization, impoverishment, and exploitation of the local peasant society, her interpretation follows a teleological narrative based on the theoretical concept of the "development of underdevelopment," an argument presented by Philip Huang in his study of the rural economy in the Yangzi Delta through the model of involution.[70]

The most comprehensive approach to the institutional structure of the Dasheng enterprise to date is *Dasheng xitong qiyeshi* (Business history of the Dasheng group; 1990), and most of the secondary sources already mentioned rely heavily on its interpretation.[71] The result of a team project under the guidance of the economic historian Xu Dixin from the Beijing Academy of

Social Sciences, this serious and detailed study, based on company records and unpublished source material, was the first to examine Dasheng exclusively as an institutional system (*xitong*).[72] The authors document the growth of the enterprise from its founding in 1895 into a full-fledged business operation that included branch mills, subsidiaries, and numerous affiliated companies. By analyzing in some detail the numerical data in Dasheng's annual reports, the study examines the profitability of the business between 1900 and the 1930s. It argues that Zhang Jian's expansionist strategy centering on the Dasheng cotton mills allowed him to gain control of the region. The authors see the increasing indebtedness of Dasheng and the financial problems of the land reclamation companies and the newly established branch mills as the main reasons for the enterprise's difficulties in the early 1920s.[73]

Dasheng xitong xiyeshi is a landmark in Chinese business studies because of the authors' serious attempt to back their argument with detailed statistical data. My analysis agrees with many of its conclusions, one of which is the possibility of regarding indebtedness as the result of too rapid expansion. However, overextension is one of those concepts that works better in a post-hoc argument than in an analysis of decision making. For example, one could blame any company's failure on overextension and ask what measures had been taken to hedge its risks. In the case of Dasheng, because of the lack of a clear overall hierarchy and because of the free flow of funds between Zhang Jian's private and his business accounts as well as between different parts of the enterprise, I would argue that the *Dasheng xitong qiyeshi* errs by taking too rigid a line in examining the financial structure of the enterprise.

The problem arises, in fact, because the authors of *Dasheng xitong qiyeshi* accepted too readily the structure of the company as it was presented to the shareholders in the company reports. I agree with the authors of this study that power rested with Zhang Jian, but they have failed to notice the complex role of the central accounts office in the operation of the enterprise, which is vital to understanding Dasheng's institutional structure.[74] In addition, the study does not give as much weight to the problem of financing the business as it does to the deposition of funds; that is to say, it fails to appreciate that although capital is employed in the operation of the business, capital itself can only be acquired at a cost and such costs may have much to do with the structure of the business and its management performance. Therefore, I argue that for the purpose of critical analysis we should not take Dasheng's holding structure at face value.

Although this book treats various issues in the field of Chinese business history, it also attempts to address certain themes of significance to the broader context of modern Chinese economic history. By understanding the institutional structure of the business enterprises, we can assess more carefully the issues of "undercapitalization" and excessive profit distributions that have often been held responsible for China's slow industrial development.[75] As I will argue, these factors did not automatically lead to the economic failure of industrial enterprises and lackluster industrial development. In fact, although this book points out the institutional problems of Chinese enterprises and their limited impact on regional economic development, it does not argue against the findings of economic historians like Thomas Rawski or David Faure whose studies have found considerable economic growth in certain areas of rural China during the Republican period.[76] My analysis will also explore how Nantong fit into Skinner's concept of macro-regions and to what extent the region experienced economic integration during the Republican period.[77] In line with economic historians who stress the disparities in the levels of development of China's various geographical regions and interactions between the traditional and modern economic sector,[78] my study confirms that industrial growth in the Nantong area had an impact on rural development but in the end never sustained long-term growth despite the area's vicinity to the economic center of Shanghai.

Finally, I need to make two disclaimers. Even though this study addresses the issue of the economic and social relationship between the Dasheng enterprise and the region, it does not analyze local agricultural data and the development of land and commodity prices to estimate growth rates and production patterns. Similarly, despite the lively debate about the Western concept of capitalism and the arguments for its existence or absence in China, or its applicability or non-applicability to Chinese history and society, I do not approach the Dasheng business group with the intention to prove the success or failure of capitalism in early twentieth-century China.[79] As R. Bin Wong and Kenneth Pomeranz have pointed out, we should not ask why China did not develop capitalism; rather, we should pay attention to the dynamics and limitations of economic expansion in China in comparison with similar developments in Europe.[80] Along this line, I suggest that we investigate the functions of private large-scale business institutions in the economic process and then evaluate particular advantages and disadvantages of their organization; this will allow us to better understand the emergence of Chinese industrial capitalism and modern Chinese business structures after 1900.

CHAPTER 2

National and Regional Context

The era in which the Dasheng cotton mills were established was one of great opportunities as well as great risks for businesses in China. The emergence of industrial enterprises as private business concerns and the new role of private entrepreneurs after 1895 were part of the transformation of Chinese state and society that roiled the last decades of the Qing dynasty. Nor did the enormous challenges the government confronted in the political, social, and economic realms end with the transition from the late imperial state to the Republic in 1911.

Within this transition, industrialization through private initiatives became a focus in the power struggle waged by the central political authority, regional officials and their supporters, and merchants and businessmen. As this chapter will show, the emergence of private industrial enterprises in China in the late 1890s was a slow and difficult process, with considerable financial risks for investors, sponsoring officials, and founding managers. To grasp the development of Dasheng as a business institution in this transition period, we need first to explore why government sponsorship of enterprises declined and private companies began to dominate the industrial sector. In addition, I will briefly discuss the topographical and socioeconomic characteristics of the Nantong area that became significant factors in Dasheng's development as a regional enterprise.

1895—A Fateful Year for Nation and Industry

In 1895, the year that Zhang Jian began to plan a cotton mill in the Nantong area, the county was home to agriculture and a cottage industry of cotton spinning and weaving, but not to any kind of industrial production. In fact, at that time only a handful of Chinese factories under government sponsorship and control struggled for survival. Apart from the imperial workshops supplying the court with silk and porcelain, any private manufacturing of goods, even in sectors with a substantial output, took place in the form of handicraft production. The first large-scale shipyards, mines, and industrial textile mills in China were not privately initiated and organized business operations but part of the government's agenda to strengthen the country's political economy. The number of these operations was extremely small, and their success very limited. This was to change from 1895 on, when the political obstacles to private Chinese entrepreneurship were lifted.

In 1895 the Sino-Japanese war over political influence in Korea ended with China's defeat and the signing of the Treaty of Shimonoseki. Japan imposed, among other conditions, an indemnity of 200 million taels on China, forced the opening of further inland cities to foreign trade, and the concession of Taiwan to Japanese control. Aside from the economic consequences of the treaty conditions for China (the indemnity was more than double the government revenues of about 81 million taels in 1894), the outcome of the Sino-Japanese war also had a severe impact on China's foreign and domestic politics. The so-called scramble for concessions began with Britain, Russia, Japan, Germany, and France demanding leases of Chinese territory. Protest by the upper stratum of Chinese society against the treaty demands finally led to the Hundred Days reform of 1898 initiated by the scholar Kang Youwei. After its failure, events unfolded quickly.[1]

The cumulative effect of the Boxer uprising in 1900, the siege of Beijing, the onerous Boxer indemnity, and demands by foreign powers for legal reforms exerted great political and financial pressure on the Qing government. In response, the Qing government started to pursue institutional and administrative reforms. The late Qing reforms of the 1900s made fundamental changes in the government and society. For example, the abolition of the imperial examination system in 1905 in effect abolished the traditional gentry class, and a promised constitution and the convening of local and provincial assemblies would have completely overhauled the basis of government. Before the reforms were completed, however, the imperial government was overthrown in the Revolution of 1911.[2]

The year 1895 was in many ways crucial for the development of privately owned industrial enterprises and the necessary adjustments of China's socioeconomic framework. Following the end of the Taiping Rebellion in 1864, concerned government officials had initiated the first attempts to build industrial enterprises. In the wake of this major political crisis, the authority of the Qing government weakened substantially, even as the political power and economic influence of governors-general began to grow because of their control of regional armies and the profits from the newly introduced *lijin* or transit tax in the provinces. This regionalization of the political power and economic interests of the highest officials outside the court played a major role during the first phase of industrial enterprises in China in the 1870s and 1880s.[3]

The little industrialization that existed in China before 1895 was focused on heavy industries serving the government's military and defense needs.[4] This was directly linked to the Self-Strengthening movement among concerned officials and their attempt to revive the national economy and military during the Tongzhi Restoration period between 1862 and 1874. When Li Hongzhang (1823–1901) was appointed governor-general of Zhili and imperial commissioner of the northern ports in 1870, he became the most ardent proponent of self-strengthening. His career over the years as a high-ranking official in various parts of the empire had given him much political and even military experience. Together with moderately reform-minded officials such as Zeng Guofan (1811–72) and Zuo Zongtang (1812–85), he demanded that the government strive to improve the military to defend China against the Western powers. These officials were not, however, proponents of an industrial revolution or a modern economy. To the contrary, they wanted to restore the traditional economy in agriculture and commerce; they had no intent of "enhancing the strength and wealth of the country at the cost of its traditional institutions."[5] Hence it is not surprising that the Self-Strengthening movement enjoyed strong support from the court despite the fact that the proposals for change came not from court circles but from officials with close ties to regional bases.[6]

Thus the initial establishment of industrial enterprises has to be interpreted as an attempt to regain military strength and restore national pride without contesting the status quo of government and society rather than as a step toward planned economic development. As part of this policy, any industrial enterprise founded before 1895 required not only the sanction or permission of, but even active supervision and sponsorship from, the government and its agents, the bureaucrats. Notable examples of this promotion of industrial enterprises under government sponsorship in the 1860s and 1870s included the Jiangnan Arsenal (Jiangnan zhizaoju) and the China

Merchants' Steamship Navigation Company (Lunchuan zhaoshangju), both in Shanghai, as well as the Kaiping Coal Mines (Kaiping meikuang) near Tianjin.

All three enterprises evince the immediate goals of the Self-Strengthening movement: the arsenal was to improve China's military strength by manufacturing modern arms, the steamship company was to facilitate grain transport for the government as well as general commercial transport, and the mines were supposed to provide the power for national transportation and limited private consumption.[7] This strategy was certainly not an ambitious program aimed at nationwide industrialization through private initiatives. The close relationship between these officially sponsored enterprises and the government's agenda is revealed by the character *ju* (governmental bureau) in their names, in contrast to *chang* (factory) or *gongsi* (industrial company), which would have indicated a private business concern.

Nevertheless, these new enterprises operated on a much larger scale than traditional manufacturing and transportation businesses and thus faced tremendous and unprecedented financial, managerial, and technological challenges. Especially in the absence of a national capital market, finding the necessary capital for large-scale operations such as mines, railways, and factories was an obstacle to industrial development. Facing a similar predicament, the Japanese government opted to establish new enterprises as government monopolies during the 1870s and 1880s, but the Qing government did not have sufficient funds for investments of this magnitude. In addition, running the new enterprises required technological and managerial skills that government officials, with their administrative background, could not provide.[8]

To solve these problems, the new industrial enterprises established in the 1870s and 1880s took the form of government-sponsored enterprises managed by merchants (*guandu shangban*). The bureaucratic term for this type of enterprise originated in the salt monopoly, in which merchants provided capital and management and officials controlled production and set trade quotas. Under this new scheme for large-scale industrial enterprises, private investors, mostly merchants, were expected to put up the capital and to manage these concerns under the supervision of officials. Apart from some government loans, the merchants bore all the financial risks of the enterprise. In addition, the officials who supervised them often followed their own, not necessarily government-directed, agenda and introduced bribes, corruption, and inflexible management into these enterprises. As Albert Feuerwerker and Guohui Zhang have shown in detail, these enterprises encountered innumerable problems because of their peculiar financial and managerial arrangements.[9] Not surprisingly, the financial returns for the private investors in these *guandu shangban* enterprises in the 1870s and 1880s were limited.

During this period of timid state-directed industrial efforts, Li Hongzhang became the most powerful patron of *guandu shangban* enterprises. The China Merchants' Steamship Navigation Company, the Kaiping Mines, and the Shanghai Cotton Cloth Mill (Shanghai jiqi zhibuju) were under his official sponsorship, and Li was able to translate his political power into a sphere of economic influence and to control these quasi-monopoly enterprises. This is not to say that Li Hongzhang's patronage had a completely negative impact. As Chi-kong Lai has shown for the China Merchants' Company, in the beginning Li's sponsorship secured sufficient financial support and autonomy for the merchant managers.[10] Only later, when Li Hongzhang became unable to prevent the government from assuming more direct control of the management, did the company encounter problems. Rent-seeking, mismanagement, and misuse of funds that accompanied the government's growing intervention in the enterprise led to decreasing merchant investment. In general, as was true of contemporary family businesses, the lack of auditing procedures and absence of a distinction between private and company funds characterized these government-sponsored enterprises.

In the 1880s, as merchants became less and less willing to risk their money in government-sponsored enterprises, the government devised a compromise and promoted *guanshang heban* (official and merchant joint management) enterprises, which it hoped would prove attractive to merchants. Under this new arrangement, merchants were to be more in control of capital investment and of management. However, this move by the government toward more flexibility and private financial as well as managerial involvement never triggered the desired outpouring of funds. In fact, the dissatisfaction of the merchants grew during the early 1890s, as even government officials acknowledged.[11]

Certainly, the more restrained presence of the government in *guanshang heban* enterprises still offered private investors an advantage in that it guaranteed official protection against inconvenient national as well as foreign competition. Nevertheless, as we shall see, creating an encouraging investment climate for private activity in the industrial sector first required the more drastic step of abolishing the general protectionist mechanism against private enterprises in China, namely, the government policy of not allowing Chinese nationals independently to establish private industrial enterprises.

The turning point came in 1895, with a new phase in industrial entrepreneurship.[12] From that year on, greater numbers of light and consumer-goods industries were founded, and there was a significant shift from government-sponsored enterprises to enterprises with private ownership and management. For example, a boom in establishing cotton mills with full Chinese ownership took place after 1895. Between 1890 and 1894 only five cotton-spinning mills had been successfully established (all but one with government involvement); by 1916, 30 new mills were in operation, all of them under private merchant management (*shangban*).[13] The statistics on weaving mills are even more impressive. Only one privately managed factory was operating in 1897; by 1916 there were 81.[14]

Why did the number of private operations in the Chinese cotton spinning and weaving sector increase so quickly after 1895? What caused the government to reduce its dominant influence through new economic policies and, if not encourage, at least make private industrial enterprises legal? Interestingly enough, the incentives for increased industrial activity and the changing ownership conditions did not originate in deliberate government reforms to strengthen a weak national economy; rather, they resulted from China's foreign policy.

The Treaty of Shimonoseki granted foreigners permission to engage in manufacturing in the treaty ports. As Shao Xunzheng has pointed out, this made it impossible for the government to prevent its own nationals from engaging in industry. Shao stresses that Li Hongzhang's fall from power in 1895 was also a vital factor.[15] As noted above, Li Hongzhang, who until 1895 was governor-general of Zhili province, had been by far the most powerful senior official active in government sponsorship of new enterprises. He was not only on good terms with the empress dowager and with the foreign powers, but as commissioner of the northern ports he was in charge of the most modern portion of the Qing navy.[16]

The Shanghai Cotton Cloth Mill is an excellent example of how Li Hongzhang's personal influence worked and the obstacles it posed to industrial development. Plans for the mill began in 1877, and like other government-sponsored enterprises, the Shanghai Cotton Cloth Mill was granted a ten-year monopoly from 1882 on.[17] However, it took another ten years before the mill began operations. The monopoly prevented the establishment of other cotton mills, and even though several mills are known to have been in operation in the early 1890s, these mills were, according to Shao Xunzheng, established not as private operations but as spin-offs of Li Hongzhang's Shanghai Cotton Cloth Mill.[18] In 1893 the Shanghai Cotton Cloth Mill was destroyed by fire and rebuilt under the new name Huasheng.[19] To curtail further competition, as late as 1894 Li Hongzhang petitioned the government to forbid further expansion of spinning operations such as the government-managed mill in Hubei province.[20]

Li Hongzhang's personal patronage of such enterprises as the Kaiping Mines, the Shanghai Arsenal, and the China Merchants' Steamship Navigation Company was crucial to their success. Li Hongzhang was powerful not only in Beijing near his power base in Zhili province but also in Shanghai. There he exerted his influence in the appointment of the Shanghai circuit intendant (*daotai*), the senior official in the local administration, and promoted his operations by networking through fellow provincials, colleagues, and fellow examination graduates.[21] Through these formal and informal relationships, Li Hongzhang was able to gain support from Shanghai and Jiangsu officials as well as from merchants and gentry attracted by the financial awards at Li's disposal or by their own interests in the enterprises. In short, as long as Li Hongzhang was in power, the operations under his supervision were protected through his patronage and through their monopoly status. However, this situation was not to last.

Since the Sino-Japanese war had arisen from Li Hongzhang's policies and was conducted by troops under his control, China's humiliating defeat in 1895 led to Li's disgrace and removal from his post as governor-general of Zhili. This created a power vacuum in Beijing, into which Governor-General Zhang Zhidong (1837–1909) of Huguang (Hunan and Hubei) stepped.[22] Zhang Zhidong, like Li Hongzhang, had championed Westernization, but it was not until he was appointed governor-general of Huguang that he found a power base to implement his ideas.[23] But although Zhang Zhidong was to become one of the leading politicians and reformers during the final years of the Qing dynasty, he never achieved Li Hongzhang's influence and power over political and economic affairs.

Zhang Zhidong obviously wanted to engage actively in establishing industrial enterprises, but he was never able to see his plans through to fruition. For example, while posted to Liangguang (Guangdong and Guangxi) in 1888, he had taken steps to set up a cotton mill in Guangdong and ordered machinery for it.[24] When he was appointed governor-general of Huguang the following year, he took the machinery with him, and the planned mill in Guangdong never materialized.[25] In the city of Wuchang, he then established the Hubei Weaving Mill (Hubei zhiguanju), for which he ordered new machinery.[26] However, when he was transferred to Liangjiang (Jiangsu, Jiangxi, and Anhui) in 1894, the newly purchased machinery was of no immediate use and was stored in a Shanghai warehouse for several years. This machinery was to play a crucial role in launching Zhang Jian's first cotton mill, as we shall see in the next chapter.

Despite the fall of Li Hongzhang and his monopolies, it took more than a decade for substantial industrialization in terms of the number of factories and their output. It would be fair to say that Zhang Jian's move into the world of industry—he began preparations for his first cotton mill in 1895—was early even by the standards of the Qing. Indeed, it was not until the post-1900 reforms that the imperial court openly encouraged business and industrial enterprise and sought to grant merchants a higher social and political status.[27] The cautious and limited approach favored by the government for encouraging Chinese merchants to open factories after the loss of the war to Japan is apparent in a government proclamation from early 1896 posted outside the Shanghai customs house for several months and later quoted in the *North China Herald*:

[By establishing factories,] it may be possible to successfully stop the flow of foreign commodities (into China) and prevent the country of being drained of its capital. It is not necessary to make a hard and fast choice of some branch of industry such as the manufacture of piece goods or silk filature. There is plenty of profit to be derived from other industries such as the manufacture of foreign candles, foreign sugar, or foreign crockery. It will be a good thing for those with small capital to manufacture several kinds of articles, with a view to accustom the popular mind (to the innovation). No capital belonging to officials will be put in, nor will other merchants or officials be mixed up in the matter. Hereafter the merchants will manage their business as they please, and the officials will have no questions to ask.[28]

This document was drawn up by the Shanghai circuit intendant to publicize Zhang Zhidong's instructions, which had received imperial approval. Obviously the imperial government considered the proliferation of factories—which in this context meant the production of goods with machines—

to be of paramount importance; it was less concerned with the type of products, consumer demand, and the market situation, which might have a substantial impact on the success or failure of any new business enterprise. This proclamation also reveals the desperate efforts of concerned government officials like Zhang Zhidong to initiate industrial production for the sake of protecting and stabilizing the national economy. However, it is doubtful that the manufacture of foreign-style candles and crockery by Chinese for the Chinese market would have prevented the large-scale draining of Chinese capital and resources abroad. For those searching for promising industrialization projects, the textile sector became the answer.

Establishing factories for textile production required considerable private capital investment from merchants and businessmen. Even without interference from the government and influential officials, the risk of investing private capital in major industrial operations such as cotton-spinning mills or silk filatures was substantial. Without an open and accessible capital market, the raising of capital was a major problem in founding private enterprises, with the exception of family businesses which recruited their capital from kinship and native-place networks.

The Dasheng enterprises reveal the strengths and weaknesses of industrial enterprises founded in the wake of 1895 and the transition that came about with privatization. As I explain in more detail in the next chapter, Dasheng was originally conceived as a regional *guanshang heban* operation; it was officially initiated by Zhang Zhidong, who planned to lend his support in the beginning. However, in contrast to the previous system under Li Hongzhang, Zhang Zhidong, the *guan* or official side in the enterprise, did not represent the government as a corporate body but was acting as an individual official. In this position he offered patronage and ineffective official protection for the enterprise, but little else.

Arguably, the watering-down of government support to the patronage of individual officials eventually led to the end of involvement by individual officials in enterprises. Zhang Zhidong was unable to offer Dasheng vital financial support, and without financial leverage his influence faded. What started as government-sponsored enterprise soon became a privatized operation of the founder's family without ever developing into a family business. Registered officially as a shareholding company with limited liability in 1907, Dasheng grew into a major industrial complex with considerable financial success and a substantial life span.

A broader view allows us to examine not only Dasheng's history as a business institution but also the impact of political and economic changes on industrialization in early twentieth-century China. China's situation at the turn of the twentieth century is often compared to Japan's development following the Meiji Restoration of 1868.[29] Although Japan was successful with industrial development after 1880, in the first decade of the restoration, like China, it lacked private capital and confronted the technical and organizational difficulties in machine production and risk-aversion by merchants who might have provided investment capital.[30] To be sure, the degree of intervention by the central and regional governments in Japan was substantially weaker. More important, however, was the Japanese government's decision not only to permit but actively to promote the founding of private industrial enterprises in the 1880s through government loans and favorable industrial policies. Thus, in contrast to the situation in China, Japan's enterprise structure changed abruptly in November 1880 when the government sold all its enterprises, with the exception of such strategically important sectors as railways, telegraphs, and arsenals, to private buyers.[31] The Chinese government never managed to draw the line so clearly; in many cases, a change from government enterprise to semi-official management and ownership preceded any process of immediate privatization. However, the post-1895 development of enterprises like the Dasheng Cotton Mill proves that, despite temporary involvement, the Chinese government was to lose control over the management and ownership of these new concerns for good.

It would be a mistake to place the blame for the slowness of China's industrialization solely on the Qing government. Other important mechanisms necessary for running modern large-scale enterprises such as an easily accessible capital market or legal protection through commercial and company laws were not properly in place before the 1910s. Needless to say, the treaty ports became the preferred locations for Chinese and foreign businessmen to establish their industrial enterprises. Chinese merchants and businessmen worked with compradors or foreign brokers in the treaty ports to gain access to financing and foreign materials and technologies. In addition, many Chinese investors took advantage of the foreign settlements and their special legal position to register their companies under the protection of foreign laws.

Because of its location and its status as a regional enterprise in rural Jiangsu province in the hinterland of a treaty port, Dasheng differed in terms of management and workforce from the mills and factories located in the urban centers. Certainly, Dasheng was not the only enterprise founded with government help that subsequently became a private operation. Whereas Dasheng rid itself of government patronage, however, some enterprises actively continued to seek and exploit patronage during the Republican period when political power became even more fragmented. The Lanzhou Mining Company (Beiyang Lanzhou guankuang youxian gongsi) and the Qixin Cement Company (Qixin yanghui gongsi) are two examples. Their founder, the official Zhou Xuexi (1869–1947), enjoyed the political patronage of Yuan Shikai (1859–1916), who, first as the Qing governor-general of Zhili and later as president of the Republic, had a great influence in the Beijing government. Yuan supported the Qixin company by partially exempting it from custom duties and arranging for it to become a major supplier of cement for the government-owned railways; this fortified the positive relationship between the most successful industrialist in northern China and the Beijing government. Although the establishment of the Nanjing government in 1927 meant a drastic political change for Zhou Xuexi, his companies were already so well established that they continued to be successful until the Japanese invasion in the late 1930s.[32]

In addition to political sponsorship, the role of the founder and his family as well as the geographical context were vital factors in the formation of regional enterprises. Whereas Zhou Xuexi combined officeholding with entrepreneurship, Zhang Jian abandoned officialdom for industry. Even more important, he attempted not only to introduce industry to the local rural communities but also to dominate development in the Nantong area through his social, financial, and political activities. In contrast to the Qixin cement factories near urban centers such as Tangshan, Guangzhou, or Shanghai, the Dasheng enterprise was a government-initiated project in a rural area that created a new power balance and changed social structures, even if it did not generate long-term economic development and growth per se.

From Salt to Cotton: The Nantong Region

The land to the north of the Yangzi River was a backward area throughout the nineteenth century. Despite its proximity to Shanghai, northern Jiangsu (Subei) differed considerably from prosperous Jiangnan, the southern part of the province. Southern Jiangsu could boast of enormous economic success in agricultural and handicraft production as well as in commerce, which went hand in hand with a strong elite culture.[33] In contrast, northern Jiangsu was often stereotyped as a region of economic poverty and cultural backwardness. Although the city of Nantong and its adjacent counties were north of the Yangzi River and the local dialect and customs were distinct from those of Jiangnan, it nevertheless did not exhibit the extreme poverty found in Subei cities further north such as Yancheng or Funing. One major advantage enjoyed by Nantong was its river connection. Nearby small ports along the Yangzi linked the region to the rest of China. However, the area remained underdeveloped in regard to other transportation facilities. Even when, in the twentieth century, railways were built in Jiangsu, they passed Nantong by.[34]

During the Qing dynasty, Nantong county was known as Tongzhou county, with Tongzhou city as the county seat.[35] When the county was elevated to the administrative level of an independent department (Tongzhou zhili zhou) in 1724, it came under the direct control of the censor in charge of the Suzhou circuit (*dao*) and the provincial governor of Jiangsu.[36] Tongzhou independent department controlled neighboring Haimen subprefecture and Rugao county.[37] Under the Republic, Tongzhou became Nantong county (Nantong xian) with Nantong city as the county seat. In the Republican period, Nantong, Haimen, and Rugao counties together with Chongming, an island in the Yangzi estuary, constituted the Nantong region as discussed in this book (see Map 1, p. 14). As we shall see, socioeconomic developments in Haimen county and Chongming island to the southeast and in Rugao county to the north were closely related to those in Nantong county.

Historically, the most significant product of the area was salt. Since the Tang dynasty, the region had been known for its salt fields. Salt production took place in the Huainan salt yards along the eastern coast under the supervision of the Lianghuai Salt Administration, the government monopoly for salt in Jiangsu province. The salt trade was the most important commercial activity in the region.[38] However, from the early nineteenth century on, the salt trade declined drastically because of rising salt prices in connection with rising tax rates and rising silver prices, new trading routes for salt, and, especially, intense salt smuggling.[39] As the salt fields were gradually abandoned by the salt producers, reeds took over.[40]

The decline in the salt trade was compounded by another long-term development in the Nantong region: throughout the ages, silt has been deposited on the seaward coast of Jiangsu, and the northern shoreline of the

Yangzi has been eroded by the river current.[41] The coastal area did not make good farmland because the soil was too saline for rice, but it could be converted to cotton and wheat cultivation. Land-reclamation companies (see Chapter 7) set up in the coastal area in the early years of the twentieth century attempted to take advantage of the declining salt trade and the geological changes by reclaiming the land for cotton cultivation. The erosion of the northern banks of the Yangzi had different consequences: the river ports perforce remained small and had to be relocated every few generations.[42] In short, the nineteenth century saw a drastic change in the local economy; the conversion from salt to cotton affected patterns of land use, occupation, production, and commerce.

Cotton was introduced quite early to the region. The Tongzhou gazetteer of 1755 encouraged "people along the river to be skillful at growing cotton."[43] However, the level and quality of cotton-textile production in the Nantong area were still far below those achieved in Songjiang prefecture, the leading center for spinning and weaving in southern Jiangsu province, near Shanghai.[44] Cotton growing was a common activity in Tongzhou by the early nineteenth century, to judge from local publications of that time, which gave detailed descriptions of and ample advice on how to plant, grow, and process cotton.[45] Over time, the quality of Tongzhou cotton improved, and Republican sources describe cotton from Nantong county as superior to that produced in other counties of the province.[46] Apart from the quality of the cotton, the humid weather conditions of the Nantong area were traditionally regarded as advantageous for cotton growing and spinning.

Farmers in Haimen county southeast of Nantong, an area that had never been fully a part of the Huainan salt production area, traditionally produced raw cotton and then wove it into various types of cloth as a highly specialized household industry.[47] Like Nantong, Haimen was also supplier of the indigo dye for the cotton cloth, which, after processing, was sold as *lanbu* (blue-dyed cotton cloth) in the local markets.[48] In the early twentieth century, Haimen cotton was considered high quality, and the bulk was sold to the Dasheng No. 3 Cotton Mill and the rest shipped for sale to Nantong and Shanghai.[49]

Cotton-related household production on Chongming island can be traced to the Ming dynasty (1368–1644).[50] During the Republican period, Chongming county included not only the island in the Yangzi River estuary but also newly reclaimed land on the southeastern tip of northern Jiangsu (present-day Qidong county).[51] Due to the sandy soil and the island's suitability for growing cotton, the quality of the cotton produced in Chongming county on the mudbanks in the Waisha, Jiulong, and Beixin districts was regarded as superior even to that of Nantong.[52]

Although I include Rugao county in the Nantong area for the broader purpose of analysis, traditionally households there did not engage in the production of cotton yarn and cloth. Neither yarn nor cloth is mentioned among the local products listed in the gazetteers covering the early and mid-nineteenth century. Indeed, cotton farming was introduced to Rugao only in the late nineteenth century, and in the Republican period Rugao cotton was still described as inferior in quality. Since there was no strong local handicraft or factory production of yarn in Rugao, most of the little cotton that was produced was exported to Nantong and Shanghai.[53]

Socioeconomic Dynamics of a Periphery

Although cotton replaced salt as Nantong's most important product and income producer and the quantities of finished yarn and cloth increased substantially, the area remained a periphery to the economic and cultural centers of the Yangzi Delta. Historians have addressed the issue of Subei as a periphery in the nineteenth and early twentieth century from various angles. Emily Honig has dealt with the emergence of demeaning cultural stereotypes and their reflection in the native-place hierarchy for Subei migrants who came to Shanghai for work in large numbers after 1900. Antonia Finnane has expanded this theme by analyzing Subei's economic and political mal-integration compared with southern Jiangsu in terms of internal colonialism.[54] As useful as these studies are, I shall concentrate only on the significant aspects of Nantong's nature as a periphery in relation to the socioeconomic conditions and infrastructure that provided the framework for Dasheng's development after 1895.

As mentioned above, the Jiangnan area was among China's most prosperous and most highly urbanized regions in the nineteenth and twentieth centuries. In contrast, the Nantong region to the north of the Yangzi River was, apart from Nantong city, dotted with only small market towns at the subcounty level and village clusters. Nantong city, the county seat, was a walled city surrounded by a moat connected to the canal system and could be crossed on foot over bridges leading to the city gates in the east, west, and south faces of the wall.[55]

Demographic figures for the Nantong region in the early twentieth century reflect both its predominantly rural population and its lack of urban centers. For example, a survey conducted by the local police bureau in 1920 quoted in the Republican gazetteer gives a population of about 108,000 for Nantong city. However, this number included inhabitants of the suburbs and villages administratively attached to the city; only some 10,000 people lived within the city walls.[56] Among the 22 other towns and larger villages listed in the county survey, only one, the town of Jinsha, had a population of similar size. The total population of Nantong county was around 1.1 million people in 1920 and 1.5 million in the early 1930s (for comparison, Shanghai city at that time had a population of 3.5 million).[57] In the 1930s, Rugao county had a population of about 1.5 million people, Haimen 0.7 million, and Chongming 0.5 million people.[58] Since it was a third larger than Nantong county, Rugao had fewer people per square kilometer. The population density in Haimen and Chongming, both substantially smaller-sized counties, was comparable to that in Nantong.[59]

Despite the incorporation of the region into the national cotton trade, before the twentieth century Nantong city did not function as the commercial core of the area, centralizing and directing all regional and interregional trade in the cotton business. Rather, it served instead as the periphery to other economic centers in southern Jiangsu. This is not to say that the region in general lacked commerce: on the contrary, the growing of cotton and the handicraft production of cotton yarn and cloth in rural households had to be trade-oriented. However, most of the business transactions between cotton producers and buyers took place near the area of production, in the villages or along the river, and not in the county seat. A 1923 survey of 96 cotton and yarn shops in the region confirms this trade distribution pattern. Only six of these establishments were situated in Nantong city.[60] Business was obviously conducted not from the city but in locations in the countryside near the farmers who were both producers of cotton and consumers of yarn. Even when the cloth trade to Manchuria through Shanghai came under the control of local cloth firms in the late nineteenth century, the majority of the firms were not located in Nantong city but in villages and suburbs closer to the areas of cloth production.[61]

If we apply G. William Skinner's model of market hierarchies and marketing systems to Nantong city, the category of the central market town would seem an obvious choice for the county seat.[62] However, as Skinner suggests, a city's administrative status did not always overlap with its position in the marketing structure. Before 1900, Nantong city was more important within the administrative hierarchy than it was within the economic hierarchy, where it should have been "a strategic site in the transportation network" with "important wholesaling functions."[63] A case in point is the fact that for the longest time Nantong city did not have its own trading port, despite its proximity to the Yangzi River. In the Ming dynasty a stone sluice gate had been built at Tianshenggang, which became essential for the regulation of the canal system.[64] Until the early twentieth century, Tianshenggang served as the region's main port and entrance to the Yangzi River. Once industry developed around Nantong city, ships transporting bulk loads of cotton, coal, and other material crowded the canal between Tianshenggang and Tangjiazha, the location of the Dasheng No. 1 Cotton Mill. Only then, in 1905, was a road built between the two places.[65] It was not until 1913 that the local chamber of commerce financed the construction of a road connecting Nantong city and Tianshenggang.[66]

Convenient transportation facilities via the river and the canal system were extremely important for the Nantong region since the production of good-quality cotton attracted buyers from outside the area. For example, in the early nineteenth century traders from Fujian and Guangdong provinces came at the end of autumn to the Tongzhou cotton fields on the sands (*shadi*) to buy ginned cotton (*huayi*). According to the 1830 gazetteer, the merchants from the south loaded the ginned cotton onto huge junks, which crowded the canals and rivers.[67] Heavy shipping traffic on the Yangzi to transport the area's produce is documented for the Republican period as well; the descriptions mention many different types and sizes of boats.[68] In addition to bulk goods such as raw cotton and yarn, they transported commercial goods such as rice, dry goods, and tobacco, and, of course, passengers between the ports near Nantong and the destinations up- and downriver. Especially notable were agents from Shanghai buying cotton on behalf of the cotton-spinning mills in that city.[69]

Despite all the economic activities related to long-distance and interregional trade, Nantong remained an economic periphery in terms of local economic institutions and their members. Certainly, the cotton trading system connected local farmers and local wholesale merchants through outside agents and their contacts indirectly to major markets all over China. The local merchants, however, never managed to dominate the regional trade systems in raw cotton, which remained in the hands of outsiders, such as wholesale merchants from the southern provinces and the Shanghai agents mentioned above. Local firms continued to play only a minor role in the cotton trade even in the early twentieth century.[70] The dominance of outside merchants was at first also visible in the cloth trade. In the most informative study of the history of Nantong *tubu* or local hand-woven cotton cloth to date, Lin Jubai mentions Shandong merchants in the nineteenth century who purchased *tubu* for export to Manchuria.[71] As Lin shows, only in the early twentieth century did a group of 25 local cloth firms from Nantong and Haimen, the so-called *guanzhuang*, manage to dominate the cloth trade to Shanghai, where the *tubu* was then sold via wholesalers to the north, in particular to the target market of Manchuria.[72]

Long-distance trade and commercial activities also left their imprint on the area's social structure through the formation of various regional organizations of merchants. In Nantong city the biggest native-place organization (*huiguan*) looked after the business interests and social needs of merchants from Anhui province, who were prominent in the cotton and banking business.[73] Founded at the end of the eighteenth century, this native-place association, the Xin'an gongshan tang (Xin'an Hall of the Public Good), occupied a large piece of land within the walled city along one of the main north-south streets; it was still featured as one of Nantong's prominent institutions on a 1925 city map.[74] Although within the city walls, the area occupied by this *huiguan* was as far away as possible from the yamen, the administrative seat of the local magistrate and the local government. The merchant association had also acquired large plots of land outside the city as burial grounds for natives of Anhui province.[75]

Another important merchant group in the Nantong area hailed from Ningbo and was represented by two *huiguan* in the villages of Hai'ergang and Yancangba. Most of the Ningbo sojourners in the Nantong area were either skilled craftsmen or traders. It appears that the *huiguan* in the region were not necessarily based in the county seat. A further example is the *huiguan* for the Guangdong merchants, traders in cotton and in the late 1920s in opium, which was originally established in Duanjiaba village and not within the walls of Nantong city. In addition to the usual services for fellow provincials, the Guangdong *huiguan* in particular maintained also its own local customs by holding an annual temple fair for Tianhou, the Empress of Heaven.[76]

Local merchants from the Nantong area never became famous as long-distance traders within China, unlike their colleagues from Anhui, Guangdong, or Ningbo. I was able to locate only one source stating that merchants from Tongzhou maintained a *huiguan* in Beijing (established in 1724).[77] Antonia Finnane has remarked on the lack of a strong indigenous merchant organization as one of the main reasons for Subei's low economic development.[78] A look at the origins of shopkeepers in the Nantong area confirms her argument. About a quarter of the managers of the 96 cotton cloth and yarn shops in Nantong, Rugao, and Haimen registered in a 1923 survey came from places outside the region such as Anhui, southern Jiangsu, or Zhejiang.[79] A high percentage of the managers of such shops in Haimen county also came from places outside the region such as Dantu, Huizhou, Ningbo, or Zhenjiang. By contrast, all the cotton cloth and yarn shops in Rugao were managed by people from this county. Since Rugao was not a traditional cotton-producing area, it probably did not attract much outside merchant interest in this sector.[80] However, a large and diversified community of sojourning merchants dominated Rugao's commerce in other trade sectors. For example, most pawnshops were run by people from Anhui, who had their own *huiguan*.[81] Natives of Zhenjiang city, mostly wealthy merchants, established a *huiguan* in Rugao under the name Jingjiang (the old name for Zhenjiang), which even had its own school from 1907 on.[82]

Since many of the extra-local merchants were involved in banking and pawnshops, a few remarks about the financial infrastructure of the region are appropriate. Cotton cultivation and the cotton trade were financed by local, traditional native banks (*qianzhuang*) well into the 1920s. The *qianzhuang* were situated throughout the area in smaller towns and villages such as Shigang and Baipu.[83] The same distribution pattern held for pawnshops (*diandang*), another traditional financial institution that catered to the needs of villagers in the Nantong region.[84] Indicative of their close ties with the cotton business is the fact that some native banks also owned big cloth firms and financed part of Dasheng's early business expansion. As the company records show, until the late 1910s Dasheng conducted financial transactions with large *qianzhuang* such as Shunkang and Deji throughout the Nantong area.[85]

One indirect result of the establishment of the Dasheng cotton mills and their growing business was the establishment of branches of the Jiangsu Provincial Bank and the Bank of China in 1915 in the county seat.[86] As latecomers to the city's commercial infrastructure, the branches of modern banks such as the Shanghai Commercial and Savings Bank, the Huaihai Bank, and the Bank of Communications were concentrated at the very edge of Nantong's city wall or even outside the walls, as a map from 1925 indicates.[87] Haimen county, which was much less industrialized than Nantong county, had no modern banking facilities at all in 1920.[88]

Although much of Subei's characterization as an economic and political periphery—the identification of Subei natives with poverty, backwardness, and boorishness—is known to us through the prejudices Subei people experienced as migrants in twentieth-century Shanghai, Shanghai did not play an important economic role for Nantong's workforce before the 1910s and 1920s. In the 1880s a regular boat service transported passengers from Shanghai to Wusong harbor, where they could catch a connecting boat to Langshan near Nantong.[89] At that time most of those who traveled to Shanghai were local cloth and yarn merchants who had business with agents and brokerages in that city.

The economic ties between the Nantong area and Shanghai intensified only in the early twentieth century, when the treaty port experienced tremendous economic growth and employment opportunities and the lure of a better livelihood and modernity there began to attract people from the countryside. In particular, people from Subei's poorest areas near Yancheng and northeast of Yangzhou migrated to Shanghai, where the majority took up menial jobs as freight haulers, night soil collectors, rickshaw pullers, and beggars.[90] Although Nantong was a periphery in comparison to southern Jiangsu, its socioeconomic conditions compared very favorably to these impoverished districts. After 1900 the increasing number of factories in Shanghai drew people from rural areas, but not particularly from the Nantong region.[91] With a general increase in commercialization and intensified trade links between Shanghai and the Nantong area—some of the bigger local cloth firms opened branches in the metropolis and Dasheng had its headquarters there—Nantong businessmen set up offices, wharfs, and storehouses in Shanghai.[92] By the early twentieth century, several steamship companies were running directly between Nantong and Shanghai and faced stiff competition for passengers and goods. As I will show in Chapter 8, the profits of these transportation businesses were so lucrative that in the mid-1930s control over the Nantong steamship lines and their wharfs came under the protection racket of Shanghai's notorious underworld organization, the Green Gang (Qing bang).[93]

The fact that migration from the Nantong area to Shanghai increased only during the Republican period is also demonstrated through the representation and organization of these natives in the metropolis. The number of workers and small shopkeepers in various trades and occupations from Nantong sojourning in Shanghai grew slowly but steadily in the first decade of the 1900s. It was not until 1933, however, that these sojourners founded their own native-place association for fellow provincials from the five counties of Tongzhou, Rugao, Chongming, Haimen, and Qidong.[94] In comparison with natives of other areas in the country, people from the Nantong region joined Shanghai's substantial immigrant population at a relatively late stage. In fact, due to their origin in the Subei periphery and prejudices against them, people from northern Jiangsu joined the industrial workforce in Shanghai rather late and did not appear as unskilled workers in the records of industrial enterprises such as cotton- and silk-spinning mills until the early 1920s.[95]

To judge from the historical genesis of private industrial enterprises in late nineteenth- and early twentieth-century China, the general political climate represented a major obstacle to industrial development and private investment. Only a radical, even if involuntary, change in government policies and the removal of officials who embodied government sponsorship and monopolizing patronage, opened the door to a slow transformation of China's economy through private entrepreneurship and industrial investment. Eventually, political and subsequent socioeconomic changes on the national level translated to the regional level.

As the case of Dasheng shows, regional industrialization was initiated because of national economic policies, which almost inadvertently resulted in privatization without a clear framework dictated by the government. Thus, many aspects of management, ownership, and control that had not been addressed by the government would have to be negotiated by the new managers and owners over time. By tracing Dasheng's evolution from an enterprise established with government cooperation in 1895 into a de facto but not yet legally recognized private shareholding company by 1901, we can explore the phasing out of government influence and the decline of official sponsorship during the transitional period. The next chapter examines this regional enterprise as a particularly interesting case of institutional development in Chinese business history.

The region itself, with its particular socioeconomic structure and dynamics as a periphery, was to have a deeper impact on the future of the enterprise than any of the people involved in the founding of Dasheng could have anticipated. Certainly, the availability of raw materials and cheap labor was an incentive to start cotton mills in the countryside. Nevertheless, the Dasheng cotton mills also experienced the disadvantages of the periphery, particularly problems with the infrastructure, land development, and a non-industrial, rural workforce. How the Dasheng factories came to be set up in such a curious place at that particular moment is the subject of the next chapter.

PART II

Factories in the Countryside

CHAPTER 3

Setting Up the Mills

The Dasheng mills were among the first major private industrial enterprises to be established in the countryside, outside the large commercial cities and treaty ports. The mills introduced large-scale industrial production through modern factories and shop-floor management to the region and to the Chinese-owned textile sector. Establishment of the production facilities thus involved the creation of three new elements: the factory as an institutional workplace, an industrial workforce, and the entrepreneurial businessman filling various managerial functions. This part of the book focuses on the two main agents in the Dasheng mills: the owner-manager and the workers. The following chapter discusses the nature of industrial labor in terms of work discipline, wages, hiring patterns, and social stratification; this chapter is devoted to the founder of the enterprise and to the political and socioeconomic aspects of becoming an entrepreneur and starting a cotton mill in late nineteenth-century China.

In this analysis of Dasheng, the issues of control and accountability will emerge as the main themes. These concerns are manifested not only in the managerial and financial side of the enterprise but also in the cultural and educational aspirations of Zhang Jian and his family. This chapter is not, however, a detailed biography of Zhang Jian; rather, it addresses the question of the extent to which his family background and roots in local society determined and helped promote his business goals. The biographical literature on Zhang Jian is ample and provides detailed, and mostly hagiographic, descriptions of his early life as a scholar and as an assistant to high government officials.[1] Zhang Jian's standing as a scholar may help to explain his elevated position in local society, but we need a broader approach to explain his sudden transformation from scholar-official to businessman. As we shall see, the founding of Dasheng required negotiations between private and government interests, political connections on the local and the national levels, and a support network of family and social ties.

A Scholar Turns Businessman

The story of Zhang Jian's venture in Nantong illustrates many general problems Chinese business had to face before the nationwide advent of industrialization. At the same time, Zhang Jian had to re-invent the role of businessman and entrepreneur and forge a new career among the changing economic and political elites of the early twentieth century. In Marion Levy's convincing characterization, Zhang Jian represents the first generation of "industrial executives" who took over business initiatives from "industrial promoters" in the government.[2] Many business decisions of this new industrial executive were based on coincidences, opportunities, political conditions, and personal connections. The Dasheng mills were not designed in the abstract or built according to a long-existing master plan. On the contrary, they were founded amid a constant struggle between insufficient private investment and waning government patronage. From land to machinery to capital, every aspect of the enterprise entailed a complicated negotiation between private efforts and government influence.

Zhang Jian was always associated with the city and the region of Nantong in contemporary literature, an association that continues today.[3] A Chinese reader would conclude that he was a Nantong native, but this was not the case. Although the Zhang lineage traced its origins to Tongzhou, since the eighteenth century the family had been linked with Changle village in Haimen, east of Nantong city, where this branch of the Zhang family had its ancestral hall (see Figs. 3.1 and 3.2).[4] To judge from the lineage endowment, the Changle branch of the Zhang family was not nearly as wealthy as another branch of the family in Jinsha, northeast of Nantong city. Still, it was not poor.[5] As head of the Zhang family's Changle branch after his father's death in 1894, Zhang Jian was in charge of the ancestral rituals, a task he took seriously.[6] From his diary, we know that he kept his main residence in Changle village throughout his life. According to his granddaughter and other informants, Zhang Jian always celebrated the New Year festival in Changle.[7]

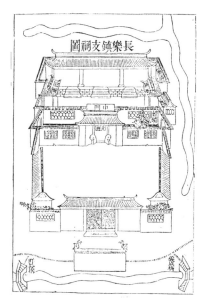

Fig. 3.1 The Zhang family's ancestral hall in Changle
(*Zhang shi jiapu*, 1903, juan shou, citu, 3b).

As a native of Haimen, Zhang Jian had to make his way in Nantong from outside. Once he had established himself as a successful businessman and local dignitary in the early twentieth century, he had a Western-style residence built in Nantong city. In Shanghai, he lodged at the impressive Dasheng office building in the International Settlement. However, his family ties were always rooted in Changle and not in Nantong.

Zhang Jian (courtesy name: Zhang Jizhi; literary names: Zhang Se'an, Zhang Seweng) was born on July 1, 1853.[8] According to Zhang's reminiscences, he came from an ordinary, rather poor peasant family that had never produced a scholar or government official.[9] However, the family cannot have been very poor since Zhang's father, Zhang Pengnian (d. 1894), had his son educated by tutors from the age of five and in his teenage years sent him to Xiting, northwest of Jinsha, for further private studies.[10] Zhang Jian was the second youngest of five sons, but he developed a close relationship only with his next older brother, Zhang Cha (1851–1939), whose support was to be a major factor in Dasheng.

Fig. 3.2 The Zhang family's ancestral hall, now a museum,
in Changle, 1993 (photograph by the author).

After many years of diligent study and success in the local civil service ex-
aminations, Zhang Jian passed the provincial examination for the *juren*
degree in 1885 after several fruitless attempts and obtained the *jinshi* degree in
the metropolitan examination in 1894.[11] Even though he headed the list of
successful candidates, a distinction that earned him the prestigious title of
zhuangyuan and the offer of the chief compiler's post at the imperial Hanlin
Academy, Zhang refused to enter government service. At that time he had
already reached the age of 41 and had been working for many years as a distinguished tutor in various scholarly academies and as a personal assistant in
the private secretariats (*mufu*) of high-ranking officials such as General Wu
Changqing (1834–84).[12] Zhang Jian's volatile career path and late start in
business were not exceptional; Xue Nanming (1850–1929) served in the private secretariat of Li Hongzhang and then in official posts before embarking
on a career as entrepreneur in the silk industry.[13]

After his father's death in 1894, Zhang Jian returned from the capital to
his native place to carry out his mourning duties. He returned with a higher
social status as a first-class scholar and some official connections, but without a strong family network, local ties, or the business or commercial experi-

ence that one would consider necessary for entrepreneurial activities. The change in career was indeed drastic.

The argument has been made that the defeat in the war with Japan in 1894–95 and the humiliating Treaty of Shimonoseki were the main reasons for Zhang Jian's decision to turn his back on government service and to enter the world of business.[14] Zhang Jian himself contributed to this view, which suggests that patriotism and concern about the national economy were the driving forces behind his sudden career change. In his essays Zhang repeatedly blamed Japan for its aggression and, to use a modern term, economic imperialism, both of which in his opinion were partly responsible for China's political and economic problems.[15] For example, his public statements on his motivations for founding Dasheng emphasized national economic independence:

Cotton mills are established in Tongzhou for the sake of the Tongzhou people's livelihood and also for the sake of [exploiting] China's economic resources. The cotton produced in Tongzhou with its pliable strength and long fibers is the very best in Asia and is needed by Japanese mills. The export of [raw] cotton and import of yarn is increasing day by day. We give up our produce in order to supply others, and they then sell to us goods that have made use of what we sold them. [This] is like bleeding yourself to fatten the tiger and then following that with exposing your flesh. If we cannot preserve our wealth, our people will become poorer day by day. What, then, can the country rely on?[16]

Zhang Jian's indignation over Japan's increasing power and his economic concerns reflect the rhetoric of the time. The people's livelihood (*minsheng*) was emerging as a key term in public discussions about China's exposure to foreign economic competition, the protection of its economic rights, and the promotion of its industrial development in the late nineteenth century. Governor-General Zhang Zhidong, for example, repeatedly stressed the need "to protect and maintain the livelihood of our people."[17] Against the background of this debate with its highly patriotic overtones, Zhang Jian frequently depicted his business as a contribution to the public good, and he wove national pride and apprehensions about China's economic fate into his arguments.

His highly moral tone most certainly reflected the attempt of the businessman to please the government and to create a positive image in public opinion. Traditionally (at least in orthodox Confucian writings), Chinese society held the merchant in much lower esteem than the scholar-official.[18]

However, with the increasing commercialization in the nineteenth century, the improved social status and upward mobility of merchants, who were even allowed to buy academic titles, had in reality blurred the distinction between merchants (*shang*) and gentry (*shen*).[19] Thus the late nineteenth century saw the emergence of the so-called class of gentry-merchants (*shenshang*) as local leaders. This term was also used for the new class of businessmen before more specific terms such as *shiyejia* (industrialist) or *qiyejia* (entrepreneur) came into use. Nantong's local newspaper was using *shenshang* to refer to Zhang Jian and his son and their business activities as late as 1922.[20]

Although the rigid traditional ranking system broke down and social interaction between merchants and gentry became common, scholarly writings and debates continued to consider the agrarian economy the most appropriate and solid foundation of the Chinese empire and assigned a much higher economic and social value to it than to industry.[21] Zhang Jian himself repeatedly evoked the dogma of the agrarian base in his writings on the state of the Chinese nation as the cure for social instability, which he sought to achieve through more efficient agricultural, commercial, and industrial activities.[22]

What are we to make of these contradictions? Zhang Jian's abandonment of officialdom to enter business was an act that required a certain amount of justification in 1895. Most certainly, the publicity given Zhang Jian and others who made this decision gradually brought about a change in the perception of the role of the businessman as someone with much larger ambitions than those found among traditional merchants. Zhang Jian's previous career as a scholar with the prestigious *zhuangyuan* title and as a government official was in itself an indirect form of capital, which I will call "reputation capital." As we shall see in Chapter 7, Zhang Jian's social prestige and reputation capital were vital to his business, political, and social endeavors. Another description of reputation capital can be found in Ma Min's excellent study of the role of the gentry-merchant in Chinese society, where he refers to Zhang Jian as the "*zhuangyuan* capitalist" (*zhuangyuan zibenjia*), who, like other former government officials and degree holders, embarked on a business career in the late nineteenth and early twentieth centuries.[23]

Zhang Jian clearly was one of the most successful of the more scholarly *shenshang*. His life-long interest in and promotion of education certainly reflect his background as a member of the scholarly elite. Thus Zhang Jian the gentry-merchant has to be seen in contrast to the more practical "comprador type" of gentry-merchants who used the knowledge and business connections they had gained as compradors (*maiban*) dealing with foreign firms in the treaty ports in the mid- and late nineteenth century to create their own business enterprises.[24] Sheng Xuanhuai, another famous businessman and contemporary of Zhang Jian, is the most successful case of a comprador-turned-businessman with excellent connections with the government.[25]

For Zhang Jian, abandoning an official career did not mean severing his official connections. In fact, he is typical of the businessman with strong political interests who emerged as the Qing government embarked on reforms meant to curtail the power of officialdom and to introduce an element of popular representation.[26] Between 1904 and 1911, major changes in China's economic, educational, and political structure led to the creation of new institutions and legal regulations. In 1904 the imperial government decreed the establishment of a national school system in connection with the abolition of the examination system in 1905.[27] At the same time study societies (*xuehui*) began to mushroom and focused their efforts on education, agriculture, or the preparation of a constitution. As Marianne Bastid has pointed out, these study societies are perhaps the best indication of a change in social mentality among the gentry, and they proved useful in the diffusion of new values and reformist ideas.[28]

Zhang Jian, as I will show in Chapter 7, is the perfect example of a member of the gentry who enlarged his field of action step by step through educational and welfare projects. In addition, he became a strong supporter of local self-government (*difang zizhi*) in the reform period of the last decade of the Qing dynasty. Very briefly, the idea behind local self-government was to rely on local elites to restructure Chinese society and thus to create a new relationship between state and society. In the imperial government's plans, local self-government was meant as an important step in the country's shift to a constitutional government.[29] Zhang Jian was a proponent of constitutional government and founded the influential Society for the Preparation of a Constitutional Government (Yubei lixian gonghui), which he ran jointly with Zheng Xiaoxu (1860–1938), a prominent political figure and one of Dasheng's most outspoken and influential shareholders.[30] Even before self-government regulations were promulgated by the imperial government in January 1909, initiatives for local self-government found their most common expression in commercial, educational, and political societies run by local activists. Zhang Jian's dedication to educational and charity projects in Nantong reflected general political and social trends among local elites.

Zhang Jian also supported the establishment of chambers of commerce (*shanghui*), another facet of the late Qing reforms. In proposing a system of one general chamber in each province with branch chambers in each prefecture, he expressed the wish that the state play a less intrusive role in commercial activities and be "supportive rather than determinative."[31] Following the establishment of the General Chamber of Commerce in Shanghai in 1902, similar organizations were soon founded in smaller towns throughout the country.[32] From the account books of the Dasheng No. 1 Cotton Mill, we know that Dasheng contributed regularly to the Nantong Chamber of Commerce.[33] Since his brother Zhang Cha and later his son, Zhang Xiaoruo (1898–1935), were directors of this local chamber of commerce, Zhang Jian was able to utilize this institution to lobby the local government to protect his personal and business domain (see Chapter 7).

At a higher political level, the provincial assemblies elected in 1909 became the institutional expression of the autonomous political power demanded by the aspiring modern elite. In the first decade of the 1900s, Zhang Jian increasingly devoted his time and energies to politics, notably in 1909 as president of the Jiangsu provincial assembly.[34] In 1911, he was one of the most independent-minded political leaders in Jiangsu; after the revolution, he served as minister of agriculture and commerce first in Sun Yatsen's and then in Yuan Shikai's government between 1912 and 1915.[35] During his ministerial career, Zhang Jian promulgated new regulations for land reclamation, which created new business opportunities along the coast for himself and his business associates (see Chapters 6 and 7). Although he held no further public office, newspaper articles and even cartoons continued to refer to his political standing and reputation as a public figure until his death in 1926.[36] In his role as minister, Zhang Jian was, along with other political figures, even immortalized in a Cantonese play about the country's difficult political situation during Yuan Shikai's presidency.[37] However politically and socially influential Zhang Jian may have become, prestige alone was not sufficient to get the factories set up quickly in 1895. On the contrary, patterns of official patronage and influence had changed and began to play a much less dominant role in the founding of businesses at the turn of the century.

Government Support Versus Private Interests

Planning for the Dasheng No. 1 Cotton Mill in Tangjiazha village northwest of Nantong city began in 1895, but it took four years before operations started in 1899. From Zhang Jian's correspondence with senior government officials, we know more about the negotiations with these officials and the struggle to obtain sufficient start-up capital than about the practical arrangements for setting up the mill. Nevertheless, these documents reveal why Zhang Jian went into business.

In late 1895, the governor-general of the Liangjiang provinces and imperial commissioner of the southern ports, Zhang Zhidong, contacted officials in Suzhou prefecture, Zhenjiang prefecture, and Tongzhou independent department and requested that they recruit local merchants to establish factories for the production of local goods.[38] The reason given by Zhang Zhidong was "to boycott the plans of the foreigners," meaning the business expansion of Westerners and Japanese into China's interior in the wake of the Treaty of Shimonoseki (see Chapter 2).[39] In answer to the question of why he had chosen Nantong for his textile enterprises, Zhang Jian later described his reaction to Zhang Zhidong's invitation: "The cotton produced in Tongzhou is the strongest and [qualitatively] the best; for this reason I decided to establish cotton spinning mills."[40] His response and the fact that the idea to found a business originated in a suggestion from the government show that the project was not based on a long-premeditated plan. It is also questionable whether Zhang's move into business was based on purely idealistic motives. We can say with certainty that Zhang Jian was not guided in his decision by contact with foreigners or personal experiences abroad. In contrast to businessmen with a comprador past, Zhang Jian had no connections with the foreign business community in Shanghai and was unable to read the English or Japanese publications on economics or industry available at the time.

Zhang Jian started with six promoters committed to helping him raise the necessary funds and look for potential investors interested in a private enterprise. Pan Huamao from Guangzhou, Guo Xun from Fujian, and Fan Fen from Ningbo were businessmen in Shanghai; Liu Guixin, Shen Xiejun (courtesy name: Shen Jingfu), and Chen Weiyong were merchants from

Nantong and Haimen.[41] These six promoters jointly committed to investing 600,000 taels; the three Shanghai investors under Fan Fen were responsible for supplying 400,000 taels, and the local investors under Shen Xiejun for 200,000 taels. In order to attract private capital, Zhang Jian wanted the enterprise to be defined as completely *shangban*, that is, under full merchant management. The six promoters were listed as managers (*jingli dongshi*) of the enterprise in the first official document from 1895, which laid out the government's plan for financing and managing the mill's setup.[42] The initial plan was soon overturned by harsh financial realities. After nine months the Cantonese and Fujian promoters backed out, and the Dasheng cotton mill became mainly a local concern.[43] In the long run, this development strengthened Dasheng's nature as a regional enterprise and economic concern; however, the withdrawal of funds delayed the mill considerably. As it turned out, convincing local merchants to buy shares was a slow and not very successful process.

Zhang Jian had to face many difficulties, not least the acquisition of expensive machinery. In his original proposal, Zhang Jian had suggested that spinning machinery with 20,000 spindles would be purchased with the capital collected by the Shanghai investors.[44] When they backed out, he sought the government's financial support to purchase the machinery. His decision has to be understood in the context of the absence of a national capital market in late nineteenth-century China and his initial lack of connections with local financial networks in the Nantong area. The request for official sponsorship proved to be a bad decision in two ways: it curtailed Dasheng's appeal as a "private" operation to potential investors, and the government was unable to give sufficient financial support.

To make things worse, in early 1896 another problem arose when Zhang Zhidong was ordered to resume the governor-generalship of the Huguang provinces; for Zhang Jian this meant the loss of his official patron and supporter. When Zhang Jian informed Zhang Zhidong's successor as governor-general of Liangjiang, Liu Kunyi (1830–1902), about his difficulties in raising funds, Liu proved to be sympathetic but unsuccessful in offering financial help.[45] After much correspondence, the pressing problem of machinery was indirectly solved through Zhang Zhidong's intervention, which, incidentally, served his own purposes very well. Zhang Zhidong "contributed" the secondhand English equipment he had originally purchased for a planned cotton mill in Wuchang. As mentioned in Chapter 2, Zhang Zhidong had been unable to use it, and it was being stored in a Shanghai warehouse.[46] Zhang Jian and the government agreed that this donation of machinery would be considered the government's provision of half the capitalization of the Dasheng mill. The remaining half was to be provided by private investors, and therefore, according to late Qing terminology, Dasheng was a *guanshang heban* enterprise.[47] The machinery was valued at 500,000 taels, and shares in this amount were to be held by the government. To complicate the situation, the government contribution came with the condition that an equal amount of private capital be raised.[48]

Zhang Jian found it difficult to raise the private capital required. In 1897, he approached Sheng Xuanhuai for funds. Sheng at that time was prominent in government-sponsored businesses as director of the Huasheng Spinning and Weaving Mill, the China Merchants' Steamship Navigation Company, and the Imperial Railroad Administration.[49] In a desperate attempt, Zhang Jian offered Sheng Xuanhuai half the machinery Zhang Zhidong had agreed to supply in return for Sheng's agreement to raise 250,000 taels.[50]

This overture clearly reflects Zhang Jian's calculation of the political situation at the time and his wish to avoid the collapse of an enterprise that so far only existed on paper. Zhang Jian was probably relying on Zhang Zhidong's goodwill to pressure Sheng Xuanhuai, since Sheng had already agreed to take over the struggling Hanyang Ironworks and its subsidiary mines in 1896 after Zhang Zhidong was unable to raise the necessary funds.[51] If that strategy had succeeded, Zhang Jian would in effect have sold a portion of Dasheng's assets provided by the government in order to claim that he had raised private capital. Apart from the fact that this transaction would have turned government assets into private funds, it would also have meant a much smaller operation than the one he had promised Zhang Zhidong in order to get the machinery. Much to Zhang Jian's dismay, however, Sheng Xuanhuai did not raise the money, and the deal fell through.[52] In the end, Zhang Jian did not succeed in raising the required private capital, but in 1899, since he at least had the machinery, he started operations anyway.

When the Dasheng mill commenced production in 1899, paid-up capital amounted to 195,100 taels and had been provided by local investors from Nantong and Haimen.[53] By 1901 their investment had risen to 239,400 taels, and by 1902 to 330,000 taels.[54] A list of the shareholders in the Dasheng No. 1 Cotton Mill between 1898 and 1903 reveals that many of the major local cloth businesses were investors. For example, Hengji, a prominent local business, owned five shares in the No. 1 mill.[55]

We can assume that these local merchants understood the cotton business in Tongzhou and invested in the Dasheng mill as part of their local business activities. In their shops, these merchants sold the yarn produced by Dasheng next to locally produced cloth (*tubu*).[56] The high-quality yarn produced on Dasheng's industrial machinery was purchased mainly by local weavers, who then wove it into *tubu* on their wooden handlooms. These local merchants brokered the link between industrial yarn production and cloth weaving in Nantong and the cloth's major markets in the Northeast (Dongbei) (see Chapter 8).

It is no coincidence that Shen Xiejun, one of Zhang Jian's most capable and staunchest supporters from the very beginning, was an influential cloth merchant and a prominent member of Nantong's merchant community.[57] Shen was the managing partner of the well-established Hengji cloth shop (*buzhuang*), which sold cotton cloth wholesale to the northeastern provinces. At the beginning of the Guangxu period (1875–1908), the cloth market had experienced a slump. Local merchants had deputed Shen Xiejun to request a reduction in the transit tax on commercial goods.[58] Despite repeated petitions, Shen had no success. Later he received support from Zhang Jian, who petitioned the government in the late 1890s to protect Chinese merchants. Zhang Jian warned that the power balance in China had recently changed and that the government could no longer afford to neglect important economic issues. As he put it: "In China nowadays officials are all merchants, and merchants can become officials."[59]

Apart from these local political initiatives, which must have made Zhang Jian popular within the business community, his diary reveals how important Shen Xiejun was to him as an advisor and close business associate. Unfortunately his discussions of business are never very specific, but the frequency of his meetings with Shen Xiejun is clear enough. For example, in 1896 Zhang Jian either met or corresponded with Shen several times every month; this cooperation was to last for years.[60] Once factory operations began, Shen immediately became senior manager in charge of raw material acquisition and distribution in the Dasheng No. 1 Cotton Mill.

There is little doubt that Zhang Jian as an outsider both to business and to Nantong needed Shen Xiejun as a mediator and as a socially and economically powerful member of Nantong's business community. In a nutshell, local support for Zhang Jian proved much more important than patronage from senior government officials. Zhang Jian paid tribute to Shen Xiejun's vital practical and moral support in an emotional obituary that documents Shen's key role in his business success:

> When I [Zhang Jian] went from scholarship into industrial enterprise, people did not trust me. At this time Shen [Xiejun] was already in the cloth business. The cloth merchants were grateful for Xiejun's efforts in having the transit tax (*lijin*) reduced, and his trust and reputation were greater than mine. At the times of utmost difficulties in my factory operations, I was dependent on Xiejun as the provider of consolation! He never said a word that discouraged me. . . . I often tell people that Tongzhou [i.e., Nantong] owes the success of its textile industry to the help of Xiejun.[61]

Shen Xiejun exemplifies the many members of Nantong's commercial community with whom Zhang Jian maintained business relations. Liu Yishan and Zhang Jingfu are other examples of important local businessmen among Dasheng's prominent shareholders. Liu Yishan owned the Liu Zhengda cloth business and invested in several of Dasheng's business operations; Zhang Jingfu was the founder and manager of the Deji company, one of the biggest cloth shops in the area, which grew out of a *qianzhuang* with the same name and became a major customer of Dasheng.[62]

In 1900 the Dasheng No. 1 mill reported its first net profit of 26,850 taels. Profits doubled during the first half of 1901.[63] At that time one share in the company was priced at 100 taels. The text on the share certificates stated a total incapitalization of 500,000 taels: 250,000 taels in form of machinery contributed by the government and 250,000 taels as private (but only eventually paid-up) capital by private investors.[64] In order to enhance the reputation and probably the trustworthiness of the newly founded enterprise, Zhang Jian's full title as Hanlin scholar (*Hanlin yuan xiuzhuan*) appeared on the share certificates between 1897 and 1907.[65] Share certificates issued in 1915 and 1919 no longer mention him.[66] Obviously by that time the company had established a solid reputation and was able to attract investors more easily than it had earlier.

Each share entitled its holder to a guaranteed dividend (*guanli*) of 8 percent per year,[67] regardless of the company's performance. This was a common practice to attract investors and had been a feature of the first substantial government-sponsored enterprises such as the China Merchants' Steamship Navigation Company.[68] As the passbooks (*xizhe*) for drawing the dividends show, the shareholders collected their fixed dividend from Dasheng at the end of each fiscal year.[69]

The cotton mill was the first enterprise in a growing industrial complex, which would gradually encompass such varied subsidiaries and affiliated enterprises as flour and oil mills, shipping lines, land reclamation companies, a publishing house, and even a distillery. As I discuss in detail in Chapter 5, all these companies were founded during the first decade of the twentieth century, and they kept their affiliation with Dasheng even after it became a limited liability company.

Because of the important role of land reclamation in guaranteeing a stable supply of cotton, it became one of Zhang Jian's major business concerns. The official founding of the Tonghai Land Reclamation Company in 1901 was preceded by several years of negotiations. This reclamation operation along the coast of Haimen was part of the reward Zhang Jian received from the government for his efforts to found a local industry. From his diary we know that in the seventh month of 1895 Zhang Zhidong came to discuss business matters with Zhang Jian.[70] Only two weeks later, Zhang Jian started the negotiations over the fee he would have to pay to the garrison that at the time occupied parts of the wasteland along the Haimen coast.

The Tonghai Land Reclamation Company began operating in 1903, but it took several years before the 120,000 mu of land Zhang had purchased were brought under cultivation.[71] The activities of the Tonghai Land Reclamation Company would eventually complement the operations of Dasheng, since they enabled Zhang Jian to provide his factories with raw material within easy reach and at competitive prices (see Chapter 7). This company is crucial for understanding Zhang Jian's strategy during the following years of establishing enterprises that supplied raw materials or by-products or provided transportation facilities for the cotton mills.

During this initial period, Zhang Jian concentrated his business activities mainly in Nantong county. The Dasheng No. 1 mill and subsidiaries like the flour mill and soap factory were located in Tangjiazha; the transportation companies' offices and the publishing house were in Nantong city. In 1904 Zhang Jian started preparations for setting up a branch mill, known as Dasheng No. 2 Cotton Mill, on Chongming island, and operations began in

1907.[72] Apparently the success of his first mill emboldened him to expand his business. Chongming island was famous for its high-quality cotton and could easily supply the new plant with raw material.

As his business grew into a conglomerate, Zhang Jian needed support from his personal network and family to fulfill the many managerial tasks. Although I will argue in the following chapters that Zhang Jian succeeded in maintaining control not through networks but through institutionalized tools within the enterprise, Dasheng's day-to-day business involved family members, without, however, giving them full access to Zhang Jian's instruments of power.

Family Ties

Zhang Jian's active involvement in provincial and national politics meant that he spent much of his time away from Nantong. His brother Zhang Cha looked after his local business interests during his absence. Although Dasheng never became a family business, family members were included in the managerial and financial administration of Dasheng and the business complex at large. However, Zhang Jian limited the involvement to core members; he depended more on a personal network of business and political associates and personal friends among the local elite (see Chapter 7). For this reason I prefer to speak of family ties rather than of a full-blown family network.

Zhang Cha has received much less attention in the literature than his brother, but he was more influential and important to the Dasheng business than has generally been assumed.[73] In 1902, at the request of his brother, he had left his official post as a minor magistrate in Jiangxi province to help manage the Dasheng No. 1 mill. Zhang Cha's role in the enterprise is examined below; here suffice it to say that his involvement increased from the mid-1910s on. For example, he became general manager of the Dasheng No. 3 branch mill, which was founded in Haimen in 1914.[74] That same year he also joined his brother in founding several land-reclamation companies along the northern Jiangsu coast.

The two brothers also worked together to direct Nantong's social and educational development. Reflecting the hierarchical status of his management positions in the various business enterprises, Zhang Cha, for example, was the vice-director of the schools and charity institutions set up by Zhang

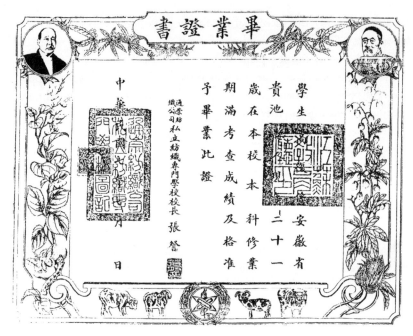

Fig. 3.3 Graduation certificate from the Nantong Textile School with the
portraits of Zhang Jian and Zhang Cha (NTFB: doc. 423, 1918).

Jian.[75] In public the two brothers assumed different roles, vividly documented in a graduation certificate of the Nantong textile school from 1918
(see Fig. 3.3).[76] The photograph of Zhang Jian on the document shows him
in a Western suit and with a cropped mustache; Zhang Cha appears in a
traditional Chinese riding jacket with skull cap and a long beard.

The contrasting images were circulated in contemporary publications and
were also featured in the men's respective biographical entries in *Who's Who
in China*, published in Shanghai in the early 1920s, and in reports in the *North
China Herald* in 1921.[77] Although Zhang Jian was the *zhuangyuan* scholar and
representative of traditional Chinese learning and government service, he
chose the image of a modernizer and promoter of "Western" ideas in public
(see Fig. 3.4). Not surprisingly, this progressive image continues today, as
can be seen, for example, in the recently erected statue of Zhang Jian at his
gravesite in Nantong city (see Fig. 3.5). In contrast, his brother, who had no
particular claim to fame in scholarship and officialdom, chose to present
himself publicly in the role of the traditional scholar (see Fig. 3.6). These

Fig. 3.4 Zhang Jian in the 1910s (Nantong youyi julebu, *Nantong shiye, jiaoyu, cishan fengjing*, 1920, unpaginated).

visual distinctions reflected the complementary aspects of their cooperation. Zhang Cha's traditional image may well have evoked trust from traditionally minded local shareholders and business associates in Dasheng; Zhang Jian's Western image and modern attire appealed to members of the reform-minded local elite, the business community in Shanghai, and the political circles in which he moved. The brothers also indirectly symbolized the nature of Dasheng as an enterprise oriented toward Western-style management and a strong adherence to Chinese traditions. This interpretation, in an ironic twist, is a rather profound statement about Dasheng's institutional character as a Chinese business in the early twentieth century, as I will discuss in Chapters 5 and 6.

Although Dasheng was not a family business, the second generation eventually became involved in the enterprise.[78] As Zhang Jian's only son, Zhang Xiaoruo was groomed to be a modern young man with a Western education and experiences abroad.[79] However, as we shall see in the last chapter, he did not live up to expectations and become a strong and capable business leader after his father's death. Instead, he preferred the world of entertainment in Shanghai to the world of business in Nantong.

Fig. 3.5 Zhang Jian's gravesite in Nantong, 1993
(photograph by the author).

Fig. 3.6 Zhang Cha in the 1910s (Nantong youyi julebu,
Nantong shiye, jiaoyu, cishan fengjing, 1920, unpaginated).

Apparently Zhang Jian never seriously considered establishing the younger generation of his family in his business. Although his own son lacked the qualities of a capable successor, Zhang Jian could have trained his brother's sons for key positions in the enterprise. However, in contrast to industrialists like the Rong brothers who made use of their extended family network to manage their various enterprises, Zhang Jian did not delegate power to the next generation.[80] For example, Zhang Ren, the older son of Zhang Cha, only headed the local industrial police guard for Tongzhou, Haimen, and Taizhou, which had been established as a private local militia to guarantee law and order during the transition to the Republic.[81] Zhang Ren died in the late 1910s, and Zhang Cha's younger son, Zhang Jingli (1911–83), did not become involved in the Dasheng business until the 1930s. Zhang Xiaoruo's death in 1935 ended his involvement in the business. As discussed in Chapter 8, Zhang Jingli then became the family's only representative in Dasheng until its transformation into a state-owned enterprise in the early 1950s.

Machinery, Land, and Technology

The issues of machinery, land, and technology are important because they were determined by the peculiar way in which the mill was founded. With the government capital in form of machinery, crucial decisions on the use of specific equipment and technology had already been taken out of the hands of the aspiring industrialist. As I will show, this did not necessarily imply a competitive disadvantage for Dasheng and suited Zhang Jian's financial priorities rather well.

Zhang Zhidong's machinery had sat in a warehouse in Shanghai's wharf area for several years. It had to be shipped from the warehouse in Pudong to the factory site at Tangjiazha village, where it was cleaned and scraped in order to remove the accumulated rust.[82] The cleaning and repair of the machinery was a costly procedure; including the transportation costs, it amounted to over 16,000 taels.[83] However, considering the cost of new equipment, the use of old and rusty, though yet unused, machinery could still be justified.

Even in the English cotton industry in the eighteenth and nineteenth century, it was not uncommon to use secondhand equipment in newly established factories in order to minimize initial fixed capital costs.[84] When

Zhang Jian established his first branch mill in Chongming in 1907, he also purchased secondhand machinery, this time from the Shanxi Central Bureau for Commercial Affairs (Shanxi shangwu zongju).[85] Since the installation of textile machinery was complicated, the original contract, which Zhang Jian acquired together with Zhang Zhidong's machinery, had included the supervision of the installation by an expert. A foreign engineer was hired at considerable expense to supervise the installation of the machinery at its new home in the Dasheng No. 1 mill in Tangjiazha.[86]

Most of this initial machinery equipment in the Dasheng mills had been manufactured by British firms and eventually was supplemented with equipment ordered from American firms in the 1910s and early 1920s. J. Hetherington & Sons Ltd., a textile-machine maker in Manchester, England, was the producer of the first 20,400 spindles installed in the No. 1 mill after 1896; by the early 1920s, the number of spindles rose to 80,000, all by the same maker.[87] As one of the major producers of machinery for every step of the production process in a cotton mill, this firm, like many other Western and Japanese suppliers, maintained an office in the middle of Shanghai's International Settlement on Hankou Road. The first 35,000 spindles of the No. 2 mill in Chongming were purchased from Howard & Bullough, another prominent British textile firm. Power in the No. 1 mill was provided by a steam engine and a Lancashire boiler. When the factory added weaving to its production process in 1915, 400 looms from the American machine manufacturers Lowell and Henry Livesey were imported.[88]

The boiler and other supplementary machinery equipment such as belts and pipes were also purchased through specialized Shanghai brokerages and transported to Tianshenggang, which became the most significant port for Dasheng on the north bank of the river. As early as 1899 trading companies like Mitsui supplied the No. 1 mill through this port with bulk goods such as coal or heavy machinery ordered in Shanghai.[89] The boiler and steam engine for the No. 2 branch mill, which had been ordered through the Swire brokerage in 1904, were transported in the same fashion and arrived in over 1,800 large and small boxes.[90] Since assembling the machinery correctly according to the plans and explanations was difficult, the brokerages always sent an experienced engineer to supervise the installation. Most likely the engineer introduced the factory technicians to the use and maintenance of the equipment.

Machinery from Hetherington & Sons, Howard & Bullough, and Lowell represented the cutting edge in textile technology at the time, not only in China but worldwide.[91] By relying on these foreign imports, Dasheng not only acquired the newest machinery but also the most up-to-date technology in cotton yarn production. In the case of the initial machinery supplied by the government, the detailed discussions between Zhang Jian and his managers on the question of which equipment to order had become redundant. However, until the 1920s, the Dasheng mills relied mainly on technical advice from Shanghai brokerages and their engineering experts when ordering new equipment.[92]

In the textile business, in China as well as all over the world, most machinery was custom-made according to the plant's specific physical arrangements and the production needs of the customer. For example, the engineer Frederick R. Pratt from the Whitin Machine Works in Whitinsville, Massachusetts, worked with Dasheng through a contract with the Gaston, Williams & Wigmore Far Eastern Division Inc., a brokerage in Shanghai. Pratt first advised and then supervised Dasheng's purchase of 25,000 spindles in 1921 from the Whitin company.[93] Consultations with the Dasheng managers took him or his representative (in 1921 a Chinese engineer named Yang Shizong) to Nantong several times.[94]

The overwhelming reliance on foreign machinery by Chinese textile mills was common at the time and necessitated by the lack of domestic manufacturers. Since agriculture-based products dominated the structure of prewar manufacturing in China, the manufacture of textile machinery developed only slowly in the wake of the domestic textile industry's development as a whole. As Thomas Rawski has pointed out, as in other industrializing nations, in China "the accumulation of mechanical and metalworking skills resulting from repair work in textile factories was a major contributor to the emergence of an engineering industry."[95]

The Dalong Machine Works owned and managed by the Yan family in Shanghai illustrate Rawski's point. The company started out by servicing steamships in the early 1900s and then switched to servicing machinery in the 1910s due to increasing demand during the boom in the textile sector and other manufacturing industries.[96] However, despite its profitable business, Dalong did not venture into machine manufacturing until the 1920s and even then had to overcome the competitive advantage of imports from well-established foreign firms. Despite its eventual success, machine manufacturing did not become the most profitable part of the Dalong company; the owner-manager decided to branch into real estate and to establish his own spinning mills.[97]

Similarly, literature on engineering and professional issues in the textile industry emerged in significant quantity only relatively late. In 1919 the successful Chinese cotton mill owner Mu Ouchu (1876–1942) (he had founded three large mills in 1915, 1918, and 1919) shared his experiences in setting up and running a mill in the newly founded professional journal published by the Chinese Cotton Mill Owners' Association (Huashang shachang lianhehui), of which he also served as president.[98] However, his report reflects his personal and practical experience and does not represent a theoretical approach to the topic. Professional manuals with titles such as *Factory Design and Management* dealing with issues from shop-floor design to insurance to time management and productivity began to appear only in the late 1920s.[99]

The slow development and spread of technical knowledge should not surprise us in an emerging industry, even though the first Chinese translations of English manuals on steam engines and mechanical engineering by translators from the Jiangnan Arsenal had been published in the late nineteenth century.[100] The establishment of technical colleges and the introduction of textile engineering into the teaching curriculum in the 1910s attest to the industry's increasing need for specialized knowledge and professional training. The first textile schools, such as the Nantong Textile School (Nantong fangzhi zhuanmen xuexiao), founded by Zhang Jian in 1912, used teaching materials based on original business documents and equipment used in the mill to which it was attached. For example, the materials on textile machinery were drawn by hand by a teacher in the Nantong school who himself was a graduate of the second class to enter the school, in 1914.[101] Because of the lack of appropriate textbooks, students studying how to prepare a contract for foreign machinery studied copies of contracts between major Chinese cotton mills and their brokerages in Shanghai.[102] Probably reflecting the late development of Chinese machine manufacturing as an industry and machine engineering as a technical profession, essays by engineers on the technical aspects of textile machinery and choices in technology began to appear in professional journals such as *Textile Weekly* only in the 1930s.[103]

Apart from machinery, land and buildings are the other major assets needed to set up a cotton mill. According to Zhang Jian, the group of local investors in Tongzhou bought the land for the No. 1 mill in Tangjiazha in 1896.[104] Unfortunately, I was not able to locate the original land deeds in Nantong, and it is not absolutely clear who became the owner of the company land. However, six land deeds for the Dasheng cotton mill are listed in a document from 1911 and state that land in Tangjiazha west of the river was systematically purchased from private owners in 1895, 1896, 1901, 1903, and 1905 at a total cost of 8,125 yuan.[105] According to this document, the cotton mill owned 142 mu in Tangjiazha, but other land deeds may well have existed. The earliest complete original land deed available to me is dated 1905 and indicates that the Industrial Company (Shiye gongsi), later established as Dasheng's shell company, sold a small plot of land to a certain Zhu family in the village of Yuchigang.[106] This plot of land had apparently come into the company's possession through Zhang Jian's land reclamation project after 1900.

Land for building the branch mills was acquired in a similar fashion. Records kept in the accounts office of the No. 2 mill in Chongming show systematic purchase from 1904 on of land on this island to establish a new work site.[107] More than 22 recorded contracts give a clear description of where the plots were located, how much land they included, the selling price, and the seller. However, although the Dasheng No. 2 mill acquired some land for the construction of factory buildings, it also rented out purchased land. For example, as the contracts show, vacant land to the northeast of the factory was leased as farmland to tenants after it had been purchased by the company in 1906.[108]

Construction work at Tangjiazha started in late 1897 and was followed by the building of workshops, the final installation of machinery, the repair of sluice gates and embankments, and the construction of roads and bridges in 1898.[109] In 1899 the factory buildings at the No. 1 mill were completed and the boiler installed; the spinning machines began operating in May of that year. Zhang Jian had an authoritarian management style, and his diary suggests that he seldom visited the factories in person. As befitted a managing director at the time, he delegated the supervisory tasks to his managers. However, in 1898 and 1899 he went to Tangjiazha every few months in order to inspect progress on the construction and was present at major events such as the installation of the boiler.[110] In similar fashion, directors of the board in German textile factories liked to visit construction sites at important junctures such as the raising of the rafters and have their picture taken.[111]

Despite his erratic presence, given his authority and prestige, Zhang Jian filled an almost ritual function in the construction of the factory compound. For example, after the buildings of the No. 1 mill were finished, he composed an auspicious couplet alluding to the importance of his business for the welfare of the country, which was later immortalized in a pair of scrolls in the famous calligraphy of the imperial tutor Weng Tonghe.[112] Other events like the installation of a generator for the mill's power supply show that Zhang Jian took his ritual role seriously and did not hesitate to perform ceremonies; on the outside this seems to contrast oddly with the use of modern technology. In proper and respectful attire, he knocked his head in reverence toward the electric light three times after the power was switched on, very much as one pays respects to the ancestors.[113] He also had ceremonies performed on behalf of the success of the construction work. In the case of the No. 3 mill, established in Haimen in 1916, Zhang Jian wrote an auspicious poem for the groundbreaking ceremony. The title clearly suggests that he composed it for the sacrifice to the Earth god held on this occasion.[114] Needless to say, as documents of modern and scientific mill management, none of the Dasheng mills' construction plans ever marked the location of a little temple or shrine on the compound, although its existence is conceivable.

This leads us finally to the question of the local response to the introduction of power-driven machinery and industrial technology in the last decade of the nineteenth century. As has already been mentioned, before the arrival of industrial factory work in the Nantong area, cotton yarn and cloth had been produced at home on simple spinning wheels and mechanical looms for private consumption and as supplemental income for rural households.[115] Although the local spinners could have perceived the new factories as a potential economic threat to their livelihood, the impression usually given in studies on Dasheng is that the introduction of machine spinning did not meet with local opposition.

Nevertheless, a commemorative volume published in Nantong in 1926 indicates that things did not go so smoothly at first. After noting the reluctance of the local elite to invest in the enterprise, this text remarks: "There were people engaged in the native cloth industry who wanted to burn down the factory, and so soldiers were sent to protect it. Only then could the Dasheng spinning mill be established."[116]

We know about Luddite-like riots by silk weavers in Guangdong against the mechanized silk filatures in the late Qing period.[117] However, it seems that the protest in Nantong was never as severe. One explanation for the lack of unrest is the fact that hand-weaving expanded because of the high quality and abundance of the machine-spun yarn. In contrast to the Guangdong silk weavers who were unable to use the fine machine-spun thread on their wooden looms, weavers in Nantong began to produce a cloth that combined the use of machine-spun yarn as weft and hand-spun yarn as warp.[118] As a result, the quality of the local hand-woven cloth improved. Thus industrial yarn production led indirectly to increased demand for products of the cottage weaving industry in Nantong at the beginning of the twentieth century; this must have taken the edge off protest.

————◆————

The difficulties Dasheng encountered during its founding are symptomatic of those many new Chinese industrial enterprises faced after 1895. The political atmosphere for private investment may have become more flexible, but the increasingly unreliable relationship between private businessmen and the government posed problems. In addition, the as yet insufficient economic, legal, and social framework prevented Chinese business from developing rapidly because of financial and proprietary issues. At a time when private investors were slow to put their money into unfamiliar business ventures, government patronage no longer guaranteed financial help. As Dasheng's case shows, after 1895 the structure of patronage broadened but did not disappear completely.[119] Although Zhang Jian received support from various officials, their influence was not strong enough to set the enterprise on firm financial grounds. To complicate things, officials-turned-entrepreneurs like Zhang Jian also had to cope with a general lack of expertise in organizing and using modern machinery and technology in the industrial setting of the factory.

At the local level, Zhang Jian's difficulties in establishing the mill point to his position as an outsider, with no previous industrial experience and no track record in Nantong. As in the case of other industrialists with a background in officialdom such as Nie Qigui (1850–1911) or Zhou Xuexi (1866–1947), reputation capital in form of the prestigious *zhuangyuan* title did not automatically guarantee more favorable business opportunities. The fact that it took Zhang Jian so long to find investors for his business shows the limits of reputation capital for acquiring capital in late imperial China.

The role the government played through its contribution of machinery and rewards of land decided the initial location and equipment of the factory without forcing Zhang Jian to make these significant business decisions. I have argued here that Zhang Jian's role in the founding of Dasheng reflects more a rational response to given circumstances than industrial activism based on patriotic sentiments. Although I do not dispute his enthusiasm and commitment, I argue that we also have to acknowledge Zhang Jian's skills as a businessman who recognizes a business opportunity and, despite initial setbacks, turns it into the cornerstone of a profitable enterprise.

Finally, we have to ask how representative Dasheng's development as a regional enterprise was. For example, the Sulun mill was established as a government enterprise in Suzhou in 1897 under the management of the *zhuangyuan* Lu Runxiang (1841–1915). However, the enterprise never achieved any substantial profits, even after its privatization in 1912.[120] The Yeqin spinning mills in Wuxi represent another case of a regional enterprise under the management of an official-turned-industrialist, in this case the former *daotai* Yang Zonghan. However, like the Sulun mills and despite the patronage of Zhang Zhidong, the enterprise never achieved a secure economic footing.[121] Both cases illustrate the limitations of decentralized official patronage, insufficient private investment, and poor capital markets. In Nantong, a combination of positive factors such as Zhang Jian's charismatic personality, the local availability of high-quality cotton, and his skillful incorporation of the local commercial community into his business plans turned Dasheng into a regional enterprise that not only survived the initial stage but became one of China's most successful private enterprises in the early twentieth century. It is now time to turn to the other important ingredient in the success story of Dasheng as a regional enterprise—its workforce and the work environment in the mills.

CHAPTER 4

The Realities of Industrial Work

This chapter examines the concrete physical and managerial organization of the factories and their workforce, with an emphasis on the Dasheng No. 1 mill.[1] The majority of the No. 1 mill's workforce consisted of unskilled workers from the surrounding villages with some background in home weaving. Thus any definition of the term *worker* must incorporate both the workers' rural background and their employment in factory work. The introduction of industrial work to a rural area confronts us with questions of how the transition from home industry to factory work came about, how workers at the factory defined themselves, and who, from management's point of view, counted as a member of the mill's workforce. These issues are closely connected to the concepts of control and accountability management applied to the work process and to the social hierarchy within the compound.

Studies on factory work by Emily Honig, Elizabeth Perry, and Gail Hershatter have examined the working and living conditions of a predominantly female workforce in big cities such as Shanghai or Tianjin during the Republican period.[2] Their detailed analyses and their strong focus on socioeconomic factors have dealt with the responses of workers to the requirements of factory work, the organization of labor protest, and the relationships of these protests to the formation of a working-class consciousness. A study of the Dasheng mills in Nantong will broaden our perspective on these issues not only because these factories were located in a rural area but also because this industrial development predates the economic booms in Shanghai and Tianjin by almost twenty years. The Dasheng mills can tell us much about the conceptualization of work and workplace among workers, employees, and management and how this process affected the company's management ethos, the lives of local workers, and the social and economic development of the surrounding communities. As we will see, certain patterns in labor relations, shop-floor management, and labor politics highlight the differences between urban and rural work environments.

Factory Compound, Management, and Hierarchies

The Dasheng No. 1 Cotton Mill was situated in Tangjiazha village, northwest of Nantong city. The mill's official name, Tongzhou Dasheng shachang (Dasheng cotton mill in Tongzhou department), which changed in 1911 to Nantong xian Dasheng shachang (Dasheng cotton mill in Nantong county), indicated that the manufacturing of cotton yarn in the mill did not take place in Nantong city.[3] However, publications from the beginning of the twentieth century on associate the Dasheng No. 1 Cotton Mill with the development of Nantong as a city and a region and do not refer to Tangjiazha as an independent place with its own community and socioeconomic structure. They create the erroneous impression that the factory compound was located in an urban setting. In fact, the rural background of the workforce was an essential ingredient of the Dasheng No. 1 mill. The same can be said of the branch mills that began production in 1907, 1921, and 1923.

Maps, photographs, and written descriptions are the main sources for piecing together a picture of the work compound as it existed in the late nineteenth and early twentieth century. In contrast to Nantong city, whose maps recorded the modern educational and public welfare institutions in which the city took pride, Tangjiazha had nothing more modern to offer than the cotton mills that dominated it.[4] The maps of the cotton mill said all there was to be said about Tangjiazha; the village, even if not consciously, was meant to be forgotten.

In 1898 a large factory compound with modern factory buildings was a novelty in China, especially in the countryside. Although the scale of operation of some silk-producing workshops during the Ming and Qing was quite substantial, these early workshops were not factories. For example, in the mid-seventeenth century, the Suzhou imperial silk workshops had 400 looms and employed 1,170 artisans who were paid in rice each month.[5] But as an enterprise these workshops were not characterized by the single hierarchical structure characteristic of a complex factory operation. The silk workshops tended to split up into subcontracting units, with the government

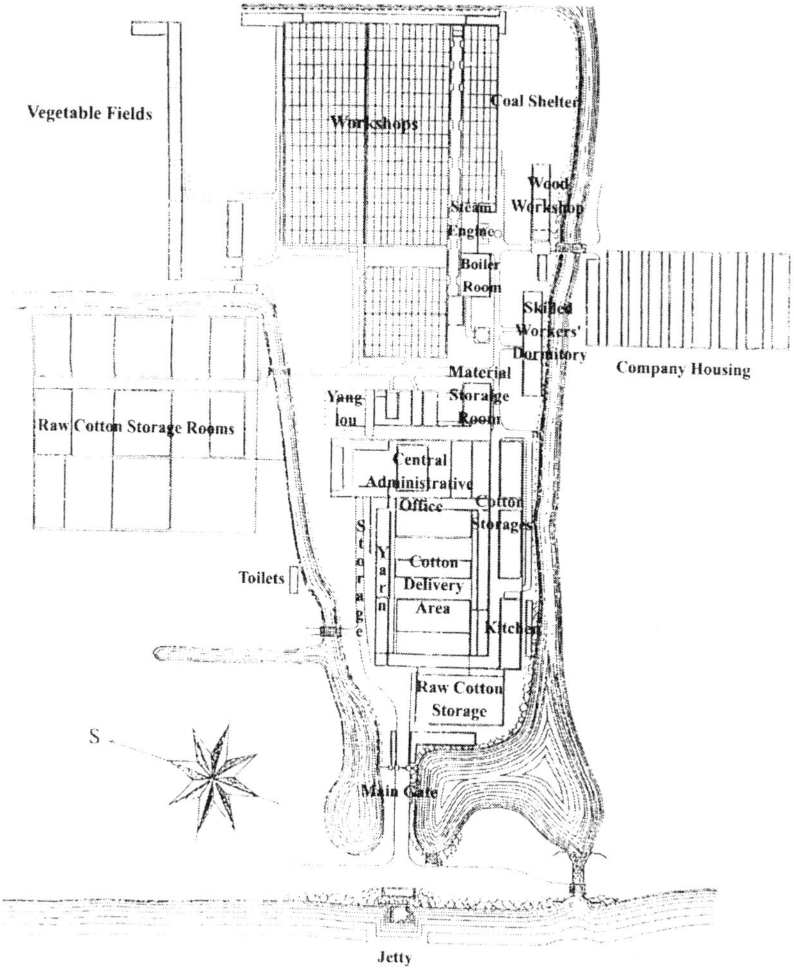

Fig. 4.1 Map of the Dasheng No. 1 Cotton Mill factory compound (adapted from *Jiangsu Tongzhou Dasheng fangzhi gufen youxian gongsi zhi tu*, 1919?).

officials responsible for their organization functioning as purchasing agents. In contrast, the Dasheng compound exhibits a complex yet strict hierarchical structure in the organization of work in relation to the layout of the shop floor. Moreover, management dictated a daily routine that created a new social hierarchy.

The earliest Chinese map of the Dasheng No. 1 Cotton Mill shows that the work compound consisted of two parts: the administration section (*hang*) and the workshops (*gongchang*) (see Fig. 4.1). Together they made up the cotton mill (*shachang*).[6] In later maps, the term *chang* as in *shachang* came to be used for the workshops.[7] To judge from the nomenclature, the administrative and trading functions of the mill were considered as important as the manufacturing side in the early days; only later, when the term *chang* came to be associated almost exclusively with production, did it acquire its current meaning of "factory" and the administrative and business side of the enterprise become overshadowed in the popular mind by the workshops.

The Dasheng No. 1 work compound was spread over 8.6 hectares (21.25 acres).[8] Someone arriving from outside Tangjiazha would most likely approach it by boat along the Tongyang canal, which was linked to the Yangzi River. The company owned a stone jetty on the canal in front of the main entrance to the compound, where boats unloaded the raw cotton from local collection stations or from Shanghai and loaded finished goods, mostly yarn, for distribution and sale. At the end of the jetty, a large wooden gate with three arches and the inscription "Dasheng Pier" (Dasheng matou) gave the compound a grand and distinctive entrance (see Figs. 4.2 and 4.3). Beyond the jetty a crowd of porters—known to Westerners and Chinese as "coolies"—waited for work.[9] They carried cotton bales from the jetty into the compound.[10] These porters were not mentioned in the company's regulations and were not on the payroll. Obviously, they were hired on a daily basis and paid according to the work they did.

For someone approaching the work compound from the village, the compound's dominant features would have been the clock tower, chimney, and walls (see Fig. 4.4). Visually, the compound was a tightly structured building complex surrounded on its northern, southern, and western sides by a bamboo fence and canals (Fig. 4.5). These canals connected the compound with the Tongyang canal east of the mill and thus eventually with the Yangzi River. Access to storage rooms, toilets, and company housing bordering the work compound was possible over three small bridges.[11] Workers entered the work compound from the main gate to the east, under a big brick gateway bearing the characters "Dasheng shachang" (Dasheng Cotton Mill).[12]

Inside the compound, the buildings were laid out in the order of the production, delivery, and distribution processes. Behind the office for raw cotton deliveries (*shouhuachu*) were cotton storage rooms (*huazhan*) on the right and yarn storage rooms (*shazhan*) and the wholesale office (*pifasuo*) on the

Fig. 4.2 The Dasheng jetty, main entrance, and clocktower in Tangjiazha, ca. 1920 (Nantong youyi julebu, *Nantong shiye, jiaoyu, cishan fengjing,* 1920, unpaginated).

Fig. 4.3 The Dasheng jetty in Tangjiazha, 1998 (photograph by the author).

Fig. 4.4 Factory grounds of the Dasheng No. 1 Cotton Mill at Tangjiazha with the training area of the company patrol force in the foreground (Nantong youyi julebu, *Nantong shiye, jiaoyu, cishan fengjing*, 1920, unpaginated).

left (Fig. 4.6). The head office (*zong banshichu*) was situated in the middle of the administrative section, surrounded by a dining hall, with separate kitchen facilities, and additional storage rooms. Behind the head office on the left was the "foreign building" (*yanglou*), the office built in a "foreign style" (*yangshi*) that served as Zhang Jian's personal office (see Fig. 4.7). In order to stress its detachment from the rest of the work compound, this office was surrounded by a bamboo fence. Because of the physical layout, ordinary workers seldom entered the administrative area; the routes from the main gate to the workshops kept them away from the offices.

Behind the management offices were storage rooms for oil, machinery parts, and other equipment and finally the workshops proper.[13] Until 1915, the workshops were housed in one-, two-, and three-story brick buildings (see Fig. 4.8).[14] The workshops' design was meant to be functional rather than aesthetic: high windows and supporting pillars, between which were placed row upon row of machinery. Brick gave way to steel girders and cement in 1915 when the Dasheng No. 1 mill incorporated weaving into its operations. The looms were too heavy for multistory workshops and had to

Fig. 4.5 Canal in the compound of the former Dasheng No. 1 Cotton Mill, 1998
(photograph by the author).

be installed in one-floor buildings with sawtooth roofs and large skylights that afforded more natural light for the more complicated weaving procedures.[15]

Each workshop was defined by the task performed in it and gave it its name: the picking room (*jianhua chang*), ginning room (*yahua chang*), blowing room (*qinghua chang*), roving room (*cusha chang*), spinning room (*xisha chang*), reeling room (*yaosha chang*), and packing room (*chengbao chang*).[16] In the picking room, the workers sorted the raw cotton according to its quality and condition. It was then taken to the ginning room where seeds, sand, and other impurities were removed. The cleaning process was continued in the blowing room, where the matted cotton was torn apart, fluffed, and cleaned again. The workers in the roving and spinning rooms were occupied with the task of producing the actual cotton yarn by entering the rope-like strands of cotton into a series of roving and spinning machines until a fine cotton thread emerged. In the reeling room, the cotton yarn was reeled from the machines' bobbins into hanks, which were finally taken to the packing room for weighing and bundling (see Fig. 4.9).

Fig. 4.6 Original storage rooms for raw cotton at the former Dasheng
No. 1 Cotton Mill, 1998 (photograph by the author).

Fig. 4.7 Zhang Jian's office in the *yanglou* on the factory compound of the former
Dasheng No. 1 Cotton Mill, 1998 (photograph by the author).

Fig. 4.8 Brick factory buildings with the tower for the boiler at the Dasheng No. 2 mill in Chongming (Nantong youyi julebu, *Nantong shiye, jiaoyu, cishan fengjing*, 1920, unpaginated).

Once weaving was added to the production process in 1915, the yarn had to go through a preparatory process before it could be used in the weaving sheds. According to an anonymous visitor to Dasheng's shop floor in the early 1920s, the yarn was again put onto the reeling machines, which wound the thread into bigger yarn cans. After feeding the yarn into sizing machines to make it stronger and more durable, it was wound onto loom-beams before being drawn into the shafts and reeds for the final weaving process.[17]

Although it is easy to understand how the production process dictated the outlay of the shop floor, it is much more difficult to assess the impact of the industrial environment on the workers' potential transformation into factory workers. A crucial aspect for understanding the dynamics on the shop floor is the issue whether and, if so, how industrial work in a factory environment helps create new identities for industrial laborers. A collection of interviews conducted with 214 former workers at the Dasheng No. 1 Cotton Mill in the 1960s enables us to reach some conclusions on how workers thought of themselves and their work.

Unskilled workers, that is, workers without vocational skills or training and previous work experience, represented the lowest stratum and the

Fig. 4.9 Label for bales of Dasheng's most popular brand of yarn, Kuixing. Considering Zhang Jian's scholarly background, the brand name is appropriate. Kuixing is the chief star of the dipper and was worshipped as the god of literature (from the author's collection).

majority of Dasheng's workforce. From the accounts of workers in the interview sample, it is obvious that unskilled workers thought of their work only in terms of the particular activity in which they were engaged and not in terms of professional identification as workers.[18] Only three of the interviewees referred to themselves as workers (*gongren*); the rest used their workshop affiliation as point of reference when asked about their life in Dasheng. For them, working in one of the workshops was "doing work" (*zuo gong*) after "entering the factory" (*jin chang*).[19] A worker "entered the factory" on the day he or she began working in the compound. From that day on, they might move slowly up a hierarchy that was closely connected to the varieties of work available in the work compound.

Even without a clearly pronounced identity, the workers in the Dasheng mill were integrated into a diversified social hierarchy on the shop floor. Different varieties of work required different skills and brought different wages. Piecework in the reeling and roving rooms tended to be more demanding than timework in the picking and ginning rooms. The work in the reeling room was extremely exhausting, not only because reeling the hanks was difficult but also because workers were paid according to the number of reels finished and thus felt under pressure to exert themselves.[20] In comparison with tasks like carding or spinning, reeling was paid at the lowest wage rate. Like most other workers in the Dasheng No. 1 mill, the reelers worked in a large room; the reeling room housed at least eighty reeling machines separated into five rows.[21] One incentive for the reelers was promotion to the roving room. The roving room, where slivers were put through a set of roving frames to produce a softer thread, was one of the noisiest and dustiest rooms in the work compound, but roving was paid at a higher rate than reeling.[22] In short, for most unskilled workers, "doing work" (zuo gong) translated into working with specific machinery in return for a wage; the work was such that it did not force on them an abstract awareness of being an industrial worker (gongren).

The reelers, the rovers, indeed almost all the workers who came from the surrounding villages, were unskilled and were trained on the shop floor in specific tasks under the supervision of the foremen (discussed in the following section). At the top of the shop-floor hierarchy were the machinists responsible for looking after machinery in certain workshops and repairing any broken parts. They had vocational skills and practical work experience, yet lacked formal textile-specific education or training; hence they fell into the middle part of the work hierarchy, above unskilled workers and below engineers. Skills acquired as a blacksmith or armorer were the usual requirement for employment as a machinist.[23] A machinist usually started in the boiler room and then moved on to the blowing room, for example, where he worked under the supervision of a more experienced machinist from Shanghai until he was promoted and assigned to a specific workshop.[24]

In addition to these skilled workers, the middle stratum of Dasheng's workforce also included administrative staff employed as accountants and their assistants, clerks, and secretaries. Since they were working in the detached administrative section (hang) of the compound, no direct communication or interaction between the unskilled workers in the workshops and the administrative staff took place. The company regulations (see below) stressed the centrality and supervising function of the administration, in particular the accounts office, over the mill's operations. The accounts office exerted strict control on a day-to-day basis by carefully examining and filing daily records from the storage rooms, registration cards from the workshops, and other aspects of the work flow.[25]

Skilled workers and administrative staff belonging to the middle stratum were not classified into blue- and white-collar workers. This is clearly reflected in their housing options. Both groups were more closely tied to the work compound than the unskilled workers because they qualified for company accommodation in either the *sushe* (dormitory) or *gongfang* (workers' housing). The *sushe*, a small building in the middle of the administrative compound, served as accommodation for unmarried staff members of the administration, for example, apprentice clerks; it also served as temporary lodgings for cotton traders and other visitors to the mill from outside. More substantial housing was provided in the *gongfang*, but only employees in the middle ranks were eligible; ordinary unskilled workers returned to their villages after their shifts.[26] These two-story, small square houses with very narrow alleys between them were built in blocks in the early 1900s. They derived their names from their positions on the compound, such as workers' houses to the east (*dong gongfang*), workers' houses to the west (*xi gongfang*), and new workers' houses (*xin gongfang*), terms still used in Tangjiazha today (see Fig. 4.10).[27]

As one rent book of the Dasheng No. 1 mill's company housing shows, almost all the tenants were identified as employees (*zhiyuan*) on the office staff, machinists (*jigong*), or bookkeepers (*jizhang*).[28] Most of the tenants and their families were not from Nantong county but from cities such as Ningbo, Wuxi, Shaoxing, Zhenjiang, and even Shanghai and Nanjing.[29] These are the places from which skilled labor and engineers were recruited.

The rent book also reveals another aspect of Dasheng's policy regarding company housing: a substantial number of tenants had occupations obviously unrelated to the mill, such as shop owner, merchant, vendor, or hairdresser. According to information from a former worker and tenant, Mr. Li Guangquan, company housing was very cheap, about one yuan per month in the 1920s, and over time tenants became virtual owners of their units.[30] Thus the accommodation was kept in the family for generations and could be "inherited" by family members, even if they themselves were no longer employed in the Dasheng mills.

In certain respects, the housing arrangements for members of the workforce on the compound bears some resemblances to the work-unit (*danwei*) system of post-1949 China. It would be easy to interpret Dasheng's company housing as the predecessor of the socialist work unit, which until recently

Fig. 4.10 Company housing on the compound of the former Dasheng
No. 1 Cotton Mill, 1998 (photograph by the author).

provided housing plus all necessary social services for workers. Recent scholarship has shown that the *danwei* system can be traced to the pre-1949 period.[31] Linan Bian has discussed the development of social service institutions and industrial welfare in China's national defense industries during the
Sino-Japanese war (1937–45), and Wen-Hsin Yeh has shown how the Bank
of China in Shanghai with its dormitory compound, welfare facilities, and
training methods took care of the needs of its middle-class employees in the
1930s.[32] Bian's argument is persuasive in terms of the industrial origin of the
work-unit system and its characteristics, and Yeh's case study is helpful in
understanding Dasheng's policies, particularly her discussion of the bank's
social services and company culture in the context of corporate leadership
through paternalistic authority.

Dasheng's housing policies have more to do with the attempt to create a
company culture based on social hierarchy for its middle management than
with the creation of a prototypical work-unit system for the whole workforce. As we shall see in the following section on factory discipline, Zhang
Jian favored a paternalistic and authoritarian approach to middle and upper
management. Unlike cotton mills in Japan, which tried to attract and retain

a labor supply by providing secure and strictly supervised company housing for young female workers from the countryside, Zhang Jian's paternalistic attitude extended only marginally to the skilled workforce and not at all to unskilled workers.[33] Since the Dasheng No. 1 mill did not offer even the most basic welfare and recreational facilities to its employees, or any housing and medical care to its unskilled workforce, the housing policies were on the whole a modest attempt to create a hierarchically oriented company culture in the mill. The cheap rents and lenient lease regulations may have been incentives for Dasheng's skilled employees to settle in Tangjiazha instead of looking for more lucrative or attractive employment in the growing textile industry of the big cities during the early Republican period. Decent housing was obviously rare in Tangjiazha. As the mill's rent book shows, employees from Zhang Jian's other companies in Tangjiazha village, for example machinists from the Fuxin Flour Mill or the Guangsheng Oil Mill and employees in the Zisheng Iron Workshop, were also eligible for company housing.[34]

The housing arrangements for the upper stratum of Dasheng's workforce reflect its distance from the skilled and unskilled workforce. Managers and their assistants in the materials department, the workshop department, and the finance department were required to live in the administrative section of the compound; the manager of the miscellaneous tasks department was allowed to choose his accommodation outside.[35] Likewise, high-ranking employees like engineers, many of them hired from places outside Nantong, were not required to live in company housing.[36]

As Dasheng's managing director, Zhang Jian had a private office next to the administrative building, but like the rest of the top managers he seldom visited the factory. In contrast to enthusiastic industrial entrepreneurs like the German machinery manufacturer Alfred Krupp, who at the beginning of his industrial career in the mid-nineteenth century lived with his family in a villa right next to the workshops in order to show solidarity with his workforce, Zhang Jian kept his family residence in Changle in Haimen county all through his life. For purposes of public image and as a demonstration of local power, he later built a grand villa in Nantong city along the Haohe canal rather than in the vicinity of the factories. In fact, once the mill started operations, Zhang Jian visited only about twice a year, and his arrival was announced by drums on the jetty and the raising of a flag. Zhang Jian was the patron and power center of the Dasheng enterprise, but, as one would expect, he entertained no visions of solidarity with his workforce or an egalitarian company culture.[37]

In short, the spatial design of the compound created and solidified the social hierarchy within Dasheng's workforce. Furthermore, with its selective housing arrangements, the compound also reflected the specific employment pattern for hiring unskilled labor. As we have seen, unskilled workers would not ordinarily come into direct contact with any member of the managerial staff. Among those interviewed in the 1960s, only machinists mentioned the existence of managers and were able to name them; the unskilled workers' experience with management was limited to contact with the *gongtou*, the male or female foreman.[38]

The *gongtou* and the hiring system they represented were of central significance to the dynamics on the shop floor and are explored in more detail below. Hiring practices and shop-floor management in the Dasheng mills relied mainly on the so-called contract work system (*baogongzhi*), only occasionally supplemented by hiring through independent contractors. As Emily Honig has shown in her study of textile mills in Shanghai, mill managers installed this system in the 1910s. A foreman was paid a flat fee by the management for delivering a required amount of output; he hired workers through subordinate foremen and paid them on his own without providing accommodation.[39] The more infamous contract labor system (*baoshenzhi*) only came about in the Shanghai textile mills in the late 1920s. Under this system, mostly exploitative contractors "bought" young women for a flat fee in the countryside and created a relationship of total dependence by hiring them out to the mills in Shanghai, providing accommodation and food, controlling their life even outside the factory, and, most important, paying them directly and retaining substantial portions of their wages.[40]

Obviously, Dasheng's location in the countryside and the lack of company housing for unskilled labor point to the development of hiring through the contract work system rather than through the contract labor system. The unskilled workforce for menial jobs in the blowing, roving, carding, cleaning, or packing rooms was hired from villages within walking distance of Tangjiazha.[41] *Gongtou* did not need to provide food and lodging for the young women workers. Nevertheless, unskilled workers in the mill were hired by the *gongtou* and their subcontractors and not by the managerial staff. The salaries employees of the company received from the accounts office are traceable in the account books, but wages for unskilled workers are not to be found as regular, separate expense categories in these company records.[42] Since the unskilled workers were subcontracted by the *gongtou*, they received their wages directly from the *gongtou*. Expenses for unskilled labor appear only as a single lump sum in the annual reports, a figure presumably compiled in the mill's accounts office by adding the company's payments to the *gongtou*.[43]

The role of the *gongtou* among the skilled workforce was quite different. The more complicated jobs, such as working at the drawing frames and weaving looms, required skilled labor that could not be recruited in sufficient numbers from the Tangjiazha area. Not surprisingly, the skilled workers (*lianggong*) for these tasks came mostly from Ningbo in Zhejiang province, which had a long tradition of and high reputation for handicraft cotton yarn and cloth production. These skilled workers were hired by their own Ningbo *gongtou* and formed an autonomous group on the shop floor and within the factory.[44] This pattern was repeated at the other Dasheng mills. When the Dasheng No. 2 mill on Chongming island opened, skilled workers from textile centers in southern Jiangsu such as Shanghai, Suzhou, and Wuxi were hired as instructors for the unskilled workers there, who had no experience working with textile machinery.[45]

Engineers were hired directly by the Dasheng management. According to letters found in the company archives, Chinese engineers for the No. 1 mill were recruited in Shanghai.[46] Once the Nantong Textile School, set up by Zhang Jian in 1912, and other textile schools in the country began producing graduates, they automatically became candidates for recruitment. At least half of Nantong's first substantial class of textile engineers (almost 70 percent came from other places in Jiangsu, Zhejiang, and Hunan province) in 1917 found employment in Shanghai or elsewhere; the rest joined the Dasheng mills at least for their initial job.[47] As mentioned above, foreign engineers were occasionally hired for a short period of time to supervise the installation of new, imported machinery. These engineers were hired through the Shanghai brokerage that had negotiated the purchase of the machinery on Dasheng's behalf.[48]

In summary, the spatial location of work and residence in Dasheng's compound said much about status. The resident community was made up of technicians, administrators, and middle management. Senior management, like the unskilled workers, commuted to the factory. The compound functioned like a miniature society: social groups formed according to their economic position and social status, all under the strict control of Zhang Jian and the senior management, who devised the company policies regulating the compound and work hierarchy.

The establishment of the Dasheng No. 1 mill with its huge compound and impressive industrial architecture changed the appearance of Tangjiazha village; in fact, what people in the area called simply the "No. 1 mill" (*yichang*) became the dominant landmark. At the same time, the work compound had an impact on Tangjiazha's socioeconomic structure. Shops and food stalls opened near the main gate of the Dasheng No. 1 mill to cater to the needs of workers before and after their shifts.[49] Because of the increased population and its need for food, in the early 1900s Tangjiazha developed into an entrepot and marketplace for rice from Anhui and southern Jiangsu, thus becoming a market for grain brokers from neighboring counties.[50] A late Qing period source describes the thriving development of Tangjiazha since the founding of the mill and other Dasheng subsidiary factories: "The residents in the vicinity of the sluice gates who work at the various factories amount to as many as three to four thousand people.... The number of trading boats along the river and markets and shops along the sluice increases day by day."[51]

The requirements of industrial production brought so many workers from outside the community (*waidiren*) to the mill that they became a common sight in Tangjiazha. These workers were despised by the local peasants because of their black clothes and their strange, unfamiliar accents. In a typical condescending and derisive reaction to strangers in the community, the locals referred to them as "worms" (*chongzi*).[52] Perhaps the professional skills and thus higher wages and higher social status of outside workers gave the locals additional reasons to envy and to reject them.

Shop-Floor Routine and Discipline

Factory work requires discipline. Discipline is required in the production process, maintained through rewards and punishments, and justified by a work ethos and moral code. Obviously, how much discipline is required of the worker and how it is maintained and justified varies according to rank and responsibility, and we shall see how different groups within the work hierarchy responded to the requirements. Work in the cottage weaving industry or on the farm certainly had its own rules and discipline.[53] Farmwork, however, was regulated by the seasonal cycles and subject to the vagaries of the weather. The Dasheng No. 1 Cotton Mill operated around the clock in two twelve-hour shifts throughout the year.[54] Agricultural work and secondary occupations took place within the household, and work routines tended to be more flexible. In contrast, by the early 1920s manufacturing at the Dasheng No. 1 mill involved up to 8,000 workers working to a strict rhythm.[55] Coordination required strict discipline.

The discipline required to run the cotton mill was laid down in the "factory regulations" (*changyue*), which served as written guidelines for unskilled workers, skilled workers, and managers. According to an entry in his diary, Zhang Jian drew up the factory regulations in late 1897.[56] These rules were apparently among the most comprehensive regulations to be laid down for an industrial enterprise in China at the time. I have not been able to locate factory regulations for those cotton mills established prior to 1895, but a set of factory regulations for the Deji and the Housheng cotton mills in Shanghai published in the late 1910s emulate the example set by Dasheng. They are, however, far less comprehensive and lack the autocratic, strongly disciplinarian spirit enforced by Zhang Jian.[57]

To the best of my knowledge, Zhang Jian designed the factory regulations apparently without consulting Western factory discipline and regulations, such as those instituted in Germany by large industrial companies like Hoechst or Bayer, covering wages, work hours, and discipline, in the 1880s.[58] I suspect that Zhang Jian was influenced more by regulations for the military and military-related, government-sponsored enterprises in China in the late nineteenth century.[59] For example, the "Regulations for the Beiyang Navy" ("Beiyang haijun zhangcheng"), published in 1888 with ample references to the regulations of the British and other European navies, dealt with such issues as shipbuilding, administrative control, promotion, rewards and punishments, accidents, financial compensation, and training and could easily have served as a blueprint for Zhang Jian's factory regulations.[60] The fact that Zhang Jian was familiar with Chinese naval affairs from his earlier career in the private secretariat of General Wu Changqing lends support to this hypothesis. The strong connection between the establishment of a modern military, based on Western models, and the creation of a new social order in schools, factories, and prisons through the introduction of new concepts of time, space, discipline, and the body has been established for Meiji Japan.[61]

The regulations for the Dasheng No. 1 Cotton Mill touched on discipline in several different contexts: time, the handling of machinery and company property, and general issues of conduct. They became important factors in defining when, where, and how the workforce was expected to perform in the factories and within the compound.

Time discipline was a significant part of the overall factory discipline. As specified in the factory regulations, unskilled workers, referred to as labor hands (*xiaogong*), child workers (*tonggong*), and female workers (*nügong*), had to work twelve hours a day in two shifts, day and night.[62] Day-shift workers had to appear at 5:30 A.M. to register with the staff in charge of work supervision (*guangong zhishi*).[63] After the workers had entered the compound, the gate was locked and late arrivals were not admitted into the compound.[64] Then a siren would sound, which was the signal for the workers to enter the workshops.

In some workshops, the shift was longer than the prescribed twelve hours. In the reeling room, for example, the shift could last thirteen hours. In the weaving shed, which was set up in 1915, the shift could be as long as fourteen hours because the production process could not be interrupted arbitrarily. However, there was no night shift in the weaving shed, probably because daylight from large factory windows and skylights made it easier to control the complicated weaving process on the looms than it would have been under insufficient, costly artificial light. Packing department workers, whose work load was much more predictable in terms of the daily output, worked only eight-hour shifts and only during the day.[65]

For the managerial staff, the regulations specified a fixed daily schedule for staff meetings. Daily meetings in the late afternoon were devoted to reviewing the proceedings of the day, and the resulting reports had to be sent to the accounts office.[66] Office apprentices, who lived in the dormitory of the administrative building, were subject to further time discipline. The door to their building was locked at 10:15 P.M., and the lights came on only at 6:00 A.M. Here time discipline was integrated with moral discipline for single men living in the compound. These rather drastic measures were obviously considered necessary in order to prevent improper activities during the night. The factory regulations stipulated that the apprentices and temporary lodgers in the dormitory be well behaved and not smoke opium, gamble, or entertain prostitutes.[67]

As a physical embodiment of the factory regulations, the Western-style clock tower erected after 1900 as part of the main gate was a prominent feature of the factory compound and became the omnipresent symbol of time discipline.[68] The clock structured the work schedule for management, and it signaled the beginnings and ends of shifts for unskilled workers.[69] As in the West, factory production, in contrast to work in the village, meant "a mechanical and totally uniform division of the working day, instead of the variable, flexible and organic rhythms of more traditional forms of labour."[70]

The 1897 factory regulations also specified how workers were to handle machinery and company property. The regulations for the ginning room, for example, stipulated that the machinery had to be oiled and the belts stretched because the lack of proper maintenance could destroy the machine.[71] Female workers in the roving room were forbidden to switch off the machines in order to reconnect broken threads.[72] Halting the loom to reconnect broken threads was a common practice among weavers working at home, but switching the power-driven machine on and off would presumably wear it out more quickly. The workers were advised to summon the *xiaogong*, who had been trained in the quick repair of broken threads.[73] The frequent advice to handle machinery with care probably reflects as much management's concern about maintenance, financial losses due to downtime for repairs, and replacement costs as the workers' inexperience with modern machinery.

Other regulations laid down in detail that the buildings and company property must be treated with care.[74] In the materials department, workers were advised to open the windows on sunny days but to keep them closed otherwise, probably in order to avoid damage through a combination of bad weather and negligence. The same paragraph ordered unskilled workers to transport heavy and bulky materials through the east and north gates of the compound, since these gates were nearer the storage rooms. Other workers were not allowed to use these gates.

The factory regulations also demanded changes in daily habits, such as greater attention to fire prevention. Fire was considered an extreme and constant danger at the Dasheng No. 1 Cotton Mill. This worry, shared by every mill owner, was reflected in the strict orders about fire prevention in every workshop. Fires could be caused not only by the careless use of oil lamps and lights but also by scraps from the iron bands holding the cotton bales together. Iron scraps swept with the cotton into the metal scutchers could easily set the cotton on fire.[75] A fire started by the scutching machines resulted, for example, in the complete destruction of the Shanghai Cotton Cloth Mill in October 1893.[76]

A strict ban on smoking, especially in the storage area, was repeated many times in the factory regulations.[77] Workers were not allowed to carry matches or lighters for fear that carelessness near the dry cotton bales and cloth bolts would spark a conflagration that would destroy the entire compound.[78] In order to enforce these fire-prevention measures, which were aimed mainly at the unskilled workers, Zhang Jian made the managers in charge of the materials, workshop, and miscellaneous tasks departments personally responsible for fire prevention.[79]

To some extent, the regulations demarcated management from skilled and unskilled workers. Regulations that sought to protect company property required managers to view every worker as a potential thief. At the end of a shift, the unskilled workers were searched as they left the compound for stolen yarn or cotton. The prohibition against offduty workers loitering around the storage rooms may also have been an attempt to curtail theft as well as to keep everyone in his or her workplace.[80]

The factory regulations also addressed the conduct of managers and their assistants. In contrast to the regulations for skilled and unskilled workers, which concentrated on behavior that was adjudged unacceptable in the workplace for practical reasons, the regulations for managers emphasized attitudes and moral values.[81] The responsibilities and authority of the managers within their respective departments were described in detail. They were required to keep their staff under tight control and to intervene decisively to prevent inefficiency or discontent. The regulations even recommended that managers gather information on their subordinates' performance behind their backs. This recommendation in the factory regulations was accompanied by a quotation from the *Zuo zhuan*, one of the Confucian classics; perhaps this was an attempt on Zhang Jian's part to lend the regulations' strongly punitive character the sanction of the classics.[82]

In addition, the regulations distinguished between performance and personal integrity in judging the managers' work. The terms used in describing the distinction are revealing: "Unintentional mistakes, guilt by association, and bad results despite good intentions" were considered "public demerits" (*gongguo*), whereas "corruption, embezzlement, violation of the regulations, laziness, and incompetence" were regarded as "personal demerits" (*siguo*).[83] Indeed, any breach of integrity was viewed seriously, and private demerits were punishable with dismissal. In contrast, poor work performance led to a reduction in the annual bonus.[84] Apparently the community of managers was to consist only of people with integrity, but once a person had been admitted into the community, public standards determined how rewards were meted out.

The appeal to a moral code as a tool of disciplining managers reflected a sharp class distinction. Zhang Jian's regulations for skilled and unskilled workers did not resemble nineteenth-century English employers' attempts to prevent immoral behavior in- and outside the factory by reforming workers' drinking habits and use of bad language. In contrast, Zhang Jian did not attempt to improve the morality of his workers.[85] The regulations for managers, however, assumed that they were people of integrity, even though in a very practical way their bonuses were tied to performance. Despite Zhang Jian's commitment to Confucianism (discussed in Chapter 7), the factory regulations for the Dasheng No. 1 mill were on the whole not a strikingly moralistic document.

Corroboration for the practical approach to workplace discipline can be found in the company regulations for the Dasheng No. 2 Cotton Mill, the branch mill operating on Chongming island since 1907.[86] These regulations omitted the moral admonitions for managers, but the description of the work in the various shops became much more detailed and generally less prohibitive.[87] The No. 2 mill was only a cotton-spinning mill and never had weaving facilities and, as the local newspaper repeatedly pointed out, had to cope with an unsophisticated and inexperienced local workforce.[88] In the tenor of the modernizing 1920s, local publications accused the people of Chongming of being "dependent on fate," superstitious, and lacking in hygiene.[89] Perhaps for this reason the regulations paid more attention to detailed job descriptions for the unskilled workers than to the moral appraisal and education of management.

Another departure from the 1897 factory regulations was the inclusion of the role of the *gongtou*. For example, the regulations for the roving room laid down that the female *gongtou* in the No. 2 mill had the authority to assign work to each worker on the shop floor. The *gongtou*'s power is clear: "Whether or not they are experienced, workers are required to obey the assignments set by the female *gongtou*. Those who disobey are fined the first time, fined double this amount for the second offense, and are replaced the third time."[90] The fine was set equal to one week's wages, and dismissed workers were not to be rehired. The regulations for the Dasheng No. 2 mill published in 1910 clearly stated the company's official acknowledgment of the *gongtou*'s authority on the shop floor. Since the *gongtou* was in effect a subcontractor, her or his incorporation into the factory regulations amounted to recognizing that the subcontractor might enforce discipline on behalf of Dasheng's management. The *gongtou* had officially become a part of the mill's lower-level management.

It is almost certain that few of the unskilled workers, even if literate, read or even knew about the factory regulations, since none of them referred to the regulations in the interviews conducted in the 1960s. However, almost every worker complained about having been disciplined and fined. Fines were levied for poor workmanship or for breaking tools and even for taking tiny amounts of cotton to be used as insulation in the soles of shoes. Many workers also complained about being fined up to two weeks' wages for falling asleep during work hours.[91]

It is clear that for the unskilled workers the prohibitive nature of the regulations was most striking. For them, discipline was equivalent to the unnecessary restriction of personal freedom: most of the unskilled workers complained that they had not been allowed to eat in the workshops, that they had to eat their meals cold, and that they were not allowed to rest during work, to chat with other workers, or to smoke inside the compound. Since the workers were under the constant supervision of the *gongtou* in the workshop, they sometimes felt compelled to go to the toilet if they wanted to have a conversation with a coworker. Obviously, the daily routine in the factory required them to give up habits they were used to when working at home.[92]

Workers also complained about the infringement of personal dignity in the form of body searches by the guards at the main gate at the end of a shift.[93] Quite understandably, they hated this rigorous routine in which even their shoes were searched. However, this was not an uncommon measure in factories at the time to curb theft of company materials and property.[94] To judge from the interview transcripts on this issue, the workers apparently did not feel guilt at taking home small scraps of cotton.[95] Given the enormous amount of cotton the mill used, they did not seem to have counted taking a handful of raw cotton for padding jackets and blankets at home as theft.

Enforcement of discipline through the *gongtou* in this and other situations turned the *gongtou* into a common target as the personification of punitive factory discipline. In the interviews, the workers expressed little sympathy for the *gongtou*'s responsibilities toward upper management.[96] In some cases the demands by the *gongtou* were certainly quite arbitrary. For example, in

1914 Ling Wenbin, a fifteen-year-old unskilled worker in the spinning room at the Dasheng No. 1 mill, was told by a fierce female *gongtou* to cut off his queue. He refused, was harassed, and eventually decided to quit.[97]

Nevertheless, the *gongtou* did not provide sufficient physical control over the whole workforce within the compound. The most visible agent of discipline and enforcement in the Dasheng No. 1 mill was the company's patrol force (*xunding*). According to the 1897 regulations, the force was to patrol the compound day and night, to watch over the gates and side entrances, to check the workers as they left the compound, and to protect the company against burglars.[98] During the day the guards were equipped with clubs, and at night they had guns. The fire squad, which was part of the patrol force, was specially trained in using the hydrant (*shuilong*) in the case of fire.

Financial rewards and favorable working conditions were used as incentives to increase the patrol force's loyalty to the management.[99] Patrol guards received their food, rifles, and seasonal uniforms. In addition, they received rewards for good results at target practice and medical treatment if they were badly injured while fulfilling their duties. If the guards were successful in arresting a worker with stolen goods, the manager of the department for miscellaneous tasks decided how the culprit was to be punished and whether he or she was to be handed over to the authorities.

Although the patrol force was on the company's payroll, members did not live in Dasheng company housing. It appears that this was a deliberate decision by the management to prevent them from striking up friendships with other members of the workforce. This assumption is corroborated by the fact that the factory regulations stipulated that local people (*turen*) were not eligible for the patrol force. In employing outsiders (*waidiren*), who could not speak the local dialect, the management was probably trying to forestall collusion with local workers. The relationship between the guards and the workers was characterized by mutual distrust and the identification of factory discipline with its enforcement through outsiders. Local workers disliked the company guards for forcing discipline on them, for enjoying a more privileged status in the work hierarchy, and for coming from outside their own community.[100]

In summary, unskilled and skilled workers in the Dasheng mills were subjected to a punitive factory discipline intended to make the factory run more efficiently. For the workers, the punitive discipline was the single most important characteristic of industrial work. Despite the undertone of complaint in the interviews, in practice Dasheng's workers seem to have had little alternative but to allow the management to ride roughshod over them.

Chen San, for example, entered the mill in 1911 as a piecer in the spinning room at the age of twelve.[101] Together with his mother and his elder brother, he had to commute a long way on foot every day from the village where his family lived and had cultivated land as farmers. Since the family did not possess a clock, they raised a cockerel to wake them up in time for work—a measure with only limited success. Chen San's statement "While at work in the compound, whatever the foreman said had to be accepted as right, it was impossible to say that it was not right" sums up his impression of factory discipline as represented by the *gongtou*.[102] Like many others, Chen was angry with the foreman, whom he called a "rat" (*laoshu*) in his interview, for imposing a fine on him. He also despised the guards at the gate who conducted the body searches, which he held responsible for crippling his brother's leg: once, during the rush to leave the compound at the end of the shift, his brother was squeezed in the crowd and hit on the head with a bamboo club by a guard. He fell and was trampled by the people rushing out. No medical help was available within the compound for his injuries, which left him lame so that he eventually had to quit work in the mill. There was no apparent protest by the workers, nor any indication that a protest in such circumstances would have attracted the sympathy of Dasheng's management.

Gender, Work, and Income

Considering the long, physically exhausting hours and the strict discipline on the shop floor, one wonders why unskilled workers, especially women, were eager to obtain work in the Dasheng No. 1 Cotton Mill. Why would one consider a factory job if there was work to be done in the fields or on the handlooms at home? Was cash income the only reason for the decision to work in the factory? In this section, I examine work as a means to create income and also look at the general economic background of the workers at Tangjiazha in order to arrive at some understanding of the importance of factory income relative to overall family income.[103] Hiring practices and career patterns, especially as they involved the employment of women and children, are connected with this issue.

From the very beginning, the Dasheng No. 1 mill employed thousands of people from the surrounding area. Based on scattered evidence from the company records and estimates based on the amount of machinery, the total workforce amounted to 3,250 people in 1899.[104] By 1925, the Dasheng No. 1 mill had over 8,000 workers with an administrative staff (including skilled workers, management, and engineers) of 400.[105]

In order to interpret these numbers in a meaningful way, we have to put them into the context of population figures for the region. If we calculate the population density based on population figures in the Nantong county gazetteer, rural Tangjiazha and its surrounding area with an average of 885 persons per square kilometer was about as densely populated as Nantong city, which had an average of 964 inhabitants per square kilometer in the early twentieth century.[106] It seems plausible to identify migration toward Tangjiazha, stimulated by the presence of the mill, from other parts of Nantong county as a reason for the relatively high population density.

One indication of the in-migration is the larger than average number of persons per household in Tangjiazha district (*qu*). If we again resort to the local gazetteer and analyze the figures from the early Republican period, the average Tangjiazha household had almost ten people, in contrast to averages of four persons per household in Nantong city and of almost six persons per household in all of Nantong county.[107] Statistically almost every seventh person in the Tangjiazha district, or 1.5 persons per household, worked at the Dasheng No. 1 mill.[108]

The interviews with former workers in the 1960s support the argument of in-migration. In several cases, unskilled workers from other parts of Nantong county had left home for economic reasons and moved to Tangjiazha in the hope of improving their standard of living through work in the mill. After they had found work as unskilled workers in the spinning or blowing rooms of Dasheng No. 1, they rented rooms from families near Tangjiazha.[109] Skilled workers, such as the machinists from southern Jiangsu, moved into company housing.[110]

Statements about people's standard of living in Tangjiazha in the early twentieth century and changes in that standard due to earnings from work in the factories need to be qualified carefully. As discussed in Chapter 2, Nantong had a traditional cottage industry producing hand-woven cotton cloth. Agriculture was the principal occupation in most of Nantong county; in addition, many rural households engaged in handicraft spinning and weaving.[111] Although we cannot put precise figures on the number of households that might have derived an income from handicraft production, we cannot ignore the possibility that, for many, such an income would have been substantial.

This assumption is corroborated by various pieces of information we can extract from the interviews with 214 former workers. According to my analysis of their cases, 43 percent of all the interviewed workers had worked in the fields or been engaged in hand-weaving before, during, or after starting to work in the Dasheng No. 1 Cotton Mill.[112] If we take these 43 percent as a total sample, 17 percent of the workers had worked in the fields and 14 percent had been engaged in hand-weaving before entering the mill, but ceased to do so once they began work in the factory. However, 64 percent started farming during their employment in the mill; in contrast, only one person took up hand-weaving. The rest of the workers, 5 percent, were farming or hand-weaving before they became factory workers and continued to do so while being employed in the mill.

This means that about half of the interviewed workers engaged in farming before or after their shift in the factory.[113] Of those workers engaged in part-time farmwork at home, 77 percent were women. One might erroneously conclude that women, rather than men, were expected to work at home in addition to their factory jobs. Instead, we must not forget that even among the total sample of Dasheng workers engaged in farmwork at one time or another, only 23 percent were men.

The interviews also provide us with some information on wages for unskilled workers. There are, of course, problems with using an interview sample as a source of wage data. The interviews were conducted to generate general narratives and were not based on a specific set of questions; thus the interview transcripts do not supply uniform information for each worker. To make things more complicated, the interviewed workers often gave only sporadic wage information without relating it to a specific year or time period.

Nevertheless, by averaging only those reports that are specific to a period and to a particular kind of work on the shop floor, it is possible to arrive at an impression of wage levels in the Dasheng mills. Between 1900 and 1910, the average wage for women in the roving room was 0.08 yuan per day; this rose to 0.12 yuan in the 1910s but decreased to 0.10 yuan in the late 1920s.[114] In the ginning room, women earned about 0.07 yuan per day in the first decade of the 1900s and 0.08 yuan per day in the 1910s and 1920s. Women's work in the reeling room was relatively well paid, with an average daily wage of 0.10 yuan in the first decade of the 1900s, 0.25 yuan in the 1910s, and 0.20 yuan in the 1920s. In general, the wage increase in the 1910s reflects Dasheng's business success during the post–World War I boom in the Chinese cotton industry, and the decline in wages in the 1920s mirrors Dasheng's financial problems in 1922 (see Chapter 6) and the overall difficulties of the Chinese textile industry due to supply problems, rising prices for raw cotton, and intense Japanese competition.[115]

In using the data extracted from the interview sample as an average basis for wages, we have to bear in mind that 77 per cent of the interviewees were women, and of these 80 percent had entered the mill as child workers between five and thirteen years old.[116] The wage data given above tell us in general more about wages for female child workers. However, the discrepancy between wages for adult females and female children was substantial. In the absence of data that would permit us to construct a complete time series on adult female workers, I can give only some examples: in 1928, a nineteen-year-old female earned between 0.10 and 0.25 yuan per day in the reeling room; in 1929 a twelve-year-old female in the same workshop earned between 0.08 and 0.10 yuan per day. This meant that wages for adult females were almost double those paid children.[117] Of course, many of these adult women workers had greater responsibilities in the workshop.

It appears at first that the discrepancies in the wages of unskilled male and unskilled female workers were not that great. However, one has to bear in mind that only 23 percent of the total interview sample were male workers, and only 36 percent of those males were unskilled workers. Moreover, 55 percent of the male unskilled workforce entered the mill as child workers and thus received the lower wages paid children. For example, in 1916 a male child worker in the roving room, age fourteen, earned 0.10 yuan per day. In 1915, a female child worker, age twelve, received 0.08 to 0.16 yuan per day for work in the same workshop. Not surprisingly, unskilled adult male workers received distinctively higher wages than unskilled adult female workers.[118] The average of the six instances among the interview sample of unskilled adult male workers' wages shows that they earned 0.26 yuan per day in the roving or reeling room, whereas unskilled adult female workers received an average wage of only 0.12 yuan per day for similar work.

Of course, the wage discrepancies between skilled and unskilled labor were even greater. Statements in the 1897 factory regulations reveal that the managers had a fixed income of 50 to 100 yuan per month and were also entitled to a 15 percent share of the annual net profits, split among at least eight managers.[119] The managers' assistants and the administrative staff received a monthly salary of between 4 and 40 yuan, depending on their specific tasks and responsibilities.[120] According to Dasheng's account books, the monthly salaries of engineers ranged between 24 and 33 yuan in 1909–10.[121]

In general Dasheng's level of remuneration was not especially attractive to engineering graduates and reflected to some extent the mills' particular location in the countryside without the standard of living and expenses of the big cities. The fourteen entries from a record produced by the textile school attached to the Shenxin mill in Shanghai in 1929 shows that job changes in cotton mills were frequent.[122] Almost half of this school's graduates worked for some time in the Dasheng No. 1 or No. 2 Cotton Mill. The six graduates employed in the Dasheng mills on average changed jobs five times in about twelve years. Most of them took jobs at Dasheng No. 1 during the first years of their professional career and then moved on to positions in cotton mills in industrial textile centers such as Shanghai and Wuxi. Presumably, an engineer would consider employment at Dasheng No. 1 more a starting job than an upward move in his career.

The role of the *gongtou* in Dasheng was also connected with a specific career pattern. Most male *gongtou* were skilled workers who had served an apprenticeship and had experience as a machinist.[123] The position was considered to be so important that job openings were advertised in professional textile magazines in 1919.[124] The career pattern for the female *gongtou* in Dasheng was quite different. Here it seems that after long service in one of the workshops hard-working and well-behaved women were promoted by middle management to the position of *gongtou*. This in-house selection process is confirmed through descriptions in the interview sample; unskilled female workers mentioned their promotion to *gongtou* not so much because they felt empowered in their new position on the shop floor but because of the raise in pay.[125] The in-house promotion also corroborates the absence of outsiders among the unskilled labor in the workshops, since the *gongtou* were themselves locals who saw no need to bring in unskilled labor from other areas.

In order to measure the economic potential of wages at Dasheng, we have to look at their purchasing power. Unfortunately, there are no detailed price indices available for Tangjiazha or Nantong for the period between 1900 and 1930.[126] I shall, therefore, resort to a price index for another part of Jiangsu province for the purpose of comparison. In the following, I use the Wujin price index.[127] Wujin was a rice-producing rather than a cotton-producing county and, in this respect, was not similar to Nantong. Nevertheless, rice produced in Wujin was sold in Shanghai and elsewhere in Jiangsu province, and so the price of rice in Wujin reflected supplier-prices, and the price series is indicative of annual price changes for much of Jiangsu, including Nantong.

In 1900, one *sheng* (liter) of polished rice cost 0.035 yuan on an annual average in Wujin. This price rose to 0.057 in 1910 and to 0.073 yuan in 1920. What can these figures tell us about the purchasing power of the wages paid by the Dasheng mills? An unskilled female worker in the roving room at the lowest end of the pay scale earned on average 2.24 yuan per month or 26.88 yuan per year late in the first decade of the 1900s. If we take 470 catties (285 kilograms) of rice as the minimum subsistence per person per year, this worker would have paid a total annual sum of 26.79 yuan at Wujin prices,[128] or roughly her annual income. At this time, an unskilled male worker in the roving room earned about 2.8 yuan per month at the lower end of the pay scale, or 33.6 yuan per year. This amount would have been more than sufficient for the purchase of one year's polished rice for one person.

However, at the upper end of the pay scale, a female worker promoted to head of the shift in the spinning room would earn a monthly wage of 5.46 yuan per month or 65.52 yuan per year during this period. This wage would have enabled the worker to buy twice the amount of rice needed for personal subsistence. At the upper end of the pay scale, the situation was even better for male workers in advanced positions on the shop floor. Their average annual income for work in the spinning room and packing room came to 100.8 yuan. With this amount they would have been able to buy almost three and a half times the amount of rice needed for personal subsistence at Wujin prices.

In general, these figures are indicative of what industrial wages might have meant to Dasheng's workforce. Unskilled workers at the lower end of the pay scale would not have been able to afford polished rice throughout the year. They could have resorted to lower grades of rice or other staples such as sweet potatoes. Many of the workers interviewed in the 1960s complained that they had had to eat noodles and vegetables instead of rice or had lived on sweet potatoes through the winter. These dietary patterns probably reflect the standard of living for workers at the lower end of the pay scale.[129] Workers at the upper end, however, would have been able to afford much more rice in their diet, even though the Wujin figures probably exaggerate somewhat the amount of rice they were able to purchase, since the price in rice-producing Wujin would probably have been lower than in rice-importing Nantong.

A comparison of Dasheng's wages with those paid textile workers in the Shanghai cotton mills, even though the data are incomplete and do not specify the workers' jobs, reveals that Dasheng's wage levels were generally lower than those in Shanghai mills during the 1910s and 1920s.[130] Thus we need to pose the question why the near-subsistence wage received by workers at the lower end of the pay scale would be reason enough for women and children to seek work in the Dasheng factories. It is possible to understand that the wage was attractive to them only if we take into consideration that half the female workers worked in their spare time in the fields at home. Thus the cash wage from the factory work, albeit near-subsistence level, was additional to the family's regular farm income, and their wages would lead to a higher family income than without the factory work. In contrast, for men the financial incentive to seek employment as an unskilled worker in Dasheng was not strong enough to make them give up cultivation and forfeit farm income. This argument is supported by Rawski's data on the trend of annual farm wages for males in Jiangsu, which establish that the real value of rural wages in Nantong, Haimen, and Chongming rose at least moderately from the mid-1920s to the early 1930s and certainly was not declining.[131] Therefore, the majority of men continued to work on the farm, unless they were skilled and could, for example as a machinist, earn almost four times the amount of wages earned by unskilled male workers at the lower end of Dasheng's pay scale.[132]

Since around 77 percent of the workforce at Dasheng No. 1 were women, female labor became a distinctive characteristic of the mill. About 55 percent of these women would have held two jobs—before setting off to work in the mill or after returning from their shift, they would do farmwork. Some even gave up their work in the mill temporarily and helped out at home during the agricultural busy seasons on a regular basis.[133] One could even argue that these women actually held three jobs since they, of course, also had housework and thus often worked 18 to 19 hours per day.[134] In the interviews the women clearly expressed their frustrations about being burdened with multiple responsibilities at the workplace, on the farm, and in the family. With regard to the issue of how the concept of industrial work was perceived and integrated into the language, it is interesting to note that the interviewed female workers used the term *gong* (work) only in reference to factory work, but not for farmwork, handicraft production, or housework.[135]

Next to female labor, child labor was another important characteristic of Dasheng's workforce. According to a survey conducted in 1930 among nineteen Chinese cotton mills all over China, the mills in Nantong had the highest proportion of child labor.[136] The survey reported that in Nantong female workers accounted for 56.5 percent of the total workforce, child workers (female and male) for 12.8 percent, and male workers for 30.7 percent. However, we have to bear in mind that more than half of the child workers were female, too. In comparison, the workforce in Shanghai mills on average consisted of only 5.7 percent children.[137] Probably representative of most workshops of the mill, a picture taken at Dasheng No. 1 in the late 1910s or early 1920s shows a huge workshop with reeling machines attended by children. Most of them are so small that they obviously have difficulties looking over the reels to the next row of machines.[138]

The answer to the question why the Dasheng mills employed a relatively high percentage of child labor lies in the career pattern for unskilled workers. As mentioned above, the overwhelming majority of unskilled female workers (80 percent of the women in the interview sample) joined the Dasheng No. 1 mill as children and then continued their careers as unskilled female workers and sometimes even as *gongtou*. Needless to say, the child workers, a welcome source of cheap labor with little responsibility for the management, brought much desired cash income for rural families whose surplus from farming was more difficult to turn into cash and subject to the usual vagaries of agriculture. The importance of a cash income explains why female workers resorted to bribing the *gongtou* with gifts of home-grown produce or money to ensure jobs for their children and other family members or to keep their own job if they had incurred the *gongtou*'s wrath.[139] The combination of factory and farmwork also forced many female workers to take their children with them into the factory to keep an eye on them. Inevitably, nasty accidents involving children happened not because they were tending machines but because they played unattended in the workshops near dangerous machinery.[140]

However, there was still another side to keeping the children in the workshops. In nineteenth-century English cotton mills, children who entered the factory at the age of nine or ten were expected to acquire skills by working next to their parents or other relatives.[141] During this informal apprenticeship, the children began as scavengers or piecers and received little or no pay until they were at least able to tie some threads on the spinning machines.[142] As the interview sample confirms, the same happened at the Dasheng No. 1 mill. Educating the next generation of workers through early, informal on-the-job training, even if the workers were still regarded as unskilled workers, was certainly a significant incentive for Dasheng's management to hire child labor. As one former worker described her training experience: "When I was ten years old, the workshop buildings were being erected. I often went with people to the compound in order to play there, and by playing around I just learned [the job]. At the age of thirteen I entered the factory to work in the spinning room."[143] Even if we cannot dismiss the welcome financial contribution of child workers to the family income, this example indicates that there was another work-related, not entirely wage-related reason for children to enter the factory at a young age.

In my interpretation of the gender, age, and wage structure of industrial work in the Dasheng No. 1 Cotton Mill, I have consciously given more room to the quantitative than to the qualitative analysis of wage and employment data, however fragmented, in order to substantiate generalizations about the motivations, incentives, and pressures behind decisions to work in a factory. At the same time, I am not oblivious to the often negative work experiences of most of the women and children. In fact, it is very difficult to discuss the factory life of women and children without being repulsed by the harsh work environment they had to deal with.

Historically, child labor was not a moral issue in China since all children were integrated into the world of work, either in- or outside the home, from a very young age. What to our age appear to be appalling conditions of child labor were common long before factories were built in China or the West. In England, legislation limiting working hours for children was first introduced with the Factory Acts of 1831 and 1850.[144] In China, where factory work was a much more recent phenomenon, the problem of child labor was not directly addressed until the creation of the Factory Act in December 1929 and its final promulgation in 1931.[145] However, the driving force behind demands to improve working conditions in Chinese factories were the foreign inspectors of the International Labor Organization from Geneva or campaigners on behalf of religious societies such as the YMCA.[146] Even after the introduction of factory legislation in the 1930s, articles in professional textile magazines indicate that the legal requirements and actual conditions on the shop floor were still worlds apart, in both rural and urban areas.[147]

Labor Organization and Labor Protest

Strikes were not nearly as numerous in Tangjiazha as in the Shanghai cotton mills, and they were fairly ineffective and quickly put down by the factory management. The absence of unrest or strikes at the Dasheng No. 1 mill until the late 1920s is remarkable. The first strike occurred in March 1928 and was sparked by management's attempt to increase the workload for workers in the reeling room without a concomitant increase in wages.[148] Consultations between the workers' deputies and the management were fruitless, and after a few days the striking workers had to give up. Lu Jingwei, secretary of the Communist party branch for Nantong county, established in 1926, had become involved in the strike movement and was consequently arrested and sentenced to fifteen years' imprisonment. However, the other strike leaders, who were also arrested and punished, were not members of the Communist party.[149] The next strike at the Dasheng No. 1 mill was a protest in 1932 that ended in violent confrontation with the company's patrol force, leaving several workers wounded or dead.[150]

Similar "stability," secured and ruthlessly enforced through Dasheng's patrol force, was the rule in the No. 2 factory on Chongming island. In 1922, when a dispute broke out between the work supervisors at the No. 2 mill, Zhang Jian personally ordered the guards to solve the problem.[151] However, we do not know whether the solution was achieved by peaceful means. Although measures taken by the factory management in the early 1930s to increase productivity on the shop floor led to serious complaints and opposition from the workers, their protest did not lead to an organized strike movement. Instead, they accepted a heavier workload, with each worker responsible for an increased number of spindles and machines, without any raise in wages.[152]

Given the general level of political discourse and activities in the Nantong area, the workers' organization had not developed sufficiently to support a serious strike movement. A candid local report on social conditions in Chongming in 1925 revealed the lack of organizational structures and procedures in the industrial workplace: "Chongming's industry is not at all developed, and there is no opportunity to study for improvement. In addition, there are no labor organizations such as unions or industrial associations. Everybody holds meetings in order to decide on the methods for each procedure."[153]

Whereas strike activities in the Shanghai cotton mills took place under the direction of the Shanghai General Union, the weakness of the workers' organization in the Nantong area resulted in unfocused protest without strategy or results. So far I have not been able to identify strong informal relationships among Dasheng workers through sisterhoods (*jiemeihui*), connections with the Green Gang, and native-place organizations as described by Emily Honig and Elizabeth Perry for workers in Shanghai's industrial enterprises during the Republican period.[154] Female workers at Dasheng certainly established informal networks by walking together in groups from the village to the factory, helping and supporting one another at work, or arranging employment for family members and friends. However, these networks were not institutionalized and did not lead to the emergence of a conscious class of factory workers. It appears that the lack of organizational structures was a reason why political activism and the wave of strikes in the late 1920s did not automatically spread from Shanghai to Tangjiazha. Politicization of the workforce in Nantong did not take place before the late 1930s, and then it came in response to the Japanese invasion.

During the Japanese occupation of the Nantong area from 1938 to 1945 and the imposed Japanese presence in the Dasheng mills (see Chapter 8), the lack of personal safety and the frequency of incidents involving Japanese soldiers led to the strengthening of informal worker organizations in- and outside the mills. Female workers would organize themselves in tight groups, walking to and from the compound together and banding together as much as possible at work, even during the breaks or while running errands in the factory. They also accompanied one another to the toilet facilities, which were located in the distant corners of the compound, and established their own watch groups on the shop floor during night shifts. Nevertheless, several women among the workers interviewed in the 1960s admitted that they had been so afraid of Japanese harassment that they quit the Dasheng No. 1 mill altogether.[155]

This leads to a more general question: to what extent were the Communist party and labor organizations able to mobilize the workforce in Dasheng, particularly during the Sino-Japanese War? In the 214 interviews with former workers, the absence of references to organized labor activism in the factories is quite striking. In 1938, the Communist party dispatched representatives from Shanghai to establish underground organizations in various localities in northern Jiangsu province. However, the party's attempt to infiltrate the Dasheng mills never really succeeded. Meng Guilin was sent to Tangjiazha with three tasks: to create an underground party organization within the Dasheng No. 1 mill, to organize anti-Japanese resistance among the workers, and to mobilize the masses in the political and economic struggle.[156] According to Meng's description of his activities in Dasheng between 1938 and 1945, his mission eventually reduced itself to anti-Japanese resistance, which simply meant sabotage of factory property and the production process. This particular form of resistance did not require formal organization, specific training, or political education.[157] It could also be interpreted as a reflection on the general lack of vibrant political activism among the workers of the Dasheng No. 1 mill. As Meng Guilin had to realize, the workers' social and economic affiliation with the factory, "their lifeblood," was not easily replaced by a new, uncertain political agenda.[158]

Another, probably even more important reason for the workers' passive behavior and reluctance to strike was their continuing involvement in farmwork at home and the particular income structure that grew out of this situation. In addition to the women's vital cash contributions to the farm-based family income, the specific employment pattern connected with Dasheng's rural-based workforce certainly took the edge off the workers' readiness to go on strike. For example, when the Dasheng No. 1 mill was hit by a severe crisis due to financial mismanagement and shortages of raw material in the early 1920s (see Chapter 6), the management halted production for several weeks and dismissed the workers temporarily. Since the majority of the unskilled workers had farmland to which they could return, they were able to rely on produce and income from their land to sustain themselves. In contrast, rural workers who moved to the big cities to obtain work in the textile mills there could no longer fall back on income from farmland when they were laid off or had to accept wage reductions and hence were more likely to form unions and strike to protect their jobs and wages.

What generalizations about factory work, worker identity, and the process of social transformation through industrialization can we draw from the Dasheng No. 1 Cotton Mill? If we look for similarities between this large-scale factory in the countryside and Chinese industrial enterprises in the urban areas, Chinese sources from the late 1910s and early 1930s indicate that in terms of industrial architecture and work organization, Dasheng No. 1 was indeed a prototype for Chinese cotton mills established later in Shanghai and other cities.[159] As recent studies suggest, changes in work discipline, work organization, and social stratification also came about in other light-industry sectors such as tobacco, match, or tool factories during the Republican period.[160]

My analysis points to the significant differences between industrial enterprises in the countryside and in the cities. In 1899 the Dasheng No. 1 Cotton Mill was in terms of the area it occupied and the size of the workforce an exceptional operation for the Tangjiazha area and even on a nationwide scale.[161] The development of an industrial workforce in China in the late nineteenth and early twentieth centuries should thus no longer be considered only in the context of an urban setting. As Dasheng's case shows, "the importance of 'place' over 'class' in East Asian constructions of worker identity" is certainly valid for the rural as well as the urban context in China.[162] At the same time, urban workers gradually developed a different consciousness with regard to their role as industrial workers. In contrast to Dasheng's workforce, the majority of unskilled workers in Chinese cotton mills located in the urban areas of Shanghai, Tianjin, and other cities were migrants from rural areas.[163] Although native-place organizations and local personal connections were vital to obtaining a job and surviving in the harsher urban environment, unlike Dasheng workers, they slowly lost their ties with the countryside and over time adapted, at least in part, to the life-style of the city.[164] Subsidiary occupations and cottage industries no longer played a role in their lives.

This leads us to another question: how, if at all, was industrial work conceptualized by management? Anyone familiar with the literature on textile mills will recognize similar problems regarding work discipline, social hierarchies, and labor relations in industrial enterprises in England, the United States, and Japan from the late eighteenth to the early twentieth centuries.[165] Zhang Jian's autocratic style reflects the earliest stage of private Chinese industrial management, which was characterized by indirect control through the *gongtou* system and the absence of scientific management. However, even in the West, for example in the German chemical industry, factory managers—instead of foremen and overseers—began to hire workers for the workshops only in the first decade of the twentieth century.[166] From a comparative point of view, still more significant is the fact that in Japan scientific management and Taylorism appeared on the shop floors only in the 1910s and 1920s and co-existed with and reinforced the corporate paternalism of Japanese labor management.[167]

As the author of the factory regulations and director of the Dasheng enterprises, Zhang Jian never addressed the issue of factory work and its impact on man, society, and environment directly. Not surprisingly, he did not deal with the problem of the workers' alienation from their work or with the workers' physical and economic hardships, since these issues were generally ignored at the time.[168] Only in one report on the Dasheng No. 2 mill from 1907 do we find a descriptive reference to the unskilled workforce.[169] There Zhang Jian pointed out the advantage of recruiting female workers from local villages. Since these women had unbound feet, they were able to walk long distances to the factory and to stand for a long time during work. In addition to good-quality cotton and cheaper land prices than could be found in Tangjiazha, Zhang Jian obviously considered a hard-working, robust female workforce a valuable asset of the mill operation in Chongming.[170] These considerations were presumably important to the management of the Dasheng No. 1 mill as well.

Reflecting the same practical concerns, the 1897 regulations for the No. 1 mill show that management regarded child workers as a normal and indispensable part of the workforce.[171] Only a Western visitor would describe his impressions of the working conditions for child workers at the Dasheng mill in 1921 in a critical way: "When I visited the extensive cotton mills erected by his Excellency Chang Ch'ien [i.e., Zhang Jian] at Nant'ungchou, Kiangsu, in December 1921 I saw that a very large number of children were employed there, with little or no provision for their safety from accidents with machinery, and in sanitary surroundings of the most primitive sort."[172] As a first-generation entrepreneur and industrialist in China, Zhang Jian certainly had no ambitions to become a philanthropic entrepreneur in the style of Robert Owen, who was genuinely interested in the welfare of his workers, especially the children in his factories at New Lanark.[173] Zhang Jian's social ambitions were always directed at the improvement of educational and welfare institutions in Nantong city (see Chapter 7) and not at the Dasheng No. 1 mill and its huge unskilled workforce in Tangjiazha. One searches in vain for company-owned schools, hospitals, or other facilities that so often characterize social policies of big companies.[174] A park, opened in the early 1920s, was the only facility donated by Zhang Jian to Tangjiazha. A local source from 1925 stated that the purpose of the park was to provide recreation for the "ordinary people" (*pingmin*) of Tangjiazha and that it was not a place for "workers" (*gongren*) from the nearby factory to loiter in.[175] The irony of this statement is that the majority of the workforce who appeared as "workers" to the villagers of Tangjiazha and who therefore were not encouraged to use the park most probably did not see themselves as "workers" but as "ordinary people" from nearby villages.

In an interview I conducted in Tangjiazha in 1995, a retired machinist from the Dasheng No. 1 mill, who had lived all his life in company housing, told me that he visited Nantong city only two or three times a year in the 1930s.[176] However, he admitted that he always called himself a local from Nantong (*Nantong ren*). Although in this case Nantong designates the city as well as the county, his remarks could indicate that skilled workers aspired to identify themselves rather with Nantong city. Tangjiazha disappeared as a memorable place. Nobody identified with it, neither Zhang Jian nor management nor the skilled workers. As for the unskilled workers, their roots remained in the village.

PART III

The Characteristics of Big Business

CHAPTER 5

The Corporate Structure

For most people—businessmen, visitors, and locals—the factories in Tang-jiazha were Dasheng. There was much more, however, to Dasheng than just the production of cotton yarn and cloth. This chapter explores these other aspects, particularly control and accountability structures, ownership, and financial and personnel management, using archival records and documents produced by the institution itself.

Certainly, the cotton mills in the Nantong area were a crucial part of the enterprise, and the Dasheng No. 1 Cotton Mill remained the backbone of the Dasheng business complex, even after the creation of affiliated enterprises. The Guangsheng Oil Mill, the Dasheng Steamship Company, and the Tonghai Land Reclamation Company were established in 1901, the Hanmolin Publishing House and the Dalong Soap Factory in 1902, the Zisheng Iron Workshop in 1905, and the Fuxin Flour Mill in 1909, to name just a few. In addition, Dasheng branch mills were opened on Chongming island in 1907 and in Haimen county in 1921. When Dasheng acquired the legal status of a limited liability enterprise in 1907, it began to develop into a business group and by 1910 comprised seventeen different affiliated companies.[1] However, neither the cotton mills, especially the No. 1 mill, nor any of the other manufacturing units was institutionally the most significant part of the business group. As I show in this chapter, financial and managerial control within the Dasheng business group was exerted from an office outside the structure of the affiliated and subsidiary companies.

Dasheng's incorporation and its continuing expansion offer valuable insights into the manifold problems faced by the directors, managers, and shareholders of a large company during the process of establishing legal identities and financial responsibilities. The fact that Dasheng was never quite a family business or a government-backed enterprise with official patronage such as the industries managed by Sheng Xuanhuai made its transformation into a corporation in the Western sense even more complicated. As a result, the Dasheng enterprise represented a new category of business institution in the early twentieth century. It transformed and applied business practices and institutional tools with historical roots in traditional Chinese business customs to the institutional framework of a limited liability shareholding company. Thus the discussion in this chapter ultimately leads to the question whether the process of incorporation is an appropriate measure of the "modernization" of business institutions and structures in China.

Legal Status as a Company

It is difficult to establish the exact date when Dasheng, or more precisely the No. 1 mill, became a privately owned legal entity. Based on my extensive searches in various archives, I think that it is safe to say that no document exists that formally dissolved the initial structure of the enterprise as a *guanshang heban* operation. The text printed on share certificates from 1897 and from 1903 states that the spinning mills "were established in Tongzhou with approval granted by edict in response to a memorial from the Imperial Commissioner of the Southern Ports [Zhang Zhidong] . . . , by contract set up for perpetuity to be jointly managed (*yongyuan heban*) by officials and gentry"[2] (see Fig. 5.1). In March 1905 the *Dagongbao* newspaper published an announcement listing the Dasheng No. 1 Cotton Mill as approved and registered by the Ministry of Commerce (Shangbu) together with ten other companies (*gongsi*) established by Zhang Jian.[3] This was the official recognition of the company registration required by the Company Law (Gongsi lü) promulgated in 1904.[4] Finally, the published report of the first shareholder meeting in 1907 reveals that the Dasheng No. 1 Cotton Mill had by that time taken the form of a stockholding company with limited liability (*gufen youxian gongsi*).[5]

The shareholders seem to have greeted the new legal status of the company with great enthusiasm. Although Dasheng had been operating with private share capital since its establishment in 1898, shareholders had no public forum within the enterprise to voice suggestions or criticisms. Zheng Xiaoxu, one of the most prominent shareholders and active in both business and national politics,[6] is quoted in the 1907 shareholder report, which

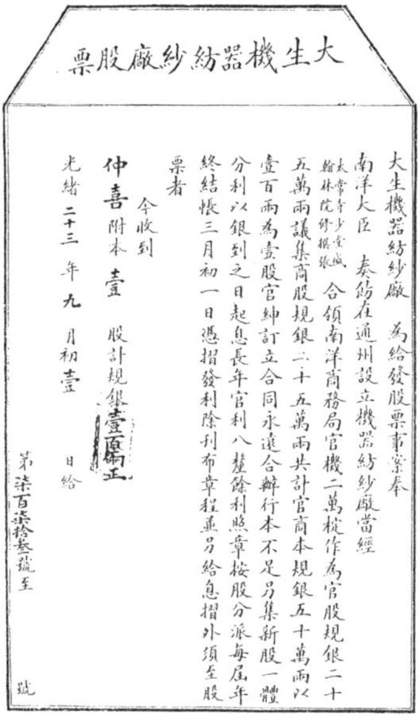

大生機器紡紗廠股票

大生機器紡紗廠　為給發股票事竊查
南洋大臣　奏明在通州設立機器紡紗廠當經
稟明合領南洋商務局官機二萬枚作為官股規銀二十
五萬兩計官商本規銀五十萬兩以
壹百兩為壹股官紳訂立合同永遠合辦本不足另集新股一體
分利以銀到之日起息長年官利八釐發利照章股分派每屆年
終結帳三月初一日憑摺發利除刊布章程並另給息摺外須在股
票者

令收到

仲喜　附本　壹　股計規銀壹佰兩正

光緒二十三年九月初壹日給

第諸百柒拾叁號至

號

Fig. 5.1 Share certificate of the Dasheng Cotton Mill
(the No. 1 mill), 1897 (NTFB: doc. 247).

documents the lively discussions at Dasheng's first shareholder meeting, as saying: "Formerly all the organization of this mill was unlimited and unregulated (*wufa*).[7] Now that we have shareholders' meetings, this unlimited and unregulated business should be changed into one that is limited and regulated throughout. We should first establish its name as Dasheng Stockholding Company with Limited Liability (Dasheng gufen youxian gongsi)."[8]

Contrary to what one might expect, the share certificates of the Dasheng No. 1 mill issued after 1907 make no mention of the new legal status of the company. The certificates refer only to the Dasheng Spinning and Weaving Company (Dasheng fangzhi gongsi) without indicating its status as a limited liability firm. Share certificates from 1915 and 1919, however, no longer mention the involvement of the government in the establishment of the company.[9]

The fact that Zhang Jian also registered the No. 2 branch mill in Chongming with the Ministry of Commerce as early as 1905, two years before this facility began operations, shows his active interest in registering his companies with the government.[10] In contrast to the Dasheng No. 1 mill, however, the Chongming branch mill seems never to have been registered as a limited liability company. That legal status is indicated neither on its share certificates nor in its loan contracts with foreign and native banks in Shanghai.[11] Perhaps, as a branch of the No. 1 mill, the No. 2 mill was automatically considered to have the same legal status as the parent company, especially since many of the shareholders of the No. 1 mill—Zhang Jian, Zhang Cha, Liu Housheng, and Zhang Zuoqi to name just a few—were also shareholders in the Chongming mill.

Did the new Company Law and its requirements of shareholder meetings empower the shareholders and decrease Zhang Jian's influence? The minutes of the meetings reveal that the shareholders were only vaguely familiar with the Company Law and with the implications of limited liability for the enterprise and for their own rights and obligations. But the shareholders who voiced an opinion at the first meeting in 1907 shared a general consensus that the law supported their claims as owners and provided them with a tool to control management—or so they thought.

For example, the shareholders used their newly won influence to protest Dasheng's generous donations to Zhang Jian's welfare and educational projects.[12] Again, Zheng Xiaoxu, a concerned and critical but by no means a majority shareholder, expressed his opinion in outspoken terms: "Subsidies spent on the costs of the Normal School . . . reflect on the virtue of the general manager [i.e. Zhang Jian] himself and have nothing to do with the company. Now in accordance with the law, we have to discuss separately new regulations for the allocation of bonuses."[13] Obviously, Zheng interpreted the law as a mechanism that would protect shareholders against arbitrary allocations of bonuses to managers and of funds by the managing director (*zongli*). However, since Zhang Jian had never had to seek appointment as the managing director by a board of directors but had slipped into this position as he transformed Dasheng from a government-sponsored into a private enterprise, Zheng Xiaoxu's criticism did not endanger Zhang Jian's position.

In fact, the report on the 1907 shareholders' meeting reveals Zhang Jian's authoritarian management of Dasheng and the ineffectiveness of the shareholders' criticism and demands for change. The 1907 document, in recognition of the No. 1 mill's incorporation, contains eight clauses composed by Zhang Jian on issues such as managing working capital and reserves and electing members of the board.[14] Interestingly enough, there is no provision for the election of the managing director, and the clause that deals with this office contains only Zhang Jian's lamentations about his untiring efforts on behalf of the shareholders and the ingratitude of men and society in general:

> I was a poor and simple person who did not think highly of himself. Without preparation and to my great surprise, I suddenly was thrown into business and became an entrepreneur of an industrial enterprise. When I had reached one, two, and then three of my goals and yet did not stop my efforts, those who know me thought I was a strange person, and those who do not know me thought I was greedy person, out for personal profit. How could I be such a strange or greedy person! People all have feelings. What has today's society come to! . . . I did not become a managing director to serve my personal benefit; in fact, I have not had any benefit [from it] at all. My thousandfold troubles and anxieties have all been for your sake, honorable gentlemen.[15]

Instead of clear regulations that lay down procedures for election and resignation of corporate officers, with these elaborate yet vague moralizing statements Zhang Jian signaled that his efforts on behalf of the company justified his present authority and that he was not prepared to let shareholders participate in any substantive decision making. In the context of the discussions at the meeting, his statement is defensive. Instead of addressing the shareholders' complaints, he appealed to their integrity and moral conscience. As the shareholders continued to question bonus allocation and salaries for the managers, Zhang Jian had other members of the board explain Dasheng's—that is, his—position. And, as we shall see in the next chapter, the company continued to fund welfare and educational projects, even when business was poor, despite protests from the shareholders.

After Dasheng's official incorporation in 1907, the annual business reports eliminated references to the earlier involvement of the government. The machinery contributed by Zhang Zhidong as the government's capital share, which before 1908 had been itemized as "official machinery capital" (*guanjigu chengben*), was now listed as "machinery capital" (*ji chengben*).[16] To my knowledge, Zhang Jian never paid either the Qing or the Republican government for the machinery, even though, as the 1924 audit makes clear, the "official machinery" (*guanji*) remained a separate category.[17] As the annual business reports show, however, dividend payments on the "official machinery" (*guanji guanli*) had stopped by 1908, an indication that this machinery had finally become the property of Dasheng.

As part of the registration process, the Company Law of 1904 required a list of the shareholders, including their names and addresses as well as the number of shares each held and the amount of capital each had contributed.[18] These regulations covered not only the initial establishment of the firm but also changes in shareholding due to expansion and growth as they occurred over time. These periodic shareholding inventories are invaluable resources for examining Dasheng's shareholding structure and the practice of disguising personal accounts as business accounts. For example, an increase in the share capital at the Dasheng No. 1 Cotton Mill from 787,000 to 1.13 million taels in 1903 was documented in an internal record of the old as well as the newly subscribed shares and their holders,[19] and an inventory from 1907 gives information about the holders of shares worth a total of 630,000 taels, which constituted the financial capital of the mill (the book value of the machinery was given as 500,000 taels).[20] Since Dasheng's incorporation was not accompanied by the subscription of new capital, its shareholding structure in 1907 can be assessed on the basis of these two records.

The relatively detailed 1903 record shows that most shares in Dasheng were not held under the personal name of a shareholder but under a business name, that is, in the name of a *tang* (family trust) or *ji* (business). For example, Zhang Jian's son, Zhang Xiaoruo, held shares under the names of five Zhang family accounts and the Zunsu *tang* as well as under the business names Ruo *ji*, Xiao *ji*, and Xuyin *ji*. Since Zhang Xiaoruo was only five years old in 1903, it is clear that these were in fact Zhang Jian's personal assets. Zhang Jian may well have been the actual owner behind many business accounts, because in the majority of cases the space for the personal name (*xingming*) of the shareholder is left blank. For example, the Fengsi *tang* represented the charity land (*yizhuang*) in possession of Zhang Jian's own family. Another shareholder, the Zunsu *tang*, was associated with Zhang Jian's family residence in Haimen county. This information is available only in Zhang Jian's obituary of 1926, which describes the distribution of his personal assets; the actual ownership of these shares is not clear from the company's register.[21] According to the 1903 record, Zhang Cha held his shares in Dasheng under the business names of Dunyu *tang*, Juru *tang*, Tui *ji*, Dun *ji*, and Yu *ji*.[22] Again, he probably operated through other business accounts that can no longer be identified. Needless to say, investors from outside the family circle adopted the same practice.

The practice of holding capital under a business account was common at least in the late Qing dynasty and not unique to Dasheng or to the Zhang family. In fact, Ming merchants used business names (*ji* or *hao*) for daily operations and held property in the name of trusts (*tang*).[23] Front men, ancestral halls, and assumed names were used to conceal the true identity of owners from the government, which imposed restrictions on the involvement of gentry in business.[24] However, Zhang Jian's motivation for using such aliases was not to escape the attention of government officials. In the early twentieth century, gentry investment in industrial enterprises had become a legal and approved activity, and the government did not tax income or capital gains. As we shall see in the next chapter, Zhang Jian's main objective was to divert the attention of shareholders and potential auditors from his personal financial dealings within the Dasheng business group.

The change to limited liability at the Dasheng No. 1 Cotton Mill evidently did not bring great changes in the organization.[25] The introduction of annual shareholder meetings appears to have been the most significant result of the legal transformation. The incorporation as a privately owned company did not affect the internal management or the overall structure of the business. The hierarchy remained basically unchanged, and the department heads were still appointed by the managing director, although now in consultation with the board of directors (*dongshiju*).[26]

In addition, the 1904 Company Law mandated the appointment of two auditors (*chazhangyuan*) to examine company finances. The law did not specify that these auditors had to be independent, only that managing directors could not simultaneously serve as auditors.[27] This meant that other members of the board could serve as auditors. Not surprisingly, in the case of Dasheng auditors were recruited among the board members and thus from within the company management under Zhang Jian's immediate influence.[28] These auditors more or less rubber-stamped Dasheng's annual reports and signed the minutes of the shareholder meetings. They were not external controllers representing the interests of shareholders and providing financial clarity and critical examination. In fact, as part of the management, the auditors were there to defend the financial decisions they had approved earlier as members of the board.

On the whole, incorporation, which we tend to associate with the "modern" business enterprise in the Western sense, did not seem to lead to significant improvements in shareholder protections or curbs on the power of the managing director. To judge from the complaints at the 1907 meeting and their complete futility, shareholders were still at a disadvantage despite the potential for openness and accountability through incorporation. The balance of power did not change in the company. The fact that from 1919 on shareholder meetings frequently took place in Zhang Jian's private villa in Nantong city symbolically confirmed his steady, strong personal hold over Dasheng and his power vis-à-vis its shareholders. Nonetheless, the shareholders' role in Chinese business in general deserves some further exploration.

As mentioned above, as was the common practice at the time, Dasheng shareholders received guaranteed dividend payments at a fixed rate (8 percent in this case) on their investment, which they collected annually in person from the accounting office at the factories.[29] Such shares are better characterized as bonds in terms of their financial returns, since the shareholders bore a minimal financial risk. Only in the early 1920s did Dasheng investors become exposed to the fluctuations of the newly opened stock exchanges. Shares of the Dasheng No. 1 mill were traded for the first time by the Shanghai Stock Merchants Association in 1917, but the volume of trade on this exchange seems to have been rather limited.[30] When the Shanghai Stock Exchange opened in 1920, shares of the Dasheng No. 1 and No. 2 Cotton Mills were listed, and their market prices were regularly reported in the *Shenbao* newspaper.[31]

To give Dasheng's management some credit, the shareholders of 1907 were not taking great risks on the company's behalf and were not inclined, due to the absence of a stock market, to withdraw their investments at short notice. On the other hand, incorporation did not seem to make the company more attractive to potential investors, even if the aim of attracting investors and thus new capital might have been the main reason behind Zhang Jian's registration of the companies. The capital of the Dasheng No. 1 mill remained unchanged at 1.13 million taels between 1903 and 1914.[32] Obviously, the new legal status did not attract tremendous interest or create greater trust among investors and did not prompt the management to increase capital through the public offering of new share subscriptions.

This observation confirms William Kirby's view that the 1904 Company Law had a limited impact on the development of Chinese enterprises and modern industries. Only a relatively small number of enterprises registered at all, and of those registered as stockholding companies with limited liability only a few were of substantial size and grew into sustainable enterprises.[33] Kirby mentions the uncertainty of how the imperial court system would settle commercial disputes of corporations as a factor deterring investors and discouraging incorporation.[34] Given these general conditions, Dasheng's early and long-term success as an incorporated company stands out even more. Two reasons for this success were the internal systems of financial and managerial organization, which allowed Zhang Jian and the managers under his command to exercise control outside the boardroom.

Internal Organization and Accounting System

Given its diverse activities (cotton and flour mills, an oil press, a publishing house) and different geographical locations (Tangjiazha, Chongming, Haimen, and Nantong city), the Dasheng business group consisted of single companies bound into the strict hierarchical structure of a corporate enterprise. As the industrial core among the Dasheng enterprises, the No. 1 cotton mill provided the blueprint for the organization of the other businesses.

Figure 5.2 summarizes the structure of the Dasheng No. 1 Cotton Mill. As an enterprise with distinctive operating units managed by salaried executives, its structure, according to the definitions proposed by Western business historians such as Alfred Chandler, is characteristic of a modern business enterprise.[35] Initially, the management structure was quite simple. Under Zhang Jian as managing director, the company was divided into four departments: material acquisition and goods distribution, shop-floor production, miscellaneous tasks, and finance.[36] Each department was headed by a senior manager (*dongshi*) directly responsible to Zhang Jian. In the factory regulations of 1897, Zhang Jian set himself eight tasks: "to mediate relations between officials and merchants, to organize [the company] so that profits may be smoothly derived, to remove obstructions, to establish regulations, to appoint and remove managers, to investigate promotions and dismissals, to evaluate merits and demerits, and to apportion rewards and punishments."[37] This description emphasizes Zhang Jian's talents in dealing with members of the imperial bureaucracy and the local business community in the early years of the enterprise. However, as we shall see in the next chapter, especially in the 1910s and early 1920s Zhang Jian's role expanded to encompass negotiations with bankers and other industrialists.

The line of command within the Dasheng No. 1 mill was strict and set the tone for autocratic, paternalistic management. Since the senior managers were extremely important, it is worth asking what kind of people Zhang Jian drew into his inner circle of power. As we know from his diaries and

Fig. 5.2 Internal structure of the Dasheng No. 1 Cotton Mill, 1900
(drawing based on *TXSZ*, "Dasheng shachang," pp. 64–70).

business documents, Zhang Jian spent little time in Tangjiazha but traveled frequently between Nantong city and Shanghai.[38] Zhang Jian's immediate representative was his brother Zhang Cha, who joined the mill in 1902 as assistant director (*xieli*) of the company.[39] From the founding of the company, Jiang Xishen was head of the finance department, Shen Xiejun of material acquisition and goods distribution, Gao Qing (1850–1912) of the shop-floor production, and Xu Xianglin of the department for miscellaneous tasks.[40]

As Zhang Jian's elder brother, Zhang Cha naturally represented family interests, and each of the senior managers had his own business in addition to working for Dasheng. As mentioned above, Shen Xiejun engaged in the wholesale cloth business in Manchuria, while he was senior manager at Dasheng responsible for the acquisition of raw cotton and the distribution of finished goods.[41] Less is known about the backgrounds of the other three managers. Gao Qing and Jiang Xishen were from Nantong and had assisted Zhang Jian in raising capital to establish Dasheng.[42] Before joining the No. 1 mill in 1896, Gao Qing had had a modest career as a scholar in Tongzhou and Haimen, not unlike Zhang Jian.[43] He later supported Zhang Jian's educational program through educational projects in Jinsha city east of Nantong, where his family had settled.

It is not surprising that Zhang Jian would choose senior managers whom he trusted and who had some professional knowledge of business. Apart from receiving salaries and bonuses, the senior managers also held shares in the company. According to the 1903 shareholding record, Shen Xiejun's cloth business held five shares in Dasheng No. 1 under the account name Heng *ji*; we can assume that the other managers held shares under the names of various business accounts as well.[44]

The No. 1 mill was controlled by Zhang Jian, supported by the administrative office (*zong banshichu*) and the accounts office (*yinqian zongzhangfang*). These two offices together served as the mill's management headquarters (see Fig. 5.2). Both were located in the factory compound and oversaw only the No. 1 mill's affairs. To judge from the factory regulations, the four departments do not seem to have interacted with one another in a strict hierarchical line. All four departments had to report to the accounts office daily. Every evening after 6:00, each department had to submit all receipts for delivered raw cotton, dispatched yarn, work materials, cash expenses, and the like to the accounts office. There the clerks registered, checked, and then summarized receipts and reports on a weekly basis. If the sums were not correct, company regulations required an investigation.[45]

Did the promulgation of the 1904 Company Law change the process of creating and controlling the accounts in the Dasheng mills? The law stipulated that companies were to produce a detailed company report at least once every year with information on income and payments (*churu zongzhang*), the company's state of trade (*maoyi qingxing jielüe*), the exact loss or profit figure, the amount of money paid out as dividends, the amount of cash reserves, and a balance sheet of the company's assets and liabilities.[46] The Dasheng No. 1 Cotton Mill complied with all these formal requirements in its annual reports.

In fact, Dasheng had fulfilled these basic publication requirements even before the 1904 legislation. For most of its first 30 years, however, the accounting system used in the company did not change significantly.[47] The same general trend in accounting practices held among Chinese enterprises in the early twentieth century. The government obviously became concerned about the caveats in the original company law, and thus the 1904 version was expanded several times, with a major revision and supplement in 1914.[48]

One would expect changes in the reporting style or at least a more detailed, lucid presentation of the accounts as a result of the introduction of new company legislation. However, the 1904 Company Law had no regulations that specified the way company accounts should be compiled and recorded; the regulations for the annual financial statement occupy just two lines.[49] Even the revised Company Law of 1914 makes no provisions for standardized bookkeeping.[50]

In short, the law required an annual company report but stipulated no uniform system for company accounting. The earliest annual reports with data organized in a more accessible, standardized way for Dasheng date only to 1931.[51] In general, modern, Western-style bookkeeping methods found their way into China in the 1930s.[52] From 1946 on, Dasheng officially used a standardized, modernized accounting system.[53] Thus when reading earlier Dasheng reports, we have to bear in mind the absence of strict legal requirements for accounting.

Nevertheless, Dasheng's accounts and reports obviously served their purpose. From the beginning, the Dasheng No. 1 Cotton Mill maintained a complex bookkeeping system that provided some internal control within the factory. Books that listed quantities and sometimes values of items such as building materials, machinery, and even raw cotton entering the factory compound seem to have served the aim of tracking inventories.[54] The next stage in the accounting procedure consisted of a variety of journals recording expenditures and revenue by their occurrence. These journals listed expenses for such items as machine oil alongside expenses for stationery and postage, transportation costs, and reimbursements to Zhang Jian and other managerial personnel.[55] Classification of expenditures and revenue types according to their origin within the company or their financial nature in the accounting system was clearly not a concern at the time.

Other account books were kept by the individual departments. For example, the finance department seems to have been in charge of the payment journal, which recorded mainly the fixed dividend (*guanli*) paid to banks and local shops that had invested in Dasheng.[56] Given the large number of small shareholders, mostly cloth shops or native banks in the Nantong area, managing the dividend payments was one of the major tasks of the accounts department. Another important account book maintained by a department was the record listing the yarn and cotton delivered to the various workshops on the compound. For example, the amount of cotton delivered to the ginning room or blowing room was recorded weekly, together with summarized expenses for production materials and wages.[57]

The accounting process in the Dasheng mills mirrored the shop-floor arrangements for the production process. Instead of establishing separate accounting categories like wages, raw materials, or production materials, the account books recorded overall inputs and outputs or expenditures and revenues for each workshop and department as they occurred. Obviously at this stage costs and quantities were not interpreted as independent abstractions that, through their processing in the accounting system, would eventually provide an institutional mechanism for managerial control.

Sidney Pollard, among others, has pointed out that during England's Industrial Revolution, accounting gave management a control mechanism for estimating costs and managing stock.[58] However, even in Western enterprises this aspect of accounting developed only gradually. For example, Alfred Chandler notes that in American cotton mills before the 1850s, accounting served only to record past transactions. Mill managers slowly introduced accounting in order to determine unit costs, but overhead and capital costs still remained mostly unknown factors.[59]

Obviously, the accounting system used in the Dasheng No. 1 mill served the purposes of managing the stock and the flow of financial transactions within the company. However, I have found no evidence that Zhang Jian or the senior managers consciously used accounting to calculate and control costs, especially when they considered business expansion. Certainly the director and the managers discussed business decisions in a rational way in their correspondence, but they did not as yet systematically analyze the accounts as a tool in business planning. The use of accounts as a record of past transactions rather than as a tool of managerial control was not a particular inefficiency of Dasheng. The concept of cost accounting found its way into Chinese industrial enterprises in general only in the 1930s when it was discussed in business-related publications and actively promoted by prominent entrepreneurs like Liu Hongsheng (1891–1956).[60]

Of course, accounting as a managerial tool became even more important once it concerned not only the mills but also Dasheng as a business group with subsidiaries and affiliated companies. As we know from the company regulations, the No. 1 mill was required to send its records to the Shanghai office, where they were compiled into an overall record (*zonglu*), which later served as the basis for the annual company report.[61] The Shanghai office (more formally, the Shanghai central accounts office [Hu zongzhangfang]) held a key position in the control of the Dasheng business complex. Although the hierarchical relationship between the accounting offices in Tangjiazha and the office in Shanghai is only vaguely defined in the 1897 company regulations, by the 1910s the Shanghai office had already developed into the center of financial control and decision making.[62] In order to understand the relationship between the Shanghai office and the corporate nature of Dasheng, we need first to consider its structural organization and its special connection with the Zhang family.

Tools of Control: The Industrial Company and the Shanghai Office

Within the Dasheng business complex, the No. 1 cotton mill functioned as the holding company for a number of subsidiaries. Although the nature of these companies appears to have been haphazard and mixed, their establishment was directly connected with the production process of the No. 1 cotton mill. The land-reclamation company provided raw cotton, the oil mill pressed the discarded cotton seeds, the flour mill used the mill's coarse cotton cloth for bagging, and the steamship company played an important role in delivery and distribution for the Dasheng No. 1 mill (see Fig. 5.3).[63]

Here the terms "holding" and "subsidiary" should not be understood in the strict legal sense of current Western business law. Both terms are useful in describing two distinctive functions within the business group. First, the Dasheng No. 1 mill held shares in these subsidiary companies, and second, it was actively involved in their management for reasons of control. The holding relationship (see Fig. 5.3) is documented in the No. 1 mill's account books and annual company reports, which list its holding of shares in these subsidiaries as assets on the balance sheet.[64] For example, a collective entry in the 1903 company report shows that the Dasheng No. 1 mill held altogether 43,658 taels in shares in the oil and flour mills and steamship line.[65] In 1905, the No. 1 mill also held 20,000 taels in shares in the land-reclamation company, 6,258 taels in the steamship company, 50,000 taels in the oil mill, and 7,400 taels in the flour mill.[66]

Investment by the No. 1 mill in the subsidiaries amounted to roughly 10 percent of the share capital of the land-reclamation company, 32 percent of the steamship company, 15 percent of the flour mill, and 17 percent of the oil mill.[67] Obviously, the No. 1 mill was not the majority shareholder in these subsidiaries, which is a necessary requirement for a holding-subsidiary relationship in contemporary business law.[68] However, shareholders of the Dasheng No. 1 mill increasingly questioned the company's investments in the subsidiaries. As a result, Zhang Jian felt the need to reassure the shareholders in the 1908 annual report that the mill's investments in the affiliated companies would not exceed 40 percent of the affiliate's share capital.[69]

Fig. 5.3 Structure of the Dasheng business complex, 1908 (drawing based on *TXSZ*, "Dasheng shachang," pp. 167–71).

Not only financial control through shareholding but also managerial control through what we could call interlocking directorships defined the relationship between holding company and subsidiaries. In almost all the subsidiary companies that came under the No. 1 mill's control, Zhang Jian and Zhang Cha held the position of managing director and assistant director, respectively. In the Guangsheng Oil Mill, a close associate of Zhang Jian from Rugao county, Sha Yuanbing (1864–1927), held the position of managing director. Zhang Jian was the assistant director.[70]

Aside from the four subsidiary companies, which were controlled by the Dasheng No. 1 Cotton Mill through shareholding and interlocking directorships, thirteen other companies were affiliated with the No. 1 mill (see Fig. 5.3). In his report to the No. 1 mill shareholders in 1908, Zhang Jian characterized the affiliations between those companies and the mill as direct (*zhijie*), close (*miqie*), or indirect (*jianjie*). Zhang Jian's classification illustrates that he not only recognized the affiliation but also wanted the shareholders to appreciate the variety of relationships between the No. 1 mill and these companies.[71]

As in the case of the subsidiaries, the relationship between the affiliated companies and the No. 1 mill was defined not through financial dependency but through the products or services the affiliated companies provided to the No. 1 mill. For example, the Zesheng Hydraulic Company was considered a directly related company because it maintained the local waterways vital for transporting the No. 1 mill's coal supplies from Shanghai to Tangjiazha. The Zisheng Iron Workshop qualified as a closely affiliated company since it repaired broken looms in the Dasheng No. 1 mill. The Yisheng Distillery is an example of an indirectly related company because it used the grain produced on land owned by the Tonghai Land Reclamation Company, another subsidiary. The distillery dealt with the Tonghai company rather than with the mill. The Dalong Soap Factory qualified as an indirectly related company because it used byproducts of the Guangsheng Oil Mill for soap production and was not directly connected with the No. 1 mill.[72]

To what extent did the Dasheng No. 1 mill, its shareholders, and Zhang Jian benefit from these associated businesses? The Tonghai Land Reclamation Company is certainly the most intriguing and complex case in terms of the No. 1 mill's financial investment. As mentioned above, the Qing government had granted Zhang Jian the salt fields along the northern Jiangsu coast on condition that he start the cotton mill operation. The intent was to use the land to grow cotton for the mill. Zhang Jian was, of course, also the managing director of the Tonghai company.[73] Thus he had good reasons to present the Tonghai company to the No. 1 mill shareholders as a promising business opportunity and to persuade them that it was right and proper to invest mill funds in Tonghai's operations.

Nevertheless, we have to examine Zhang Jian's decision carefully in the light of legal definitions and questions of control within the Dasheng business complex. According to the 1905 annual report of the No. 1 mill, a total of 20,000 taels was invested in the Tonghai company in the form of shares (*gufen*).[74] A check of the annual reports of the Tonghai company reveals that the sum received from the No. 1 mill had a book value ranging from 21,792 taels in 1906 to 28,043 taels in 1910.[75] In addition, according to the balance sheet of the Tonghai company, the funds from the Dasheng No. 1 mill were invested in the form of a deposit (*cun*) and not in the form of shares.

This accounting detail is of great significance in analyzing the financial relationship between the two companies. Since the records of the Tonghai company are not complete, it is hard to tell whether and how changes to the funds invested by the No. 1 mill might have been made in the 1910s. In 1918 the Tonghai company's records show that Zhang Jian and Zhang Cha owned 18 percent of Tonghai's share capital; a total of 59 shareholders are listed, but, surprisingly, the Dasheng No. 1 Cotton Mill is not among them.[76] In other words, Zhang Jian had quite deliberately misled the Dasheng shareholders about the mill's investment in the Tonghai company, which he controlled in much the same autocratic way that he controlled the No. 1 mill.[77]

The important point here is that funds provided by Dasheng shareholders for the Tonghai business operation were not invested as equity but turned into deposits, which did not yield a guaranteed dividend at a fixed rate and would be much more difficult to retrieve from the subsidiary. In addition, deposits, unlike shares, did not result in voting rights at shareholder meetings. In a nutshell, Zhang Jian elicited funds from the No. 1 mill shareholders, who were apprehensive about these investments in subsidiaries in the first place, without giving them rights of representation and easy access to their investment. Given his interest in Tonghai (see Chapter 7), it seems plausible that Zhang Jian might have preferred this type of financial investment, which did not entail increased control for the No. 1 mill shareholders over the Tonghai company.

Growing concern about the No. 1 mill's financial involvement in subsidiaries and affiliated companies prompted its worried shareholders to demand institutional changes. In 1907 the shareholders proposed the establishment of a holding company within the Dasheng business complex: the Tonghai Industrial Company (Tonghai shiye gongsi), hereafter referred to as the Industrial Company.

The proposal for the Industrial Company came from the influential shareholder Zheng Xiaoxu. Zheng was also involved in other modern enterprises in the Shanghai area, such as the Jiangnan Arsenal, the Shanghai Commercial Press (Shanghai shangwu yinshuguan), and the Shanghai Commercial and Savings Bank (Shanghai shangye chuxu yinhang). His business experience enabled him to make solid and critical judgments of the No. 1 mill's investment strategies. At the 1907 shareholders' meeting, he commented that "the volume of transactions between the subsidiary companies and Dasheng [the No. 1 mill] has become too large." It was now necessary "to draw a clear line by taking all the debts of the various companies as the share capital of the Tonghai Industrial Limited Liability Company." By giving the Industrial Company "its own name and thus its independence, [the subsidiaries] will not again be dragged into Dasheng's [the No. 1 mill's] affairs."[78] Obviously he and the other shareholders wanted to protect funds they had invested in the No. 1 mill and prevent its management from transferring them to the smaller and financially much weaker subsidiaries.

The 1907 shareholders' meeting voted to use the mill's accumulated reserves and the 600,000 taels set aside to pay the dividends for 1906 as starting capital for the Industrial Company. The proposal was carried over the strong protests of those shareholders who wanted the dividend distributed. Since the Dasheng No. 1 Cotton Mill was providing the total capitalization of the Industrial Company, its shareholders automatically became shareholders of the new company, and de facto both companies became inseparable.[79]

In reality, however, this transfer of funds within the Dasheng business complex resulted in the establishment not so much of a new company but of a separate account. This is obvious in the 1907 balance sheet of the No. 1 mill. There the assets of the Industrial Company were recorded as having a book value of only 123,924 taels and not the 600,000 taels authorized at the shareholders' meeting.[80] A look at the balance sheet for the previous year explains the drastic cut. In 1906 the Dasheng No. 1 mill held deposits totaling 495,467 taels in various affiliated industrial companies in Tongzhou and Haimen.[81] The affiliated companies owed this amount to the No. 1 mill. When the shareholders of the No. 1 mill voted to transfer 600,000 taels to the Industrial Company, that company in effect paid Dasheng 495,467 taels for the debts owed by the affiliated companies. Therefore, when the 1907 balance sheet records Dasheng's assets in the Industrial Company as 123,923 taels rather than 600,000 taels, it means that the No. 1 mill wrote off the 495,467 taels as bad debts (the figures shown in the two balance sheets do not total 600,000; no explanation is given for the discrepancy of 19,390 taels).[82]

The share capital for the Industrial Company was thus mainly provided through the transfer of funds between the companies in question. Since Zhang Jian was managing director of the Industrial Company, its management and shareholders were identical with those of the Dasheng No. 1 mill. The Industrial Company published neither annual reports nor minutes of

Fig 5.4 The Dasheng business complex and the Shanghai office, 1908.

shareholder meetings because there were no shareholder meetings until 1937.[83] One reason is that deposits by the No. 1 mill in the Industrial Company were fairly stable and did not exceed 172,000 taels.[84] In fact, without a business of its own, without binding regulations, without shareholder meetings, without its own accounting, office, and staff, the Industrial Company was not even a company.[85] It was nothing more than an account carried on the No. 1 mill's books for the explicit purpose of absorbing the mill's debts from loans to financially weak subsidiaries and affiliated companies.[86] In the end, in contrast to the shareholders' intention, the Industrial Company did not protect their financial interests; rather, it allowed Zhang Jian and his managers to pursue their own investment strategies within the Dasheng business complex.

Although the subsidiary and affiliated companies were linked in various ways to the Dasheng No. 1 mill, they reported not to the No. 1 mill in Tangjiazha but to the Shanghai office, an institution outside the Dasheng business group and under Zhang Jian's personal supervision (see Fig. 5.4). As the central accounts office, the Shanghai office fulfilled several functions within the Dasheng business complex (the mills, affiliated businesses, and even some of the subsidiaries). Surprisingly, the tasks of the Shanghai office were not specified in the company regulations, which so meticulously regulated the organization of the shop floor, workforce, and production.[87] As we shall see, however, there were reasons Zhang Jian was not interested in regulating and publicizing the activities of this particular office.

First, the Shanghai office acted as the head office of the business complex. As the voluminous correspondence between the Shanghai office and the

Dasheng No. 1 mill shows, the senior managers of the No. 1 mill, the head of the Shanghai office, and Zhang Jian communicated frequently.[88] For instance, the senior manager of the department for material acquisition and goods distribution in the No. 1 mill, Shen Xiejun, wrote in mid-1903 to the head of the Shanghai office, Lin Lansheng, to discuss the need to buy machinery and equipment, salaries, and the stagnant cloth market in Manchuria.[89] Two months later, Shen Xiejun wrote to inform Lin Lansheng that the inventory had been carefully completed and enclosed an account for inspection.[90]

Second, the Shanghai office acted as paymaster and broker in Shanghai for the various affiliated companies. The head of the Shanghai office and the senior accountants there seem to have been well informed about the financial situation in the Dasheng mills and in critical situations wrote directly to the managing director. Yun Zuqi, a senior accountant in the Shanghai office, complained to Zhang Jian about the increasing indebtedness to native banks in Hangzhou and Changzhou and the interest payments due.[91] The senior accountants in Shanghai also decided how money transactions would be entered in the mill's accounts. For example, Yun Zuqi told Shen Xiejun to enter a payment of 6,000 taels from a business (*hao*) in Zhejiang province under "remittances" (*huikuan*) in the revenue column.[92]

All payments to the foreign brokerages in Shanghai and to the native banks on behalf of the Dasheng No. 1 mill and its subsidiaries and affiliated companies were made through the Shanghai office. For this purpose, the Shanghai office kept passbooks recording all the funds deposited with native banks in Shanghai; the deposits were certified by stamping the respective bank's seal in the book.[93] Furthermore, account books such as the receipt book for cash payments (*songyin huidan*) show that the Shanghai office handled monetary transactions by balancing bills or delivering interest payments.[94] The fact that some entries identify the payments as "in the name of Dasheng" (Dasheng *mingxia*) confirms that the Shanghai office acted directly on behalf of the No. 1 mill. The Shanghai office also took care of accounts held by the Dasheng mills with modern banks in Shanghai such as the Shanghai Commercial and Savings Bank.[95]

Ordering machinery, arranging the visits of foreign engineers, editing the annual reports, and representing the various Dasheng companies in Shanghai by maintaining an office on Jiujiang Road in the International Settlement were some of the other tasks the office performed.[96] Yet, the Shanghai office did much more than what one would expect of an agent in a metropolis: it kept records of deposits left with it, negotiated loans on behalf of subsidiary companies, and sold shares of affiliated and subsidiary companies in Shanghai. For example, one account book entitled "internal transactions" (*neiliu*) documents the delivery of share certificates (*gupiao*) of the Tonghai Land Reclamation Company to private persons in Shanghai in 1903, handed over in sets of eighteen sheets each.[97]

The Shanghai office also handled the transportation and sales of products. For example, a page on the Dalong Soap Factory from an account book for affiliated companies (*fenhu*) reveals that the Shanghai office sold five crates of soap to a wholesale company on behalf of Dalong. The Shanghai office also recorded in-house loans and payments for transportation costs between affiliated companies and cleared one item against another. In one particular case, the Dasheng Steamship Company's charges to the Zisheng Iron Workshop were deducted from a loan from Zisheng to the steamship company and the net balance was transferred from Zisheng's account.[98]

Various shareholder reports also indicate that the Shanghai office itself acted as an independent business, investing funds and receiving interest on deposits at several of the No. 1 mill's affiliated and subsidiary companies such as the Zisheng Iron Workshop, the Tonghai Land Reclamation Company, and the Fuxin Flour Mill. These investments were rather modest and never exceeded 50,000 taels in any of those companies.[99] The account books of the Dasheng No. 2 Cotton Mill in Chongming show that the mill received considerable sums as interest payments from the Shanghai office, and the Shanghai office in turn received substantial interest payments from the No. 2 mill (almost 30,000 taels in 1904). In the following years, the Shanghai office received continuing payments of 5,600 taels from the Chongming mill for its services as an intermediary searching on behalf of the mill for new shareholders and bank loans in Shanghai.[100]

Evidence that the Shanghai office directly managed the accounts of affiliated companies can be found in the account books of Tongrentai, a salt-producing company founded by Zhang Jian in 1903 with capital provided mainly by major shareholders of the Dasheng No. 1 mill. Zhang Jian himself owned 7.5 percent of the starting capital in shares, and the Tonghai Land Reclamation Company held 10 percent of the shares.[101] One of Tongrentai's account books kept by the Shanghai office lists its income and expenses for the years between 1904 and 1908.[102] In addition to payments of a fixed dividend to the Tonghai Land Reclamation Company, the book also records dividends of 720 taels paid Zhang Jian as one of the major investors.

Zhang Jian's relationship with the Shanghai office leads us to its most significant function: it was his private office and looked after his personal and family accounts and managed his financial transactions. The Shanghai office kept books entitled "miscellaneous accounts" (*zahu*) on Zhang Jian's noncommercial projects such as the Nantong Normal School and the Tongzhou Girls' School, which received payments through the office in 1909 and 1910. The same books document other money transaction for private matters. For example, an entry labeled "Zhang *gong shou*" (into the hands of his Excellency Zhang Jian) records a payment of 2,000 taels to Zhang Jian for the Constitutional Society, which he was running at that time.[103]

Zhang Jian frequently instructed the Shanghai office on how sums of money should be recorded in the account books. In a succession of letters, he told the head of the Shanghai office to transfer sums of 1,000, 2,000, or 3,000 taels to the account of the Guan *ji* business, which appears to have been one of his private accounts disguised as a business account.[104] Even more significant is the fact that Zhang Jian did not specify from what accounts these sums were to be drawn, for what purposes the transfers were made, or whether the transfers were of a personal or a business nature. He felt free to demand transfers between company accounts and his own accounts, and the head accountant obviously knew exactly what to do. The lack of documentation in such transfers of funds suggests the laxness of accountability. As Chapter 6 illustrates in detail, the combined management of business and private accounts was to have a serious impact on the financial soundness of the Dasheng mills in the late 1910s and early 1920s.

The Shanghai office was a crucial part of the "modern" Dasheng business complex, but it had roots in traditional business practices. The accounting office (*zhangfang*) was not a new business institution in twentieth-century China. Unfortunately, we know little about the internal operations of such offices before 1900. In the traditional silk industry, the *zhangfang*, in this context translated as "accounting houses," acted as the basic suppliers of financing for the processing of silk.[105] In the eighteenth and nineteenth centuries, accounting houses, which were owned by wealthy merchants, would provide silk weavers with looms and raw materials and then pay them for the finished products on delivery.[106]

As Lillian Li has demonstrated, the accounting houses maintained a close relationship with the silk-weaving households, sometimes on a quasi-permanent basis.[107] Although the accounting houses were engaged in large-scale financing, the number of looms under the supervision of each *zhangfang* was relatively small and never exceeded 600 looms.[108] Thus we should evaluate the *zhangfang* not so much in the context of large-scale production but rather in the context of financing it. If we apply Li's definition of the *zhangfang*'s function as that of "a middleman, handling transactions at various stages in the [silk-]manufacturing process,"[109] then we can define the *zhangfang* in Dasheng as a middleman in financial and managerial matters that linked Zhang Jian and his family closely with the companies of the business complex.

A comparison with the development of the *zhangfang* in other family-run businesses will serve to highlight the nature of the Shanghai office. In the late nineteenth and early twentieth centuries, the institution of the accounting office was a feature of large family enterprises such as the Yekaitai medicine store, established and run for generations by the prominent Ye family in Hankou.[110] Although the production of various medical products was divided into six departments, the managerial operations of the store in Hankou and its branches in, among other places, Wuchang and Shanghai were divided into five departments. The *zhangfang* at the top of the company's hierarchy presided over the departments of customer service and sales, both retail and wholesale, as well as long-distance trading and raw materials acquisition. As at Dasheng, the manager of the accounting office lived on the premises, and all the financial transactions of the business were under his control.[111]

The Meng family's Ruifuxiang business is another example of a thriving operation in which business and personal matters were handled from one office. The Ruifuxiang company had stores selling medicine, cosmetics, and imported goods in Beijing and other major Chinese cities in the early twentieth century.[112] By 1925 the store had some 26 branches, one of which was among the biggest piece-goods establishments in Beijing. Meng Luochuan, the general manager, controlled this highly diversified business complex through a personalized network of trustworthy subordinates, a strict chain of managerial coordination, and a formal structure of meetings and written reports.[113] He was assisted by his own family accounting office, which was in charge of the accounts of both his private estate and his own businesses.[114]

As in Zhang Jian's case, the accounting office was an institution of control over private as well as business interests.

Eventually other corporate enterprises in Republican China followed Dasheng's example and adopted the institution of the *zhangfang*. For example, in the 1910s and 1920s, the industrialist Liu Hongsheng used his central accounts office in Shanghai, which was headed by his brother, as a tool to control his diversified business complex, which consisted of cement and match factories and wharf companies.[115]

As we have seen, the traditional accounts office served several important purposes in a family business. As this institution was adapted to an industrial joint-stock enterprise with limited liability, one would expect conflicts of interest between the shareholders and the managing director (who was also the founder). However, in Zhang Jian's case, his personal authority and control were not curtailed by but embedded in the Shanghai office as an institutionalized tool of control. In fact, the internal organization of the Shanghai office and its placement outside the formal structure of the Dasheng business complex allowed Zhang Jian to exert full vertical authority, to use a modern management expression. How personal relationships and networks shaped the dynamics of power in the Shanghai office and affected the issue of accountability is the subject of the next section.

Ownership and Accountability

In the West the issue of control in an enterprise is assumed to be closely linked to the issue of ownership. The Dasheng business complex is a perfect example of the fact that Chinese enterprises, even those with a corporate structure, do not necessarily fulfill this assumption. In fact, ownership and control are two completely separate issues in the context of Chinese business. A closer look at the ownership of Dasheng will demonstrate this.

Both Zhang Jian and his brother held shares in the Dasheng No. 1 Cotton Mill and its branch mills.[116] In addition, the brothers held shares in every subsidiary and every land reclamation company (a total of 22 enterprises by 1916). These shares were held either in their own name or in the business name of a *tang* or *ji* or through their involvement in other companies that held shares in the Dasheng mills. Based on documents available in the Nantong archives, I estimate that the Zhang family, considering all the equity linked in one way or another to its accounts, owned about 10 percent of all the shares in the Dasheng business complex.

Even allowing for a considerable margin of error because some of the family accounts may not have been identified, control was clearly not tied to a majority shareholding. The 1907 inventory of shareholdings in the No. 1 mill supports this argument with straightforward numbers. A total of 553 shareholders had subscribed the capital stock of 630,000 taels. The largest single shareholder was the Salt Bureau, with an investment of 23,000 taels in public funds (*gongkuan*); this is roughly 4 percent of the total capital. Then follows a group of seventeen shareholders with investments of 8,000–15,000 taels each (1.3–2.4 percent each, or 27 percent altogether). The remaining 435,000 taels, or 69 percent, of the capital stock had been subscribed by 535 shareholders, who individually owned less than 5,000 taels each in equity. The overwhelming majority of these shareholders owned between one and five shares at 100 taels each. Accounts that can be linked to Zhang Jian's family in one form or another reveal an ownership of 40,300 taels, or 6.4 percent of the total capital stock, still a modest percentage even though it was higher than that of the largest single shareholder.[117]

The fact that control over the Dasheng business complex was not connected to a majority shareholding emphasizes the important function of the Shanghai office as the primary tool of control. In an oversimplified way, one could argue that managerial control through a separate institution replaced financial control through equity in the enterprise. Certainly, the issue of managerial control is also linked to the issue of costs, in particular to the costs of controlling managers. The delegation of decision-making authority and its supervision incur "agency costs." These can be divided into the direct costs of supervising the managers and the indirect costs of "managerial opportunism," which arise from the inability to supervise managers with perfect efficiency.[118] In this respect, the Shanghai office enabled Zhang Jian to reduce agency costs because it made strict, immediate supervision of managers throughout the business complex possible and thus lessened the impact of managerial opportunism.

Obviously, the head of the Shanghai office held an extremely important position. His position outside the formal business structure of Dasheng associated him with Zhang Jian and his family in a unique way. Zhang Jian never stayed in Shanghai for long periods of time and never acquired a home in the city. His control over the many companies in the group was secured through constant direct communication with Wu Jichen (1873–1935), the head of the Shanghai office. The correspondence between the two gives ample evidence of such communication. Through almost daily contacts via letters and sometimes telegrams, Wu Jichen kept Zhang Jian up to date on the business climate in Shanghai and the general market conditions for cotton prices and yarn sales. Whenever Zhang Jian visited Shanghai for personal meetings, he stayed at the Shanghai office, a grand, impressive Western-style building that housed not only Wu Jichen's apartment but also other companies in which Zhang Jian was financially involved such as the Huaihai Bank.[119]

As the head of the Shanghai office, Wu Jichen was personally and exclusively accountable to Zhang Jian and not to the shareholders or the management. He occupied the position of *zhangfang xiansheng*, or Mr. Accounts Office, the traditional, popular term for the man in charge of private and business accounts in the *zhangfang*.[120] Most holders of this office were either family members or someone recommended by a close friend who guaranteed the person's reliability.[121] Wu Jichen's relationship with Zhang Jian was certainly characterized by close cooperation and trust. According to Wu Jichen's elaborate obituary, which was composed by one of Zhang Jian's associates, Meng Lin, in 1935, "the Shanghai office always remained the center of trust."[122] Even if he was not equal to Zhang Jian in social standing and financial influence, Wu's family background and interests made him an ideal candidate for the position.

Wu Jichen was not a simple, narrow-minded bookkeeper but a sophisticated person with a sharp business mind and excellent managerial skills. He came from Dantu (present-day Zhenjiang city), a port on the southern bank of the Yangzi River in Jiangsu.[123] Like Zhang Jian, Wu Jichen was a connoisseur of the arts and a famous book collector.[124] He started as an assistant manager to his predecessor, Lin Lansheng, and took over the Shanghai office around 1910. The importance of native place in the business world is shown by the fact that Wu's assistant, Fan Xujing, was also from Zhenjiang. As a former banker, Fan had excellent connections with the Zhenjiang group (*bang*) of local native banks and thus was able to arrange loans for Dasheng from them, especially between 1918 and 1920 during expansion of the mill business.[125]

Wu Jichen gained enormous power during the early 1920s, when Zhang Jian was busy with matters related to regional politics and development. When the Dasheng cotton mills faced a serious financial crisis in the early 1920s (see Chapter 6), the transferring of funds and mortgaging of real estate in particular became Wu Jichen's major task in the office.[126] Wu Jichen was also an important shareholder in several industrial enterprises such as the Nanyang Tobacco Company and a member of the board of the Shanghai Commercial and Savings Bank.[127] His importance for the Dasheng business complex and Zhang Jian is obvious from board meetings of the Chinese Cotton Mill Owners' Association, at which he represented the Dasheng mills in Zhang Jian's absence.[128]

Relationships between Zhang Jian and Wu Jichen were not without friction, however. For example, when Wu suggested that they use the No. 3 branch mill as security for a large bank loan, he evidently felt that he had to explain to Zhang Jian that this suggestion was not motivated by personal interest.[129] This unsolicited statement was probably necessary because Wu was a shareholder and assistant director of the No. 3 mill. Wu Jichen again assured Zhang Jian of his loyalty when he wrote to him in 1923 that he would argue with the shareholders on behalf of Zhang Jian and the company.[130]

In spite of these occasional conflicts of interest, Wu Jichen acknowledged Zhang's authority as the ultimate patron of the company when he wrote Zhang Jian's son, Zhang Xiaoruo, in 1920: "His Excellency [Zhang Jian] is a person held in high esteem by people outside [the company]. I have to handle affairs with utmost care and not by rashness cause outside people to be contemptuous. If I do not do this, in future, not only will negotiations become more difficult, but, and this is of even greater consequence to us, also His Excellency's reputation will be affected."[131] In my opinion, Wu Jichen's statement should be interpreted not only as respectful and loyal support of his boss but also as a sign that he recognized that Zhang Jian's social reputation was an important part of Dasheng's business capital.

For his efforts, Wu Jichen received generous remuneration. The official salary found in the account books under "expenses for the Shanghai office" was obviously only one part of his income. In addition to his annual salary of 800 taels, Wu received also a generous bonus and lavish office expenses, which enabled him to discuss the purchase of a Packard or Cadillac automobile for business use.[132] Wu Jichen's financial rewards certainly also reflect the fact that, as in a traditional family business, the Shanghai office managed financial affairs for other members of the family as well, such as Zhang Jian's son and his brother Zhang Cha. We know from their correspondence with Wu Jichen that both withdrew money from accounts, which are not specified but seem to have been private family accounts like the Dunyu *tang* account (see Fig. 5.5).[133] The son asked for money to pay the upkeep on his residence, and Zhang Cha asked Wu Jichen to transfer money to an account that seems to have been part of his land-reclamation projects.[134] However, their correspondence also reveals that son and brother had no say in the major business decisions of the office, which were made solely by Zhang Jian in consultation with Wu Jichen.

From a historical perspective, the vital role of the head of the accounts office in relation to the family is confirmed by cases like the Yuanfahang business. One of the biggest rice wholesalers in Hong Kong, it was founded in the 1850s by Gao Manhua from Shantou.[135] After the death of the founder, the business continued under joint ownership of his nine sons, with the second son, Gao Shunqin, acting as owner-director (*shitou*).[136] As the business developed into a large enterprise, the director's office (*shitou fang*) became the center of control under the manager Chen Chunquan, who had been with the family for a long time.[137] The relationship between Chen and the family seems to have been characterized by great mutual trust. For example, Chen started businesses of his own like the Yudesheng Bank in which the Gao family invested. According to Gao Shunqin's son Gao Zhenbai, Chen Chunquan "decided on strategies."[138] Chen was in charge of the accounts, which also meant that he was in charge of the private accounts of the family held at the director's office. As Gao Zhenbai recollects, Chen Chunquan managed his father's accounts under the name Shun *ji*, which between 1883 and 1933 had deposits of more than one million yuan.[139] Whenever Gao Shunqin or other family members wanted to withdraw money, Chen would pay them. Chen in return complained about overspending by family members and the charging of debts to family accounts, loyally reminding the family of the founder's hardships during the early years of the business.[140] However, without final authority over the accounts, he had to oblige the family.

If power stemming from control of a business is expressed through wealth, then Zhang Jian was a powerful man—he remained a wealthy man until the end of his life, despite Dasheng's financial crisis in 1922. How wealthy is difficult to measure because of the complex accounting system. In addition, Zhang Jian always portrayed himself as a frugal person from a modest family background who more or less by chance had become a businessman. In fact, Zhang Jian was quite careful not to display his personal wealth through conspicuous consumption. His grand villa in Nantong city

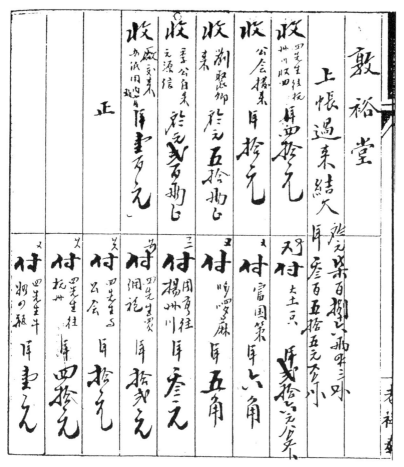

Fig. 5.5 Page from the account book for one of Zhang Jian's private accounts
under the name Dunyu *tang* (NTD: B 401-311-2, 1897–1900, p. 59).

was not built until 1915, and in contrast to his son, he never pursued an expensive urban lifestyle (see Chapter 8). Zhang Jian's contemporaries who
have been interviewed for local oral history projects since the mid-1980s continue to popularize this frugal image by describing Zhang Jian's simple diet
and his habit of binding scraps of paper into the booklets in which he kept
his diary.[141]

In combination with his claims of frugality and self-sacrifice, Zhang Jian
tried to convince shareholders as well as the general public of his morally

superior motives in pursuing business. The following statement from the factory regulations, published in 1910, purveys his untiring dedication to building a successful enterprise solely for the benefit of shareholders and business associates:

In the midst of the many mouths that violently attacked me, and at a place where the attitude was blind and bigoted, my position deteriorated as I tried harder and harder before all this was achieved. I did not do this [for the benefit] of a single person or family, as you honorable gentlemen already know! With firmness and determination, one can rise above defeat and achieve success. With wasteful negligence and concern only for one's private ends, even success will end in defeat. How can success and defeat be the glory or shame of only one person, my humble self?[142]

The traditional perceptions of merchants and commercial activities as morally tainted might have prompted Zhang Jian to make these humble and self-deprecating statements. Obviously they also helped smooth negotiations with dissatisfied shareholders, fractious managers, and skeptical business associates.

Considering the modest shareholdings of the family in Dasheng, just how wealthy were Zhang Jian and his family? A special issue of the Nantong newspaper, published for his funeral in October 1926, is the only source that gives information about the real estate assets and other possessions of the Zhang family.[143] One article describes Zhang Jian's and Zhang Cha's provisions for distribution of the family's property. It is interesting that the will was made public at a time when Zhang Jian's elder brother was still alive and representing the family. Each brother had expanded his own family residence over many years, but according to the will the descendants of both brothers were to share the family land and real estate. Most of the buildings were to go to the eastern branch of the family, that is, to Zhang Cha's branch; Zhang Jian's books and art collections were destined for his son's, western branch of the family. The land was to remain "eternally under the mutual management of both branches" but divided by right of ownership.[144] The deeds for sacrificial land and for the land on which the girls' school was built and the land set aside for its upkeep, altogether 707 mu of land, were to stay with Zhang Xiaoruo's branch. The son's branch was also to receive the deeds to 1,560 mu of various categories of land rented to tenants. Zhang Cha's branch of the family was to receive the deeds to 1,575 mu of land rented to tenants, as well as to several large properties in Nantong city and the rental income from them. In the end, Zhang Jian's son received more land because his share included the fields of the ancestral trust, whereas Zhang Cha's branch of the family obtained not only agricultural land but also all the urban real estate.[145]

Although it is difficult to assign a concrete value to the urban real estate, this settlement suggests that Zhang Cha, rather than Zhang Jian and his branch, controlled more of the family's finances and assets. The impression that Zhang Cha's personal wealth surpassed that of Zhang Jian was confirmed by Zhang Jian's granddaughter, Zhang Rouwu, in an interview in 1995: "Zhang Cha had the money, and Zhang Jian had the reputation" (*Sanfang you qian, sifang you ming*).[146] Corroboration of this can be seen in the mansions the two built in Nantong. Zhang Cha established his grand residence in the southern section of the city two years before Zhang Jian built his in 1915.[147] The fact that the residences faced each other across the Haohe canal—Zhang Cha's being larger and more impressive than Zhang Jian's—tells us something about both brothers' wealth and their competition for status and recognition in local society, a subject further discussed in Chapter 7.

Zhang Jian's will also specified the distribution of his business assets. All his shares in the cotton mills, oil mill, flour mill, and land-reclamation companies were to be divided equally between the western branch of the family, represented by the Zunsu *tang* (the business name of Zhang Xiaoruo's account), and the eastern branch, represented by the Dunyu *tang* account.[148] It appears that by 1926 Zhang Jian's shares in these firms were worth around 200,000 taels. Neither Zhang Jian nor his brother could have accumulated these assets from their company salaries, bonuses, and interest income. The amount of real estate and financial assets, owned not only by Zhang Jian but by the family as a whole, points to additional sources of income from other business opportunities and investments in land reclamation, which I analyze in the following chapter.

Further evidence of the extensiveness of the family's financial assets came to light in 1928, two years after Zhang Jian's death, when *Tonghai xinbao*, a local newspaper, reported that the provincial authorities were investigating Zhang Cha's private property.[149] According to the newspaper, Zhang Cha was said to have private financial assets of more than 2 million yuan, in addition to real estate estimated at another million yuan in Haimen and other counties, acquired mainly through the purchase of reclaimed land.[150] Obviously, the very size of Zhang Cha's holdings lent themselves to suspicions that he might not have acquired them legally, but in the climate of this period that would not in itself have led to a government investigation. As one might suspect, there was a hidden agenda at work here. The investigation was apparently initiated by the Guomindang government in retaliation for Zhang Jian's and Zhang Cha's financial support of Sun Chuanfang (1885–1935), the Beiyang warlord, who in 1926 had controlled the five provinces around the lower Yangzi, including the Nantong area (see Chapter 8). Sun Chuanfang was the political enemy of Chiang Kai-shek (1887–1975) and was one of Chiang's primary targets during the Northern Expedition. This military campaign, which began in the summer of 1926 and moved from Guangdong province toward the Yangzi region, eliminated Chiang's political enemies and established him in power. With the help of Zhang Zuolin, the warlord in control of Manchuria, Sun Chuanfang was able to hold on to power in the economically strategic provinces around the Yangzi until March 1927, when Chiang Kai-shek's troops took over the area, including the cities of Nanjing and Shanghai.[151] Because of Sun Chuanfang's defeat, Zhang Cha had lost power and support in local and provincial politics by 1928. Obviously fearing further investigations and pressure from the new Guomindang government in Nanjing, Zhang Cha fled to Beijing and returned to Shanghai only in 1931. It is not clear what happened to his land and financial assets after his move north. Apparently most of his property remained in the hands of the Zhang family, since his son stayed in Nantong and began to work for the Dasheng No. 1 mill in the 1930s.

Next to the incorporation process itself, the relationship between control and ownership is one of the central issues for understanding business in China. Recent scholarship has shown that because of the strong family influence the control of equity was rarely separated from the control of management and that succession disputes were of great significance for the continuity of the company.[152] Historians generally agree that the influence of shareholders in China's first stockholding companies, such as the China Merchants' Steamship Navigation Company, was restricted and limited. The general scholarly evaluation of Dasheng is much more positive. Historians like Zhu Yingui have, however, praised Zhang Jian's role in introducing incorporation too uncritically by seeing this step as automatically empowering shareholders and restricting the power of Zhang Jian, who "himself set the boundaries of his influence."[153]

In contrast, I argue that another conclusion is plausible: although the Dasheng No. 1 Cotton Mill adopted the legal form of a limited liability company as early as 1907, it was not managed in such a way as to allow the shareholders to curtail the power of the founder-director. The mills and the Dasheng business group as a whole obviously continued traditional business practices and institutions characteristic of Chinese family enterprises. In addition, members of the Zhang family remained involved in the financial and managerial organization of the company, even as a hierarchy of salaried executives came into existence to manage the different parts of the business on a day-to-day basis. In fact, despite Dasheng's incorporation, the gap between ownership and control widened considerably until the early 1920s because of Zhang Jian's skillful institutional use of the Shanghai office.

Nevertheless, Dasheng was in many ways a new type of business in early twentieth-century China: it satisfied the new legal requirements by adopting limited liability, holding shareholder meetings, publishing annual company reports, and observing the existing regulations for accounting. These "modern" aspects of Dasheng's internal management, that is, modern by Western standards of business organization and legislation, complemented the "modern" aspects of its factory management and shop-floor discipline discussed above.

Despite the modern, rational, and efficient appearance of Dasheng's workshops and administrative offices, however, they ultimately were run under Zhang Jian's personal patronage. As a business group with cross-asset subsidization, Dasheng is an excellent example of management by paternalism, which was institutionalized through the Shanghai office.[154] If we consider paternalism in the contexts of individual control, freedom of choice, and accountability, then it is obvious why the Shanghai office never was subjected to the strict company regulations that directed every other aspect of the business. For Zhang Jian, direct control over information and channels of command and financial flexibility without strict accountability were this office's functions. It would have been awkward to acknowledge these aspects of the Shanghai office in Dasheng's official company regulations. Not surprisingly, the Shanghai office as an institution of control worked only as long as Zhang Jian dominated the business. Once third parties such as creditor-banks began to restructure management, the function of the Shanghai office as a traditional institution within a modern corporate enterprise came under attack (see Chapter 6).

Until recently, China business historians have tried to capture the essence of Chinese enterprises by focusing on personal relations, particularly in family businesses. Frequently, a business organization is more or less reduced to being a network, often in the context of a search for the "spirit of Chinese capitalism."[155] Scholars have argued that "kinship and collegiality in China play roles analogous to those played by law and individuality in the West," and the growth of the Chinese economy has been explained in terms of increased economic opportunities and the simultaneous expansion of networks.[156] Scholars who discuss Zhang Jian and his relationship with the Dasheng business complex always refer to his clout as a public figure and to his personal connections in the political and intellectual arena.[157] Of course, business always involves networks, and as I have shown, personal relationships played a significant role in the management of the enterprise's various parts. However, Dasheng's internal organization into departments and its overall structure, with the Shanghai office as the controlling unit, suggest that "networking" is an inadequate explanation. Essentially, in Dasheng, we find conflicts of interest between the founder-director and his shareholders and divided loyalties between people whose positions relied either on the authority of the founder or on the holding of shares.

Private influence was also a problem in Western firms in the late nineteenth and early twentieth centuries. For example, Leslie Hannah has demonstrated that in Britain in 1914 the majority of registered joint stock companies "were private rather than public companies."[158] Even now, the fact that networks play an important role in Western joint-stock companies influences the general debate over the future of corporations.[159] And most certainly, poor disclosure and weak regulations are well-known and persistent problems of companies and the stock market in contemporary China. Tumultuous shareholder meetings with angry minority shareholders are not unknown.[160] Even Japanese corporations have only recently started to respond to shareholder complaints and concerns through improved disclosure and regular meetings, especially since economic developments have forced them to rely more on investors than on banks as a source of funds.[161]

Dasheng's structure within the new institutional framework allowed Zhang Jian to dominate the enterprise without having to consider shareholders' interests. As the analysis of financial records in the next chapter shows, Zhang Jian was held answerable neither to the shareholders nor to the company's accountants. Thus, with Dasheng we witness the conflict between accountability and paternalism in the emergence of a new business institution in twentieth-century China.

CHAPTER 6

Business Performance and Crisis Management

As we saw in the preceding chapter, accountability and control practices defined and sustained the role of an authoritarian director in the Dasheng
business complex. In this chapter, we will investigate how these institutional
mechanisms created an environment for financial strategies that almost led
to the bankruptcy of one of China's most successful industrial enterprises in
the early Republican period. Dasheng's financial vulnerability became apparent during the crisis in the Chinese textile industry in 1923–24. In the words
of Marie-Claire Bergère, this crisis "brought into question not only the future of Chinese industry but also its recent past and the nature of the progress accomplished."[1] In contrast to many Chinese industrial enterprises,
Dasheng managed to survive this crisis and others that followed.

How profitable and financially sound was Dasheng in the 1910s and 1920s?
In retrospect and from the vantage point of the outsider, from 1900 on the
Dasheng No. 1 mill operated at a fairly stable profit, which improved dramatically during the postwar boom of 1919–20. The subsidiaries and affiliated companies were also profitable, and plans were made to found two new
branch mills, which materialized in the early 1920s. In 1921 profits dropped
sharply, and from 1922 on the company operated at a substantial loss. Borrowing from banks to cover the losses led in the end to a takeover of
Dasheng by a banking consortium in 1924. How did an enterprise that
seemed so profitable get into such a predicament?

This troubled period is often neglected in the literature or explained away
as the result of external economic factors such as fluctuations in raw cotton
and yarn prices and foreign competition.[2] In a recent article, Tang Keke and
Qian Jiang have argued indirectly along the same lines by linking Dasheng's

financial problems to increasing raw material costs.[3] In contrast to these traditional interpretations, this chapter uses a detailed analysis of account and
balance sheets to argue that internal financial practices led to Dasheng's crisis in 1922.

Of course, external economic factors did play a role. However, the events
leading up to the debacle did not happen randomly. Although it may seem
that the crisis caught the company—shareholders, management, and even
Zhang Jian himself—by surprise, many financial problems and inappropriate decisions developed out of Dasheng's established business practices and
were already visible in the 1910s. I begin by explaining how and why things
went wrong in the Dasheng cotton mills by exploring their profitability and
indebtedness and then present a structural analysis of expenditures and production costs. Although my analysis focuses on the No. 1 cotton mill because of its centrality in the business complex, we need to investigate the crisis in the context of the whole business group and not just the mill business.
Thus the third part of this chapter relates the crisis in the land-reclamation
companies to the cotton mills' development. After exploring the financial
crisis and the flow of funds from Dasheng's books, I conclude by discussing
the input of the banks and their loan strategies during the 1920s.

Profitability and Indebtedness

Profitability and indebtedness are the two most obvious indices of business
performance. For contemporary observers, the profit-and-loss accounts in
the annual business reports of the Dasheng No. 1 mill provided information
on the company's surpluses or losses in a particular fiscal year.[4] These statements recorded the annual net profit. In contrast to present-day accounting
practices, items such as depreciation of assets were deducted only after 1907,
and taxation figured only in the form of the so-called transit tax (*lijuan*) paid
for raw cotton and yarn.[5] The annual net profit should not be confused with
the retained profit (net profit minus bonuses, reserves, and donations),
which was carried forward to the next year and appeared as an accumulated
sum under the company's liabilities on the balance sheet.

As Fig. 6.1 shows, from 1900 on the No. 1 mill made an annual profit,
which rose steadily to its first peak of 483,070 taels in 1905.[6] Profits decreased sharply to only 55,904 taels in 1907 because of machinery purchases
and repairs and the establishment of the No. 2 branch mill. From then until

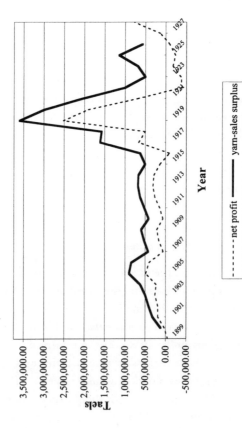

Fig. 6.1 Net profit and yarn-sales surplus of the Dasheng No. 1 Cotton Mill, 1899–1928 (based on the mill's annual company reports in *DSQXDX*). See Table A1, p. 295.

the mid-1910s, the No. 1 mill made moderate profits before plunging into debt in 1916 with a loss of 97,080 taels. This loss is linked to an expansion in the No. 1 mill as the numbers of spindles was increased, 400 looms for weaving were purchased, and new factory workshops for the new spinning and weaving machinery were built.[7] According to a supplementary report on the mill's financial situation, the loss was accompanied by an increase in assets of 850,000 taels in machinery and buildings in 1916.[8] In 1917, profits rose dramatically to 661,769 taels and reached a record high of 2.5 million taels in 1919. In 1920 a profit of 1.9 million taels was recorded, but 1921 brought a 64 percent decline in profits to 691,092 taels. The negative trend continued from 1922 until 1926; only in 1927 did the mill move into the black again.

How does Dasheng's profit history compare with that of commercial cotton production as a whole? One would expect the overall profitability of the company to follow the general market conditions closely. In the case of the Dasheng No. 1 mill, however, the returns in the form of revenues from yarn sales were only partly responsible for the company's overall profitability.

The figure for Dasheng's income from yarn sales was based on a peculiar bookkeeping principle.[9] Throughout the company's history, purchases of raw cotton were not listed under expenditures in the annual profit-and-loss accounts presented to the shareholders. Instead, these expenses were subtracted from the income for yarn sales, and the surplus was then entered as a lump sum.[10] This surplus (*jinhua chusha heyu*) was recorded under income as a net figure in the profit-and-loss accounts.

Figure 6.1 shows the No. 1 mill's income from yarn sales less the payments for raw cotton, which I shall refer to as the "yarn-sales surplus." Between 1900 and 1921, the yarn-sales surplus closely parallels the changes in the annual profit. After a steady increase, the yarn-sales surplus peaked at 894,202 taels in 1905, then dropped to slightly more than half this level to 425,759 taels in 1907. During the following years, the yarn-sales surplus generated a steady but moderate income. The year 1916 is an exception: despite a yarn-sales surplus of 623,849 taels, the company recorded a loss because of its substantial expansion. In 1917 the yarn-sales surplus rose dramatically and reached a peak of 3.6 million taels in 1919.

The gradually widening gap between the two lines in Fig. 6.1 beginning in 1916 illustrates a significant change in the relationship between the two factors. During the mill's early history, the gap between net profits and the yarn-sales surplus was fairly small, an indication that the yarn-sales surplus

counted for a substantial percentage of the mill's annual net profit. For example, in 1905 annual profits were 54 percent of the yarn-sales surplus, and
in 1912, 42 percent. However, from 1916 on, this percentage decreased significantly, for example, to 32 percent in 1918 and 1919. The widening gap between the two figures reveals that factors other than market conditions for
yarn sales were curtailing the mill's net profits. A case in point is 1922, when
the No. 1 mill had severe net losses despite a substantial yarn-sales surplus of
996,813 taels. And in 1925, even a yarn-sales surplus of 1.1 million taels could
not prevent an overall net loss of 241,454 taels for Dasheng No. 1.[11] If significant income from product sales could not prevent the company from sliding
into the red, then we have to ask why.

Between 1917 and 1921, the excellent yarn-sales surpluses mitigated the extent to which the Dasheng No. 1 mill was suffering from indebtedness. Figure 6.2 shows the aggregate amount of loans and the annual interest the
company owed on these loans.[12] After 1900 debts rose slowly to 1.5 million
taels in 1909, then decreased again and averaged roughly 1 million taels per
year until the mid-1910s. In 1915 the company's indebtedness amounted to
1.83 million taels per year and rose steadily to 2.9 million taels in 1920. After
that date the No. 1 mill's indebtedness skyrocketed to 9.15 million taels in
1925 and decreased only slightly to 8.1 million taels in the following year.

As Fig. 6.2 shows, interest payments rose with the increasing indebtedness. Between 1900 and 1905, the annual interest amounted to less than
100,000 taels per year. Following a rise to 152,489 taels in 1906, interest payments remained fairly stable at an annual average of roughly 100,000 taels.
After 1915 interest payments grew sharply to the maximum of 1 million taels
in 1922. The dramatic increase in bank loans after 1922 did not, however, lead
to commensurate growth in interest payments. With Dasheng's insolvency
and the takeover by the banks, the amount and scheduling of the No. 1 mill's
interest payments were repeatedly renegotiated and extended, as the company encountered difficulties in meeting the annual interest payments.

It is difficult to comment on the interest rates charged by Dasheng's
creditors, since until 1921 loans were recorded only as one lump sum on the
balance sheet, whether they were short- or long-term loans. Presumably, different creditors charged different interest rates.[13] It is, however, obvious that
from 1919 to 1922 interest rates rose significantly. On average, during the first
years of its operation the No. 1 mill had to pay interest rates of more than 10

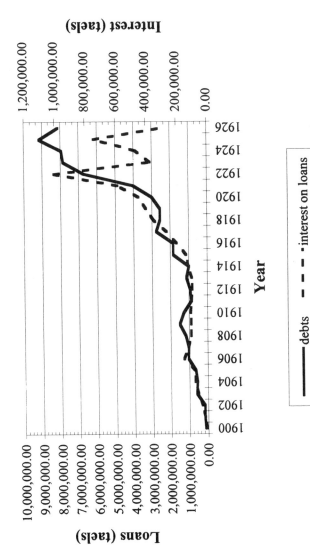

Fig. 6.2 Debts and interest payments of the Dasheng No. 1 Cotton Mill, 1900–1926 (based on the mill's annual company reports in DSQXDX). See Table A2, p. 296.

percent per year. In the textile industry rates of up to 12 percent were considered normal.[14] Between 1908 and 1913, the average interest rate for the No. 1 mill remained at a stable 9 percent. After 1919 the average interest rate went well over 10 percent per year and culminated in 14.9 percent on loans from modern Chinese banks in 1922.

If we compare the figures for the yarn-sales surplus in Fig. 6.1 and the interest due on loans in Fig. 6.2, it is obvious that the interest payments reduced the No. 1 mill's overall net profits substantially. For example, in 1906, 18 percent of the yarn-sales surplus went to cover the interest payments, and even in 1919, 11 percent of the record income from the yarn-sales surplus had to be used to service interest payments. This ratio increased to 15 percent in 1920 and 28 percent in 1921. In 1922, 106 percent of the yarn-sales surplus of 996,813 taels would have been necessary to cover the annual interest payments of 1.002 million taels.[15] The unbalanced ratio between income from yarn-sales surplus and expenditures on interest payments explains the phenomenon of decreasing net profits despite sound income figures for the No. 1 mill.

The two branch mills, the No. 2 mill in Chongming opened in 1907 and the No. 3 mill operating in Haimen after 1921, faced a similar situation (see Fig. 6.3). In fact, since the two branch mills were financially not independently managed business units but closely linked to the No. 1 mill, their financial history up to the 1922 crisis reflected that of the No. 1 mill. Although the No. 2 and No. 3 branch mills were not subsidiaries through majority shareholdings, the Dasheng No. 1 mill had deposits in both companies, for example, 302,000 taels in the No. 2 mill in 1909 and 155,000 taels in the No. 3 mill in 1918.[16] In addition, Zhang Jian was managing director of all three mills. Like the No. 1 mill, the No. 2 mill achieved a record net profit in 1919, operated at a loss in 1922 and managed to achieve a meager profit only after 1926. The No. 3 mill started in 1921 with an annual loss of 90,324 taels. The mill's profit performance remained unstable until 1925, when it finally began to operate at a modest profit.[17]

As Fig. 6.4 indicates, the branch mills mirrored the No. 1 mill's financial performance fairly closely in terms of indebtedness. The debts of the No. 2 mill fluctuated over the years, before they reached a maximum of 1.2 million taels in the crisis year of 1922. The debts of the No. 3 mill increased substantially after 1921, the year of its official opening. The No. 2 mill had debts of

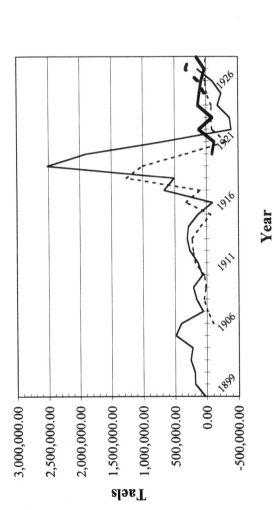

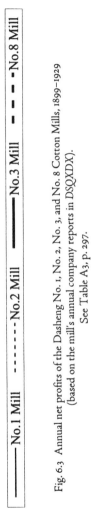

Fig. 6.3 Annual net profits of the Dasheng No. 1, No. 2, No. 3, and No. 8 Cotton Mills, 1899–1929 (based on the mill's annual company reports in DSQXDX).

See Table A3, p. 297.

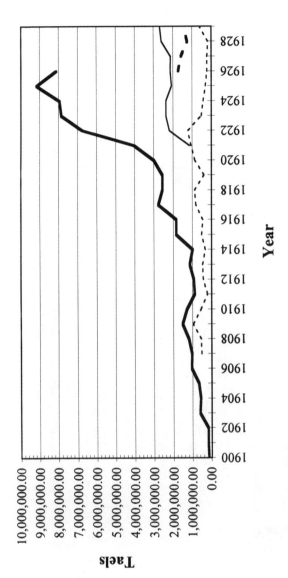

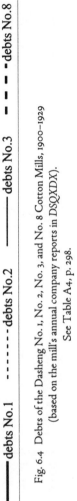

Fig. 6.4 Debts of the Dasheng No. 1, No. 2, No. 3, and No. 8 Cotton Mills, 1900–1929 (based on the mill's annual company reports in DSQXDX).
See Table A4, p. 298.

less than 600,000 taels after 1923; the indebtedness of the No. 3 mill remained at over 2 million taels from 1922 until 1929. As I shall explain in more detail below, both branch mills eventually became part of the loan arrangements of the bank consortium that controlled the Dasheng No. 1 mill after 1924. Not surprisingly, as a brand-new operation with up-to-date machinery and buildings, the No. 3 mill presented collateral of much higher value for the mortgage than did the older and much less well equipped No. 2 mill.[18]

The preceding descriptions give a rough idea of the basic financial development of the Dasheng cotton mills between 1900 and the late 1920s. However, the mills operated under the umbrella of the Dasheng business complex and were linked financially and managerially to the subsidiary and affiliated companies. Did these arrangements have an impact on the financial performance of the subsidiaries?

Information on the various non-textile subsidiaries is not available in a complete series of company reports and must be extracted from single reports and internal account books. I draw here on the examples of the Fuxin Flour Mill, the Guangsheng Oil Mill, and the Zisheng Iron Workshop in order to show that their performance displays a pattern similar to that of the cotton mills. For example, according to the annual report of the Fuxin company for 1918, the flour mill made a net profit of 20,225 yuan, which is not surprising since 1918 was the beginning of the postwar boom. More important is the fact that the Fuxin company suffered from an imbalance in the ratio between expenses for interest payments and the surplus income from flour sales. Fuxin had accumulated a debt of 312,380 taels in 1918, and the interest payments of 38,670 taels were equivalent to 21 percent of the flour-sales surplus of 188,864 taels in this particular year.[19]

The situation in the Guangsheng Oil Mill was similar. In 1919 the company achieved an oil-sales surplus of 273,432 taels, but the interest to be paid on loans amounted to 30,640 taels, or 11 percent.[20] This ratio deteriorated significantly. The company's business is documented for the years 1924 to 1926, and we have data on the oil mill's performance after the crisis at the Dasheng No. 1 mill. The Guangsheng company had a loss of 48,071 taels in 1924; interest payments amounted to 40,971 taels or 47 percent of the oil-sales surplus of 87,058 taels. Although Guangsheng relied on the by-products of the cotton mills and was thus affected by price changes on the raw cotton market, the 1924 report shows clearly that the total amount of debt was considered the biggest financial burden for the company. Like the

Dasheng No. 1 mill, Guangsheng had received loans that it was unable to repay, and creditors had to provide another loan of 100,000 taels as working capital. Guangsheng was able to achieve a small profit in 1925 but was again in the red in 1926. By then interest payments amounted to 49 percent of the annual oil-sales surplus. In short, Guangsheng's situation remained precarious throughout the 1920s.[21]

The Zisheng Iron Workshop did not suffer from indebtedness to the extent the other subsidiaries did. Although only reports for the period between 1911 and 1915 and one report for 1934 are available, the sound financial structure of the company is obvious.[22] In 1911 only 4 percent of Zisheng's iron-sales surplus went to cover interest payments; the equivalent figure for 1913 is 0.5 percent and for 1914, 1.4 percent. Even in 1934 Zisheng's interest payments on loans still accounted for only 1.3 percent of its annual iron-sales surplus.[23]

This healthy financial structure reflects the nature of the Zisheng Iron Workshop as a business. Zisheng was a very small operation—it was a workshop rather than a factory—with total assets of less than 100,000 taels in the 1910s.[24] Although Zhang Jian described the company to the shareholders as a supplier of tools and provider of repair services for the No. 1 mill, Zisheng produced mainly cooking utensils. It was not a capital-intensive operation, and it generated only moderate profits. Moreover, the majority of the loans extended to Zisheng came from within the Dasheng business complex. For example, in 1914 and 1915 the Shanghai office and the Industrial Company contributed more than half of the total loans of 16,700 taels.[25] Although from a profit-generating point of view, small industrial companies like Zisheng played only a minor part within the Dasheng business group, as we shall see below, they played an important role in its overall financial structure and flow of funds.

In summary, the mills and the other industrial enterprises achieved sound net profits from 1900 to 1920. The losses of 1916 resulted from the purchases of new machinery; the yarn-sales surplus actually increased by 24 percent over the previous year. At the same time, all the enterprises were plagued by an increasingly high ratio of indebtedness and consequently high interest payments, which cut deeply into the companies' net profits. Obviously, the yarn-sales surplus dropped sharply in 1922, and the mills immediately started to operate in the red. This analysis has shown how it was possible for an enterprise with healthy profits to be on the verge of bankruptcy in 1922. Why did management pay no attention to these financial developments and not take preventive measures?

Expenditures and the Problem of Production Costs

Aside from interest payments, Dasheng's major expenditures were payments for labor, fuel, and raw materials. Operational costs did have an impact, but in comparison to interest payments on debts, they were less decisive factors in the No. 1 mill's business performance, especially in the early 1920s. Besides dividend payments, in this section I discuss depreciation, reserves, and bonuses, which were recorded as part of the appropriation account in Dasheng's annual profit-and-loss account.

The available data on each of these categories vary. Information about labor and production costs is vital for a labor-intensive operation like a cotton mill, but it is difficult to evaluate workers' wages from the information provided in Dasheng's annual reports, since the profit-and-loss accounts recorded only the total wage bill as a lump sum. Nor do we have exact figures on the numbers of workers and their working hours. At best, only a rough estimate of labor costs in relation to the output is possible. The salaries of the managing director and senior managers, foreign engineers, and the patrol force were listed separately in the accounts. Fuel costs were subsumed under an entry for coal each year. Expenditures in the profit-and-loss account also included several smaller entries such as expenses for meals, apparently for the senior management, small welfare and charity donations, machinery repairs, insurance fees, and the commodity tax; these are not examined separately in this section. Dividends were listed under annual expenditures as a cost, as were reserves, depreciation, and bonuses. These expenditures were set aside from the annual overall net profit.

As noted above, raw material costs were not listed separately but were subtracted from the sales income and then included in the annual accounts as the sales surplus. For this reason, we have so far compared major items of expenditure to the "cotton-purchase yarn-sales surplus" and not with cotton purchases or yarn sales per se. In the following discussion on expenditures for wages, salaries, fuel, and dividends, I make comparisons with the No. 1 mill's overall expenditures excluding raw material costs. Nevertheless, the price of cotton in relation to the price of yarn must be considered a major factor in the profitability of the mill. Since there is no information on expenditures for raw cotton in the annual reports, I shall extrapolate these data from other sources.

If we relate wage costs to yarn sales, 1917 stands out as the year with the highest increase in the wage bill (see Fig. 6.5). The steep increase of 37 percent over the previous year can be attributed to the expansion of the No. 1 mill in 1916 which, as mentioned above, resulted in a net loss for the mill that year. The new power looms not only added cloth production to the mill's repertoire but also required the hiring of more skilled workers. The wage bill thus reflects an increase in the number of more highly skilled workers rather than an increase in the number of hours worked or the wages of an existing workforce. Wages increased steadily almost year by year until 1921, when they amounted to 20 percent of the No. 1 mill's total expenses.[26] Since in the same year interest payments amounted to 29 percent of the total expenses, these two cost factors together accounted for about 50 percent of Dasheng's overall expenditures, excluding raw material.

Salaries for Zhang Jian and the management followed the remuneration scales laid down in the factory regulations. The bill rose fairly steadily between 1900 and 1926,[27] and salaries increased faster than wages (see Fig. 6.5). For example, even in a financially tight year such as 1916 salaries rose by 11.5 percent. As I will demonstrate below, the managerial structure of the No. 1 mill did not change until 1924, and we can assume a more or less constant number of managers until then. Thus the increase in the salary bill directly reflected increasing compensation for management. For example, despite the No. 1 mill's losses in 1922, the salary bill increased by 10 percent over the previous year, whereas the wage bill decreased by 11 percent. Obviously, in contrast to the wages, salaries were not tied to the overall performance of the company. However, as a percentage of the annual total costs, salaries became less and less significant over the years. For example, in 1922 the salary bill accounted for only 3 percent of Dasheng's overall expenditures, excluding raw material.

A similar tendency is visible in regard to the fuel costs (see Fig. 6.5). Expenditures on coal were recorded as an annual lump sum; no records of the quantities purchased for the mill were kept. Coal was frequently shipped in bulk loads from Shanghai to the factory site at Tangjiazha; Dasheng used Chinese as well as imported coal purchased through Shanghai brokerages.[28]

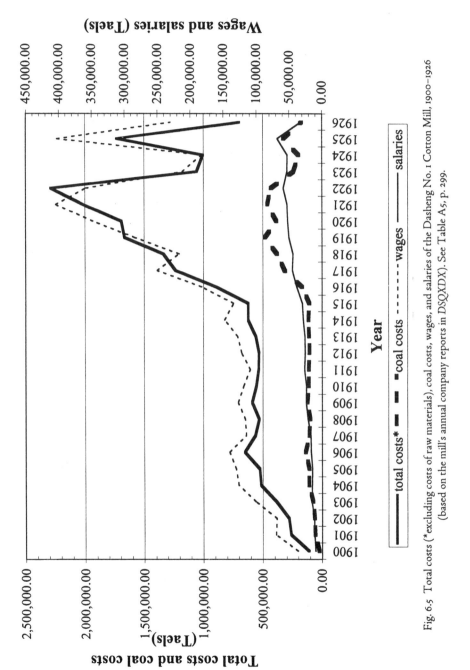

Fig. 6.5 Total costs (*excluding costs of raw materials), coal costs, wages, and salaries of the Dasheng No. 1 Cotton Mill, 1900–1926 (based on the mill's annual company reports in DSQXDX). See Table A5, p. 299.

Between 1904 and 1915, the No. 1 mill's annual expenses on coal fluctuated only slightly; they reached their first peak in 1917, with an increase of 89 percent over the previous year. This sharp increase makes sense in the context of the newly purchased equipment and additional boilers, which required additional fuel. Annual expenses for coal increased until 1919, then fell slightly in the early 1920s, and dropped dramatically after the 1922 crisis. Coal accounted for 20 percent of Dasheng's total annual costs in 1910, 19 percent in 1916, 29 percent in 1919, and 19 percent in 1922, excluding raw material. These figures, of course, ignore fluctuations in fuel prices.

The peak in coal costs in 1919 reflects the price trend for Chinese and imported coal. In that year, the average price of imported coal rose by roughly 10 percent and for Chinese coal by almost 6 percent.[29] The postwar boom created strong local and overseas demand for coal. Using the average price data for Chinese and imported coal per ton, we can compile a rough quantitative estimate of Dasheng's coal purchases. At first it appears that the growth in the No. 1 mill's expenditures on coal from the mid-1910s to 1919 and later was due to an increase in the price of coal. However, whereas expenditures on coal decreased by 20 percent in 1920 over the previous year, the quantity of coal purchased dropped by 32 percent.[30] This means that the No. 1 mill actually bought much less coal than the decrease of the lump sum in the account suggests. The amount of coal purchased increased again in 1921 but then decreased significantly for several years. In 1919 Dasheng's fuel costs accounted for 29 percent of its total expenditures, almost twice as much as the wage costs for that year.[31] In 1921 expenditures on coal amounted to 23 percent and in 1922 to 20 percent of the No. 1 mill's total costs, excluding raw material.

As an incorporated enterprise, the Dasheng No. 1 mill had to pay annual dividends, which represent another form of expenses in the company's profit-and-loss accounts. For the twelve years between 1904 and 1916, the annual amount paid to shareholders as "fixed dividends" (*guanli*) remained a constant 90,400 taels (see Fig. 6.6). This pattern should not surprise us when we take into consideration the peculiar way Chinese business attracted shareholders: "fixed dividends" were paid according to a rate of interest determined when the shares were sold; dividends did not reflect variations in the company's performance.[32] The sum of 90,400 taels amounted exactly to the 8 percent that was the standard interest rate on guaranteed shares in

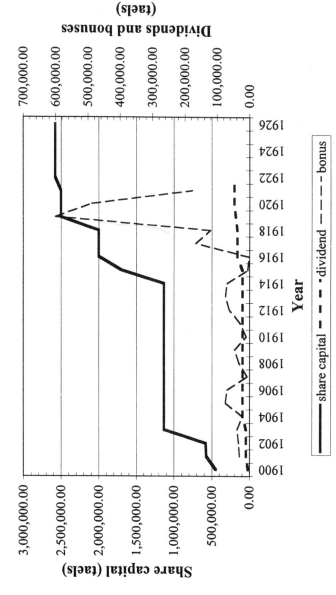

Fig. 6.6 Total share capital, annual dividends, and annual bonuses of the Dasheng No. 1 Cotton Mill, 1900–1926 (based on the mill's annual company reports in *DSQXDX*).

See Table A6, p. 300.

industrial enterprises. In 1918, dividends increased to a regular 160,000 taels at 8 percent per annum and stayed at 200,000 taels per year between 1920 and 1922.[33]

As Fig. 6.6 makes clear, these increases in dividend payments mirrored more or less exactly the increases in the company's equity in the years 1904, 1916, and 1920. Dividend payments amounted to 18 percent of Dasheng's overall expenditures in 1916, but for only 9 percent in 1922. Because of the negative business performance, dividend payments were suspended after 1922. The reaction of the shareholders of the No. 1 mill to this drastic step was not recorded. According to the 1924 auditors' report, the shareholders were to be compensated with new shares of the No. 1 mill.[34] However, it is not clear from the report whether these new shares also paid a fixed dividend; since no *guanli* payments are recorded after 1922, we may assume that the shareholders had to accept regular shares, which were subject to price fluctuations on the Shanghai stock exchange.

Figure 6.7 summarizes the general development of Dasheng's total expenditures in comparison with the expenditures other than interest (both excluding raw material costs). Between 1900 and 1918, the two follow each other fairly closely, an indication that the interest payments did not account for a large portion of the No. 1 mill's total expenditures. However, after 1918 the gap between the two graphs widens increasingly, a reflection of the increasing share of interest payments. After 1921, it becomes obvious that interest payments accounted for almost half of the mill's total costs. For example, by 1922 costs other than interest amounted to 56 percent and interest payments to 44 percent of the mill's total expenditures, excluding raw material costs.

Funds were set aside from the net profits for specific purposes in the so-called appropriation section of the profit-and-loss account. This section of the Dasheng No. 1 mill's annual business report consisted of four items: retained profits, reserves, depreciation funds, and bonuses. The expenses for these items should not be considered direct costs as such, but they were deducted from the annual net profit or loss. An analysis of the appropriation fund can show us how the No. 1 mill's net profits were distributed, for what purposes, to whom, and in what amounts.

The category of bonuses (*huahong*) in the Dasheng No. 1 mill's annual report referred to payments to shareholders as well as to awards for the

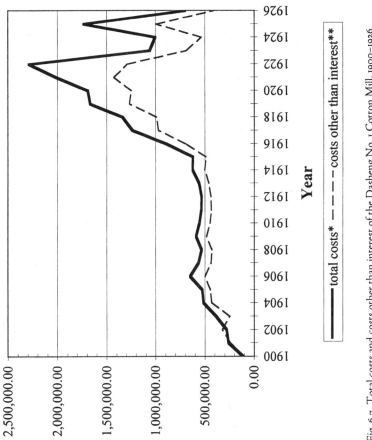

Fig. 6.7 Total costs and costs other than interest of the Dasheng No. 1 Cotton Mill, 1900–1926 (based on the mill's annual company reports in *DSQXDX*). See Table A7, p. 301.

managers and managing director of the company. The factory regulations stipulated that after the deduction of reserves and insurance, 77 percent of the net profits should be returned to the shareholders as bonuses, 15 percent to senior management, and 8 percent to middle management.[35] However, as Fig. 6.6 shows, from 1900 to 1917 bonuses varied greatly from year to year, although, according to the regulations, their distribution should have been pegged to a fixed percentage of the net profits. For example, 15 percent of the net profits were distributed as bonuses in 1905 and 1910. However, in 1915 only 4 percent of the net profits were paid out, and, not surprisingly, in 1916 no bonuses at all were distributed because of the company's losses. Between 1917 and 1921 bonus payments resumed, but at a much higher percentage of the net profit. The bonuses amounted to 24 percent of the net profits in 1919 and 26 percent in 1920 and 1921. In 1922, the generous bonus distributions halted.

Depreciation (*zhejiu*) is significant as a general indicator of a firm's long-term business strategies. The funds set aside annually by the Dasheng No. 1 mill for recapturing the loss in the value of its productive assets are noted in Fig. 6.8. This practice began only in 1907, the year of Dasheng's incorporation. Clearly, the annual amounts budgeted for this purpose were stable; they were also insufficient, to judge from the rough baseline of 5 percent depreciation used in contemporary Western corporations. Apart from the year 1919, the No. 1 mill set aside 25,000 taels annually. This would have covered only a minimal percentage of the company's productive assets. For example, in 1910 the No. 1 mill's total depreciation fund was equivalent to 4.4 percent of the total value of its machinery value; this dropped to 2.1 percent in 1917 and a mere 1.5 percent in 1921.[36] Although the concept of depreciation was unknown in traditional Chinese business accounting and emerged only slowly in the 1900s, even in the late 1910s and early 1920s Dasheng's depreciation measures were negligible, especially if we consider the substantial overall growth in the No. 1 mill's productive assets, which included real estate.

Unspecified reserves (*gongji*) set aside under appropriations experienced a somewhat similar fate. The amount set aside as reserves each year mirrored increases and decreases in net profits, with the highest rate of reserves retained in the record years of 1919 and 1920. For example, 7.3 percent of net profits was set aside in 1911; the ratio rose to 10 percent in 1919 and then dropped to 5.7 percent in 1921, before set-asides for this purpose were suspended from 1922 on.

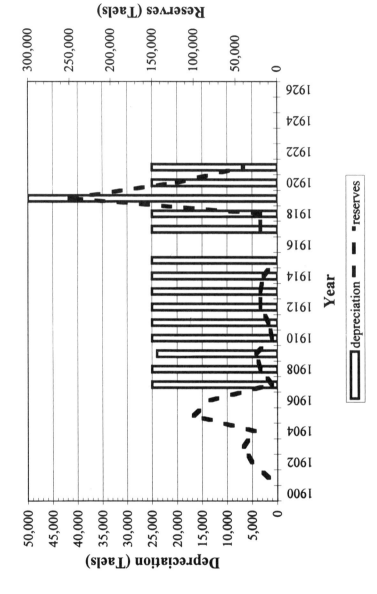

Fig. 6.8 Depreciation and reserves of the Dasheng No. 1 Cotton Mill, 1900–1926 (based on the mill's annual company reports in DSQXDX). See Table A8, p. 302.

In general, the funds set aside for depreciation and reserves were, particularly by today's accounting standards, far too low to have had a substantial impact on Dasheng's performance. Confronting a similar situation today, a stockholder would worry that the lack of sufficient risk hedging through solid depreciation funds and accumulated reserves boded ill for the company. The minutes of Dasheng's annual meeting in 1920 reveal that the shareholders were concerned not about the low depreciation rate but about the increase in reserves because it reduced the profits to be distributed to them.[37]

Finally, what impact did raw material and yarn prices have on the No. 1 mill's performance? This issue is particularly significant for existing interpretations of the crisis that affected the Chinese cotton industry nationwide in 1922–23. Marie-Claire Bergère, for example, in her study on China's economic and social transformation between 1911 and 1937, sees the rising price of raw cotton in 1922 as the "determining factor in the cotton mills' crisis" and cites difficulties in the supplies of raw material and insufficient financial support from traditional banks as major problems.[38] Mori Tokihiko's complex analysis of national trends in prices and costs in China's textile sector also focuses on external economic factors and their negative role in what he calls the "1923 crisis."[39] Although these studies present valid arguments for the plight of many urban Chinese textile mills in 1923, I shall contend in the following paragraphs that rising raw material prices were not the major factor in Dasheng's problematic financial development, which began well before the industry-wide predicament.

One probable reason for Dasheng's failure to track the cost of cotton and the income from yarn sales separately was that Dasheng received a considerable amount of raw cotton directly from affiliated land-reclamation companies. In addition, the Dasheng No. 1 mill had established four wholesale cotton-purchasing stations in the Nantong area to supplement supplies from the land-reclamation companies.[40] The local supply seems rarely to have been sufficient, however, and raw cotton had to be purchased from Hubei and Shandong and even from overseas. In one case among many, invoices show that the No. 1 mill ordered and received 100 bales of American cotton worth US$19,750, shipped from New Orleans to Shanghai, through the agent Joring & Bekker in November 1919.[41] The payment was handled by the Shanghai Commercial and Savings Bank (hereafter, the Shanghai Bank) under the personal supervision of its managing director, Chen Guangfu.[42] One would expect that expenditures on raw materials, in particular if ordered in bulk from abroad, would appear in the annual report, but this was not the case.

Two items in the annual report are helpful for the purpose of determining how much raw cotton Dasheng purchased and at what prices: the values of raw cotton and yarn inventories were listed among the company's assets on the balance sheet. Figure 6.9 showing various inventories between 1900 and 1926 gives an idea about how much of Dasheng's funds were tied up in stock. Stocks of ginned cotton and yarn were recorded throughout the No. 1 mill's history; stocks of finished goods, that is, yarn and cloth, were listed in the annual reports only between 1911 and 1922. We have to be careful with all these figures since they are expressed as monetary values rather than as quantities. In the absence of explanatory documentation, we can only assume that current prices were used for the annual evaluation of stocks rather than a more precise and complicated evaluation based on historical costs.

Stocks of ginned cotton and yarn fluctuated widely between 1900 and 1916. After 1917, the inventories, at least in terms of value, at the No. 1 mill were kept at a high level, reaching 2.3 million taels in 1919; the lowest value was the 1.25 million taels recorded for 1921. In 1925 the value of stocks reached an all-time high of 2.8 million taels. The increase in the values of stocks during the years after 1917 should be interpreted as an increase in funds tied up in fixed assets. In other words, a significant part of the No. 1 mill's assets was unproductively piling up in the form of ginned cotton and yarn in the storage rooms. In 1925, the value of ginned cotton and yarn stock exceeded Dasheng's share capital. This unhealthy development is visible as early as the mid-1910s and not just in the crisis years of the early 1920s, when an unfavorable market situation might have led to reduced production and sales. The figure of 1.15 million taels for the yarn and cloth inventory in 1920 is particularly telling: obviously, overproduction triggered by the postwar boom and a saturated market were keeping finished goods in Dasheng's warehouses.

However, the value of these inventories was set by company accountants, who could have easily manipulated the numbers through over- or underestimation in order to balance the mill's books. In addition, we still know nothing about the amounts and prices of raw cotton used at the Dasheng No. 1 mill. Needless to say, the cost of raw cotton must have accounted for a substantial portion of the total cost of yarn production. Although data are

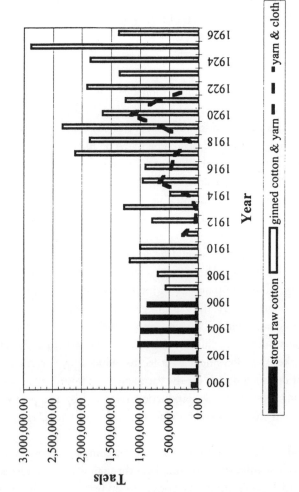

Fig. 6.9 Cash values of inventories of yarn and raw cotton at the Dasheng No. 1 Cotton Mill, 1900–1926 (based on the mill's annual company reports in *DSQXDX*). See Table A9, p. 303.

Table 6.1

Costs at Dasheng in 1899

(per one bale of 12-count yarn in taels)

Category	Cost (taels)	Percentage of total costs (%)
Fixed costs		
Raw material	45.9	68.0
Work materials	1.8	2.6
Fuel (coal)	1.38	2.0
Variable costs		
Wages	4.4	6.6
Salaries	0.76	1.1
Overhead expenses	0.20	0.3
Surplus value		
Dividend (*guanli*)	1.1	1.6
Dividend	2.5	3.7
Levies (*juanshui*)	1.0	1.5
Net balance	8.46	12.6
Net sales value	67.5	100.0

SOURCE: Dasheng company records for 1899 from *Dasheng xitong qiyeshi*, pp. 152–53.

too scanty for a detailed analysis, we can compare figures extracted from Dasheng's company archives for the year 1899 (Table 6.1) with Arno Pearse's estimates for the Chinese cotton industry in 1928 (Table 6.2). In both cases, raw cotton costs amount to 68 percent of the total yarn costs per unit. These two estimates contradict a more recent estimate of 85 percent given by Tang Keke and Qian Jiang.[43] Before we continue our analysis of inventory values at Dasheng, this difference requires an explanation.

Pearse, in his study on the Chinese cotton industry, provided data for Shanghai on the seasonal prices of cotton and yarn from 1921 to 1929. He assumed 350 catties of cotton were needed to make one bale of yarn, and thus he estimated the percentage cost of raw cotton per bale of yarn at various prices. To judge from the data in Table 6.3, cotton prices in those years were more elastic and fluctuated more vigorously than yarn prices. For example, when the price of cotton rose 91 percent from 24.50 taels per picul in January 1921 to 46.75 taels per picul in January 1924, the price of yarn went up only 36 percent, from 133 taels to 180.2 taels per bale.

Table 6.2
Cotton Costs per Bale, 1928
(per picul in taels)

Category	Cost (taels)	Percentage of total costs (%)
Raw materials		
Cotton	131.25	68.4
Spinning and other costs		
Labor	9.00	4.7
Tax	3.80	2.0
Interest	8.00	4.2
Overhead	5.00	2.6
Electricity	3.20	1.7
Materials	3.50	1.8
Net balance	28.25	14.7
Total value	192.00	100.0

SOURCE: Pearse, *The Cotton Industry of Japan and China*, p. 191.

Table 6.3
Cost of Cotton as Portion of Cost of One Bale of Yarn, 1921–29

Date	(a) Unit cost of cotton (taels/picul)	(b) Unit cost of yarn (taels/bale)	(c) Cost of cotton per unit of yarn (taels)	(d) Percentage [(c)/(d)] (%)
1921				
Jan. 15	24.50	133.00	85.75	64.47
April	23.50	133.20	82.25	61.75
July	28.00	153.70	98.00	63.76
Oct.	37.50	162.20	131.25	80.92
1922				
Jan. 15	34.00	144.40	119.00	82.41
April	36.00	145.80	126.00	86.42
July	35.50	141.60	124.25	87.75
Oct.	29.00	127.20	101.50	79.80
1923				
Jan. 15	39.00	148.00	136.50	92.23
April	38.00	145.90	133.00	91.16
July	39.50	148.70	138.25	92.97
Oct.	40.50	158.00	141.75	89.72

Table 6.3, *cont.*

Date	(a) Unit cost of cotton (taels/picul)	(b) Unit cost of yarn (taels/bale)	(c) Cost of cotton per unit of yarn (taels)	(d) Percentage [(c)/(d)] (%)
1924				
Jan. 15	46.75	180.20	163.63	90.80
April	45.70	174.30	159.95	91.77
July	38.55	159.80	134.92	84.43
Oct.	35.70	151.90	124.95	82.26
1925				
Jan. 15	40.30	164.60	141.05	85.69
April	43.00	169.20	150.50	88.95
July	38.60	167.00	135.10	80.90
Oct.	36.70	159.50	128.45	80.53
1926				
Jan. 15	33.15	149.60	116.03	77.56
April	31.65	143.50	110.78	77.20
July	31.75	144.00	111.13	77.17
Oct.	30.55	137.90	106.93	77.54
1927				
Jan. 15	28.75	129.20	100.63	77.88
April	31.30	136.70	109.55	80.14
July	36.05	143.00	126.17	88.23
Oct.	37.70	151.80	131.95	86.92
1928				
Jan. 15	35.40	151.50	123.90	81.78
April	38.75	158.00	135.63	85.84
July	39.00	161.80	136.50	84.36
Oct.	33.90	158.90	118.65	74.67
1929				
Jan. 15	33.85	161.40	118.48	73.40
April	33.95	162.80	118.83	72.99
July	35.15	164.70	123.03	74.70

SOURCE: Based on price figures for cotton and yarn in Pearse, *The Cotton Industry of Japan and China*, p. 157. According to Pearse, 3.5 piculs of cotton were needed to produce one bale of 16-count yarn weighing 400 pounds.

Therefore, when the price of cotton was at its lowest in April 1921, the cost of cotton amounted to roughly 62 percent of the cost of yarn. However, when the price of cotton was at its highest, in April 1924, the analogous

Table 6.4
Prices for Raw Cotton and Yarn (16-count) at Wujin, 1915–27
(*yuan*)

Year	Raw cotton (*yuan*/catty)	Index (1910–14 = 100)	Yarn (*yuan*/bale)	Index (1910–14 = 100)
1915	0.231	93.5	3.28	91.6
1916	0.230	93.1	3.39	94.7
1917	0.246	99.6	4.30	120.1
1918	0.264	106.8	5.44	151.9
1919	0.240	97.1	6.55	183.0
1920	0.234	94.7	5.83	162.8
1921	0.255	103.2	5.08	141.9
1922	0.260	105.2	4.81	134.4
1923	0.285	115.4	5.36	149.7
1924	0.340	137.7	5.91	165.1
1925	0.300	121.5	5.86	163.6
1926	0.340	137.7	5.00	139.6
1927	0.494	200.0	4.843	135.0

SOURCE: Raw cotton and yarn prices from Zhang Liluan, "Jiangsu Wujin wujia zhi yanjiu," appendix, p. 215.

figure was 92 percent. According to Pearse's table, in the years when the cost of cotton was high, no profit was to be made in yarn manufacturing. However, cotton costs were extremely high relative to yarn prices only between 1922 and 1925, Dasheng's years of red ink. For most of the No. 1 mill's production period, say, 1910 to 1920, the price of cotton would not have been nearly as high as in 1924. Again, without price statistics for Dasheng and the Nantong area itself, we have to resort to an extraneous source for comparison. The figures extrapolated from the price series of Wujin, a city on the southern bank of the Yangzi River in Jiangsu province, are shown in Table 6.4.

At a five-year average, the price index for raw cotton at Wujin dropped from 100 (1910–14) to 98 (1915–19) and then rose to 111 (1920–24) and 153 (1925–27). The comparison with the price of yarn is highly significant for our understanding of the profitability of yarn manufacturing. The index for Wujin yarn prices rose from 100 (1910–14) to 128 (1915–19) to 151 (1920–24) and then dropped slightly to 146 (1925–27). That is to say, for most of the period up to 1924, the price of cotton was relatively stable as the price of yarn rose by about 50 percent. In the years that followed, the price of yarn remained fairly constant while the price of cotton soared. Therefore, given the figures of Table 6.3, for most of the period we should not expect cotton costs to account for more than 68 percent of yarn costs on average as documented for Dasheng in 1899.

What do these figures mean in terms of Dasheng's business performance? As we have seen, none of the expenditures in Dasheng posed an immediate danger to the business performance of the company through runaway growth. The expansion of production in 1916 and the postwar boom in 1919 were certainly responsible for substantial increases in the mill's costs for coal, wages, and salaries. However, these costs have to be set against the growth in income. The most significant point here is that the cost of raw cotton did not hamper the mill's growth in the first two decades of the twentieth century. My estimates of raw cotton prices are based on data from a geographical area with a different agricultural structure: Wujin was not a cotton-producing area; rice in summer and wheat in winter were its major crops.[44] However, this means that Wujin prices for raw cotton must have been higher than those in the cotton-producing area around Nantong. In addition, we should bear in mind that a substantial percentage of Dasheng's raw cotton came directly from the affiliated land-reclamation companies at in-house prices (see Chapter 7). Thus my estimates for the percentage of yarn costs in Dasheng's production costs are on the high side.

Although Dasheng's depreciation, reserves, and inventory policies appear in hindsight to be signs of future problems, any manufacturer in the Chinese textile industry would have opted to expand based on the price trends up to the early 1920s. However, as the case of Dasheng will demonstrate, he would have been tied up by loan payments when rising prices of cotton and stable yarn prices shaved his profit margin. The mill's financial crisis in 1922, however, resulted in part from the activities of the land-reclamation companies, a vital part of the Dasheng business complex. As I shall demonstrate, much more than cotton linked these companies financially to the mills.

Prelude to the Crisis

Financial problems in 1921 and 1922 affected two different parts of the Dasheng business group, the cotton mills and the land-reclamation companies. The crises were closely related in terms of their internal and external causes and the way a solution was sought. It appears that the financial entanglement of the land-reclamation companies in the Dasheng mills but not the scarcity of cotton following the typhoon in 1921 was most detrimental to the mills' business.

Land reclamation was a major business concern of Zhang Jian. In 1901 he founded the first of his land-reclamation companies under the name Tonghai, which became a subsidiary of the Dasheng cotton mills. After Zhang Jian as minister of agriculture and commerce tried to stimulate land reclamation by improving legal conditions in 1914, new companies were founded in quick succession.[45] About forty new land-reclamation companies sprang up along the northern coast of Jiangsu province, where the land under tenant cultivation became an important source of raw cotton.[46] As the scant records of the reclamation companies show, the shareholders were also recruited from Zhang Jian's personal and business networks. For example, the 1918 shareholder report of the Tonghai Land Reclamation Company listed Zhang Jian and Zhang Cha as the biggest shareholders, with 618 shares, or 18 percent, of the share capital, followed by the Dasheng mill managers and local yarn traders with smaller stakes.[47]

The land-reclamation companies varied greatly in size and funding. Turning brackish coastal fields, previously used for salt production, into agricultural land for growing cotton was an expensive and laborious undertaking that left the land-reclamation companies in constant need of capital. Many did even not get off the ground because of insufficient funding.[48]

Among the companies founded after 1914, Dayoujin (founded 1914), Dayu (1916), Dalai (1917), Huacheng (1918), and Dafeng (1919) were the biggest enterprises, but none of them achieved long-term success.[49] Like most other land-reclamation companies in the area, they went seriously into debt in early 1921.[50] All five companies had been established by Zhang Jian and Zhang Cha and were under their directorship.[51] Compared to the other land-reclamation companies, these five companies appear at first sight to have started out promisingly with paid-up capital ranging from Dalai's 700,000 yuan to Dafeng's 1.94 million.[52] However, if we measure the capitalization against the size of each of the five companies, the situation looks much bleaker. Huacheng (600,000 mu), Dayu (480,000 mu), Dafeng (450,000 mu), and Dayoujin (269,000 mu) had the four biggest landholdings of all the land-reclamation companies along the Jiangsu coast and would thus have needed a much more solid capital base in order to be able to transform their land. According to figures from a 1935 survey, by that point

Huacheng had managed to reclaim and cultivate only 34 percent of its land, Dayu 27 percent, and Dafeng 46 percent.[53]

After a rocky start, the Dayoujin company, with 110,000 mu under cultivation in 1914, made a profit of only 18,540 yuan in 1918. Like the Dasheng No. 1 mill, Dayoujin suffered from an unfavorable balance between income and interest payments. For example, in 1918, with a debt of 566,914 yuan the company had to use almost 50 percent, or 57,977 yuan, of its net income of 117,727 yuan to cover the interest payments on the loans.[54] From the late 1920s on, the company was reported to be heavily in debt, with most of its property mortgaged and control over the land in the hands of creditors.[55] The Dalai company with 130,000 mu of land and 70,000 mu under cultivation shared the same fate. Founded in 1917 by Zhang Cha, the company had debts of 420,000 yuan by 1936 and was under the control of a banking consortium.[56] By 1931 the Dafeng company was also under the complete control of its creditors.[57]

Apart from the enormous costs connected with the cultivation and irrigation of wasteland on a very large scale, many companies were not able to bring land under cultivation as fast as they had planned and thus lost out on rental income. In addition, at the demand of the shareholders the company regulations stated that after reclamation the land had to be divided and returned to the shareholders in proportion to their original investment. The companies continued to manage the land on behalf of the shareholder-owners, but this practice diminished the company's ability to raise sufficient capital for the ongoing reclamation process and to obtain a steady income from rents.

When this detrimental arrangement was aggravated by severe external damage to the reclaimed land and the cotton crops by spring storms and floods, the first crisis began to unfold in 1921.[58] Not one of the annual reports of the Dayoujin, Dayu, Huacheng, Dalai, and Dafeng companies records the provision of reserves or special funds.[59] Obviously, no financial precautions were taken against the precarious nature of the land-reclamation business.

For all these reasons, the five companies were in severe danger of bankruptcy in 1921. In fact, the situation was so serious that the Dasheng No. 1 Cotton Mill officially invested in the land-reclamation companies for the first time and tried to save them with a substantial loan of 1.28 million taels.[60] The amount increased to 1.33 million taels the following year.[61] In fact, Dasheng's investment changed the five companies' status from affiliated to subsidiary companies. However, this loan was insufficient. Financial help from banking institutions became necessary.

In the process of dealing with the banks, Dasheng's accounts office in Shanghai became the linchpin of negotiations and the tool for supervising the financial arrangements concerning the land-reclamation companies. The head of Dasheng's accounts office, Wu Jichen, assumed a particularly influential role. In early 1921, Zhang Jia'ao, then the assistant general manager of the Bank of China and one of the most prominent members of Shanghai's financial world, contacted Wu Jichen in order to discuss the future of the five land-reclamation companies.[62] On a trip south from his bank's head office in Beijing, Zhang had inspected the area in question, most probably assessing the value of the land as a prospective collateral. Arriving in Shanghai, Zhang Jia'ao contacted members of the banking community, modern banks as well as *qianzhuang*, and initiated the formation of a banking consortium in the summer of 1921. The consortium, or *yintuan*, included the Shanghai Bank of Communications, the Shanghai Bank, and the Bank of China.[63]

In July 1921 this consortium entered into a loan agreement with the five land-reclamation companies. The contract was signed by Song Hanzhang from the Bank of China and Tian Qiyuan as representatives of the consortium, by the managers of the five land-reclamation companies, and by Zhang Jian and Zhang Cha as the managing directors of the companies. All the managers were trusted business partners of Zhang Jian or, like Xu Jingren and Zhang Zuosan, managers in the Dasheng mills. The contract stated that between July and October 1921 the consortium would raise 3 million yuan by issuing bonds for the companies against an 8 percent annual interest and collateral of 1.05 million mu in as-yet undivided reclamation land.[64] The purpose of this loan arrangement was "to settle old debts and to expand reclamation work."[65]

The consortium's three major Chinese banks were members of the Shanghai Bankers' Association, which had been founded in 1917. Zhang Jia'ao in particular promoted the association's journal, *Yinhang zhoubao* (Bankers' weekly), which reported in great detail on the land-reclamation companies and the banks involved between 1922 and 1928.[66] Numerous articles described the reasons for the companies' indebtedness—extensive borrowing with no chance of redeeming the debt or paying the interest on it—quite sympathetically. In the journal, the consortium liked to have its commitment to national economic goals described with statements such as "at this critical time when the agriculture of our nation is just beginning to prosper, we [i.e., the banks] cannot help but offer our support."[67] Altruism was certainly not enough to motivate major Chinese banks to invest in a group of heavily indebted agricultural enterprises with an uncertain future; there had to be a serious business agenda behind the banks' helping hand.

The extremely incomplete records of the land-reclamation companies point to direct investments by leading members of the banks and the Dasheng enterprises. For example, when the Huacheng Land Reclamation Company was established in 1917, the 25 promoters (faqiren) issued a statement of purpose and set out the investment rules with the intention of attracting new shareholders. Among the promoters were Zhang Jian, Zhang Cha, Wu Jichen, and Chen Guangfu, the managing director of the Shanghai Bank.[68] Promoting the establishment of the company meant not only lending one's good name to the undertaking as a sign of its trustworthiness but also putting up the initial share capital. As the report stated, each promoter had invested 50,000 yuan and was entitled to draw a bonus on it in the future. However, as the first accounting report from 1917 shows, only two-thirds of the company's starting capital of 1.25 million yuan was paid up in the first year.[69]

This means that long before the Shanghai Bank became involved in the land-reclamation companies as part of the consortium in 1921, Chen Guangfu had already invested in them and thus most probably had a strong interest in keeping these companies in business. Based on the existing documentation, it is impossible to say whether Chen Guangfu invested his own money or the funds of the Shanghai Bank. In either case he clearly considered land reclamation a viable business investment.

The investments by Zhang Jian, his brother, and Wu Jichen in Huacheng confirm the close relationship between the land-reclamation companies and the Dasheng cotton mills. These three powerful managers of the Dasheng business group had also invested in other land-reclamation companies.[70] The Huacheng company itself had small investments in other land-reclamation companies such as Dagang or Xintong, and Zhang Jian even borrowed money from Huacheng through a personal business account.[71]

The close relationship between the land-reclamation companies and Dasheng was not only recognized but even strengthened by the banking consortium's arrangements. The 1921 loan contract required that the loan should be administered through Dasheng's Shanghai office and that Wu

Jichen should act as temporary auditor for the land-reclamation companies on behalf of the banks. In addition, the contract stipulated that Wu Jichen be in charge of distributing the loan among the five companies.[72]

It would appear that by 1922 the five land-reclamation companies had become subsidiaries of the Dasheng No. 1 Cotton Mill, since there is no evidence that they ever paid back the loan of 1.33 million yuan to the No. 1 mill. Financially the five companies were controlled by the banks since they were not able to redeem their debts and to pay all the interest on the consortium's loans. In 1932 the companies still owed 1.84 million yuan in principal and 0.94 million yuan in interest to the consortium.[73] In order to control them efficiently, the banks operated through Dasheng's headquarters in Shanghai. One can assume that the close contact allowed the banks to familiarize themselves with Dasheng's internal structure and to observe its financial development. When the Dasheng mill operations faced their own crisis in 1922, the Bank of China, the Shanghai Bank, and the Bank of Communications were certainly not unprepared to get involved in the industrial side of the business.

1922: A Crisis Hidden in the Books

The year 1922 posed a great challenge to China's textile industry. Rising raw material prices because of scarce supplies and increasing foreign and domestic demand for cotton pointed to land reclamation as a potential remedy.[74] Unfortunately, by then the land-reclamation companies had become financially the weakest part of the Dasheng business complex. As I shall argue here, Dasheng's imminent bankruptcy was not just a matter of rising cotton prices, constant or falling yarn prices, and increasing foreign competition; rather, it stemmed mainly from its business and accounting practices, a cause that sheds new light on the viability of "modern" industrial enterprises in Republican China.

Dasheng's extensive indebtedness was aggravated but not primarily caused by the negative impact of rising costs. Heavy indebtedness was not, however, a sheer coincidence or accident but the result of the company's financial strategy. Why did Dasheng end up in a crisis that seriously threatened its viability? And how was the enterprise able to maintain an obviously precarious financial situation with the consent of shareholders, creditors, and managers?

Table 6.5
Indebtedness of the Dasheng No. 1 Cotton Mill, 1921
(*taels*)

Liabilities		Assets	
Loans	–4,016,602	13 affiliated companies	–425,816
		No. 3 mill	–399,033
		No. 6 mill	–120,195
		No. 8 mill	–483,393
		Land-reclamation companies	–1,278,505
		Banks and *qianzhuang*	–441,518
		Private accounts	–719,674
		Industrial Company	–114,870
TOTAL	–4,016,602		–3,983,004

SOURCE: Balance sheet of the No. 1 mill's 1921 annual company report in *DSQXDX*, pp. 143–48.

The company's insolvency became dramatically apparent in 1922 when the company announced that it was 400,000 taels in the red.[75] The Dasheng No. 1 mill was unable to pay dividends to its shareholders, to meet all its interest payments, and to add to its reserves or depreciation funds—in short, the company needed outside credits to prevent bankruptcy. However, payments of the principal and interest on outstanding loans had created a new problem: the Dasheng No. 1 mill had a cash flow crisis despite good sales. In 1924, an auditing report commissioned by the shareholders commented on this predicament: "With high costs and little [new input of] share capital, everything depends on the loans; no wonder that [the company] finds it difficult to go on."[76]

In 1921, Dasheng had operated with strongly diminishing returns but still achieved an overall profit. The mill's balance sheet for 1921 reported a lump sum of 4.02 million taels as loans among its liabilities (see Table 6.5).[77] This entry did not list the creditors individually, but from business correspondence we know that Chinese banks, modern as well as traditional, advanced the loans. For example, in 1921, the Shanghai Bank loaned the Dasheng No. 1 mill 200,000 gold dollars, or 798,000 taels, to purchase new spinning machines from the Within Machine Works in Massachusetts.[78]

According to figures extrapolated from the 1921 balance sheet (Table 6.5), Dasheng held a total of 3.98 million taels in other companies as current

Table 6.6
Indebtedness of the Dasheng No. 1 Cotton Mill, 1922
(*taels*)

Liabilities		Assets	
Mortgages	−3,973,750	Land-reclamation companies	−1,334,215
Credit	−1,360,902	No. 6 mill	− 136,888
Loans	−1,139,234	No. 8 mill	−1,107,618
Banks and *qianzhuang*	−414,551	Industrial Company	−100,460
Temporary loans	−209,511	Advances	−1,753,243
		Loans due for collection	−1,012,592
		Temporary loans	−379,685
TOTAL	−7,098,948		−5,824,701

SOURCE: Balance sheet of the No. 1 mill's 1922 annual company report in *DSQXDX*, pp. 148–53.

assets. Among these assets, 1.28 million taels in loans to various land-reclamation companies was the largest item.[79] An examination of the annual business reports for the previous five years shows that at least during that period the No. 1 mill had not invested directly in land-reclamation companies; the huge investment in 1921 was due to the precarious financial situation of those companies. Additionally, Dasheng had current assets of almost 720,000 taels in private accounts, 441,000 taels in various banking institutions, and 115,000 taels in its shell company, the Industrial Company.

Of course, most of these assets were investments made before 1921. Two new investments were a loan of 483,000 taels to the No. 8 mill, which at that time was still at the planning stage, and another loan of 120,000 taels to the No. 6 mill, which in 1921 existed only on paper. The No. 1 mill also had assets of about 400,000 taels in the No. 3 mill, which started operations in 1921, and about 426,000 taels as loans to various small affiliated companies.

The balance sheet for 1922, the year of Dasheng's crisis, records dramatic changes, and a record loss (see Table 6.6).[80] The overall loan liabilities now amounted to 7.1 million taels; of this, 3.97 million were loans secured by mortgages, including a mortgage on the No. 2 mill, 1.36 million in credits, 1.14 million in unspecified loans, and the rest in various bank loans and short-term credits. Dasheng's loan liabilities had increased by roughly 3 million taels over the previous year. Complicating any attempt to understand where these 3 million taels went is the fact that the headings under which items are listed on the balance sheets differ greatly from year to year. In order to analyze the accounts, one has to equate differently named items and risk a margin of error in terms of mistaken identification.

So, where did the loans of 3 million taels go? According to the extrapolated numbers presented in Table 6.6, the No. 1 mill held current assets in outside operations of 5.82 million taels in 1922, of which 1.33 million taels were investments in the various land-reclamation companies. The amount invested in the No. 8 mill had increased significantly to 1.1 million taels; the investment in the No. 6 mill remained almost the same at 137,000 taels. The No. 1 mill's current assets in the Industrial Company dropped slightly to 100,000 taels. The lion's share of Dasheng's deposits with other companies in 1922 are found in three entries labeled "various advances" (*gexiang diankuan*), "loans due for collection" (*cuishou gekuan*), and "temporary loans" (*zanji qiankuan*).[81] The "various advances" consisted of long-term deposits; as the name implies, "temporary loans" were short-term advances; "loans due for collection" were overdue for repayment. Dasheng thus held current assets of 3.1 million taels under these three extremely general entries, which neither identify the companies nor the persons to whom the money had been lent. I would argue that the 1.9 million taels in the No. 1 mill's assets in private accounts, bank accounts, and affiliated companies from the previous year were now included under these three entries. If this is correct, the 1.8 million increase in current assets in 1922 consists of an additional 0.6 million taels invested in the No. 8 mill and a 1.2 million tael increase in current assets held in various private and company accounts.

This increasing indebtedness and its impact on the asset side of Dasheng's balance sheet feature prominently in the business report for 1923. Dasheng's overall liabilities rose by 0.74 million taels to 7.8 million taels (Table 6.7).[82] The company raised loans of 4.4 million taels by mortgaging real estate, machinery, raw cotton, and finished cotton products as well as financial securities to the banks. Another 3.4 million taels came through loans from private accounts and affiliated industrial companies. On the asset side of the 1923 balance sheet, this increase in funds was reflected in an overall increase of current assets to 6.4 million taels.

More documentation is available for the next year; in addition to the annual company report, we have the report on the audit commissioned by the shareholders of the Dasheng No. 1 mill at their 1922 meeting.[83] The auditors,

Table 6.7
Indebtedness of the Dasheng No. 1 Cotton Mill, 1923
(*taels*)

Liabilities		Assets	
Mortgage fixed assets	−1,523,000	Charity	−683,152
Mortgage in bonds	−1,451,319	No. 8 mill	−1,581,071
No. 8 mill	−100,000	Industrial companies	−1,462,319
Industrial companies	−1,151,599	Various loans	−1,287,516
Various loans	−1,720,637	Temporary loans	−203,272
Temporary loans	−448,677	Current assets	−1,167,304
Mortgage yarn & cloth	−1,448,940		
TOTAL	−7,844,172		−6,384,634

SOURCE: Balance sheet of the No. 1 mill's 1923 annual company report in *DSQXDX*, pp. 163–66.

sent by a consortium of creditor banks, produced a detailed statement of the Dasheng No. 1 mill's assets and liabilities in 1924 in order to evaluate the financial condition of the enterprise. This report provides invaluable information and enables us to identify some of the owners of the business accounts and the flow of funds in which they were involved.

In 1924, the Dasheng No. 1 Cotton Mill had liabilities of 7.9 million taels, only 0.1 million taels more than in 1923, in the form of bank loans secured by mortgages or unsecured loans from private persons and other companies (see Table 6.8).[84] The funds Dasheng held as current assets with other companies amounted to 5.9 million taels. Between 1923 and 1924, the categories used in the accounts had changed again and are even less informative to the outsider; it is difficult to decide on the basis of the balance sheet to which accounts the money was distributed. In this respect, the auditing report proves to be especially helpful, although it is, of course, not possible to identify all financial sources.

The investment of 1.64 million taels by the No. 1 mill in the No. 8 mill noted in the 1924 annual report can be equated with various entries in the auditors' report; there it is valued at 1.48 million taels, that is 10 percent less than the nominal value on the balance sheet.[85] Deposits with the No. 6 mill are not recorded among the assets in the 1923 and 1924 balance sheets, but the auditors' report records 0.15 million taels as assets in the No. 6 mill, now listed together with the other industrial companies.[86]

Table 6.8
Indebtedness of the Dasheng No. 1 Cotton Mill, 1924
(*taels*)

Liabilities		Assets	
Mortgage fixed assets	-2,250,276	Charity	-576,453
Mortgage bonds	-1,088,261	No. 8 mill	-1,642,667
No. 8 mill	-141,839	Industrial companies	-1,550,236
Industrial companies	-1,014,723	Various loans	-1,261,487
Various loans	-1,323,509	Temporary loans	-117,823
Temporary loans	-379,106	Current assets	-809,594
Mortgage yarn & cloth	-1,745,286		
TOTAL	-7,943,000		-5,958,260

SOURCE: Balance sheet of the No. 1 mill's 1924 annual company report in *DSQXDX*, pp. 166–70.

In comparison with the 1922 balance sheet, the absence of loans to the land-reclamation companies in 1924 is striking. This does not, however, mean that no money was invested in those companies. On the contrary, we can see from the auditors' report that loans to the land-reclamation companies were split up and included within the entries "various loans" and "industrial companies" among Dasheng's liabilities. In fact, analysis of the auditors' report reveals that 1.07 million taels of the total 2.3 million taels under those two entries was invested in various land-reclamation companies, a fact that would not have been clear to readers of the 1924 annual company report.[87]

However, Dasheng's funds invested in the land-reclamation companies on the asset side were problematic as well. The precarious financial situation of the land-reclamation companies is obvious from the auditors' evaluation of these companies' assets in the books.[88] The item "various loans" (*gehu qiankuan*), valued at 1.26 million taels on Dasheng's 1924 balance sheet (see Table 6.8), is explained by a detailed list in the auditors' report. For example, Dasheng No. 1 had lent 5,000 taels to the Laiyuan company, which it secured with shares of the Dafeng Land Reclamation Company nominally worth 56,000 taels, eleven times the value of the loan. This was no exceptional case: under his personal account Gong *ji*, Zhang Jian borrowed 139,777 taels from Dasheng using shares of the Huacheng, Tongsui, Dafeng, Dagang, and Dayu land-reclamation companies with a nominal value of 206,000 taels, about 1.5 times the value of the loan, as collateral.[89] Since the value of the securities was so much higher than the loan, we can assume that the land-reclamation companies and their shares were worth much less than their book value. This suspicion is confirmed by the fact that even the banks, in their effort to exercise careful risk management, found it difficult to assess the real value of the land offered as collateral by the land-reclamation companies. For example, one year after signing the original contract in 1921, the consortium complained that the value of the land offered as collateral by the Dayoujin company was too low and that the land would no longer qualify as a security. The consortium demanded that the Dayoujin company put up an additional 20,000 mu of land as collateral.[90]

The practice of putting private accounts under the name of a business makes it difficult to identify the owner of the account. The list in the auditors' report shows that the No. 1 mill lent 80,742 taels to Dunsu *tang*, Zhang Jian's business account, in 1924. In return, Dunsu *tang* offered 22,500 taels worth of shares in land-reclamation companies plus 90,000 taels of shares in the Bank of China as securities. Another identifiable private account in the list is the Tui *ji*, the personal account of Zhang Cha, which borrowed 9,730 taels from the No. 1 mill against shares of the No. 3 mill in Haimen. As the auditors' report noted, these had yet to be paid up completely.[91] Another of Zhang Jian's private accounts was the Ji gong, which had borrowed 242,152 taels against shares in the No. 1 and No. 2 mills, the Bank of China, a real estate company, and a piece of land.[92] Over 0.5 million taels in loans can be traced through the auditors' report to Zhang Jian's private accounts. This custom was practiced in many of the other Dasheng enterprises as well. For example, one of the detailed account books of the Dasheng No. 2 mill lists another of Zhang Jian's personal accounts, the Zunsu *tang*, as the receiver of 23,000 taels in loans in 1922.[93]

Although many of the account names recorded in the auditors' report sound familiar from other documents, it is not absolutely certain that they belonged to the Zhang family. Nevertheless, the actual amount of money hidden in Zhang Jian's private accounts was probably much higher than the 0.5 million taels that I have been able to document. The No. 1 mill made small loans without security requirements to various business associates and personal friends of Zhang Jian such as Liu Housheng and Shen Shou (1874–1921), who specialized in artistic embroidery and opened a school for women in Nantong in 1914. The Dasheng No. 1 mill functioned almost like a bank, serving customers connected with the business and its director. In contrast to transactions of a regular bank, however, it is impossible to say whether these private loans, which totaled 155,000 taels, were ever repaid.[94]

The small companies affiliated with Dasheng also continued to receive funds, according to the auditors' report. For example, the No. 1 mill lent 0.47 million taels to the Zisheng Iron Workshop and the electrical plant; the total lent to the affiliated companies came to 0.81 million taels.[95] The securities offered for these loans, including the collateral with a book value of 1.15 million taels offered by the land-reclamation companies, obviously did not satisfy the auditors. They remarked that "the loans under this entry need quickly to be put into order, either by taking over property to be sold off or by taking over land and putting it under its own [i.e. Dasheng's] management."[96] The auditors demanded that the bank committee approve any further arrangements concerning these loans. The auditors' remark confirms my suspicion that the affiliated companies in the Dasheng business group were not obliged to follow the same, strict financial requirements that outside companies would have had to observe to obtain a loan from Dasheng.

In the years of financial difficulties, the welfare projects were introduced into the accounts to improve the balance. In the boom years of 1919, 1920, and 1921, only a modest amount of 22,000 taels was recorded as assets held in various school projects. In 1922 not a single charity institution or project was recorded as a company asset. Suddenly in 1923, the sum of 683,000 taels was listed as "advances to public welfare projects" (*gongyi cishan diankuan*) on Dasheng's balance sheet under its assets (see Table 6.7). No new welfare or educational projects had been founded in 1923 or the previous year, however. In 1924, these charitable "investments" continued to appear in the balance sheet, with 0.58 million taels listed under assets (see Table 6.8). This amount must be interpreted as a cumulative figure for expenditures on welfare projects during the previous twenty years; it was not, of course, a real asset.

The auditors' report confirms this suspicion by listing a theater in Nantong, road construction in Haimen and Nantong, the textile school, famine relief, and the local hospital as the recipients of these loans.[97] I know of no evidence of repayments of these moneys. Nor were these charity projects marketable assets that could be sold to redeem Dasheng's debts. The funds directed to welfare projects were treated as real loans solely as a cosmetic device to improve the asset side of the balance sheet.

My conjecture that too much money was invested in projects from which it could not be retrieved is corroborated by a statement in the auditors' report. Obviously, the auditors shared the same serious concerns about the value and liquidity of Dasheng's assets: "Although securities have been received from the debtors, they cannot be turned into ready cash from one moment to the next, and since for the creditors cash must be provided, in reality it is very difficult to pay them back."[98] This statement defines Dasheng's securities as bad assets and summarizes the financial dilemma of the No. 1 mill in the early 1920s.

From a detailed analysis of the crisis years, it is possible to identify a financial strategy that was simultaneously deleterious to the overall performance of Dasheng and yet beneficial to Zhang Jian. Because of the more detailed documentation available for 1924, I will use that year as an example. The question that immediately arises is: How did Dasheng use the 7.9 million taels of loans granted to the enterprise?

First, the extensive investment in the branch mills and the almost total lack of returns on this investment were enormous burdens. The loan of 1.64 million taels to the No. 8 mill went to a branch enterprise that was to begin operations only two years later, and the No. 6 mill, which received 0.15 million taels, never materialized. Second, the land-reclamation companies received loans of 1.07 million taels, which were insufficiently secured, and the real value of their shares offered as collateral was much less than their nominal value. Third, the private draining of funds represented a significant decrease in actual company assets. According to my calculations, 0.5 million taels went to Zhang Jian through accounts in his personal name or through family accounts, and I suspect that the actual amount was much higher. Funds invested in charity projects with no real business value amounted to 0.57 million taels, and Zhang Jian put additional money in the accounts of his non-textile subsidiary companies, which did not offer proper securities for the 0.81 million taels they received as loans. I would argue that of all the loans advanced by Dasheng by 1924, 4.74 million taels were bad (noncollectible) debts. This is a significant amount, especially when we consider that it is equivalent to around 60 percent of the total value of the loans received by the No. 1 mill.

Despite these obvious examples of bad practices, the auditors never directly criticized Zhang Jian or Dasheng's accounting methods. It is questionable to what extent the auditors were able to identify the owners behind the numerous accounts that received funds from the Dasheng mills. In holding the first audit in the history of the Dasheng No. 1 mill and publishing the results in 1926, the banks presumably wanted to clarify the cotton mills' financial situation and its obligations. In the words of the auditors, the report was designed to help the banks decide on "how from now on [i.e., 1926] the debts and the rights of the creditors should be administered and how business should proceed."[99]

The strategy of liberal transfers of funds, of course, did not improve the company's strained business situation in the early 1920s. I call this pattern of indebtedness with a high percentage of bad debts and unsound investments in assets a strategy because clearly it was authorized by Zhang Jian and institutionalized in the Dasheng business complex through its peculiar accounting system supervised by the Shanghai office, which was under his personal control. Obviously, the system had operated until around 1920 without causing financial disaster. Land reclamation did not begin to play an important role in the Dasheng business until 1914. As long as the business was expanding, the transfer of funds between companies must have seemed the ideal solution to the problems of providing capital and financing cash flows. When external factors impaired the economic stability of the enterprise, the whole strategy of intercompany financing collapsed.

Once the creditor-banks became involved in Dasheng, they began to turn into serious investment banks that needed to install managerial and financial mechanisms that maximized their returns and minimized the financial risks without jeopardizing the enterprise's overall profitability. As we shall see, managerial reforms as well as careful assessment and management of collateral played a vital role in this process.

Under Control of the Banks

The 1922 financial crisis was the beginning of a serious long-term involvement of the banks in the Dasheng business complex and led to financial as well as managerial changes.[100] As in the case of the land-reclamation companies, the Shanghai Bank was one of the Dasheng mills' most important creditors during the crisis. Apart from the personal connection between Zhang Jian and Chen Guangfu, Dasheng's business relationship with the Shanghai Bank had been established for some time through modest shareholding and investment. Zhang Jian had been one of the initial shareholders in the bank, although his holdings were nominal, amounting to only 1,500 yuan in 1916 and to 5,000 yuan in 1921.[101] However, Dasheng as a company

and several of its managers such as Xu Jingren and Wu Jichen were also investors in the bank. The relation between the Shanghai Bank and Dasheng
was obviously characterized by mutual obligation. No doubt, Wu Jichen's
position as vice-chairman of the bank's board at the time of Dasheng's crisis
in 1922 and 1923 facilitated the loan negotiations.[102] Wu Youchun, Wu
Jichen's nephew, confirmed this assumption: "Not only did Dasheng help by
way of investments, but it also maintained a surplus in its current accounts;
therefore, when Dasheng later ran into difficulties over its cash flow, the
Shanghai Bank offered help."[103]

In 1922 the Shanghai Bank gave the Dasheng No. 1 Cotton Mill loans totaling 513,532 taels.[104] Because of the business group's continuing financial
problems and its inability to pay the interest on these loans, additional loans
and long-term support from outside sources were needed. In order to give
themselves as creditors a more formal structure and in order to facilitate
their dealings with Dasheng, the Jincheng Bank, the Bank of China, the
Shanghai Bank, and the Bank of Communications together with the Yongfeng and Yongju *qianzhuang* formed a banking consortium in 1925.[105] The
three major banks controlling the five land-reclamation companies were
now, with the addition of the Jincheng Bank, also in charge of Dasheng. It
took much longer to form a consortium for the mills than it had for the
land-reclamation companies, possibly because of the greater capital requirements of the mills.

After auditing each of the cotton mills and uniting them under one
managerial structure and financial scheme, the banks split their managerial
responsibilities for the mills according to their individual share of the loan
capital. The No. 1 and No. 2 cotton mills came under the management of
the Yongzhong Company, which consisted of the Yongfeng *qianzhuang*, the
Bank of China, and the Bank of Communications; the Yongju *qianzhuang*
was in charge of the No. 3 mill; and the Jincheng Bank together with the
Yongfeng *qianzhuang* took over the No. 8 mill.[106] Each banking group chose
its own representative to organize and supervise the financial and managerial
changes in its respective mill(s). The banking consortium remained in control of Dasheng until 1937 (see Chapter 8). The rise in the total value of the
loans to 8.3 million yuan in 1935 indicates that the financial grip of the banks
on Dasheng became even tighter during the late 1920s and early 1930s.[107]

From the creditor-banks' perspective, some of Dasheng's inherent financial problems should have been obvious to any sensitive reader of the audi-

tors' report of 1924. In their introduction to the report, the auditors stated that they had found it necessary to investigate not only the Shanghai accounts office but also the accounts offices of the mills, and they admitted that the investigation had been difficult and troublesome.[108] But although the auditors identified overextension (payments for new machinery and the establishment of the No. 8 mill in 1921/22 as the cotton market was deteriorating) and indebtedness as the reasons for Dasheng's negative performance, they did not relate these issues to Dasheng's mechanisms of financial control and internal management under Zhang Jian.

Securities in form of land, factory buildings, machinery, raw cotton, and cloth served as the banks' insurance against the possibility of the debtor-companies' going out of business. In contrast to unsecured loans, which carried a higher interest rate, loans based on securities in form of assets were discounted by the banks. Given the banks' risks when issuing unsecured loans, it is not surprising that, for example, in 1922 unsecured loans to the Dasheng mills amounted to only 8.5 percent of the total loans issued to the enterprise.[109]

Nevertheless, even with sufficient securities the banks had to wait a long time before their loans were redeemed. For example, although the mortgage period had been extended, 1.2 million taels of the secured loan issued by the Yongzhong banking group to Dasheng in 1925 remained unpaid in 1934. Consequently, Yongzhong gave Dasheng another year to come up with the required payments and to redeem its mortgaged assets.[110]

The banks evaluated the securities offered as collateral cautiously and assigned them a value that gave the banks a financial advantage and investment incentive. For example, in 1922 Dasheng put up the entire assets of its No. 1 and No. 2 cotton mills as security for a combined loan of 3.9 million taels.[111] Since the machinery in both factories alone had a value of 3.4 million taels, the mortgage arrangement seems to have been quite safe and profitable for the banks.[112] In contrast, the land provided by the land-reclamation companies as collateral did not always prove to be worth the stated value. Not only were large parts of the reclaimed land inferior in quality, but it probably would have been much more difficult to find a single buyer for the land if the banks had been forced to sell the collateral.

In 1922 the Shanghai Bank lent 2 million taels to the Dasheng No. 3 Cotton Mill in Haimen. According to a former employee of the bank, Zhang Jian personally urged Chen Guangfu to help this affiliated mill, which had started operations in 1921 and was in immediate danger of collapse.[113] Despite this personal appeal, the Shanghai Bank demanded the No. 3 mill's machinery, yarn, and raw cotton as securities and made it a condition that its own financial experts be installed in the central accounts office of the Haimen factory. These employees reported directly to the bank, an indication that the bank did not trust the mill's management.[114]

These loan conditions were a departure from credit arrangements in the 1910s. For example, a contract between the Dasheng No. 1 mill and the Yokohama Specie Bank in 1912 for a loan of 200,000 taels did not lead to the involvement of the bank in Dasheng's internal management. The contract established only that "the complete mill, all construction, landed property, buildings, machinery as well as the total financial assets of the Dasheng Cotton Mill in Nantong are to be handed over to the Yokohama Specie Bank as items of guarantee."[115]

Obviously, as the loans grew increasingly larger in the early 1920s, the banks began to stipulate conditions in addition to the provision of securities in the form of company assets. For example, the Jincheng Bank carefully evaluated Dasheng's financial situation in order to assess the company's credit rating as well as to forecast prospective profits. The bank was obviously (and, in the event, rightfully) concerned that Dasheng would be unable to repay a short-term loan of 700,000 taels in 1922. To minimize its financial risks and to exert tighter control over Dasheng, the Jincheng bank initiated a restructuring of Dasheng's top management.[116] In 1922 the Jincheng Bank demanded that Zhang Jian and Zhang Cha appoint Xu Jingweng as overseer of the No. 1 and No. 2 mills with the task of reorganizing them on behalf of the bank.[117] To judge from a letter written in the Jincheng Bank, this seems to have required some delicacy:

It has set things [i.e., the reorganization of the Dasheng cotton mills] back that Zhang Cha seemed unwilling to give up his power, and consequently people in charge were not able to get on with the task. Zhang Jian, however, has been more straightforward. He has taken a broader view of things and is not one to "give up his meals for having choked once in his throat." So, our authority is now just about complete.[118]

This remark reveals that at this point Zhang Cha was much more involved in internal business politics at Dasheng's headquarters than was Zhang Jian. Unlike his brother, he obviously had no intention of handing over financial control and thus the management of the enterprise to representatives of the bank.

An interesting side effect of the removal of members of the Zhang family network from the company's top management was a strengthening of the manager's position in the Shanghai office. In a loan contract between the Zhongnan, Dalu, Yanye, and Jincheng banks and the Dasheng cotton mill in 1923, Wu Jichen's position takes on new significance. One part of the real estate in Baoshan county securing the loan of 213,300 taels was offered by the Wu gong *ji* business account, that is, Wu Jichen's own business account, together with the Qianhe company on behalf of the Dasheng mill.[119] Wu Jichen was putting up his private property as a collateral for Dasheng. He also acted together with Shen Yanmou, the assistant manager of the Shanghai accounts office, as a guarantor for a loan of 400,000 taels by the Shanghai Bank to the Dasheng No. 8 mill in 1926.[120] Thus it was not Zhang Cha as the chairman of the board but Wu Jichen who functioned as the guarantor for Dasheng. After Zhang Jian's death in 1926 and the curbing of the family influence, the power of the director of the Shanghai office apparently became stronger. The banks had obviously realized that gaining power over the Dasheng business complex meant controlling its Shanghai office.

How little confidence the banks had in the mills' management even after the first set of reforms can be seen from an eight-point program designed by Li Shengbo, Dasheng's managing director after 1924. The Dasheng No. 1 mill was specifically advised to adhere to scientific management and to adopt cost accounting; the No. 2 mill in Chongming was advised to add weaving to its production process. The program also stated that the loans advanced by the banks to both mills were subject to a monthly interest rate of 8 percent; any remaining profits were to be added to the monthly payments.[121]

The fact that the banking consortium once more insisted on strict bookkeeping procedures in 1934 indicates the lack of serious changes in Dasheng's accounting system despite pressure from the creditor-banks. Among other things, the revised regulations stipulated that checks had to be issued for all payments, no matter whether the expenditures occurred in Nantong or Shanghai; and that cotton purchases, wage payments, and daily expenses within the factories had first to be entered on an advice note and verified before a check was issued.[122] In contrast to Dasheng's former accounting practices, the banks also required a detailed monthly statement about the costs of produced yarn and cloth and exact information about the mill's sales income from yarn and cloth. Obviously, even in the 1930s Dasheng's accounting system was still not organized in a way that allowed the banks to use it as a tool of control.

The banks had little confidence in the financial and managerial control of the land-reclamation companies as well. Auditors and accountants were sent to the coastal areas as representatives of the consortium and installed on the premises of each land-reclamation company in order to audit the books and to assess the general financial situation of the company. Since the original loan contracts had not specified accounting standards, the banks were particularly concerned that both sides adhere to clear and uniform methods.[123] In spring 1922, when the financial situation of the land-reclamation companies was still deteriorating, the consortium used the annual shareholder meetings of the five companies to announce its five-point rescue program: all land sales had to be reported to the consortium, expenses had to be cut, shareholders were not to receive any dividends, all activities connected with the salt business were to cease, and land reclamation was to continue in order to generate income.[124]

The investment activities of modern banks in the Dasheng business group during the 1920s did not preclude a role for traditional banking institutions. A few, large *qianzhuang* joined the consortium as equal partners. For example, in 1923 and 1924 the Yongzhong banking group loaned the Dasheng mills funds for working capital. As is obvious from the 1923 and 1924 balance sheets, the mill's yarn and cloth were put up as securities for the 1.74 million–tael loan.[125] The Yongfeng *qianzhuang* was a partner in the Yongzhong banking group and raised the major share of this loan; according to Zhu Zhenhua's study, Yongfeng performed extremely well between 1921 and 1926 and received deposits of up to 10 million yuan.[126]

The financial power of the Yongfeng *qianzhuang* explains why Li Shengbo, the son of Yongfeng manager Li Jisheng, was put in charge of the Dasheng No. 1 mill as the representative of the banking consortium in 1925. As Zhu Zhenhua has pointed out, Li Shengbo's personal influence in mobilizing financial help in Shanghai and restoring creditors' faith in Dasheng was substantial. When Dasheng proved unable to meet the required repayments, he succeeded in negotiating a temporary suspension of interest payments. The Bank of China, the Jincheng, and other banks consequently reduced the interest rates on their loans by 15 and by 20 percent.[127] The banks were not acting out of sheer altruism, however. They added the missed interest payments to Dasheng's capital under liabilities on the balance sheet, where it was recorded as interest completely unpaid or partially unpaid.[128]

The banks were prepared to extend their loans since they considered the property and real estate of the spinning mills attractive securities. In addition, interest payments from Dasheng, even if incomplete, constituted a considerable annual income for the banks. The banks tried, however, to assess Dasheng's credit rating as well as their own risk. For example, during the 1922 crisis, the Jincheng Bank used the assessment of Xu Jingren, which listed in great detail the machinery assets of all three Dasheng mills. It then calculated how much credit the bank could offer to each mill. In order to reduce its own risk, the Jincheng bank decided to cooperate with the Yanye Bank. Both banks jointly offered a loan of 0.45 million taels provided that Dasheng agreed that the banks' representatives would assume control of management and accounting and that all future income and expenditures would be managed by the creditors.[129] With regard to the No. 1 and No. 8 spinning mills, the Jincheng Bank concluded in 1922 that "all in all, if we compare the assets with the liabilities of these mills, there is an adequate surplus; if we can sincerely institute reforms, we need not worry about the lack of investors. However, if we do not do what we say, then we shall lose the investors' support."[130] Obviously, the Dasheng enterprise was an attractive investment because of its real estate assets, which lowered the banks' overall risk. This statement also points to the fact that the precarious financial situation in 1922 was aggravated by a deep loss of public confidence in Dasheng among shareholders, former investors, and present creditors in Shanghai's business circles. Zhang Jian's clout in the financial and political world was no longer able to smooth things over in the early 1920s.

Dasheng was only one of many spinning mills in Shanghai, Wuxi, and Changzhou receiving financial help from modern banking institutions during the Republican period. For example, the expansion of the Shenxin mills in Wuxi under the Rong family's management was aided by strong financial support from the Shanghai Bank and the Bank of China.[131] A loan contract from 1931 illustrates the conditions under which both banks agreed to raise 400,000 taels for the Wuxi mills. The mills received the loan at a rate of 7.75 percent annual interest, to be paid semi-annually, by mortgaging all their fixed assets—land, buildings, and machinery. As in the case of Dasheng, the creditor-banks inserted themselves into the mills' management. The banks required that their own inventory manager take control of the mill's warehouses and bring order to the recordkeeping system for raw cotton, yarn, and finished cloth. The recording of expenses and income from these items was to be supervised by an accountant dispatched by the banks.[132] The control of the banks had extended beyond the account books and reached the shop floor.

———— ◆ ————

Dasheng's financial performance between 1900 and the mid-1920s is sobering: high capital costs through increasing indebtedness reduced Dasheng's net profit severely. In addition to the skimming of company funds by the founder, land-reclamation companies and Zhang Jian's other business interests received the major share of loans. Dasheng's risk hedging was also insufficient. Annual reserves and depreciation funds were not adjusted to the company's accumulating assets, and with increasing indebtedness there was no financial backup once disaster struck. Insufficient risk management forced Dasheng to turn to the banks for loans.

Some of these factors have been described by the authors of the *Dasheng xitong qiyeshi*. Their study examines the mill's increasing indebtedness and correctly identifies rising interest payments, hasty expansion, and substantial deposits with affiliated companies as detrimental to Dasheng's business performance and as the main factors in the crisis of 1922.[133] Even beyond these elements, however, the most crucial reason for Dasheng's failure was the transfer of funds between company accounts and private accounts and personal business interests.

External factors exacerbated an already precarious situation. Dasheng's expansion strategy in the 1920s was plagued by bad planning and bad luck. First, for reasons that are not clear, the company planned further branch mills at a time when the No. 1 mill was facing liquidity problems. It is possible that this expansion was intended to forestall competitors who wanted to establish mills in the region. Dasheng enjoyed quasi-monopoly protection in Nantong until the early 1920s, when the Jiu'an company became its first local competitor, and this may have spurred plans for new facilities.[134]

Second, bad luck in the form of natural disasters devastated the cotton crop in coastal Jiangsu in 1921, and bad harvests in other provinces seem to have hit Dasheng at a time when it could ill afford additional expenses. Since cotton was the main product of the land-reclamation companies, Dasheng was hit twice: the cultivated land of the companies was badly damaged and required costly repairs; at the same time the mills lost their steady supply of raw material and had to resort to more expensive outside sources.

In terms of the national economic framework, Dasheng illustrates the general trend during the 1920s and 1930s for modern banks to expand their investment portfolios to include industrial enterprises and thus to become vital to financing the nation's industrial development. For example, the Jincheng Bank invested in several cotton and coal businesses during that time, putting over two million yuan in the Yuyuan cotton mill in Tianjin alone between 1919 and 1922.[135] By 1933 the Shanghai Bank had invested 22.5 million yuan in cotton mills nationwide, and the Bank of China had lent 22.1 million yuan to various textile enterprises.[136]

The dealings of major modern Chinese banks with the land-reclamation companies and the Dasheng cotton mills corroborates the growth of financial and economic integration during the Republican period that Thomas Rawski has noted.[137] As the banks' portfolio began to include industrial and agricultural enterprises in the less well-developed countryside of northern Jiangsu, they opened branches in the area and monitored cotton, yarn, and land prices. In turn, Dasheng's Shanghai office brought the mills with all their affiliated and subsidiary companies into close contact with that metropolis's capital market. Consortiums became the preferred response of banks in the 1920s and 1930s to deal with the greater demand for financial capital and to protect themselves by sharing the investment risk.

The banks' invasive role in Dasheng also illustrates the power struggle between modern and traditional business structures and practices. From the mid-1910s onward, the newly founded Chinese banks had been eager to emulate foreign banks and embrace their concepts of modern and efficient business management.[138] Not surprisingly, conflict arose when the banks had to deal with enterprises like Dasheng, which combined characteristics of the traditional family business with those of a modern business operation. From the banks' point of view, curbing the power of the Zhang family network went hand in hand with gaining control over the Shanghai office, the heart of the Dasheng operation. It is significant that during the restructuring process the banks did not demolish the accounts office but strengthened their own ties with it by making the head of this office their representative and main negotiator.

It appears that by 1922 Zhang Jian had slowly pulled out of the official management of the company, leaving the day-to-day business to the banks but with his own financial assets and interests untouched. Business contacts and loan arrangements were still initiated through personal contacts and networking; yet even Chen Guangfu was unable to save Zhang Jian's position in Dasheng once his bank had decided to reform Dasheng's management by undermining the power of the founder-director. Shareholders who had had to tolerate unfavorable profit distributions under Zhang Jian welcomed the reforms in management and accounting under the consortium: yet the prescribed, rigid profit distribution was intended to benefit the banks and left the shareholders as powerless as before.

In short, even the changes and reforms forced on the enterprise in the 1920s did not automatically turn Dasheng into a truly modern and transparent business institution. However, even in the West the accounting practices and information policies of corporations at the beginning of the twentieth century left much to be desired. For example, between 1900 and 1929, shareholders of the Distillers Company Limited in England were given little information concerning the expansion of the company through investments in other companies. In addition, information on the activities of these subsidiary companies was largely nonexistent in its financial reports, and there was no formal depreciation policy.[139]

Of course, belief in the transparency and accountability of contemporary Western corporations has been damaged since the scandalous collapse of the Enron Corporation because of "fun-house accounting" by reckless managers and auditors.[140] The Enron debacle has been attributed to a combination of aggressive accounting—listing loans as trades on the balance sheet—and an auditing firm with conflicts of interest. Dasheng, in similar fashion, pursued deceptive accounting—listing nonperforming loans as assets—without any outside auditing, at least until the banks became involved. The Enron case has shown that irregular accounting methods still have drastic financial consequences for the shareholders. If in the year 2001 the disaster of "Enron proves how meaningless financial statements have become,"[141] we should be less surprised at Zhang Jian's and Dasheng's attempt to stretch the meaning and interpretation of financial statements in early twentieth-century China.

PART IV

Enterprise and Region

CHAPTER 7

Socioeconomic Control Beyond the Factories

Dominating local industry and society as the largest employer, buyer of raw cotton, and industrial producer of yarn and cloth, Dasheng had an impact on the region's economy at many different levels far beyond the mill compound. Yet, there is also another aspect to the regional nature of Dasheng. Any enterprise on the scale of Dasheng leaves its imprint on the social development of its locality. Indeed, in regional enterprises business and local society are closely linked spheres. This is especially true of enterprises like Dasheng that are under the strict, paternalistic control of a charismatic managing director.

Zhang Jian's interest in local community development, both urban and rural, is apparent in the many modernization projects he initiated and in his restructuring of Nantong city's social and cultural image. As in his management of business institutions, there are issues of control and accountability in his social projects as well. Zhang Jian and his family headed the local elite and had political and social connections on the regional and national levels. These ties lent credibility to his claim to be working for the common good, both locally and nationally.

This chapter begins by analyzing Zhang Jian's land-reclamation projects, which shaped local society along the northern Jiangsu coast by introducing aspects of industrial discipline and hierarchy to these agricultural communities and their organization. The remainder of the chapter discusses the development of Nantong as a city. Urban planning, modern buildings, and social services made the city a model hailed by Chinese and Western contemporaries alike. Indeed, even today, publications by the local government and party authorities base the reappraisal of Zhang Jian as a businessman and industrialist on his remaking of Nantong. Instead of uncritically accepting the praise of Zhang Jian and his achievements, I shall concentrate on investigating the viability of his modernizing efforts, the perception of them among the local population and in public discourse, and their contributions to his personal image, which was part of the social capital he used to support Dasheng.

Recently, a stream of publications has addressed various aspects of urban culture and urban development in Republican China, focusing on Shanghai and Beijing and provincial capitals such as Chengdu and Guangzhou.[1] Certainly, this chapter cannot discuss all the cultural, political, and social issues that accompanied the emergence of the modern city in China and were relevant to Nantong. My aim, rather, is to show the social and cultural embeddedness of Dasheng as a business institution and its consequences for the Nantong region. I will argue that despite Nantong's progressive and enlightened image, its modernization did not lead to the creation of an autonomous civil society. In fact, modernization did not challenge state power and was carried out in a hierarchical and controlled social environment, directed by the local elite under the guidance of the Zhang family. The extent to which these efforts sustained Zhang Jian's business and economic interests is a recurrent theme in this chapter.

Agricultural Enterprises: Cotton Cultivation and Land Reclamation

The land-reclamation companies were important suppliers of raw materials to the textile mills and eventually became financial tools for the Dasheng enterprise. However, these agricultural businesses did more than just provide for the needs of the Dasheng mills. Zhang Jian had more in mind than just procuring good-quality cotton at low prices: he envisioned, at least according to his writings, local economic development that would sustain and promote agriculture, according to Confucian thought the root of the well-being of the state, and at the same time benefit local industry. Thus in developing agriculture in the Nantong area, Zhang Jian envisioned the creation of a "stable" rural society that complemented his "civilizing" efforts in Nantong city.[2]

As noted in Chapter 2, cotton cultivation had flourished in the area long before the introduction of commercial land reclamation. In its first years, Dasheng relied on crops from the nearby villages of Liuhaisha, Baipu, Pingchao, Liuqiao, and Tangjiazha and immediately became the largest consumer of locally produced raw cotton. Tongzhou cotton was valued for its whiteness and its strong yet soft fibers; the highest grade of Tongzhou cotton was called "chicken feet" (*jijiao*) and earned the highest prices on the Shanghai market.[3]

Additional supplies of raw cotton were available from scattered fields in Nantong, Haimen, and Chongming counties; the expanding mills demanded increasingly larger amounts of raw material, as did the rest of the growing cotton industry in China. Dasheng's supply system, however, was not without problems: the collection and purchasing system required extensive supervision and, most important, could not guarantee a steady supply of cotton from one harvest to the next. Land-reclamation companies were hailed as the solution to this predicament; they were envisioned as reliable, professionally supervised suppliers of cotton on a large scale that would reduce Dasheng's expenditures on cotton imported from elsewhere in China and overseas. At least, that was the plan.

The plan came at the right time politically. Salt production had declined along the northern Jiangsu coast in the late nineteenth century, and it had been suggested that abandoned saltfields be converted to agricultural production to help develop the Nantong area (see Chapter 2). Although in the Qing private land reclamation was illegal, Zhang Jian, because of his initial commitment to government-sponsored industrialization, had obtained a special dispensation for the Tonghai Land Reclamation Company, and the company began operations in 1901.[4] Nor was this an isolated case. Agricultural education and agricultural experimentation were much discussed during the reform period between 1901 and 1911.[5] In 1903, for example, the financier Zhang Bishi (1840–1916) submitted a twelve-point memorial to the court and the Board of Trade; among other things, he proposed that merchants be recruited to promote the opening of hill land for cultivation and to develop irrigation and water conservation.[6]

The legal framework that impeded land reclamation did not change until the early years of the Republic. Not surprisingly, Zhang Jian played a role in lifting the ban on private land reclamation. After new laws encouraging commercial land reclamation were introduced under his tenure as minister of agriculture and commerce in 1914, he embarked on the strategic expansion of his operations together with Zhang Cha. He approached reclamation in the same way that he had approached industrial expansion.[7] The results were impressive. Between 1914 and 1933, more than 50 new land-reclamation companies were founded along the northern Jiangsu coast, 20 of them within the boundaries of Nantong, Haimen, and Rugao counties.[8] Fifteen of these, including eight of the eleven largest and most important, companies were founded by the Zhang brothers or in the names of their sons. Zhang Jian was personally in charge of five of these companies; Zhang Cha supervised most of the rest. As in their industrial enterprises, interlocking directorships were a characteristic of these companies as well. Some ten land-reclamation companies were founded by friends and business associates of Zhang Jian. With three exceptions, the cultivation companies run by outsiders to Nantong and Zhang Jian's business circle were less significant in terms of size and capital.[9] Obviously, the cultivation business along the northern Jiangsu coast, particularly within the wider Nantong area, was firmly in the hands of the Zhang family.

A look at a map from the 1920s reveals the extent to which these companies changed the physical appearance of the coastal area of northern Jiangsu (see Map 2). Even more significant is the fact that these commercial agricultural enterprises had a lasting impact on the social and economic organization of people living on the reclaimed land, that is, the former salt producers, the new tenants, and the land-company supervisors.

The Tonghai company provides a useful example of the physical, economic, and social structures of the companies, as well as their organization and day-to-day operations. According to a description dating from 1905, the company was spread over an area of 123,279 mu, roughly 8,382 hectares, and occupied a large part of Haimen county and a lesser though still significant part of Nantong county.[10]

The first step in land reclamation was a costly undertaking. Before beginning the reconstruction, the Tonghai company had to compensate not only the former salt producers but also a military garrison for the loss of their fields and training grounds. In contrast to the difficulties Zhang Jian encountered in raising funds for the Dasheng cotton mill, raising local capital proved to be much easier in the case of Tonghai. The initial capital in 1901 amounted to 156,000 taels, which increased over time to 300,000 taels in 1909.[11] The greater attractiveness of the land-reclamation companies to investors has to be seen in the context of Chinese business culture; land—in contrast to an uncertain industrial business venture—was viewed as the safest form of financial investment.

However, the paid-up capital is less impressive if we consider the substantial costs of the basic construction work.[12] Once Tonghai had taken

Fig. 7.1 Reclamation work on Tonghai company land (Nantong youyi julebu, *Nantong shiye, jiaoyu, cishan fengjing*, 1920, unpaginated).

possession of the land, it was separated by dikes running from north to south into seven sections. Each section bordered the sea in the east and comprised the fields behind the dike to the company's inland border in the west.[13] The next step was to dig irrigation ditches and construct drainages, roads, and bridges. Only then could the task of soil improvement be tackled.

The process of transforming coastal land into agricultural fields required several years of hard work. A photograph dating to the early 1900s (see Fig. 7.1) gives an impression of what the future arable looked like during the initial recovery process. The sandy coastal soil, sparsely grown with grass, is dotted with pools of stagnant, brackish water. Although the porous soil was particularly suitable for growing cotton, it was too saline to permit cultivation. Zhang Jian planned and constructed a series of dikes and sluice gates that kept the seawater out and provided proper drainage for the fields.[14] In order to decrease the salinity of the soil further, the reclaimed land was planted with reeds such as artemisia and other salt-resistant grasses for the first four years.[15] After all these procedures were completed, the land was finally ready for the newly recruited tenants of the Tonghai company to grow cotton and wheat.[16]

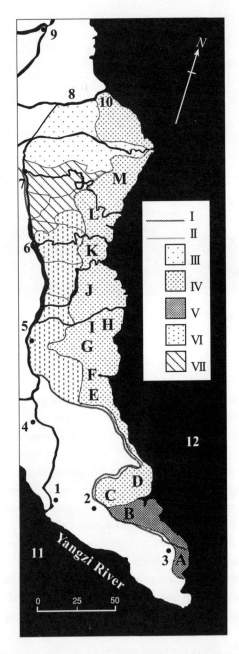

Map 2 Major land-reclamation companies and land use along the northern Jiangsu coast in the late 1910s and early 1920s (adpated from Amano, "Kōhoku no enkon kōshi kō," p. 90; and Sun, *Subei yanken shi chugao*, map following p. 93).

KEY TO MAP 2

Cities and Waterways

1 Nantong	4 Rugao	7 Funing	10 Chenjiagang
2 Jinsha	5 Dongtai	8 Huai river	11 Yangzi River
3 Lüsi	6 Yancheng	9 Donghai	12 East China Sea

Land-Reclamation Companies

A Tonghai	E Dalai	H Suiji	K Dayou
B Dayoujin	F Taiyuan	I Tongsui	L Dagang
C Huafeng	G Zhongfu	J Dafeng	M Huacheng
D Dayu			

Land-Use Types

I Fan gong dike

II The line indicates the distribution of coastal reclamation land under management/ownership of land reclamation companies to the east and the area of individually owned or leased reclamation land to the west

III Area with cereal crops and wheat and beans grown in rotation

IV Area with one cotton crop per year (parts of it were grown in rotation as cotton with wheat, cotton with maize, cotton with bur clover or cotton with broad beans)

V Area with two crops of cotton and wheat (parts of it were grown in rotation as cotton with broad beans, cotton with early season rice or cotton with bur clover)

VI Area with two crops of wheat and rice

VII Area with one crop of paddy rice per year

Nothing was left to chance. The dikes and the drainage system gave the area a distinctive and regulated outlook. As the maps and land deeds of the Tonghai company show, the dike sections and the borders of each plot of land were drawn in a straight and geometrical fashion, and the whole area under the company's control was intersected by drainage canals arranged in a regular grid.[17] Paths and roads were built in straight lines and led directly to the administrative center of each section.[18]

Certainly, the regularity and orderly arrangement of fields and settlements in an area completely shaped and controlled by man are not surprising. However, the extent to which the coastal area and its communities reflect the impact of human control and the absence of natural growth is quite amazing. The geometrical arrangement of drainage canals, roads, and even villages is still visible today (see Fig. 7.2). An obvious example of this kind of rural restructuring is Haifuzhen village, literally the "village retrieved from the sea," which was built on company land after a typhoon destroyed the previous settlement at this location (see Fig. 7.3).[19] The streets within the

Fig. 7.2 Canal in the area of the former Tonghai Land Reclamation
Company, 1995 (photograph by the author).

village were designed to intersect at right angles, and this arrangement left
little leeway for the gradual or random building of residential dwellings. A
walk through the village nowadays, with its perfectly straight main road and
the total absence of irregular side paths and buildings defying the street grid-
pattern, conveys a sense of its artificial orderliness. To contemporary observers in the early twentieth century accustomed to irregularities of natural villages, it must have appeared even more exceptional.

Zhang Jian's progressive plans for his cultivation companies materialized
in a previously underdeveloped and rather inaccessible part of the northern
Jiangsu countryside. Before he began, it took more than three days to reach
the coastal area of Haimen from Nantong city, and there were no proper
roads. One of the achievements of the Tonghai company land was that it
connected Haifuzhen village for the first time with a direct road to the
county seat of Haimen to the south and Nantong city to the north.[20]

The origins of the new settlers who produced much-needed cotton for
the Dasheng textile mills were diverse. Obviously, the salt workers needed a
new means of livelihood and constituted a pool of prospective applicants. As

Fig. 7.3 Straight road in Haifuzhen village, 1995
(photograph by the author).

a source from the 1930s indicates, because of the decline in government-
regulated salt production and rising production costs, most of the salters
perforce had to consider the new forms of employment that came along with
the cultivation projects:

> Ever since [the founding] of the republic, the Salt Administration has made a ruling
> to reduce salt production in the Huainan area year after year. Moreover, because
> reed prices have soared, the profits gained from iron-pan drying in this area are far
> inferior to those from sun-drying in the Huaibei area. Therefore one land-
> reclamation company followed another, turning stove [land] into reclaimed [land].
> Nowadays only slightly more than 20 or 30 percent of the salt workers have not yet
> found another line of work.[21]

As in the case of the Dasheng mills, Zhang Jian left nothing to chance. In
1903, he drew up a set of regulations for Tonghai giving detailed instructions
on hiring tenants. According to the regulations on the recruitment of tenants for company lands within the boundaries of Nantong county, 70 percent were to be recruited from among the former salt workers (*zaomin*) and
30 percent from among the former squatters on the uncultivated coastal

shore (*shamin*). For Tonghai company land within the boundaries of Haimen county, these proportions were reversed.[22] Obviously, Zhang Jian was
aware of tensions and competition between the two groups, since the salt
workers had most probably contested the presence of squatters on the sands
and their illegal use of land before it was opened for reclamation. Although
his companies would have provided both groups with work, Zhang Jian
definitely wanted them to be as spatially separated as possible. As the company regulations expressly stated, "If people from the sands and the salt
workers are mixed together, the company will not be strong."[23]

Salt workers and squatters were not, however, necessarily qualified for
the new agricultural tasks, which demanded substantial experience. In the
event, the Tonghai company and the many other new companies founded in
the 1910s needed to recruit tenants from a much larger pool of people. Indeed, the evidence suggests a huge gap between the hiring process prescribed
in the official company regulations and actual practice.

According to anthropologist Haruhiko Nishizawa, more than 80 percent
of the labor force on reclaimed lands in northern coastal Jiangsu migrated
from Haimen and Qidong counties; former salt workers and squatters accounted for only about 15 percent of the new tenants.[24] In the early 1920s,
more than 90 percent of the tenants of the Dafeng company came from the
Haimen and Qidong counties, with farmers from Haimen in the majority.[25]
The total numbers tell a story of substantial migration within the area: by
1928, about one million farmers from outside the reclamation area had found
a new livelihood on the land-reclamation companies' land. In the case of the
Tonghai company alone, some 80,000–90,000 people moved onto its land
in the years following its establishment.[26]

Not surprisingly, differences in local origins led to friction between the
tenants and the local population, who spoke a different dialect. According to
Qiao Qiming's survey of farm tenancy in Jiangsu between 1922 and 1925, 95.9
percent of the farmers in Nantong—excluding those in the land-reclamation
companies—were native to the area.[27] Based on his interviews with former
tenants of the Dafeng Land Reclamation Company, Nishizawa argues that
since the number of farmers from Haimen was much larger than the local
population, local people adopted some aspects of the Haimen dialect. However, both groups kept to themselves, and there was no intermarriage. To
the contrary, confrontation and disputes about issues like water control of-

ten ended in fistfights between the locals and the tenants from Haimen, who as immigrants to the area found strength in solidarity.[28]

Since the reclamation companies wanted to rent their land to tenants as soon as the basic construction and reclamation work had been finished, the question arises whether enough people were willing to live and work as tenants in an underdeveloped area. Because of the high population and concentration of holdings in the hands of large landlords in the area, the tenancy rate in Nantong was relatively high, and it was difficult for tenants to buy land.[29] Qiao Qiming's survey of tenancy in Jiangsu tracks a growth in tenancy rates in Nantong county from 61.5 percent in 1914 to 64.4 percent in 1924.[30] This trend is confirmed by the data published by Feng Hefa in 1935, who gives the percentage of tenant farmers for the county as 55 percent.[31] In Haimen county the percentage of tenant farmers was only slightly lower, at 50 percent.[32] This compares with an average rate of 40.7 percent in Wuxi county in southern Jiangsu province. Tenancy was definitely more common in the Nantong area than in most of the southern part of the province.[33]

The higher tenancy and lower ownership rates in the Nantong area should not be interpreted simplistically as a sign of a lower standard of living; we need to look more closely at tenancy on the reclaimed lands before we can reach a judgment about living standards. It is difficult to give an exact figure for the number of tenants or households living on company land. A report by the Cultivation Commission of Jiangsu Province, published in 1936, offers a number of 4,485 households for the Tonghai company, with an average of 20 mu under cultivation by each household.[34] The company regulations required a farmer to pay a refundable cash deposit before becoming a tenant, plus a nonrefundable fee on each mu of rented land for drawing up the lease.[35] The absolute sums to be paid by the tenants differed from company to company, and rents depended on the quality of the soil. In the case of the Tonghai company, for example, the available land was divided into three categories according to quality: already cultivated land, land not yet protected by a dike, and land on the mudbanks. According to a report from 1925, the average unit (called a *tiao*) rented out by the Tonghai company to tenants was equal to 25 mu.[36]

How does this amount of land compare with the situation in the rest of the county? According to Qiao Qiming, the average amount of land cultivated by a tenant farmer in Nantong county amounted to 19 mu in 1905, 15 mu in 1914, and only 11.8 mu in 1924. Moreover, the average amount of land farmed by an owner-cultivator in Nantong county decreased from 16.6 mu in 1905 to 12.8 mu in 1914 to 10 mu in 1924.[37] The complex reasons for this trend are not our concerns here, but the favorable situation of tenants of the land-reclamation companies is clear. At the same time, a substantial part of the 25 mu of company land would have included fields of medium and low quality.

The larger amount of land available through the land-reclamation companies must have been an incentive for farmers to begin a new and possibly better life on these reclaimed lands. There were, of course, considerable start-up costs involved in resettlement. For example, aside from the registration fee of 6 yuan per mu to obtain the surface rights to the land, the tenant had to build accommodations for his household and to provide his own farm tools, seeds, and fertilizers. Only tenants with serious intentions and a certain amount of capital were able to settle on Tonghai company land. As we know from oral history reports, the farmers who became tenants of the land reclamation companies did not come from among the poorest, much less the landless, people of the area. In fact, many of the Tonghai company's tenants had exchanged their old farmland in return for a larger amount of the reclaimed land. Although many lived in reed huts in the beginning, most were able to build a brick house after several years. Over time, families also moved from Tonghai to other reclamation companies in the north such as Dafeng, selling the cultivation rights to their improved land at Tonghai at a profit in exchange for a larger amount of newly reclaimed land at Dafeng.[38] Thus, successful tenants with sufficient start-up capital and enough family manpower were able to improve their economic position by profitably switching to new land as it became available with the expansion of land-reclamation companies along the coast.

Day-to-day farming decisions were left to the tenants, even though they were not free to choose what to grow on their land. There were generally two crops a year, a main crop of cotton in the fall and a secondary crop of wheat and beans in the spring.[39] Tenants paid rents to the company twice a year, after the autumn and spring harvests. Instead of paying the spring rent in kind, many tenants preferred to keep the crop and to pay cash to the company.[40] In October the tenants paid the main autumn rent in kind by delivering a fixed share of the cotton harvest to the company. In general, tenants were allowed to retain 60 percent of the cotton crop, and the Tong-

hai company claimed 40 percent.[41] In order to ensure that the company received its proper share, company inspectors examined the tenants' fields before the harvest and in discussion with the tenants decided on the amount of
cotton per mu to be handed over to the company.[42] Estimating the volume
of incoming rent (*yizu*) was a difficult process and required great experience
and agricultural knowledge on the part of the inspectors. At the same time,
the estimates almost always antagonized the tenants, who felt the company
representatives were biased. According to Qiu Yunzhang, a former inspector
for Tonghai, the negotiations were often so tedious that he gave his estimate
to the company accountant in a secret code in order to escape disputes with
the tenant accompanying them.[43]

Despite the regulations, some tenants wanted to concentrate more on
secondary crops, since they obtained better prices for these products on the
local markets or needed them for private use. The company allowed millet to
be grown on the strips of land in front or back of the tenants' dwellings but
not together with cotton in the main fields. In order to secure a steady supply of raw cotton, the company exercised strict control over cropping patterns. Farmers who violated the rules and thus damaged the quality and
amount of cotton were reported to management and at harvest time had to
pay an additional one-sixth in kind as rent and penalty to the company.[44]

Complaints by tenants can only be reconstructed indirectly because of the
lack of written sources, but on the whole relationships between tenants and
company management seemed to have been tense. Tenants could borrow
food and cash from the company in times of bad harvests.[45] These credit arrangements tied the tenants as debtors even closer to the company and its
land, very much like landlords and traditional credit institutions in the villages. Tonghai's tenants complained about the high interest rates charged on
these loans and about the obligation to follow the company's cropping instructions, since they limited the tenants' income from growing vegetables and
other cash crops.[46] Zhang Jian repeatedly expressed his concern about tenants' not paying rent and the serious disputes between managers and tenants
over the amounts of cotton the company claimed tenants owed.[47]

Like the industries under Zhang Jian's control, Tonghai and the other
land-reclamation companies had strict managerial and administrative hierarchies defined by the authoritarian spirit of the founder's company regulations. In the Dasheng textile mills, native place and residential origin very
much decided a person's occupation and his or her social status within the

compound. In the land-reclamation companies, the division between management and tenants was also reflected in different places of origin. The managers and staff of the Tonghai Land Reclamation Company were recruited from outside the area, mostly from Anhui and Zhejiang provinces or from Shanghai and other Jiangsu counties. According to one oral history report, these employees normally obtained their jobs through connections (*guanxi*), for example, a recommendation from a major shareholder.[48] Once the banks became the main creditors of the land-reclamation companies in the 1920s and early 1930s, they sent their own employees from Shanghai to become involved in management.[49] For example, the Futai *qianzhuang* of Shanghai stationed its accountant, Ye Xuyuan, at the Tonghai company in 1933 after the bank took over 1,050 mu of mortgaged land because Tonghai had defaulted on a loan. The accountant's particular task was to supervise the selling of the raw cotton and use the proceeds to pay Tonghai's debts; this gave him an excellent opportunity to observe the financial transactions as well as the day-to-day business of the company.[50]

Each of Tonghai's seven dike sections was under the supervision of a dike manager (*ti jingli*), with seven to eight assistants, employed in the construction, miscellaneous tasks, and reclamation departments. The managers of each section in turn relied on a large number of farmhands hired for manual labor and supervised a number of students from Zhang Jian's agricultural school. All seven dike managers had an office within their respective section and were accountable to and under the control of the company headquarters situated east of Haifuzhen village.[51]

The headquarters of the Tonghai company accommodated the general manager and his staff in impressive office buildings. Their progressive design symbolized Zhang Jian's ambition of imprinting discipline and modern-style efficiency on his enterprises and the people under its control. According to Ye Xuyuan, the former accountant, the central headquarters occupied buildings with 110 rooms on 60 mu of land near Haifuzhen. A proper road with trees planted on both sides led to the complex, where two large cannons hanging over the front entrance, flanked by two tiger-headed tablets, greeted the visitor.[52] Tiger-headed tablets (*hutoupai*) were the traditional insignia of a public office and warned against disorder and misbehavior. The Tonghai headquarters assumed the responsibility for law and order on its land and among the local population and did not hesitate to display its intimidating authority. Ye Xuyuan observed that the headquarters' complex "had very much the awe-inspiring atmosphere of a yamen" (the county magistrate's office).[53]

The administrative and legal aura of the Tonghai headquarters was complemented by a ritual function. At the center of the complex stood a large assembly hall with a rare white bark pine planted in front of it, which Zhang Jian named the Hall of Reverence for Agricultural Farmland (Muchou tang).[54] Since the characters for *muchou* also carry the meaning of "revering the past," the ritual aspect of this assembly hall might be interpreted as a symbolic link between Zhang Jian, his land-reclamation activities, and the cultural importance of agriculture as an expression of civilization in China's past. To put it with slight exaggeration, in a way the assembly hall took the place of an ancestral hall at the Tonghai headquarters.

Although the land-reclamation companies provided a different spatial framework for the social and disciplinary organization of their workforce, as in the mills the life of the tenants was heavily regulated by disciplinary measures. Although Zhang Jian designed the Tonghai company regulations (*Tonghai kenmu gongsi zhaodian zhangcheng*) mainly to provide rules for hiring tenants and for distributing and reclaiming land, a separate part of the regulations called the "tenant agreement" (*dianyue*) regulated the morals and work discipline of the tenants in more or less the same way the factory regulations regulated the mill workers.

The general aim of the agreement was "to have the tenants enjoy together permanent fairness and gain." The agreement comprised two categories of regulations: matters of exhortation (*quan zhi shi*) and matters of punishment (*xing zhi shi*).[55] Tenants were admonished, for example, to exert themselves and "not to waste time."[56] Other regulations contained exact specifications for the building of tenant housing and recommended that the toilet not be too close to the dwelling for hygienic reasons. In an authoritarian tone, the regulations stated expressly that tenants must maintain their physical health in order to be able to give their best at work in the fields.[57] The regulations also covered the planting of trees appropriate to the soil and climate as well as the rearing of animals for private consumption.

The prohibitive part of the regulations clearly gave top priority to the maintenance of moral standards through the fighting of vices. However, the harshest punishment was set aside for growing millet instead of cotton; that led to immediate eviction. Opium smoking also led to an immediate, but unspecified, punishment. Small shops selling opium and allowing gambling on their premises were first to be fined; their owners were to be handed over to the state authorities if they were discovered a second time; and on the third offense, they were evicted. Disobedience toward seniors, theft of company property or livestock from adjacent areas, and involvement in violent brawls resulted in the same punishments. Tenants were forbidden to make changes to trails, ditches, or roads on company land and, in case of violation, had to make restitution and provide labor service ranging from one day to seven days to the company. The head of the household was held responsible for damage committed by children under the age of twelve.[58]

Zhang Jian's tenant agreement reflected his authoritarian and patronizing management style as well as the practical requirements of land-reclamation companies as profit-oriented business institutions—not only the continuing improvement of the soil and the quality and quantity of its major crops and the maintenance of dikes and irrigation canals but also a general work environment ensuring high productivity and the smooth functioning of the operation. Although tenants could not be supervised as constantly and strictly as workers on the shop floor, middle management nevertheless played an important supervisory role. This was not laid down in the rules but is documented in oral histories.

Most of the Tonghai company's managerial staff came from Anhui province; over time, because of their commercial and financial expertise, they moved into the highest positions in the headquarters' accounts office.[59] According to Qiu Yunzhang's recollections, employees from Anhui also monopolized the accountants' positions in the branch offices. The hierarchical and social division between tenants and company employees was enforced by different dialects and social customs because of their different origins; apparently Zhang Jian wanted as much distance between management and tenants as possible. Any socializing beyond the necessary professional contact was to be avoided. Thus, as Qiu Yunzhang remembers, Tonghai's employees were not allowed to attend the weddings, funerals, or festivals of tenants. In addition, company inspectors were not allowed to consume any food or drink provided by tenants when they were estimating the size of the harvest. This rule was strictly enforced. The company sent food and tea to the inspectors working in the fields every day at 10:00 A.M. and wheelbarrows to take them home after work at 4:00 P.M.[60]

In order to enforce the many regulations and prohibitions over the vast area occupied by the company, the Tonghai company had its own patrol force of 140 guards organized into three divisions. Many of the guards came from outside the Nantong and Haimen area. They were stationed at the administrative headquarters south of the arms depot and received a generous monthly salary.[61] Initially, the Tonghai company had established a small guard station in each of the sections. However, as one oral history report puts it, without strict supervision, these scattered police guards "were up to no good" and had to be reintegrated into the main force at the headquarters. From then on, tenants, who received a small plot of land as compensation for their service, took over the guard stations and notified the company of irregularities.[62]

To a considerable extent, the Tonghai company assumed the executive and legislative functions of local civil administration over the company land and its inhabitants. Of course, officially the company had no legal authority acknowledged by the state. However, whenever disputes arose among the tenants, they first sought mediation through the company representative in charge of the section.[63] If the matter could not be resolved at this level, the tenants would then take the matter to Tonghai's headquarters near Haifu-zhen village. Most of the cases were settled at this stage; the few that could not be were passed to the local government authorities. The lack of existing communities and the subsequent slow growth of natural village communities and their intrinsic social hierarchies might have helped Tonghai establish and ensure the company's authority in the areas of law and order.

In the context of social controls, the school system introduced by the Tonghai company is another example of Zhang Jian's efforts to shape the agricultural communities according to his paternalistic aspirations. The tenant agreement stipulated that a primary school was to be established in every section, and the tenants' children were to receive four years of basic education.[64] This institutionalized program of providing primary education for tenants' children was later imitated by other land-reclamation companies. According to a 1935 survey cited by Wang Shuhuai, fifteen land-reclamation companies along the northern Jiangsu coast operated a total of 58 primary schools, with an average of about 90 pupils per school at that time.[65] However, when we consider that this works out to 5,162 children in the entire land-reclamation area, the success of the project appears more modest.

Certainly, the small number of schools and the low level of attendance reflects the state of education in the Nantong area during the late imperial and Republican periods. According to Qiao Qiming's tenancy survey, which includes all farming households in Nantong county, 29 percent of children in tenant households attended lower primary school, compared to 64.6 percent of children from landowning households. As one would expect, attendance at the higher primary school was even lower: only 4.9 percent of children from tenant households and 19.8 percent of children from landowning households.[66]

On the surface Zhang Jian's program to establish schools in his land-reclamation companies appears to be an act of sheer altruism and philanthropy for the benefit of modernization and regional development. Nevertheless, his aspirations were, of course, anchored in the context of Chinese society and its social order. Zhang Jian did not interpret education as a means of equal access to career choices independent of social status. On the contrary, and not surprisingly, education for him was a means to keep people in their place within society. His educational programs were part of his life-long promotion of local self-government as a sociopolitical model for the good of society and nation. And as we will see below, his view was shared by many of his contemporaries in the local elite. Of significance here is the fact that education paired with control constituted Zhang Jian's paternalistic and authoritarian vision of development, in the industrial as well as in the agricultural context. His introduction to the tenant agreement's rules on education is a perfect case in point. The opening sentence reads: "When only a few people are able to read and write, rowdiness follows easily; but when many people are able to read and write, families prosper easily."[67] Obviously, his promotion of education on Tonghai land was also based on practical considerations. At the same time, his pleas for education as a tool to secure public order and social stability allowed him to justify his exercise of social control over the Tonghai tenants, since it would benefit them and ultimately society at large.

Another piece of evidence demonstrating Zhang Jian's paternalistic approach to education is his suggestion for continuing education in the tenant agreement. He decided that after four years of primary school "some [of the students] enter an agricultural school, some enter an engineering school, and some do neither, whatever suits them."[68] Although one could interpret Zhang Jian's proposal as a practical way to improve the skills of his tenants and prospective staff for the benefit of the company, it also confirms his attitude toward the social status of the tenant families: by acquiring knowledge useful either for farming or construction on reclamation land, their children would stay connected to the land and the occupational options it could offer. Zhang Jian's opinions reflect general attitudes toward new forms of education at the time. In contrast to education for the elite, for people with low social status obtaining knowledge for its own sake was not a desirable aim in itself; rather, their education had to have a practical orientation. Most important, the recipients of this education were not to harbor ambitions outside their inherited place in rural society.

Despite the complex and to a certain degree problematic nature of Zhang Jian's land-reclamation projects, his promotion of agriculture and his successes in land cultivation did create new opportunities for a large number of people. The creation of a stable and prosperous livelihood for the local population through land reclamation was one of Zhang Jian's favorite subjects. He discussed it at length in his personal writings, and it features prominently in published descriptions of his political life.[69] The following passage, recorded by his biographer, illustrates Zhang Jian's motivation for land reclamation based on his impression of the situation in the Nantong region:

In my childhood, I lived the life of a peasant family in Haimen. Although Tongzhou [Nantong] and Haimen are bordering areas, their people are totally different. Tongzhou [Nantong] people do not care to move away from their native land; they rarely move to other places to make a living. . . . People from Haimen are different. After establishing the Dasheng cotton mills, I often went to Shanghai, where I came to realize that 90 percent of the people who pull rickshaws and push carts are people from Haimen or Chongming. I have investigated their living conditions and found that they lead a very tough life. The reason why they go to Shanghai to make a living is just that they have no land they can cultivate, and that forces them to leave.[70]

Although we have to acknowledge Zhang Jian's empathy with the hard life of rickshaw pullers, his observation was factually wrong. It is true that about 80 to 90 percent of the rickshaw pullers came from northern Jiangsu,[71] but, as Hanchao Lu notes in his detailed study on Republican Shanghai, the majority of rickshaw pullers came from the poorest counties in the northernmost part of Jiangsu province, such as Dongfang, Yancheng, or Funing; immigrants from Haimen and Nantong were economically better off and for the most part had better jobs.[72] Nevertheless, those forced to work as rickshaw pullers in Shanghai often remained unmarried or had to leave their families behind in the village. Thus it is fair to say that through the land-reclamation companies, Zhang Jian created opportunities for many farmers from Haimen and Qidong counties to remain with their families and farm. Otherwise, many more might have migrated to Shanghai and been exposed to the harsh realities of urban life in the early twentieth century.

In our discussion of Dasheng as a business institution, it is important to remember that the land-reclamation operations were intended to make money, despite Zhang Jian's social and moral aspirations. As for their economic impact, here it suffices to say that the monopoly exercised by the Dasheng textile mills was certainly enhanced by the guaranteed supply of cotton from the land-reclamation companies at below market prices. As Zhang Jian put it succinctly, "the land-reclamation business is, on the one hand, a plan to develop the region and, on the other hand, a plan to achieve profit for the entrepreneur."[73]

The most important social consequence of the land-reclamation companies was their establishment of distinct hierarchies and strict social and economic controls over the communities in the area. Zhang Jian ran the land-reclamation companies with the same institutional tools he used in his industrial enterprises. Dike sections, grid patterns, and prescribed growth created a framework for the organization of space, which was complemented by regulations organizing behavior and productivity. Zhang Jian managed to translate his system of industrial discipline into an effective disciplinary system for agricultural enterprises operating in a different physical and cultural context but along the same institutional principles.

The fact that Zhang Jian presented his land-reclamation companies as elements in the larger projects of local self-government and development gave his projects an aura of social responsibility and commitment. Company management and civil administration became almost inseparable in the area. I would argue that the agricultural context allowed Zhang Jian to achieve greater influence in the reclamation area than in the factory compound. Whereas unskilled mill workers returned home after their shift, the tenants experienced the company's presence in every aspect of their lives and at all times.

The Model City: Nantong's Social Modernization

Once Zhang Jian's industrial and agricultural projects were well under way, Nantong city became the focus of his efforts to create a modern urban center for the region.[74] With its many educational and welfare facilities, cultural institutions, impressive infrastructure, and modern architecture, Nantong city had become a symbol of Zhang Jian's vision of regional development by the late 1910s and early 1920s. In his strategy, economic development was to be combined with social development for the public good. All of Zhang Jian's civic projects simultaneously introduced aspects of modernity and scientific rationality with regard to urban planning, municipal administration, education, and management of institutions. Thus it is not surprising that in the 1920s the word "model" (*mofan*) was widely applied to the city in contemporary Chinese and foreign publications.

As we know from newspaper articles and diaries, visitors to Nantong in the late 1910s and 1920s were strongly impressed by the variety of welfare institutions and modern facilities. Clearly for them, these facilities set this particular town apart from the underdeveloped surroundings of rural northern Jiangsu. The amazement expressed by a Western visitor to Nantong in 1922 is typical:

Landing on a rock-built jetty, the visitor to Nantungchow is taken by motor-bus to the city over a new highway built up like a dyke to protect the land from the overflow of the Yangzi. Once in the city, he is whisked about around the lakes and over the graceful, 12-arch bridge which spans them; is taken to inspect the various schools of many kinds and the institutions for the aged infirm, the blind, and the orphans; is put up at a new and clean Chinese hotel. . . . Throughout China there is no other city built as Nantungchow has been, under the personal direction of one man. At every turn is to be seen the embodiment of the ideas of His Excellency Chang Chien [Zhang Jian]. Everything is typical of modern thought and development.[75]

Like many others, Chinese as well as Westerners, this visitor attributed the "modern thought and development" displayed in the city to the personal influence of Zhang Jian. In a sense, one can almost speak of a "Nantong culture," characterized by Zhang Jian's intention to turn this economically and socially rather backward area into a modern, developed region with Nantong city as the experimental model and showcase.

Nantong's political and cultural history during the late imperial and Republican periods has been dealt with elsewhere.[76] The following pages focus instead on analyzing how Zhang Jian exerted control over much of Nantong's public domain, whether accountability came into play, and how his social activities in the city were connected to his business interests.

Another question of concern here is whether these new institutions had a serious impact on the life of people in Nantong city. To be sure, many of the city's institutions compared favorably not only with those prevalent in the

Nantong area but also with national standards in the early Republic. One would assume that welfare and educational institutions most benefited the poor and needy in Nantong city and its surroundings, since Zhang Jian was said to have succeeded "in transforming his wretched birthplace into a modern industrial town where there is not a single beggar and where everyone is prosperous."[77] As we will see, this was not quite the case.

A look at local gazetteers, guidebooks, and anniversary publications from the early Republican period proves that Nantong indeed had facilities of which it could be proud. A map from the early 1920s shows the cluster of welfare institutions in the inner city of Nantong, and their floor plans, like the factory plans, can be found in the local gazetteer published in the mid-1920s.[78] Because of its history as an imperial county seat, the walled city of Nantong was a confined urban space and had little to do with the factory sites in Tangjiazha and other parts of the region. On the other hand, Zhang Jian's factories are notable for the absence of medical, educational, and recreational facilities; almost all his welfare and charity projects were concentrated in the heart of the city.[79]

As in the case of the land-reclamation companies, education became one of the most important symbols and vehicles of modernization in Nantong city. Zhang Jian became famous for his efforts to modernize the existing school system, and his plans to expand it beyond the city walls through a regular network of primary schools in the area featured prominently in his writings.[80] Despite his ambitious plans, however, most of the new schools were located within Nantong city, and the network of rural schools never materialized. Thus a guidebook from 1920 stressed that only Nantong city was well equipped with primary schools and four institutions of higher learning: a normal, an agricultural, a commercial, and a medical school.[81] In contrast, the rest of the county was poorly equipped with schools above the lower primary level and could boast, for example, only 60 higher primary schools.[82]

Who could afford to attend these schools and institutions? It is not surprising that the modernized school system in Nantong benefited mostly the inhabitants of that city. The schools set up by Zhang Jian were not free of charge. In fact, the fees clearly limited access to the schools to Nantong residents with considerable disposable income. Advertisements in the local newspaper by the Nantong Women's Normal School to recruit new students corroborate this point: in 1915 the school charged a student 12 yuan as an administration fee plus 16 yuan for meals and, if necessary, 40 yuan for board, per year.[83] Even the minimum cost of 28 yuan per year for fees and meals was equivalent to almost ten months' wages of an unskilled worker in the Dasheng cotton mills. In contrast, it was about a quarter of the monthly salary of a manager.[84]

Other cultural and educational facilities founded by Zhang Jian operated in a similar fashion. Because of his own scholarly career and continuing interests in classical literature, poetry, and calligraphy, the establishment of a public library in Nantong was one of Zhang Jian's pet projects. The library, housed in spacious buildings, opened its doors to the public in 1912. As one of its first catalogues shows, most of the books were donated by the Zhang brothers and institutions under their patronage, with contributions from a few other prominent figures of Nantong's cultural elite.[85] However, access to the books was not free of charge. Short-term borrowers had to pay two copper coins per day, and long-term readers were charged a fee of two yuan per year.[86] Again, although contemporary sources advertised the library as an educational facility for the whole community of Nantong, it clearly favored the "middle class" of the city, which could afford the required fees. Arguably, the selective access ensured that the modern, pristine premises of the library were not overrun by the poor and socially less acceptable.

From reading contemporary reports, one might conclude that Zhang Jian the generous donor sponsored these institutions throughout his lifetime. However, in most cases, for example, the schools, the expenses for their day-to-day operation were covered by the government or by fees charged to the students—a common practice in educational philanthropy at the time. Not surprisingly, the schools receiving Zhang Jian's particular patronage were modern schools based on Western models, such as the Normal School and specialized vocational and professional institutions such as the Agricultural and Medical schools. These new schools, founded mostly in the 1910s, brought prestige to Nantong and Zhang Jian but catered to a selective, limited pool of applicants from among the urban, educated residents with professional aspirations. In contrast, the school that contributed the most to the general education of the local population and had the largest number of pupils (310 altogether), the No. 7 Middle School, was neither founded nor sponsored by Zhang Jian, and its annual budget of almost 24,000 yuan was completely paid by the government.[87]

Although many of Zhang Jian's projects occupied a prominent place in Nantong's urban landscape because they were housed in impressive modern, often Western-style buildings, the founding of new schools was relatively easy and inexpensive. Instead of a new facility, in many cases the school building was provided by turning a temple into a classroom. This was the case with the Nantong Normal School, which Zhang Jian opened in 1902 by transforming the Thousand Buddha Temple (Qianfo *si*) into a building with classrooms. Nantong's religious community evidently did not protest, and even if protest had occurred, Zhang Jian's positive relationship with the more prominent Buddhist monasteries and clergy in the area would probably have served him well. Buddhist, Daoist, and other types of temples served traditionally as public venues for classes of charitable schools. In the eighteenth and nineteenth centuries, renovating a temple was often considered a less expensive option than building a new schoolhouse in an urban area with high real estate prices.[88] Turning temples into classrooms became an even more common practice during the educational reforms of the late Qing and early Republican period when large numbers of newly founded schools needed readily available and inexpensive accommodation. In the early twentieth century, more than 60 school buildings in Nantong county had previously served as temples.[89]

Most of Nantong's welfare institutions were initiated but not financially supported on a long-term basis by Zhang Jian. For example, the orphanage east of Tangjiazha, which served the city of Nantong as well as its surroundings, was founded by Zhang Jian and Zhang Cha in 1906.[90] Its substantial annual budget of 24,000 yuan had to be funded from several sources, particularly the county government and the rental income from land, another traditional form of financing schools in China. The orphanage had been given 24 mu of land, which it rented to tenants in order to pay salaries and daily expenses. It also received some interest income from an unspecified source.[91]

Many of the welfare projects initiated by the Zhang brothers operated without their continuing financial sponsorship. The old peoples' home relied completely on rental income and, like the home for crippled persons, raised its own funds. Zhang Jian's home for the moral improvement of fallen women relied on donations and taxes from local prostitutes.[92] The expenses of a school run by Buddhist monks that Zhang Jian founded at the Temple of Abundant Truth (Guangjiao *si*) on Wolf Hill (Langshan) near Nantong city were covered by the temple through the income from sales of incense and other religious paraphernalia.[93] As Zhang Jian became increasingly interested in Buddhism during the later part of his life, he supported the temple through his patronage and educated two of the monks at the Nantong Normal School to become teachers and finally also administrators and managers of public affairs in the Langshan area.[94]

One project described in contemporary sources as "completely managed by the founders," Zhang Jian and his brother, was the workhouse for the poor in Nantong city. Strangely enough, this institution is the only one for which we have no information on the annual budget. According to one description, the residents labored in nine different workshops and produced simple consumer goods like fans.[95] The production must have been substantial since a national travel guide from 1926 recommended both the workhouse for the poor as well as the prison workshops, also founded by Zhang Jian, as places to buy handicraft items in Nantong city.[96] Perhaps the workhouse made a profit from its manufacturing operation and did not need outside financial help.

Beyond his role as donor and patron, Zhang Jian used his projects in Nantong city to introduce his vision of social order and modern efficiency to local urban society: on the inside through strict rules and on the outside through modern architecture. The welfare institutions founded by Zhang Jian had regulations like those of his factories.[97] Many of those regulations were published by Zhang Jian's own publishing house and circulated in print to reinforce his authoritarian approach to social development in the context of urban modernization. For example, the rules for the orphanage specified in detail the duties and obligations of the orphans with regard to work, education, and behavior. Even the Gengsu theater, founded by Zhang Jian because of his personal interest in classical Chinese opera, had a set of rules to educate the audience; theatergoers were enjoined, for example, not to spit on the floor or to shout improperly.[98]

The external characteristics of institutional discipline are obvious from maps found in Nantong's local gazetteer from the mid-1920s. The workhouse and the home for prostitutes resembled a factory compound in their disciplined, almost militaristic appearance.[99] In a similar fashion, the new prison, which was built in Nantong under Zhang Jian's supervision in 1917, was structured like a factory compound with seven different workshops (*chang*) for, among other things, the production of soap and wooden and bamboo utensils, and even for tailoring and weaving.[100] Michel Foucault has demonstrated the influence of military discipline on industrial discipline in

Western societies and their rigid control of the individual's autonomy over the use of his or her body, space, and time.[101] Without addressing this complex issue in more detail, I think that, as in the case of his industrial and agricultural companies, Zhang Jian's educational, welfare, and cultural organizations illustrate his attempt to introduce a disciplined society. Nantong's new prison presents the perfect example of how profit-oriented factory production and institutional enforcement of punitive discipline went hand in hand in the name of the public good and modern social development.

Based on the cases analyzed here, we have to redefine Zhang Jian's role in the modernization of Nantong city through educational and welfare institutions. His academic background as a Hanlin scholar, his social position as a local dignitary, and his financial resources enabled him to initiate a variety of projects ostensibly for the benefit of the Nantong community. However, these were often convenient ways for Zhang Jian to exert his influence without having to commit himself too deeply financially. Instead, the local government frequently provided operational funding, or the institution might survive on rental income, whereas the land from which rent was drawn might remain in his possession.[102] In some instances, when he did subsidize the institution, his position might enable him to claim part of its potential profits.

Zhang Jian's elevated social position derived from his enthusiasm for setting up educational and welfare projects and reflected his aspirations to local political and moral leadership. His position gave him clout and prestige beyond Nantong city and the region, which he was able to use in Shanghai to benefit his businesses, as well as to further his political power at the provincial and national levels. However, good deeds alone would not have been sufficient to transform Nantong city into Zhang Jian's private domain. For that, he utilized existing networks and made strategic use of public relations.

Local Networks and Nantong Culture

Nantong as a city developed independently from the industrial enterprises in the countryside. The last years of the Qing dynasty and the early Republican period witnessed the emergence of a new social stratum, which for reasons of simplicity I shall call the "middle class," although, of course, the term is an anachronism. Nantong's new middle class consisted of merchants and business people connected with the cotton trade, engineers employed in the mills, teachers in the new professional schools, small shareholders with stakes in Zhang Jian's companies, and members of the gentry now busy with committees organizing local self-government, to name just a few. With the founding of Nantong's new welfare, cultural, and educational institutions in the early twentieth century, organizations and associations began to spring up everywhere, and the publication of newspapers mushroomed. Obviously, in the wake of political reform and socioeconomic modernization, concerned community members needed forums to express their opinions.

The city and region of Nantong serve as a good example for evaluating the extent to which professional associations (*fatuan*) were able to take root in society during the early Republican period. Chambers of commerce, farmers' associations, study societies, and welfare committees had by then spread throughout the Nantong area. These government-sponsored institutions, in the words of Keith Schoppa, were intended "to control the localities more effectively by co-opting elite political roles" and at the same time "offered greater promise of local initiative and autonomy" to the local elites.[103] They addressed the agenda of different occupational groups but saw their work in the context of service to the public. In particular the chambers of commerce wielded considerable political and economic clout even as they tackled community-related issues.[104] The interests of merchants and businessmen in the region were represented by the general chamber of commerce (*zongshanghui*) based in Nantong, which represented the four counties of Nantong, Chongming, Haimen, and Taixing.[105]

Zhang Jian's personal networks dominated the chamber of commerce. Zhang Cha was its president, and the list of board members reads like a Who's Who of Zhang Jian's business associates and friends. Senior managers of the Dasheng mills such as Shen Jingfu and Xu Jingren, the director of the Shanghai accounts office, Wu Jichen, and Zhang Jian's son, Zhang Xiaoruo, as well as representatives from his affiliated companies like the Guangsheng Oil Mill and from institutions under his sponsorship such as the Nantong Club decided through their financial and social influence the policies and activities of this chamber.[106] The chamber's income was based on fees from cloth, cotton, and yarn merchants and on monthly fees from shops. Zhang Jian paid his dues through the accounts of the Dasheng No. 1 mill; some of the companies in the Dasheng group such as the Tongming Electrical Company even held small deposits with the chamber, in this case, 1,300 yuan in 1930.[107]

The power of the chamber of commerce as an organization, beginning in the late Qing period, to negotiate local economic disputes and the social and political implications of this power should not be underestimated. For example, when the Anhui merchant Zhu Chou tried to establish a mill on Chongming island in 1902, Zhang Jian successfully mobilized the Shanghai Chamber of Commerce to intervene on his behalf.[108] Zhang Jian argued, successfully, that the area would not sustain the business of two competing companies. Without doubt, his business clout in Shanghai and his national reputation helped him in promoting his claim. Only after 1924 do sources mention the Datong Spinning and Weaving Company (Datong fangzhi gongsi) as the first "outsider" textile mill in Chongming.[109] The curtailing of local competition in the Nantong area through the chamber of commerce, whose authority was conferred and supported by the state, obviously worked to the advantage of Zhang Jian.

Another example of significant power exercised by a local organization in Nantong operating with the explicit approval of the state is the farmers' association (*nonghui*). Like the chamber of commerce, the farmers' association assumed functions formerly performed by the local government. As we know from lawsuits filed in Nantong, the farmers' association had been granted authority to decide land disputes. The parties in disputes about the ownership and rights to land first turned to the association for a decision. Only when an appeal was rejected was the case referred to the county magistrate.[110]

Apart from making use of local networks institutionalized in the various associations and organizations, Zhang Jian also relied on more informal local networks for support, in particular for his educational projects, by taking advantage of his close relationships, both business and social, with distinguished members of the local elite. For example, Sha Yuanbing (1864–1927), a highly respected holder of the *jinshi* degree from neighboring Rugao county, became a close friend of Zhang Jian and supported his plans to expand the local educational system by establishing the first normal school in Rugao.[111] Needless to say, the men were connected through mutual business interests; Sha Yuanbing served as director general of the Guangsheng Oil Mill, a subsidiary of the Dasheng No. 1 mill.[112]

Zhang Jian's association with leaders of the scholarly elite in the Nantong region not only earned him practical support for his educational projects but also contributed substantially to his elevated public image. The scholar Fan Dangshi (1854–1904) of Nantong is just one example of how Zhang Jian, after starting his career as a businessman, continued to socialize with famous literati of the region. Like Zhang Jian, Fan Dangshi supported the political and educational reforms of the late Qing dynasty.[113] Both men had studied together, and as the holder of a *juren* degree, Fan Dangshi enjoyed a great reputation for scholarship and thus social prestige in the area. Through their highly visible association, Fan Dangshi's sophistication and merits indirectly reflected on Zhang Jian's own aspirations to dominate local culture.

Zhang Jian maintained his presence and cultural authority over local society through the exchange and circulation of his calligraphy, artwork, and poetry, through prominent inscriptions on private and public buildings, and through his voluminous publications. Traditionally, the assumption of a leadership role based on scholarly achievements automatically implied leadership based on moral and cultural superiority. As one would expect of a man with his academic background, Zhang Jian was always eager to display his cultural and moral sophistication, which complemented, and to an extent even overshadowed, his business persona in public opinion. By managing to attract attention and support from both the commercial and the cultural elites as well as from the local government, Zhang Jian was able to capture the Nantong public arena for his own purposes. All three realms—business, culture, and local politics—became part of what I call Zhang Jian's "Nantong culture." Although only a rather imaginary concept in the beginning, Nantong culture began to reinforce itself through the various modernization projects and architectural monuments and gained momentum as a concept in public discourse about local development and self-government in the 1910s and 1920s.

In this context, the design and arrangement of public spaces in Nantong city became important aspects of Zhang Jian's modernization program. In order to give the city a distinctive appearance through its architecture, Zhang Jian hired architect Sun Zhixia (1882–1975), a graduate of the Nantong Normal School and one of the first Chinese architects to be inspired by Western architecture.[114] The issues of urban planning, social transformation, and modernity in Republican China are too complex to address here; suffice it to say that the architecture of the buildings erected under Zhang Jian's supervision served several purposes: it expressed the self-perceptions and social hierarchies of the buildings' occupants as well as the ideological program behind the functional use of the buildings.

The functional modern architecture of educational and welfare institutions in Nantong city is discussed above. The architecture of cultural and

Fig. 7.4 Zhang Jian's residence in Nantong city along the Haohe canal (Nantong
youyi julebu, *Nantong shiye, jiaoyu, cishan fengjing*, 1920, unpaginated).

private buildings catered more to the tastes of Nantong's middle class and its
social aspirations, which were influenced by developments in nearby
cosmopolitan Shanghai. Sun Zhixia's design for the Nantong Friendship
Club (Nantong youyi julebu), built in 1921, imitates the Renaissance-style
architecture of the German Club "Concordia" on the Bund in Shanghai.[115]
In similar fashion, Nantong's noveaux riches documented their wealth and
social position by introducing the villa (*bieshu*) to Nantong's urban architecture. With Western-style facades and Chinese-style interiors, these
buildings presented a modern appearance as large detached houses without
courtyards, ostensibly situated in the scenic spots along the canal, one of
Nantong's main thoroughfares.[116] Zhang Jian, Zhang Cha, and prominent
Dasheng investors such as Liu Yishan and Gao Anjiu all built villas within
the walled city (see Fig. 7.4 and Fig. 7.5). Since Zhang Jian and his brother
were newcomers to Nantong in terms of native place and economic status,
the location of their villas in the center of the old walled city could be
interpreted as confirmation that they had arrived.[117]

Of course, welfare institutions and associations existed in Nantong long

Fig. 7.5 Zhang Cha's residence in Nantong city along the Haohe canal (Nantong youyi julebu, *Nantong shiye, jiaoyu, cishan fengjing*, 1920, unpaginated).

before the arrival of Zhang Jian. Local gazetteers document the existence of institutions such as foundling homes in the late seventeenth century.[118] Associations such as temple societies, charitable societies, and merchant organizations enabled people to gain representation as a professional or social group. For example, local cloth merchants formed their own professional association (*huabu hang*), and merchants from outside the Nantong region gathered into organizations based on native place (*huiguan*) (see Fig. 7.6).[119] However, in contrast to the chambers of commerce of the early twentieth century, these associations did not receive their authority from the government and were thus limited in their negotiation of private interests vis-à-vis the state.

Local associations and organizations can be found in the surrounding counties as well. In the nineteenth century, members of the local gentry in Rugao city became increasingly involved in the management of public institutions and founded an orphanage, several old people's homes, and charity associations.[120] At the same time trade associations (*gongsuo*) for the metal trade and for tobacco, incense, money, timber, and meat shops were founded.[121] However, in the wake of the Qing reforms, organizations were

Fig. 7.6 Entrance to the compound of the Xin'an gongshangtang, the former
Anhui *huiguan* in Nantong city, 1995 (photograph by the author).

less successful in the rural, poorer parts of the Nantong area. As one of
many examples, a 1925 source complained that the members of the Chongming farmers' association, established in the early twentieth century, were
in fact not farmers, and that real farmers would not join the association.[122]
The success of the various organizations and associations in Nantong city
certainly owes much to the participating residents and their middle-class
status, agenda, and expectations.

Newspapers and the Public Realm

Newspapers, local publications, and public discourse in general publicized
Zhang Jian's modernization efforts and helped consolidate his personal domain. Almost every organization or institution in the city published its own
history or annual reports: the general chamber of commerce for the Nantong area published its annual records; the orphanage, its guidelines; and the
agricultural school, a description of its general activities, to name a few.[123] In
addition, publications celebrating Nantong's achievements in community
development became increasingly popular and numerous in the late 1910s
and 1920s. In this context it is no exaggeration to say that Zhang Jian's Nan-

tong Friendship Club was the city's informal public relations agency. The club was responsible for editing and publishing local guidebooks as well as materials concerning Zhang Jian such as the anniversary books documenting his success in modernizing Nantong.[124] The club's publications in Nantong appeared through Hanmolin, Zhang Jian's publishing company. The more sophisticated books with photographs and English explanations, aimed at a wider audience and even foreign readers, were published by the Commercial Press in Shanghai.[125]

The emergence of a widespread commercial and noncommercial printing culture leads ineluctably to the discussion of the role of the public sphere in modernization and urban development in China. The changing relationship between state and local society in late imperial and Republican China as reflected in the public discourse is a particularly complex issue and has attracted much attention in the literature.[126] The problematic use of the Western concept of "public sphere" and its application to Chinese society in the early twentieth century has been at the center of an energetic debate among China historians since the 1990s.[127] Without rehashing the details of this now somewhat stale debate, in the following pages I use the term "public sphere" in the most general meaning given it by Jürgen Habermas as "a domain of our social life in which such a thing as public opinion can be formed."[128]

In terms of the influence exerted by Nantong's various organizations and their publications on public opinion, I argue that at the beginning of the twentieth century we are dealing with several separate, coexisting public spheres with limited access instead of one freely accessible public sphere in the city. However, these separate public spheres were ultimately subsumed under the new Nantong culture controlled by Zhang Jian. Crossing the boundaries between official bureaucracy and local society, chairing or at least represented in all organizations, committees, and institutions, he was able to take control of Nantong's local society while simultaneously enhancing his profile in national public opinion.

For this reason, Zhang Jian's reputation was, of course, propagated in national publications with a circulation beyond the Nantong region. For example, the jubilee volume celebrating the fiftieth anniversary of the widely read and distinguished *Shenbao* newspaper in 1922 contained a preface written by Zhang Jian in his own renowned calligraphy.[129] Other contributors to the issue included the most illustrious writers of early Republican China, such as Hu Shi with an essay on philosophy, Ma Yinchu on finance, and

Liang Qichao and Sun Yat-sen on politics. Zhang Jian thus continued to be linked to China's intellectual and political elite in the 1910s and 1920s, even though by that time he was concentrating more on local reforms than on national politics.

Zhang Jian and his social enterprises in Nantong were also widely acknowledged by the foreign community. Westerners saw in him the personification of their concept of a modern China and a solution to all social ills they identified with traditional Chinese society. Spurred by enthusiastic reports from missionaries and social activists on Nantong, Westerners could not refrain from praising Zhang Jian as "the twentieth century Aladdin."[130] The *North China Herald*'s long, respectful obituary stressed his political, social, and welfare—but not industrial—commitments and referred to the land-reclamation projects as the heart of his enterprise.[131]

To be sure, we should not pay too much attention to the praise of Westerners, who accepted all the positive reports about Nantong and Zhang Jian at face value. Yet, their reaction demonstrates the success of Zhang Jian's public relations strategy. Even more important, Western reactions found their way back into the Nantong papers and there reinforced the image promoted by the local media. For example, the travel report of Gretchen Fitkin, who is quoted above, found its way into the *Tonghai xinbao* newspaper in an article titled "China's Model County in the Eyes of a Foreigner."[132]

Zhang Jian's control over Nantong's society also left its imprint on the local newspaper culture. Nantong newspapers and other local publications in the early twentieth century were not an open forum accessible to the public and differing opinions; rather, they were heavily dependent on Zhang Jian and his patronage. Although Zhang Jian did not own the *Tonghai xinbao*, the area's most important newspaper covering Nantong city and the surrounding counties, he had a close ally in the newspaper in Chen Baochu, a prominent landlord with substantial investments in the Dasheng cotton mills, who, together with three associates, published the paper.[133] Chen Baochu's appointment as director of Dasheng in 1941 under the Wang Jingwei regime during the Japanese occupation (see Chapter 8) makes his relationship with Zhang Jian and the enterprise even more significant. Not surprisingly, the *Tonghai xinbao* never published a word of criticism of Zhang Jian. Nor did it ever discuss the situation of the factories and sensitive social issues such as labor and housing conditions. If Zhang Jian's companies were mentioned in the newspapers at all, it was because new equipment had been acquired or because a foreign engineer had arrived at the mill.[134] Since Zhang Jian was the most prominent dignitary in Nantong, the newspapers reported on his welfare and educational commitments almost daily. No donation was too small to be overlooked. For example, in January 1915, the *Tonghai xinbao* reported that he had donated "sixteen yuan plus a pair of old shoes" to the old people's home in Nantong.[135] This announcement presented Zhang Jian the way he wanted to be seen in the public: a donor who added a personal touch to his support of the poor and needy.

The image of benevolence and social concern extended to his companies, whose donations for flood relief or other charitable purposes were documented by the newspaper in great detail. This method of indirect advertising—Zhang Jian was always identified with his industrial enterprises—was far more successful than the direct promotion of his businesses could have been. Zhang Jian was not exceptional in enhancing his business reputation through charity work. For example, the owner of several cotton mills and vice-president of the Chinese Cotton Mill Owners' Association, Nie Yuntai (1880–1953), campaigned for the establishment of vocational schools and for many years was director of the YMCA in China.[136] The famous Shanghai comprador-turned-investor Zhu Baosan (1848–1926) was a cofounder of the Chinese Red Cross society and was active on behalf of many other welfare and educational institutions.[137] Another example is Jian Zhaonan (1870–1923), the founder of the Nanyang Brothers Tobacco Company. According to Sherman Cochran's detailed study of the enterprise, in terms of business strategies "one of the most elaborate and expensive investments in publicity was made in the form of philanthropy."[138] The Nanyang company made charitable contributions to needy Cantonese and, for example, sent ten steamships to the aid of flood victims. To prevent misidentification of the source of the aid, the boats were floating advertisements for Nanyang products.[139]

The skillfully designed public image of Nantong and its commercial and social achievements under Zhang Jian's patronage emerge even more clearly when we examine the images of other counties in the northern Jiangsu area in the press. For example, although Rugao county was economically quite successful, it does not come close to Nantong in terms of public self-representation. Looking at the local Rugao newspaper, the *Gaoming bao* (The Rugao announcer), one immediately notices the absence of commercial advertising.[140] There is no news about local business development or charity events, and reports of robberies, private lawsuits, and moral issues dominate its pages.

At the same time the Rugao newspaper, in contrast to the *Tonghai xinbao*, was critical of local powerholders and institutions and did not hesitate to discuss public issues in a controversial manner. Since this newspaper was managed by the vice-president of the county assembly and had a circulation of only 700 to 800 copies, its critical stance on public affairs might be explained by the publisher's own political stance and social background.[141] Most significant, however, is the fact that by providing an open, critical forum for public discussion, the newspaper de facto contributed to changes in the local power structure. For example, according to an article under the provocative headline "The Power of the Newspaper," the paper had accused the chamber of commerce in the town of Dingyan of corruption. This public report resulted in a meeting and the election of a new president of the chamber.[142] The Rugao newspaper claimed to speak for the commercial world of Dingyan and to represent its opinion. In comparison, the media in Nantong never openly challenged the existing power structures.

Zhang Jian's carefully constructed public image as a person concerned about and in charge of the welfare of the local area and its people even found its way into the textbooks used in Nantong's schools. In a Tongzhou history textbook from 1904, Zhang Jian features prominently in two lessons on the development of local industry and education.[143] The text emphasizes his industrial, agricultural, and social concerns, his love for the country, and his solidarity with the countryside as well as the success of his industrial enterprises and his efforts to improve local education. As the text tells us, the schools relied completely on the profits derived from Zhang Jian's industrial operations in Tangjiazha, and "he did not have to ask the people for a single penny."[144] Obviously, the reality of school fees and government funding had not found its way into the textbooks.

With this last example of public representation, the narrative has come full circle: not only did Zhang Jian control the organization of educational institutions, but, like a historical figure, he became an object of study for the children in school. Thus at a relatively early stage of his modernization efforts, he had already acquired the status of an exemplary persona, a "model," so to speak, who controlled Nantong's society as much through his practical achievements in the realm of industry, agriculture, education, and welfare as through the social and cultural representation of his vision in Nantong's press and public space. Zhang Jian used the public sphere and its tool, the print media, to create a framework that allowed him to present even his profit-oriented business projects in the altruistic light of community development and self-government, which enhanced his public profile locally as well as nationally. The obituaries and the public memory created in the wake of his death in August 1926 confirm this interpretation.[145] The arrangements for the burial and the memorial ceremony were meticulously set out by the local government not only to celebrate a prominent personality but also to celebrate itself, Nantong's modern institutions and the people who represented them. Zhang Jian had become a symbol and was patronized in the local media as "son of the county."[146]

Yet, at the same time this framework also helped to create a false picture of security, especially with regard to Zhang Jian's land-reclamation companies and the Dasheng textile mills. Like internal company publications, the newspapers did not offer transparent information on Zhang Jian's enterprises. Their reports on the land-reclamation companies covered only the process of reclaiming coastal land and the establishment of new settlements. Nor did the newspapers discuss the financial situation of the Dasheng textile mills or the crisis in the early 1920s. Because of Zhang Jian's control of Nantong's various public spheres in the welfare and cultural institutions, associations, and media, the availability of information left much to be desired. It seems that in all his endeavors Zhang Jian was beyond criticism or, in words familiar to us from a business context, not accountable to the people under his control.

In the wake of China's economic reforms in the 1980s and 1990s, Chinese scholars have paid much attention to the image of Nantong during the Republican period and the question of the extent to which Zhang Jian and his business projects influenced its development. In an article on the "Nantong model" (Nantong *moshi*) in 1988, Zhang Kaiyuan saw the Dasheng industrial enterprises as directly responsible for the regional socioeconomic development of Nantong.[147] His argument about Nantong as a model for regional modernization was, of course, embedded in the political and economic context of the Four Modernizations (*sige xiandaihua*) policy under Deng Xiaoping. In more recent publications, scholars such as Mao Jiaqi have stressed the overall benefit of Zhang Jian's enterprises for the region's development in terms of industrialization, agriculture, education, and welfare.[148] Qin Shao's work has introduced the cultural and political atmosphere of Nantong, and Kathy Walker has studied the region's economy in the context of merchant capitalism and peasant struggle.[149] In my view, we need to join the cultural and economic interpretations of developments in Nantong in order to understand the central role of the Dasheng enterprise and the complex nature of Zhang Jian's economic and social control.

Zhang Jian skillfully designed and shaped Nantong culture in the early twentieth century as an intermediate space in which he was able to combine his private interests with his public role. Zhang Jian transformed his vision of managerial paternalism in the factories into social paternalism in the region's main city and countryside, or as Meng Lin, his contemporary and friend, put it: "Se Weng [Zhang Jian] held the two realms of companies (*gongsi*) and area (*difang*) in one hand."[150] Through his industrial, land-reclamation, and social-cultural projects, he gradually extended his influence from the site of the cotton mills in Tangjiazha to the countryside in Nantong, Haimen, and Chongming and then finally to Nantong city. The Japanese traveler Imazeki Tempō, who described his impressions of Nantong in 1924 under the title "China's Industrial Kingdom, 'Nantong,'" obviously sensed the particular power structure of the region.[151] However, like all the other observers, he was thoroughly taken in by Zhang Jian's sophistication and prestige and saw his "kingdom" as a viable way of economic and social community development.

But just how viable was this regional development in the long term? Despite undeniable improvements in Nantong's infrastructure, significant social and economic development on a wider scale in the Nantong region, outside the city boundaries, did not occur. To be fair, Zhang Jian did not start with a ready-made plan for regional development based on existing models. When the opportunity arose, he started a cotton mill, and his approaches to education, political involvement, and charity followed from that, as he secured his business and private interests by controlling public opinion and its representation in society. Or as Zhang Jian himself put it simply: "From 1895 on I became involved in industry, after 1901 I became involved in education, and after 1907 I also devoted my considerations to charity."[152]

Fig. 7.7   Zhang Jian's residence-turned-museum in Nantong city, 1998
(photograph by the author).

The case of Zhang Jian's regional paternalism and Nantong's emergence as a modern city in the early twentieth century also sheds light on urban development, the public sphere, and civil society in Republican China. The findings in this chapter confirm the critical reappraisal of the concept of public sphere and its application to Chinese society of Frederic Wakeman.[153] Despite a substantial number of organizations and print media, an independent, openly accessible public sphere did not exist in Nantong. In this context, we need to remind ourselves that as a businessman even Zhang Jian was not autonomous but operated under the umbrella of state control without challenging its structures. Although his paternalistic patronage in Nantong depended on and was secured through his political role in local society, he continued to negotiate with and seek support from provincial and national authorities to represent and protect his business interests once issues beyond the immediate local level were involved. In contrast to public sphere and civil society in the Western context, commerce and business during the Republican period were never free from political interference, as Stephanie Chung has shown in her study on south Chinese business communities and their relationship to the state.[154]

In my conversations with senior citizens in Nantong in the mid-1990s, it became clear that for them Zhang Jian still symbolizes the historical beginnings of modern Nantong. Most of them could easily point out the now often decrepit buildings that had housed his welfare institutions and projects. Today Zhang Jian's former residence serves as home to the Nantong Museum (see Fig. 7.7). And as one would expect with a locally prominent figure, many people claimed to know quite a bit of gossip about his family. In the folklore of combined hearsay, hagiography, and personal experience, Zhang Jian remains the uncontested patron saint of Nantong. Not surprisingly, this narrative has become the official version in local histories and essay collections and at commemorative conferences.

CHAPTER 8

Enterprise in Transition: Dasheng

After Zhang Jian

Zhang Jian's skillful control of Dasheng's management and finances created a new form of business institution that combined characteristics of the family business and those of the corporation. This mixture created a problem, however. One significant advantage of incorporation is that it facilitates the continuation of the firm beyond the departure of a particular leader of the corporation. Personal control combined with lack of accountability rendered Zhang Jian the indispensable center of the enterprise, despite the fact that Dasheng was a shareholding company with limited liability, and Zhang Jian's death in 1926 became a turning point in the history of the company. How would Dasheng do business in the absence of its charismatic patron?

The purpose of this chapter is not to provide a detailed account of Dasheng's history after Zhang Jian's death. Rather, it focuses on the development of Dasheng as a modern enterprise between the 1920s and its nationalization in the early 1950s and its transition from an institution characterized by highly personalized control to an institution increasingly dominated by modern banks and government agencies. Dasheng illustrates the inability of enterprises in China to escape the impact of war and the ensuing economic and political crises, all of which left their imprint on the company's internal structure as well as on its interaction with the state and society at large. Even so, Dasheng's development in the postwar period documents the continuation of family power, which for a time survived the substantial structural changes of this period.

In the years following Zhang Jian's death in 1926, Dasheng was exposed to unprecedented political changes with the rise of Chiang Kai-shek.

Chiang's successful Northern Expedition in 1927 became a watershed in the history of the Republic and led to the establishment of a centralized Guomindang government in Nanjing and a new political and social framework during the so-called Nanjing decade (1927–37). These political and social changes challenged the continued existence of the Dasheng business group in various ways. On the one hand, no longer was there a charismatic figure to protect the enterprise through patronage and influence that reached far beyond Nantong. As the political landscape became more fragmented and more difficult, interference from local warlords and sabotage and extortion by criminal racketeers in Shanghai presented new challenges for Dasheng. On the other hand, even Zhang Jian would have had problems dealing with the extraordinary challenges of Japanese imperialism and the civil war. These factors were much larger in scope and posed a more immediate threat to the financial and physical survival of the enterprise than any of its previous crises.

Ultimately, this final chapter considers the development of Chinese modern business in the transition period from the Republic to the socialist state. In order to understand the historical trajectory of Chinese enterprises, in particular the transformation of large, private industrial enterprises into state-owned enterprises after 1949, we need to understand what happened to these businesses during the Japanese occupation and the civil war and the extent to which these experiences determined their evolution in the early years of the People's Republic.

The Impact of Politics and the Problem of Succession

Politics had their most dramatic impact on Dasheng in the 1930s. Since these events happened after Zhang Jian's death, the secondary literature often conveys the impression that Zhang Jian was able to avoid entanglements with local warlords and their messy campaigns in the early 1920s. Zhang Jian was, however, exposed to political pressures during the last two years of his life. Dasheng's involvement in the local opium business through its affiliated banking operation is, not surprisingly, suppressed in the copious literature on Dasheng and the Zhang family. Even indirect connections with opium would have tainted Dasheng's and Zhang Jian's image. There might be another reason: the activities of the Green Gang in the 1930s that led to its takeover of one of Dasheng's affiliated companies allow observers to view Dasheng as a victim of political circumstances; the events of the mid-1920s cast Zhang Jian in a much more ambiguous light. His cooperation with the local warlord may have been forced on him, but it was nonetheless profitable. When the county and the adjacent areas north of the Yangzi River came under the control of the warlord Sun Chuanfang, the winner in the Jiangsu-Zhejiang war in the fall of 1924, opium became an important commodity in Nantong. Nationwide, opium was cheaper than in previous years, and consumption increased. De facto, there were no restrictions "imposed on any branch of the traffic except by a few magistrates here and there," as a contemporary source remarked.[1] Farmers throughout China cultivated the "black rice" because it offered far greater returns than the cultivation of wheat. Since poppy farmers usually paid higher land taxes as well as a variety of related taxes, opium cultivation was encouraged (and sometimes coerced) by landlords, merchants, civil officials, warlords, and bandits.[2]

This nationwide development encouraged organizations like the International Anti-Opium Association in Beijing to launch a detailed investigation of the patterns of regional opium cultivation, consumption, and distribution in the mid-1920s. Although the investigation was based on field reports by foreign missionaries from all provinces, public health and morality were not the association's major concerns; instead it focused on the economic aspects of the local opium business. The association's report in its quarterly publication *Opium Cultivation and Traffic in China* provides crucial information on the link between Dasheng and the opium trade in Nantong during 1925 and 1926.[3]

With its access to the Yangzi River, its canal system, and its long coastline, the Nantong area was an ideal place for shipping opium grown and transported from the interior provinces. Nantong became the final and crucial stop along the Yangzi River before the opium reached Shanghai, the narcotics capital of the time.[4] Poppy cultivation in the area under Sun Chuanfang's control was rather limited, and, according to the report, "opium is eaten and smoked, but not grown. Farmers are afraid of official squeeze and military blackmail."[5] Sun Chuanfang specialized in the transportation and trading of opium instead. For example, he was involved in the Three Prosperities Company (Sanxin gongsi), an opium wholesale company founded by the Shanghai gangsters Huang Jinrong, Zhang Xiaolin, and Du Yuesheng together with opium merchants from Shantou in Guangdong in 1925. For providing military escorts for the company's opium transports, the warlord received an annual payment of 1.5 million yuan.[6]

According to the International Anti-Opium Association's report, opium produced in Sichuan and Guangdong entered the area at Lüsi, a port on the Yangzi River in Haimen county surrounded by Zhang Jian's land-reclamation companies. From there the opium was "conveyed by motor car under escort of troops. The opium is stored at the Huai Hai Bank which is nicknamed the 'Opium Bank.'"[7] The troops were under the command of Sun Chuanfang, who in 1925 had assumed control over the area's opium trade by creating a monopoly, the Nantong Combine. And the Opium Bank was the respectable Huaihai Industrial Bank (Huaihai shiye yinhang), which Zhang Jian had founded in 1919 in part with capital provided by sharehold-ers in the Dasheng No. 1 mill.[8]

Sun Chuanfang defended the creation of the Nantong Combine as a means of protecting the area from the bad influence of the Shanghai under-world. This was quite a common excuse. For example, General Zhang Zongchang portrayed opium farming in Shandong, the province under his control, as a patriotic act because it generated revenue for the troops and kept foreign opium and drugs such as morphine out of the area.[9]

For Sun Chuanfang, the most attractive aspect of the monopoly was cer-tainly the revenue he gained for his military endeavors, which covered his costs for troops and equipment as well as personal expenditures.[10] According to the 1925–26 report, the Nantong Combine received an estimated income of 40 million yuan from the opium trade for the transport of some 40,000 cases of opium.[11] The Nantong Combine was a huge business operation, with 800 "selling houses" (i.e., local retail branches), with the county defense commissioner / chief of police serving as the president and Sun Chuanfang's front man. That official's involvement gave the Nantong Combine the aura of a government agency, very much like Zhang Zongchang's monopoly, which had been named the Provincial Opium Suppression Bureau.[12]

Banks were absolutely vital to the opium trade at such a large scale. Both small traditional banks and modern national and foreign banks were needed to deposit and transfer large funds on behalf of the monopolies, their power-ful patrons, and business partners. The Huaihai Bank, with its location in the city of Nantong, was able to fulfill these tasks easily. The bank had branches in major cities throughout Jiangsu, including a branch in Dasheng's headquarters in Shanghai's International Settlement. From the bank's open-ing, Zhang Jian's son, Zhang Xiaoruo, headed it and represented the family in its financial operations. Even more important for the bank in terms of connections and the ability to raise funds were Zhang Jian's prestige in Shanghai's financial world and his close relationships with prominent bankers like Chen Guangfu.

Since the founding of the Dasheng mills and their expansion into a business group, Zhang Jian had successfully kept local politics at bay by controlling local society. His paternalistic and autocratic style set the tone for his business as well as for his vision of Nantong's economic, social, and political development. Why, then, did Zhang Jian collaborate with a warlord in a business that neither guaranteed his economic independence nor met his own supposedly high moral standards?

I would argue that for Dasheng and Zhang Jian the opportunity to earn revenues from these opium-related deposits and fund transfers came at a time of great need. Between 1922 and 1926, Dasheng experienced its worst financial crisis, which also affected the performance of the Huaihai Bank. The bank had been founded expressly to serve as Dasheng's "organ of financial transactions" (*jinrong huodong jiguan*), and the majority of its shareholders were associated with the Dasheng mills and affiliated enterprises.[13] According to Huaihai's first business report in 1920, the bank's capital amounted to a modest 303,270 yuan. This increased dramatically during the next year.[14] When bankruptcy threatened Dasheng, the bank faced an acute crisis. The Huaihai Bank had underwritten substantial loans to many of Zhang Jian's land-reclamation companies, which turned out to be risky, debt-ridden operations linked in turn to the mills through additional loan arrangements.[15] When many of these companies defaulted in the mid-1920s, the Huaihai Bank was left with collateral in the form of reclaimed land, which was difficult for the bank to redeem and turn into cash.

In short, the Huaihai Bank was in dire financial straits when Sun Chuanfang gained control of the local opium trade through the Nantong Combine. The Huaihai Bank's relationship with the warlord is ignored in the secondary literature, and, of course, hard evidence in the form of bank documents is difficult to come by—its account books do not label funds or deposits as "opium funds." Despite the lack of concrete numbers for 1925 and 1926, revenue derived from the opium trade of the Nantong Combine undoubtedly helped the bank stay in business. The fact that the bank's operations ceased soon after Zhang Jian's death underscores its fragile financial situation. During the war, more than half of the bank's remaining funds were consolidated with Dasheng and administered by a special committee of the board of directors.[16]

Although Zhang Jian's son was the director of the Huaihai Bank, considering Zhang Jian's personal contacts and correspondence with Sun Chuanfang, it is unlikely that he was unaware of the bank's affiliation with the Nantong Combine. It is less likely that Zhang Jian actively sought Sun Chuanfang as a business partner. Zhang Jian, like other local leaders in Jiangsu, supported Sun Chuanfang's political program, even though he did not support the idea of warlordism per se and probably chose cooperation for practical reasons.[17] Zhang Jian was, for example, concerned about the political stability and the maintenance of law and order in the Nantong area. In a letter to Sun dated July 1926 Zhang Jian complained about bandit gangs, mostly salt and opium smugglers, who were terrorizing both northern and southern Jiangsu.[18] Pointing to the importance of stability, he then asked the warlord to take appropriate military action.

To my knowledge, Zhang Jian never openly criticized the organized opium trade. In fact, he seems to have preferred an opium monopoly conducted under the strict rules and supervision of a warlord and his troops to unregulated opium smuggling, which caused more disturbance and violence among the general population. Like many other members of China's local elite who lived within a warlord's sphere of influence, Zhang Jian probably considered Sun Chuanfang a lesser evil than the chaos of political and economic competition in a power vacuum. For his part, Sun Chuanfang was well aware of Zhang Jian's social status and paid the appropriate respect. When Sun visited Zhang Jian in Nantong city, the warlord received an enthusiastic reception at banquets, at the Gengsu theater, and through special newspaper coverage.[19] In turn, Zhang Jian became part of Sun's informal advisory committee, together with other prominent figures such as Zhang Taiyan and Zhang Jia'ao.[20] Zhang Jian must have felt under pressure to comply with Sun Chuanfang's demands and to accommodate Sun's political and economic interests in his carefully organized domain. In the short run, cooperation had financial advantages for Dasheng. Eventually, however, both enterprise and family paid a high price for it.

The deaths of Zhang Jian in 1926 and Sun Chuanfang in 1927 ended this particular link between warlord politics and business. Now the enterprise (and the political world) had to face a new problem, succession. With its ambiguous form as a corporate enterprise under strong personal control, leadership was supposed to remain in the Zhang family to some extent. It was difficult to fill the larger-than-life position occupied by Zhang Jian with his charismatic personality and connections to the political, financial, and business elite of late imperial and Republican China from within the family circle. His successor had to take charge of the Shanghai accounts office, the institutional anchor of Zhang Jian's power and control.

As noted in Chapter 6, in the wake of the 1922 crisis the bank consortium cemented its power by removing both Zhang Jian and Zhang Cha from their positions in Dasheng and enthroning Li Shengbo as general manager of the Dasheng mills. However, the banks kept Wu Jichen in his position as the head of the Shanghai accounts office and made him directly responsible and accountable to the consortium. Although the accounts office in Shanghai continued to be part of the enterprise until the end of the war, it never again came under the exclusive control of a member of the Zhang family.

Dasheng's real crisis began to unfold in 1935. As the shareholder reports show, Wu Jichen's death that year created a serious power vacuum in Dasheng's management.[21] In fact, Wu Jichen had not only controlled the Dasheng business but also served as private financial advisor and steward to the Zhang family after Zhang Jian's death. For example, according to Zhang Jian's granddaughter, Zhang Rouwu, Wu Jichen traveled from Shanghai to Nantong from time to time to discuss financial matters with her mother, Chen Shiyun.[22] It is difficult to say whether loyalty to Zhang Jian or personal gains motivated Wu Jichen's actions, or whether it was a combination of both, which in my view seems most likely.

One reason Wu Jichen was able to gain such enormous influence and power in company and family matters after Zhang Jian's death was, next to his professional experience, the lack of strong and suitable successors from within the family circle. Zhang Jian's only son, Zhang Xiaoruo, did not possess his father's business acumen. For the most part, he merely took over his father's positions in the welfare and cultural institutions in Nantong but not in Dasheng and the other businesses. The differences between father and son could not have been more pronounced: the father refused to expose his children to modern city life by moving his family to Shanghai and remained in Nantong instead; the son took up residence in Shanghai in 1926 and obviously preferred the amenities of life and entertainments in the metropolis.[23] Apparently the death of his father allowed Zhang Xiaoruo to detach himself from the family's business interests and affairs in Nantong and pursue his own life-style in Shanghai.

Succession problems are common in family businesses, regardless of the cultural context. An extensive literature deals with issues such as the life cycle of family firms, their handling of corporate governance and conflict management, and strategic planning.[24] Although Dasheng was not a family enterprise, with its high degree of personal control, the Zhang family would have been well advised to groom a successor from within its larger kinship network early on to monitor the family's overall interests. Unfortunately, Zhang Xiaoruo was Zhang Jian's only direct male descendant. The father seems to have planned, at least in the early stages, to prepare his son for a business career. However, in contrast to several sons of the Rong family, who were sent to the Lowell Textile College in the United States and other professional institutions to be trained for positions in the family's vast textile business, Zhang Xiaoruo never received any specific professional training related to the cotton industry.[25]

As a child Zhang Xiaoruo received a traditional education and entered Aurora University in Shanghai in 1913.[26] Although apparently without strong professional ambitions, Zhang Xiaoruo assisted his father without official designation during his term as minister of agriculture and commerce. In 1917 Zhang Xiaoruo was sent to New Haven, Connecticut, to take a business course at Arnold College, a school then best known for its physical education program.[27] However, the attempt to turn Zhang Xiaoruo into a businessman seems to have been futile. An indication of this is a story related by Xu Gengqi (1892–1977), a member of the young and upwardly mobile elite in Nantong city who befriended Zhang Xiaoruo and went to study at Columbia University in 1921.[28] His son, Xu Zhongzheng, recalls that his father criticized Zhang Xiaoruo for leading a life of leisure in America instead of dedicating himself to his studies. After his return to Nantong, Xu Gengqi obtained a position in the Huaihai Bank before moving on to a higher position at the Central Bank in Shanghai, whereas Zhang Xiaoruo's studies abroad did not lead to a significant position in the Dasheng enterprise.[29]

Ignored by his father after his return, Zhang Xiaoruo focused on the political realm and became involved in Nantong's local self-government association, which he chaired.[30] When Zhang Jian founded the Huaihai Industrial Bank in 1919, he appointed his son director and manager of the Nantong branch. Yet, despite this appointment, Zhang Xiaoruo still found time to spend most of 1923 and 1924 traveling around the world, allegedly for the purpose of investigating Western industries. The trip led to poems and travel reports rather than more business-oriented insights with practical implications.[31]

Zhang Xiaoruo maintained a permanent residence in Shanghai and moved in social circles of which his father most probably would have disapproved. The difference in the public images of the father and the son is evident in contemporary accounts. In the 1920 edition of *Who's Who in China*, Zhang Xiaoruo is described as "a good Chinese scholar, well conversant with Chinese poems, a good tennis player and popular socially. Imbued with the spirit of Americanism, Mr. Chang [Zhang] has set himself [as] an example for Chinese young men in society and family."[32] References to business skills are notably absent. After his father's death, Zhang Xiaoruo took over some of Zhang Jian's honorary positions such as the directorship of Nantong University.[33] He also "inherited" his father's position as chairman of the board of the Dasheng No. 1 Cotton Mill and was a member of the consolidated board of directors of the Dasheng Nos. 1, 2, and 3 mills from 1927 on. However, according to the minutes of the board meetings between 1927 and 1934, Zhang Xiaoruo rarely attended these gatherings and often was represented by Wu Jichen, who even addressed the shareholders at their 1931 annual meeting in Shanghai on his behalf.[34] Since the chairman only delivered a formal, ghostwritten address at the beginning of the meeting and rarely participated in the discussions, Zhang Xiaoruo's absence does not seem to have had a serious impact on Dasheng's business management. Nevertheless, formally he continued to represent his family in the company.

The role of Zhang Xiaoruo, the only son and somewhat predestined successor, has gone almost undiscussed, and interviews with Zhang Xiaoruo's contemporaries have yielded little useful information. This gap in the otherwise abundant biographical and local historical literature probably results from an attempt to keep the image of the Zhang family clean and untainted. In fact, Zhang Xiaoruo's activities in Shanghai in the early 1920s drew him into a new set of acquaintances with time, money, and influence on their hands and somewhat shady professional aspirations. In 1924 he was one of the Four Lords (*si gongzi*) in Shanghai, a group of flamboyant young men with influential fathers who attracted a lot of attention in Shanghai society. The other three were Yuan Hanyun, son of Yuan Shikai, the first president of the Republic, Zhang Xueliang, son of the Manchurian warlord Zhang Zuolin, and Lu Xiaojia, son of the warlord Lu Yongxiang, who controlled Zhejiang.

The group was in contact, and more often in conflict, with the Shanghai Green Gang, particularly its most infamous leader, Huang Jinrong.[35]

Zhang Xiaoruo's life ended in a scandal; he was shot in his home on Rue Lafayette (present-day Fuxing Road) in the French concession by his servant, Wu Yigao. Zhang Xiaoruo's mistress Li Fuchu also suffered serious injuries and died several days later.[36] According to unsubstantiated rumors, the motive for the murder was Wu Yigao's jealousy over an extramarital affair, but the details of the case never made their way into the Nantong newspaper. Wu Yigao had served the Zhang family for many years, and the suggestion that he killed Zhang Xiaoruo because his son had not been promoted in the Dada Steamship Company sounds equally suspicious.[37] The French concession police never found a convincing explanation for the murder.[38] By this time Zhang Xiaoruo had become so alienated from his family in Nantong that his eldest daughter, Zhang Rouwu, had to travel from Nantong to Shanghai and bring the coffin back by boat for burial since her mother was ill and unable to leave Nantong.[39] Today Zhang Xiaoruo is buried near his father's grave in a park-like cemetery in a suburb of Nantong (see Fig. 8.1).

Zhang Xiaoruo's socializing with people in contact with members of the Green Gang and his suspicious death deserve attention in the context of Dasheng's business activities in Shanghai in the early 1930s. Unlike Zhang Jian, Zhang Xiaoruo was unable to shield the enterprise from serious interference from the Green Gang, which in the 1920s emerged as a reckless, powerful economic and political force in Shanghai. The fate of the Dada Steamship Company (Dada lunbu gongsi), an enterprise affiliated with the Dasheng business group (see Chapter 5), is a case in point. According to Brian Martin's detailed study of the Shanghai Green Gang, in the 1920s and 1930s all the major gang bosses were interested in gaining control over the shipping business in the city and in establishing rackets along the docks and wharfs of Shanghai's waterfront. Du Yuesheng, who emerged as the gang's major and most notorious patron in 1925, appears to have focused on Dada as part of his strategy of acquiring transportation facilities for his opium monopoly in Shanghai and expanding his business into the hinterlands.[40]

Founded by Zhang Jian in 1905, the Dada Steamship Company served the transportation needs of the Dasheng mills and remained a fairly small operation, financially supported by the No. 1 cotton mill, during its early years.[41] After building a commercial dock at Tianshenggang, a port on the

Fig. 8.1 Zhang Xiaoruo's gravesite in Nantong, 1993
(photograph by the author).

Yangzi River, which according to the manager of Sichuan's Minsheng Shipping Company, Hu Zuofu, became "the best along the Yangzi,"[42] Zhang Jian established a Shanghai branch of the company and built a jetty for its steamships on the famous wharf at Shiliubu on the west bank of the Huangpu river. During the 1910s, the company expanded its business to other ports on the lower Yangzi and also managed Zhang Jian's smaller shipping companies, which transported customers and goods on ten short-distance routes and along the local canal system.[43] By 1920, Dada ships annually transported 400,000–500,000 piculs of raw cotton produced in the Nantong area from Tianshenggang to Shanghai.[44]

Commonly referred to as Dada wharf (Dada *matou*), the company's jetty in Shanghai became the hub for goods shipments and passenger travel in the lower Yangzi area (see Fig. 8.2).[45] In the early 1920s, the Dada company increased its annual revenues by adding passenger service between Shanghai and Yangzhou, by monopolizing the transportation of equipment and raw material for all the companies in the Dasheng business group, and by shipping wheat, cotton, and most of the fresh produce from northern Jiangsu to

Fig. 8.2 Passenger ship of the Dada Steamship Company (Nantong youyi julebu,
Nantong shiye, jiaoyu, cishan fengjing, 1920, unpaginated).

Shanghai. In 1927, when the company had achieved a cumulative profit of
almost 1.7 million taels, Zhang Xiaoruo became the new chairman of the
board after his father's death.[46] With its profitable business—symptomatic
of the growth in the steamship shipping business at the time—and the inexperienced son in charge, Dada must have looked like an extremely promising
business opportunity to Du Yuesheng in the early 1930s.[47]

An incident in 1932 presented itself as a handy opportunity for Du Yuesheng to get a toehold in Dada's business. That year the Dada company lost
two steamers to fire, resulting in the death of over a thousand passengers.[48]
This incident allowed Du Yuesheng to interfere actively in Dada's business.
First, the heavy fines imposed on the company by the authorities made the
shareholders search for someone to hold responsible for the disaster and in
the end led to a restructuring of the board of directors. Du Yuesheng acquired shares in the company and was able to install one of his associates,
Yang Guanbei, as company manager. With the help—intentional or not—
of disgruntled shareholders, Du managed to reform the board of directors to
further his own interests.[49]

By the end of 1932 Du Yuesheng had managed to eliminate the influence
of the Zhang family in the company. The Green Gang's absolute control

over stevedores, dockworkers, and their foremen (who also operated as labor contractors) allowed Du Yuesheng to manipulate Dada's workforce at Shiliubu. Following a shutdown of the Dada wharf, the new, "reformed" board emerged stronger than before: Du Yuesheng himself became chairman of the board of directors, and Zhang Xiaoruo was left with the nominal position of managing director, with no real influence in the business.[50]

The development of the Dada Steamship Company elucidates the problem of succession in Dasheng as well as the increase in political interference in business after the end of the Northern Expedition in 1927, which established Chiang Kai-shek's power in Shanghai and the surrounding areas. Without doubt, Du Yuesheng's Green Gang and his close links with local Guomindang authorities helped him to take over the enterprise and to manipulate the business to serve his own agenda. Du Yuesheng was also a skillful businessman, and by the late 1930s the company had grown into a trading and shipping conglomerate monopolizing commerce and transport in the Subei region.[51] The fact that Zhang Xiaoruo and his family did not possess the necessary political connections to the Guomindang probably played a role in their failure to oppose Du Yuesheng's takeover.

A case in point is Zhang Jian's elder brother Zhang Cha, who was branded a *tuhao lieshen* (local bully and evil gentry) by the Guomindang government for his support of the Beiyang warlord Sun Chuanfang, whose army controlled Shanghai until late 1926. As mentioned above, after Chiang Kai-shek's victory in 1927 and his ousting of Sun, Zhang Cha came under investigation. He fled to Beijing in 1928 and continued to avoid Nantong and Shanghai until his death in 1939.[52] His case is reminiscent of that of the industrialist Fu Xiao'an, the managing director of the China Merchants' Steamship Navigation Company and chairman of the Shanghai General Chamber of Commerce, who had supported Sun Chuanfang and the northern warlord Wu Peifu. During the Northern Expedition, Fu fled to Dalian.[53] The Green Gang quickly changed its allegiance from Sun Chuanfang to the Guomindang in early 1927. To my knowledge, Zhang Xiaoruo made no efforts to forge ties with the new political power brokers under Chiang Kai-shek. Although Zhang Xiaoruo had socialized with Zhang Xueliang,[54] who opposed many of his father's political ideas and, as his successor in the Northeast in 1928, formed an alliance with Chiang Kai-shek, this connection does not seem to have improved Zhang Xiaoruo's standing with the Guomindang authorities.

Because of the changes in the overall economic and political situation, the second generation faced a much more complex and difficult situation in the 1930s than Zhang Jian had in the early 1900s. Lacking the founder's business talents, charisma, political connections, and social prestige, Zhang Xiaoruo was not able to fulfill the family's expectations. Even so, considering Zhang Jian's support for Sun Chuanfang, he, too, would have been hard-pressed to defend Dasheng against the depredations of the Green Gang. Charisma and social status would have counted for little against racketeering under the political protection of the Guomindang.

However, Zhang Xiaoruo's life-style and his activities in Shanghai did little to further Dasheng's business interests. Lacking the connections of his father, Zhang Xiaoruo and the enterprises under his leadership became easy prey for the "gangster entrepreneur," as Brian Martin characterizes Du Yuesheng. The question whether a dispute with Green Gang members or with business partners supported by the gang was behind Zhang Xiaoruo's murder in 1935 must remain open here due to lack of evidence.

Changing Markets and Consumers

External factors in the form of economic changes created problems of a different kind for Dasheng. Changes in the markets for cotton yarn and cloth had a major financial impact on the enterprise in the 1930s. After the financial crisis of the early 1920s, Dasheng continued to operate under the supervision of the Shanghai consortium. Burdened with high interest payments to its creditors for many years, Dasheng managed to achieve only very modest profits in the late 1920s. The crisis in the Manchurian textile market in 1931 aggravated the enterprise's financial condition and for the first time challenged the viability of its sales and distribution networks.

As we have seen, the management's lack of planning and failure to estimate production costs and sales income had become obvious in the 1922 crisis. Even under the direction of the banking consortium, however, Dasheng does not seem to have devoted much attention to planning and marketing strategies. The crisis in the Manchurian textile market illustrates the limited scope of the changes introduced by the banks despite their announcement of new "scientific" management, particularly with regard to product management. Dasheng was not alone in encountering problems in the 1930s. Since developments in the Chinese textile sector in the 1930s are discussed in great detail in the literature, however, I will touch on them only briefly.[55]

Nantong's connection with the Manchurian (Dongbei) market dates to the late nineteenth century when Yingkou on the Liaodong peninsula was designated a treaty port in 1861 and cotton cloth produced in northern Jiangsu's handicraft industry found its way to this new market. Merchants from Manchuria traded soybeans and other goods produced in the Northeast and bought the local Nantong cloth through Shanghai brokers. The trade relationship between northern Jiangsu and Manchuria continued in a slightly different form in the early twentieth century when cotton yarn produced in the Dasheng mills was used to produce cloth destined for the Manchurian market in great quantities. The flooding of the Manchurian market with Japanese yarn and cloth after 1928 led to a dramatic decline in the sale of imports from the Nantong area and thus in the sales of the products of the Dasheng mills.[56]

Since its establishment in 1895, the Dasheng No. 1 mill had followed a strategy of *tuchan tuxiao* (local production and local sales). Cotton grown locally in the Nantong area was used to produce cotton yarn, which was then sold through yarn merchants to local households that produced *tubu*. Until the 1920s, the Dasheng mills produced mainly the coarse 10-, 12-, and 14-count yarn suitable for the wooden looms used in handicraft production. Local weavers preferred Dasheng machine-spun yarn to local hand-spun yarn because of its superior quality. Because of its sturdiness and thickness, Nantong *tubu* became popular in the cool climate of the Dongbei region.[57] Until the late 1920s, about 80 percent of Dasheng's output of 12-count yarn, its most popular yarn, was sold within the Nantong region; the rest was marketed in Jiangxi, Zhejang, and Fujian provinces and in Wuhan.[58]

However, by the late 1920s Dasheng's locally oriented marketing strategies were in trouble. First, as Kubo Tōru has shown, China's textile industry shifted from the production of coarse low count yarn to the production of fine, high-quality, high-count yarn in the 1920s following the importation of Japanese machinery.[59] According to Linda Grove, this phase of relatively successful import substitution led to the expansion and development of the Chinese textile industry during the interwar period.[60] In addition, the Shanghai market increasingly turned to high-count, high-quality Japanese yarn, which also began to penetrate the Nantong market and become popular with the local weavers. From 1928 on, the increasing sales of Japanese cotton cloth in northeastern and northern China caused a drastic falloff in the sales of Nantong cloth in those areas. For example, by 1928 sales of Nantong

cloth in Manchuria had declined by 55 percent. Following the Mukden incident in 1931 and the Japanese occupation of Manchukuo in 1932, the control
of the Manchurian economy by Japanese authorities placed Chinese competitors in the yarn and cloth market at a further disadvantage.[61]

Dasheng's management, recruited from and under the supervision of the
banking consortium, attempted to improve its business performance by
making changes in its product line as well as in its marketing and distribution system. First, Dasheng was forced to find new markets for its yarn. By
1934, 61.5 percent of the yarn was sold in Jiangxi and Sichuan provinces and
the cities of Guangzhou, Tianjin, and Xuzhou. This change to geographically more diverse markets brought concomitant changes in distribution,
transportation, and marketing. Dasheng began to use brokers working on a
commission. For example, it contracted with the Tongcheng Company in
Tianjin to develop the North China market for Dasheng's Red Devil
(Honggui) brand of cotton yarn and its other products.[62]

As Chinese consumers began to demand high-quality yarn, Dasheng reduced the production of 12-count yarn and expanded its offerings of fine,
high-count yarns. In 1931 the No. 1 mill produced for the first time a significant amount of 20-count yarn, in fact more than twice the amount of 12-
count yarn that year.[63] The management also tried to promote machine-
spun cloth made of 16-count yarn produced in the Dasheng No. 3 mill in
Haimen. However, the local Nantong market preferred *tubu*, and in the
Manchurian market, Dasheng yard goods competed with Japanese machine-
woven cloth. According to the report of Lin Zuobo, a Nantong cloth merchant who conducted market research in Manchuria in 1931, imports of 16-
and 20-count Japanese cloth were in great demand in Yingkou, since they
were superior in quality and cheaper than the cloth produced by Dasheng.[64]

Facing increasing competition and changing markets, the management of
the Dasheng cotton mills began, for the first time, to pay attention to customer psychology and advertising strategies. For example, in addition to
promoting its brand names in pamphlets and professional journals, the management tried to increase sales by adding small gifts or free samples to its
packages of yarn.[65] Not surprisingly, these measures did not improve sales
significantly, and lowering output and reducing the workforce became additional, more drastic methods of cutting production costs. The Dasheng
No. 1 mill used only 34.5 percent of its spindle capacity and only 61 percent
of its loom capacity in the production of yarn and cloth in 1933. On the rec-

ommendation of the Chinese Cotton Mill Owners' Association, the No. 2 mill reduced its workforce by 23 percent, and the No. 3 mill halted production for several days.[66]

The company's most drastic step to improve its position was its concerted effort to control local distribution channels by establishing a contract system with local yarn shops (*shazhuang*) in 1934. According to the first clause of the contract, the shops agreed to sell Dasheng yarn exclusively and to promote it as the shop's major commodity while refraining from trading in non-Dasheng products. The second clause guaranteed the shops a cash bonus per bale of Dasheng yarn sold. Not surprisingly, Dasheng's attempt to monopolize the local distribution system failed to secure a niche for Dasheng's yarn products in a market dominated by qualitatively and commercially more competitive brands, domestic and foreign. Instead, the yarn shops avoided Dasheng's rules by buying and selling other yarn brands through middlemen like the Chinese merchants who sold yarn produced in Japanese cotton mills in Shanghai in the Nantong area.[67]

The decline in Dasheng's profits in the late 1920s and 1930s was not solely the result of external trends. Since management introduced necessary structural changes only after great delay, they were unable to ameliorate the company's financial situation immediately. The report of the shareholders' meeting in 1933 mentions that Dasheng's management had undertaken to improve the company's competitiveness by, among other actions, upgrading equipment, adding looms for fine-cloth production, and reducing production costs.[68] This special attention from management was no coincidence. Dasheng's continuing indebtedness to creditor-banks of the consortium, high interest payments, and its losses in what had been its most substantial and profitable market—12-count yarns—forced it into the red that year.

Dasheng failed to restructure its product range and expand its distribution system in the mid-1920s when major changes in the Chinese textile market began to occur. Indeed, as a regional enterprise Dasheng had relied too long on its monopolies of local raw materials and local sales of finished products. Under Zhang Jian, these quasi-monopoly arrangements had protected Dasheng from Chinese as well as from foreign competitors in the local market between 1895 and the early 1920s. The banks who took control in the early 1920s seem to have been concerned primarily with improving the finances of the business group rather than restructuring the mill business to meet the changing demands of the Chinese textile market. Obviously, the new management did not realize in time that the changing political and economic environment was seriously challenging Dasheng's strength as a regional business. The limitations of such an enterprise soon began to show: external economic pressures forced Dasheng to abandon its focus on the regional market and to reorient itself toward the national market. In the process, it had to confront the same obstacles and opportunities as its Chinese and foreign competitors.

Business Survival During War and Occupation

The financial situation of the Dasheng mills remained precarious throughout the 1930s, but the war with Japan and the subsequent occupation presented the most serious threat yet to Dasheng's business—indeed, to its very existence. The Japanese launched their offensive in central China in August 1937. On March 17, 1938, Japanese troops entered the Nantong area near Langshan (Wolf Hill) on the northern banks of the Yangzi River. Thus began the occupation period for this region and its populace; before it ended in 1945, it would bring much personal suffering and economic hardship. As the largest and only major industrial employer in the area, the Dasheng cotton mills were affected by the occupation in two ways. First, as a business institution, Dasheng was vulnerable to the general economic side effects of the Japanese occupation. Second, once a new Japanese management had been installed in the mills, it tried to gain control over Dasheng's workforce by coercing the local population into cooperation.

With the fall of Shanghai to the Japanese in October 1937, the situation for Chinese industrial enterprises in the city and surrounding hinterlands became dangerous. Although none of the Dasheng mills was located near the ongoing battle at that time, the board of directors worried about possible damage to the mills. In order to protect Dasheng property, the board decided to pre-empt a Japanese strike by registering Dasheng as a foreign-owned company in Shanghai's International Settlement in November 1937.[69]

Protected by extraterritoriality, the International Settlement served as a safe haven or "solitary island" (*gudao*) for political and economic refugees and their assets until December 1941, when Japan declared war on the Allied powers. Numerous Chinese businessmen took to the foreign concessions in 1938 and used foreign registry to secure their property from the Japanese, especially since only a few entrepreneurs were able to move their factories into the territory under foreign jurisdiction.[70] The fact that Dasheng's central accounts office had operated from a building in the International Settlement since the 1910s may have facilitated the board's decision.

Like many other Chinese enterprises, Dasheng used an unpaid debt to a foreign firm as a pretext for the transfer of ownership. Dasheng owed a German firm, the Allgemeine Elektrizitäts Gesellschaft (AEG), which was represented under the name of the Aiyiji brokerage, 172,000 British pounds for the purchase of an electrical generator and boiler for the spinning mills in Tangjiazha and Chongming.[71] Given the political alliance between Germany and Japan, German registration must have seemed the most advantageous tactic to Dasheng.

After declaring its inability to pay the debt and transferring the mills with all their property to the German creditor as collateral, Dasheng was officially registered as a German operation in the German consulate in January 1938.[72] As Parks Coble has shown, foreign business registration through debt consolidation was quite often sought by Chinese entrepreneurs who perceived it as a relatively easy form of protection with little financial risk since it allowed them to continue de facto as the owners. It was certainly a much easier option than dismantling factories and transporting them to the unoccupied part of China, which was time-consuming, costly, and dangerous because of the Japanese bombardment of shipping traffic along the Yangzi River.[73] Some Chinese companies like the Dalong machine works in Shanghai went even further and adopted an English name (Union Iron & Foundry Works) as well as a new Chinese name (Taili) to signal the transfer to foreign ownership.[74] Dasheng indicated the German registration in its official name (all the collateral mill companies were now "managed" by the Aiyiji brokerage representing AEG) and paid the salaries of two German managers, a Mr. Neumann and a Mr. Onnermann, who acted as the official front men. In addition, Dasheng's headquarters in Shanghai paid the brokerage a monthly "management" fee of 200 British pounds for this legal arrangement.[75]

However, almost nothing changed in the day-to-day management and business of the Dasheng mills. None of the 214 former Dasheng workers interviewed in the 1960s ever mentioned any impact, positive or negative, of the new German owners on their life in the workshops and around the compound.[76] It is even possible that the workers were unaware of the transfer of ownership. The only obvious sign of change was a display of swastikas in the workshops and on the company clock tower at the Tangjiazha compound. The somewhat naïve intention behind this action by the Chinese management was to prevent attacks by Japanese airplanes and to signal to Japanese troops that Dasheng was off-limits as German property. For the same reason, enamel plates in Japanese reading "Property Owned by Germans" (*Doitsu jin shoyū zaisan*) were attached to the mills.[77] These measures failed to ward off Japanese interest in the mills for long, especially when chance turned them into a financially more profitable operation.

This fortunate opportunity presented itself in the form of rampant wartime inflation, which allowed Dasheng to redeem the majority of its debts to various creditor-banks. Inflation substantially lowered the burden of Dasheng's interest payments and allowed it to consolidate its previously rather unstable financial situation. Although I cannot establish exact figures for 1938 and 1939, since the publication of shareholders' and business reports was not continued on a regular basis between 1938 and 1944, business correspondence documents that Dasheng was able to pay off its debts.[78] The most significant aspect of debt consolidation through inflation for Dasheng was, however, that it finally escaped the financial and managerial control exerted by members of the banking consortium since the early 1920s.

Unfortunately, because of its financial recovery, Dasheng was now an even more attractive object for the Japanese, who from mid-1938 on established tight political and economic control over the Nantong area. Since the Japanese were not able to declare the German registration a fraud, they forced Dasheng to enter partnership negotiations with a Japanese textile mill, the Kanegafuchi Company. Forcing Chinese enterprises into cooperative arrangements (*hezuo*) with a Japanese business partner was a common tactic of the Japanese authorities in Shanghai. In 1938 alone, seventeen Chinese-owned textile enterprises outside the foreign concessions had to form partnerships with Japanese textile mills.[79]

In March 1939 the Dasheng enterprise came under joint supervision of the military control commission of the local Japanese secret police, the Special Services, and a new factory management team appointed by and working on behalf of the Kanegafuchi Company. The militarization of Dasheng enforced by the new management went hand in hand with increasing Japanese control over the local economy and thus over Dasheng's resources. As Parks Coble has shown, the phrase "Using the war to feed the war" (*yizhan yangzhan*) summarizes Japan's procurement policy for products needed back in Japan, in particular cotton, salt, iron, and coal.[80] In the spirit of the New Order in Asia propagated in late 1938, the Japanese government established development companies like the Jiangbei xingye gongsi (Company for promoting industry in Northern Jiangsu) as an "investment program designed to marshal the resources of north China for the Japanese military."[81] The Jiangbei company was supposed to aid the Japanese army in controlling the local trade in raw cotton and cotton yarn and serve the occupier's economic interests.[82] The implementation of these new economic arrangements and institutions had a significant, practical impact on the Dasheng cotton mills, as we shall see next.

Collaboration and Resistance on the Shop Floor

Issues of resistance and collaboration feature strongly in the interviews conducted in the 1960s. Nearly all of the 214 former Dasheng workers related traumatic experiences under the Japanese occupation.[83] These interviews were conducted under the influence of political campaigns in the 1960s in which workers were encouraged to describe their fight against capitalist exploitation, right-wing Guomindang terror, and the Japanese occupation. These patriotic, highly politicized narratives—which, for that reason, need to be interpreted with care—present Chinese workers as heroes of the anti-Japanese resistance and as exemplary participants in the early Communist movement.[84]

Many of the Dasheng workers' distressing experiences with the Japanese managers and their representatives were related not only to the presence of the Japanese occupation forces but also to the use of factory discipline and the militarization of the company patrol force as tools of control. This interpretation does not deny the great suffering of the Chinese population under the Japanese occupation but instead tries to explain how the occupation affected factory workers and how we should interpret their specific reactions on the shop floor in the context of local political and patriotic activism.

In order to gain a tight grip on Dasheng's workforce, the new Japanese managers decided to deal first with the existing *gongtou* system based on local labor and the power it gave to Chinese male and female foremen on the shop floor. In order to destroy their influence and to create loyalty to the new Japanese management, the Kanegafuchi Company dismissed all *gongtou* in the four Dasheng mills and replaced them with *gongtou* hired from large urban textile mills in Shanghai, Qingdao, and other centers of China's textile industry.[85]

By employing these mainly male foremen from outside the Nantong area, the Japanese management intended to control the local workforce more strictly and to undermine local anti-Japanese solidarity on the shop floor. Even more important, these foremen, because of their previous employment in large urban mills, had ample experience with instilling a rigid factory discipline among unruly workers. Reflecting this change was a shift in terminology. *Gongtou* in Dasheng subsequently were called *namowen* (number one); this term for *gongtou*, commonly used in Shanghai cotton mills, had previously not been a familiar expression in Nantong.[86]

According to Meng Guilin, a former Dasheng worker and a party member, the newly appointed Chinese *gongtou* became the immediate object of the workers' disdain and hatred because "Chinese were being used to control Chinese" (*yi Hua zhi Hua*).[87] Additionally, in order to enforce loyalty to the new Japanese management, the Kanegafuchi Company introduced another level of lower management by hiring Japanese supervisors from textile mills in Japan to deal with the Chinese *gongtou*. Although some Chinese sources refer to them as *gongtou*, these Japanese foremen performed supervisory work (*lingong*), and they clearly had more authority and power than the Chinese *gongtou*.[88] Among the unskilled Chinese workers, the Japanese supervisors represented the Japanese management and the political agenda of the occupation forces in a direct and confrontational way. The fact that some of these Japanese supervisors wore army hats at work turned them into a perfect symbol of the workers' oppression through factory discipline combined with political oppression through the Japanese occupation army.[89]

On a day-to-day basis, the workers' complaints against the Japanese management differed little from their complaints against the previous Chinese management under the old *gongtou* system with Chinese foremen in the 1910s and 1920s. In the interview sample, former workers complained about being bossed around, scolded, and sometimes beaten by the *gongtou*. Like their predecessors, the Japanese supervisors punished sleeping on the job and mistakes at work, now more often than before with excessive force. As they had under Zhang Jian, the workers complained about having to show their work identification cards to the guards at the gate, who would check that the photograph matched the person. The only difference was that the guards were now Japanese.[90] And as before, workers complained about being searched when they left the factory compound, but this also was a rather familiar aspect of factory discipline and had always been an issue. Whereas the workers had defended pilferage as an act of survival and protest against the strict management under the old system, however, theft was now a heroic deed with a political and even nationalistic dimension. According to Meng Guilin, a slogan circulating among the workers stated this baldly: "Taking yarn and cloth from the Japanese is a patriotic act."[91]

In this context sabotage became the most common form of what one might call patriotic resistance, and it created a new dynamic in labor relations on Dasheng's shop floor. In fact, the desire to interrupt production and thus to reduce the profits of the Japanese management forced the unskilled workers to re-evaluate their relationship with the Chinese *gongtou* in the early 1940s. Acts such as temporarily stopping the machines, running reeling machines at low speed, and not replacing full spindles required the cooperation of the *gongtou* in charge of the workshop. The unskilled workers' appeal to the patriotic conscience of the *gongtou* with slogans such as "After all, we are all Chinese" created a form of solidarity between *gongtou* and unskilled workers on Dasheng's shop floor, united against the same, Japanese enemy.[92]

Patriotic sabotage, however loosely defined, even led to an unprecedented alliance between the company patrol force and the unskilled workers. After the Kanegafuchi management assumed control over Dasheng, the local military authorities allowed the managers to use Japanese soldiers to guard the factory compound and Japanese property. At the same time, the management used the existing Dasheng patrol force as a supplement to the Japanese guards. As in the case of the Chinese and Japanese *gongtou*, the use of Japanese and Chinese guards created an interesting new social dynamic, bridging to some extent the intended alienation between Chinese workers and Chinese guards.[93]

In order to facilitate the theft of yarn and cloth, the workers started to pay off the Chinese guards, most of whom came from Shanghai. As a former female worker described it, the theft and sale of stolen yarn became a serious sideline business for workers in the Dasheng mills in the early 1940s. For example, she managed to smuggle out up to twelve hanks of yarn by hiding them on her body and in her clothes.[94] The workers would pay the Chinese guards for letting them leave the compound without a search or for distracting the Japanese guards at an opportune moment. As the interviews also indicate, the cooperation of the Chinese guards was clearly motivated by financial incentives and not by the guards' patriotism. The workers always referred to the Chinese guards as representatives of Japanese discipline.[95]

The workers' most serious grievances concerned the Japanese soldiers who were stationed in the area but who were not part of the company patrol force itself. Young female workers, who had to walk long distances from their villages to the factory sites, experienced verbal and physical harassment, often ending in rape and sometimes even in murder.[96] Almost all the workers told, either from personal experience or hearsay, of crimes committed by Japanese soldiers. This aspect of an oppressive occupation regime severely affected not only the daily life of Dasheng workers but also that of the other inhabitants of Nantong and the surrounding counties and was common in most of occupied China at the time.[97]

Transformation of Ownership and Control

The final years of the war proved to be even more difficult for Dasheng, despite the newly forged political alliance between Japan and the Wang Jingwei regime in 1943, which included, among other things, the return of companies confiscated by the Japanese to their original owners. In June 1943, the Japanese army looted the Dasheng mills in order to supply their own arms-production factories in Shanghai with machine motors, machine carriages, and building materials before "returning" (*fahuan*) them to Chinese ownership. The enterprise now came under the leadership of Chen Baochu, who acted as director of the board on behalf of the collaborationist Wang Jingwei regime and thus was labeled a "traitor" (*hanjian*) after 1945.[98]

As noted in the preceding chapter, Chen Baochu had been a close business associate of Zhang Jian as well as the publisher of the *Tonghai xinbao*. He had served as a member of the board of the No. 3 mill since 1935.[99] With the support of the Wang Jingwei regime, Chen Baochu assumed control of Dasheng's financial and personnel management. One of his first acts was to restore Dasheng's patrol force to its previous strength and status. In addition, he also came to control the local production and trading of raw cotton and cotton yarn by serving as head of the Dasheng yarn-cotton exchange (*shahua jiaohuanchu*).[100]

From a more general economic and political perspective, the yarn-cotton exchange is an example of centralized economic institutions and market mechanisms introduced during the war years, long before China's state-controlled economy of the post-1949 period.[101] In the words of Christian

Henriot, Japan's "new policy toward China" in 1943 gave the Wang Jingwei regime the opportunity to "assert itself on the economic stage" by attempting to implement a controlled economy (*tongzhi jingji*).[102] For example, due to a drastic drop in the raw cotton crop in China after 1941 and intense Chinese and Japanese competition for the material, owners of cotton cloth or yarn in central China were ordered to sell their goods at fixed prices to government agencies. Raw cotton was collected in similar fashion by the Association of Raw Cotton Purchasing Guilds under the supervision of the Monopoly Committee for Cotton from November 1943 on. As Henriot points out, the system of compulsory purchase was plagued by many serious problems, from painfully slow payments, devalued by rampant inflation, to artificially low prices for cloth and yarn, which led to the financial collapse of hundreds of cotton yarn and cloth shops and smaller spinning mills. The system also proved to be completely ineffective in providing cotton mills with the much-needed raw materials and in holding prices down, which kept rising because of speculation, inflation, and a booming black market.[103]

In the Nantong area, the yarn-cotton exchange was designed primarily to ensure the Dasheng cotton mills a sufficient supply of raw cotton. According to a former Dasheng worker, Chen Baochu used a network of local merchants who favored the Wang Jingwei regime to exchange Dasheng yarn for raw cotton at a fixed ratio. This exchange resulted—according to this source—in enormous profits for Chen Baochu and the merchants, who had bought the raw cotton at low prices from local farmers.[104] However, given the continuing crisis in the cotton industry at the time and the lack of data, it is difficult to say whether Chen Baochu profited that much from the arrangement or whether blatant corruption was simply one charge against collaborators in the post-1949 narrative.[105]

Despite the return of Chinese management in 1943, workers continued to complain of harsh treatment by the Chinese *gongtou*.[106] As before, the *gongtou* wielded power over the shop floor and accepted bribes for granting jobs, and the Chinese guards continued to search workers.[107] The Dasheng company patrol force remained an institutional tool of work discipline and control. However, because of the new management's close relationship with the Wang Jingwei regime, the patrol force was now a local political tool as well, representing and supporting the political agenda of the Wang Jingwei regime.[108] At the end of the war in 1945, the patrol force switched its alliance to the Guomindang. When the Communists arrived in Tangjiazha in early

1949, they had to contend with the patrol force and had to rely on the work-ers to help them disarm the much better equipped patrol force.[109]

The end of the war in 1945 also brought the return of Zhang family members to the management of the business. After Zhang Xiaoruo's death in 1935, Zhang Jingli, the son of Zhang Cha and only surviving male family representative in the enterprise, had occupied a rather subordinate position on the board of the Dasheng No. 1 mill; he made no important business de-cisions for the enterprise, probably because of his youth. On arrival of the Japanese, he—like all the other managers and administrators in Dasheng—was dismissed from his position and replaced by staff presumably more loyal to the Japanese management.[110] We know very little about his life during the war, except that he opened a *qianzhuang* in Shanghai.[111] In 1946, Zhang Jingli returned from Shanghai to Nantong in order to serve as one of the executive managers of the No. 1 mill as well as general manager of Dasheng.[112]

Not only Zhang Jingli but also the other executives who returned to Nantong in 1945–46 to resume work at Dasheng are listed in company documents as residents of Shanghai.[113] Since many of the managers had business interests and even property in Shanghai, this city seemed to have offered them a better chance for surviving the war. During his years in Shanghai, Zhang Jingli kept a low profile and severed his associations with Dasheng and with relatives still resident in Nantong. By distancing them-selves from the Japanese management and avoiding any form of cooperation with the Japanese occupation forces or the Wang Jingwei regime, Zhang Jingli and his relatives kept the name of the Zhang family free from the taint of collaboration and were thus well prepared to make a fresh start in the en-terprise after 1945.

Company documents compiled after the end of the war reveal interesting information about the Dasheng shareholders and the registration of their shares. According to a 1947 ledger, 1,402 shareholders (*gudong hu*), listed either under their own name or under the name of their business account, held 630,000 shares at a value of 10 yuan each in the No. 1 mill.[114] The residential addresses of 1,181 (84 percent) of the shareholders are in Shanghai. This is a significant departure from the pattern that held until the late 1920s, when the majority of Dasheng's shareholders came from Nantong and the surrounding counties. With the demise of the local yarn and cloth market in the 1930s, the yarn and cloth merchants who had traditionally been Dasheng shareholders apparently sold their shares. In addition, with the banking consortium directing Dasheng's development from the mid-1920s on, shares were more easily traded outside the Nantong area, particularly in Shanghai. Since many shareholders with the same surname are listed under one address in the prewar foreign concessions, protection of their financial assets might have been a primary concern for registering their address in Shanghai.[115] This pattern of shareholding held true for the Dasheng branch mills as well.

One thing that did not change during the Japanese occupation was the way shares were held by the Zhang family through personal as well as business accounts.[116] According to business records from 1951, Zhang Jingli and the granddaughter and grandson of Zhang Jian, Zhang Rouwu and Zhang Xuwu, still jointly owned roughly 11 percent of Dasheng's share capital.[117]

The influence and public role of the Zhang family also revived after 1945. Zhang Xiaoruo's widow in Nantong, the mother of Zhang Rouwu, made local history by heroically hiding the local Communist activist Wang Minzhi in the family villa at the outbreak of the civil war in 1945.[118] In 1948, the then-chairman of Dasheng's board, Hong Lanyou, a minister in the Guomindang government, wanted to move Dasheng's machinery to Taiwan, but he was opposed by Zhang Jingli, who refused to move the business or his family abroad.[119] Hong Lanyou then went to Hong Kong and tried to convince Zhang Jingli to move Dasheng's assets to the colony (as many other textile industrialists did), but again without success. According to Zhang Jingli's autobiography, patriotism, respect for the achievements of his uncle and father, and love of his native place directed his decision to stay.[120] Because of his refusal to leave Nantong, the Communists viewed Zhang Jingli as a person who could be trusted to help in the rebuilding of the local economy and society after 1949. As managing director, he supervised the first factory reforms introduced in 1950. After Dasheng's restructuring into a cooperative in 1951, Zhang Jingli became a representative of the Chinese Communist party and the government with the explicit mission of convincing other private industrial enterprises of the benefits of nationalization and public ownership.[121]

With the rise of Chiang Kai-shek and the consolidation of his political power in Central China in 1927, the conditions for doing business changed. As Parks Coble has shown, although the Guomindang did not allow capitalists a political role in the Nanjing government, it did not hesitate to take advantage of their wealth and economic activities, often through pressure and sometimes through coercion.[122] The Japanese occupation and the war had an even more damaging and lasting impact on Chinese business, the lives of entrepreneurs, and the existence of their industrial companies. What in particular can we learn from an examination of Dasheng's case?

Recent studies suggest that the responses of Chinese entrepreneurs to the war depended on the location of their businesses, on the control and public influence exercised by company representatives, and on the existence of branches and business connections overseas.[123] Prominent industrial families like the Rong from Wuxi, who owned a diverse business empire with several flour and textile mills in Shanghai, Wuxi, and other cities, were able to save at least part of their business operations during the war.[124] In contrast, since all the Dasheng mills were concentrated in the rural area outside Shanghai and could not easily be moved to the International Settlement or China's interior, the business had to cope with the Japanese occupation forces. Dasheng also suffered from an overwhelming concentration in textiles and did not have branches or affiliated business operations overseas. More important, whereas dynamic members of the Rong family actively tried to see their enterprises through the war period, the influence of the Zhang family had been weakened by the banking consortium and the lack of suitable successors in its second generation.

Neither Zhang Jian nor his brother nor their sons were able to negotiate with the Guomindang government. Certainly, other Chinese industrial enterprises had to deal with the changed political situation after 1927. For example, the Nationalist government criticized Rong Zongjing severely and tried to intervene in his businesses, but, to quote Sherman Cochran, he "used his social network to limit, redirect, or deflect official policies."[125] Other entrepreneurs such as Liu Hongsheng in the case of the China Steamship Navigation Company openly cooperated with the Green Gang as long as it enabled them to continue.[126] In short, whereas other entrepreneurs were able to use their political and social connections to help their enterprises and family business interests, the lack of dynamic leadership and the inability of the second generation to establish useful political and social contacts left Dasheng prone to interference from the Green Gang, the Japanese, and the Wang Jingwei regime.

As for labor relations and political activism in Chinese industries during the war and occupation, I suggest that a re-evaluation of protest and resistance is needed. The Sino-Japanese war is often discussed to explain why the

Communist revolution finally succeeded and why the Guomindang failed to hold on to power. As I show in Chapter 4, despite Dasheng's huge industrial workforce, the Communists could not overcome the workers' continuing identification with their rural background and the socioeconomic structure of the Nantong area. The Japanese skillfully adapted the *gongtou* system to their own agenda of maintaining work discipline and preventing the formation of solidarity among the workforce. Anti-Japanese sabotage united workers with different interests and different status, but only for a time; it never led to the creation of new, lasting forms of alliances based on shared political or social values among the workers.

In general, the post-1926 period illustrates again Dasheng's problems as an enterprise characterized by a combination of corporate and traditional business structures. As one would expect, the enterprise never really disassociated itself from the family. Whereas industrialist families like the Rong sent employees with a different surname to represent their interests in their mills or in the cotton association controlled by the Wang Jingwei regime in Shanghai, the Zhang family must have secretly been relieved to see Chen Baochu act as general manager until 1945, because at least he was not able to implicate the family.[127]

As Dasheng was increasingly integrated into national economic programs and a state-controlled cotton market and industry after 1949, the regional component of the enterprise became less and less significant. With the political and social changes introduced by the socialist party-state, the family was no longer as influential in the Nantong area. At the same time, the government's new economic and legal framework ceased to sustain the enterprise as a corporate institution and thus the family's financial power, which derived from it. Dasheng ceased to be a private, regional enterprise.

CONCLUSION

Beyond 1949: Modern Enterprises and
Regional Businesses in China

Times have changed for Nantong and its enterprises. The Chinese and foreign businessmen who travel to Nantong in chauffeured cars are not in the cotton business. Their destination is neither the Dasheng No. 1 nor the No. 3 mill, both of which still operate as state-owned enterprises, but the development area (*kaifa qu*) southeast of the city. There the economic reforms of the 1980s and 1990s brought growth and foreign investment in the form of a huge container port, a Japanese joint venture for producing automobile parts, and other companies manufacturing light industrial products such as pharmaceuticals, textiles, and electronics. Although the infrastructure of the Nantong area is slowly improving, the importance of the river for passenger traffic has declined rapidly due to faster and cheaper transportation options on newly built expressways in the Yangzi Delta. However, Nantong city and the counties north of the river are still not connected to China's railway system. The railway line, optimistically indicated on a 1992 map for investors, had not been built by 2003.[1]

Although township-village enterprises have brought economic growth to the Nantong area (even if at a lower level than in southern Jiangsu), the Dasheng mills now face hard times. Because of serious domestic and international competition in the textile market, their profits are meager. At the same time, as state-owned enterprises the two mills are under great pressure to fulfill their financial and social responsibilities to a huge local workforce, both active and retired, at a time when government support has decreased because of Zhu Rongji's economic reforms. In stark contrast to the dire economic realities of the present, company brochures proudly refer to their more successful past and advertise Nantong as "the cradle of the Chinese national textile industry" and pay tribute to Zhang Jian as a "famous modern industrialist."[2]

What do the continuities and discontinuities between the Dasheng cotton mills at the turn of the century, the state-owned mills of the present, and the new businesses such as township-village enterprises tell us about the emergence of the modern firm in China? The answer to that question depends on the structure, shop-floor management, accounting practices, and family and business networks of these enterprises and their relationship with the state and local society.

A central finding of this book is that the deliberate institutionalization of Dasheng after 1900 played a vital role in the running of the company as a modern enterprise. The founding of the first cotton mill was heavily influenced by such external factors as government approval, regional infrastructure, availability of land, and support by local investors, but the subsequent management and expansion of the enterprise reflected a hierarchical approach combined with functional authoritarianism. In return, the institutionalization of control in the enterprise, its structure and function, explains the specific forms of ownership and accountability in place in Dasheng during the early twentieth century.

Analysis of the Dasheng business suggests a new interpretation of the emergence of the modern firm in late imperial and Republican China and offers a useful comparative framework for the interpretation of regional enterprises in contemporary China. Dasheng differed from existing forms of businesses in the late nineteenth century in that it successfully combined characteristics of the traditional Chinese family firm and the modern corporation according to Western standards. The juxtaposition of personalized power through control over managerial hierarchies and shareholders with a lack of accountability in financial and managerial matters led to the development of a paternalistic, autocratic form of management despite the legal shell of incorporation. Most significant, however, is the fact that the financial and managerial power of the founder-director did not depend solely on his position within the hierarchy or on his social networks: it was institutionalized through the Shanghai office.

This discussion of Dasheng has traced the emergence of institutionalized personal control as an important characteristic of the modern Chinese firm and contributes to the ongoing debate about hierarchies and social networks in Chinese business. In a study of six Western, Japanese, and Chinese corporations in pre-1937 China, Sherman Cochran argues convincingly that each of the companies—and each in very different ways—relied simultaneously on networks and on hierarchies.[3] Cochran's interpretation of the modern firm in China (he uses the term "corporation") is important because he demonstrates that "corporations did not all make linear transitions, fully liberating themselves from social networks and becoming exclusively dependent on managerial hierarchies, nor did they do the reverse."[4]

Within limits, Dasheng supports Cochran's argument concerning the interaction between hierarchies and social networks. However, with its particular institutionalized tool of control through the Shanghai office, Dasheng radically challenges the conventional assumption of the dominance of networks in Chinese business. For example, in studies of overseas Chinese businesses, sociologists Gary G. Hamilton and S. Gordon Redding have argued that networking is the most decisive characteristic of the Chinese economy and contrast the Chinese business based on social networks with the Western corporation based on hierarchical organization.[5] Without denying the importance of networks in Chinese business, I suggest that we need to pay more attention to hierarchical and institutional aspects of the firm, based on analyses of company records, in order fully to explain the institutional, financial, and managerial structures of modern enterprises. Dasheng's case shows that the cultural approach to Chinese business provides too narrow a perspective.

As we have seen, on the shop floor, the institutional factor was enforced physically through the factory compound and psychologically through written rules. The factory regulations were a vital tool both because they laid down guidelines and because they prescribed punishments. The shop-floor management of the production process was not supposed to be arbitrary or dominated by personal relations. Operations at the Dasheng No. 1 Cotton Mill were not, however, completely free from the influence of personal networks, either among the managers or the workers on the shop floor.

Cochran's analysis vividly demonstrates the limitations of Chinese social networks because of internal disputes and particularism based on family ties and native-place connections;[6] Dasheng's development in the early twentieth century illustrates a structural solution to this problem: through institutionalized control via the accounts office, Zhang Jian was able to bypass dissent from the shareholders and managers. Although he made use of particularistic forms of social networks, managers, business associates, and family members were ultimately subjected to the control mechanism of the accounts office.

Indeed, the analysis presented in this book takes the institutional interpretation a step further and develops a new argument. According to Cochran, "the interaction between corporations and networks was dynamic because neither controlled the other."[7] Although this accurately characterizes his case studies, analysis of Dasheng shows that the institutional tool of the accounts office allowed for the centralized control of corporate, supposedly nonpersonal, managerial hierarchies *and* social networks. As I have suggested here, Zhang Jian's control of his sphere of influence reached beyond the various factories, the reclamation companies, and his social ambitions as projected onto Nantong city.

The case of Dasheng also shows that professionalism in management not only evolved automatically from within the traditional family business but could develop gradually as part of the institutionalization process itself, even if the managerial staff was still part of the director's network. The labor market for professional managers did not emerge in Chinese enterprises before the late 1920s. This is not surprising, however; according to Sidney Pollard's findings, management as a profession emerged only slowly in England during the nineteenth century.[8]

The uses to which accounting was put illustrate the issue of professionalism. As I have shown, accounting was used less to control costs than to control the flow of funds. Cost accounting never seems to have been an aim in itself. Through the accounts office, Zhang Jian centralized financial and major managerial decisions and separated them from the day-to-day business in Nantong and elsewhere. However, he was an old-style manager in the sense that he did not separate the management of Dasheng's business accounts from his private accounts. Most important, Zhang Jian's control of the Shanghai office freed him from accountability to bookkeepers, managers, and finally the shareholders of the company.

If the separation of private and business accounts and accountability to shareholders are the characteristics of a modern business enterprise, then Dasheng certainly was not modern in these respects. Since disguised family accounts continued to exist and be used even after Dasheng's reorganization in 1947 under the supervision of professional accountants, it is questionable whether the company ever became fully transparent and accountable. Therefore, I suggest that the term "corporation" and its common definition based on Western legal, financial, and managerial concepts is not the most appropriate way to describe Chinese corporate industrial enterprises in the early twentieth century, even if they qualify in many other ways as modern enterprises according to Western standards.

Thus the Dasheng case also suggests caution in assuming a straightforward convergence of business institutions in the processes of industrialization and modernization across time and space from one culture to another. Dasheng's institutional development demonstrates neither the total acceptance of the Western corporate model nor the continuation of a distinctively Chinese business form in early twentieth-century China. This is not to imply, however, that the Chinese economy of the early twentieth century was less efficient or less successful because it did not have full-blown corporations supported by legal institutions as in the West. In fact, Kenneth Pomeranz, in his superb comparative study, has shown that we must beware of overestimating the role of corporations in the economic rise of Europe. As he points out, in the nineteenth century family firms still played a major role in Britain's economic activities (with the exception of trade and colonization in Africa), and corporations as financing mechanisms did not become important in Europe until large-scale capital was needed for railway projects at a relatively late stage of industrialization.[9] And as I have indicated in previous chapters, remnants of traditional ways of accounting and management survived in Western corporations for many years, and current standards of accountability and transparency did not become common until well into the twentieth century.

This takes us finally to a more general evaluation of the Dasheng enterprise within Chinese business history and its significance for our understanding of business in contemporary China. It is obvious that Zhang Jian's background in officialdom did not jeopardize his success as entrepreneur. Zhang Jian can be described as a "modern" entrepreneur comparable to, for example, Henry Ford, if we define "modern" as guiding the management of the shop floor and of the administration via hierarchy, regulations, and discipline. However, we must also acknowledge all the traditional aspects of the enterprise and its director when evaluating Zhang Jian as a first-generation entrepreneur and Dasheng as a first-generation enterprise. Even if we do not attach normative value to the term "modern," autocratic and authoritarian leadership combined with patronage run counter to our general interpretation of modern management styles.

Traditional autocratic leadership styles serve their purposes, however, and should not be considered irrational. The example of Dasheng shows that personal control and lack of accountability as such do not compromise business success in the short run, regardless of how strong the legal framework and its enforcement are. Yet, as Dasheng's case also demonstrates, personal control and lack of accountability do not promote long-term growth and success for business enterprises, particularly with regard to structural and financial expansion.

To what extent do Dasheng's success in the first two decades of the twentieth century and its subsequent development represent the norm or the exception for modern enterprises in China and regional enterprises in particular? As officials-turned-entrepreneurs, Nie Qigui and Zhou Xuexi faced the same political conditions and challenges as Zhang Jian. However, their cotton mills, mining operations, and cement companies were geographically scattered and never attained the regional focus of Dasheng in the Nantong area. The development and gradual expansion of their businesses were not related to the socioeconomic development of a particular town or region or linked to an entrepreneurial personality as eminent as Zhang Jian. In addition, unlike Zhang Jian, both entrepreneurs remained closely tied to the world of officialdom (Zhou Xuexi never gave up his official post), and this was reflected in the management and staffing of their enterprises.[10]

The industrial companies established and managed by the Rong family in Wuxi and Shanghai immediately come to mind as successful modern businesses with a strong regional and personal focus. The charismatic team of brothers Rong Zongjing and Rong Desheng managed the Shenxin Cotton Mills in Shanghai, which by the 1930s had become the largest Chinese-owned cotton textile enterprise and accounted for some 10 percent of spinning in China.[11] The Rong business was always primarily identified with the family's native place, Wuxi, and qualifies as a regional enterprise because of its close local ties and networks, even though most of the Shenxin mills were located and financed in Shanghai. However, the Shenxin mills present a very different case of institutional development in regard to incorporation, since they were founded twenty years later than Dasheng (in 1915) and were structured as a family business. Several studies have stressed the continuation of the Rong enterprises as a family business after Shenxin abandoned its limited liability status. Disagreement with the shareholders about profit distribution and business expansion led Rong Zongjing to conclude that an unincorporated business structure without interference from outsiders would be more suitable to the family circle's business goals.[12] Yet, in terms of their operations the Rong factories are often cited as the prime example of modern factory work, probably because in the 1930s and 1940s the mills in Wuxi created a much stronger company culture with housing facilities and social welfare programs for workers than Dasheng ever wanted to.[13]

Thus, Dasheng, with its move away from official influence and family domination and its strong regional focus, stands out more as an exception than as the norm. At the same time, it encountered and dealt with the same general problems that all Chinese enterprises had to address in the early twentieth century, regardless of their institutional structure and origins. For this reason, Dasheng also tells us something about the roles of the family in Chinese business and of family structures in long-term business survival.

Historians have pointed to the reluctance of Chinese family businesses to adopt a modern business structure. As David Faure has concluded, some companies adopted a modern structure such as limited liability to enhance their image, but the structure had little impact as long as the family was able to wield control and to settle succession disputes.[14] As I have shown in this book, succession problems and the issue of family influence played a role in a corporate firm like Dasheng. Personal control and lack of accountability worked as long as the founder-director was alive and able to wield control. His death left the company in limbo, without strong centralized leadership, because Zhang Jian's personal control had prevented any member of management or the family from preparing to take over direction of the firm, and his only son proved to be an unwilling successor. Thus, despite its corporate shell, Dasheng had to face the issue of succession that in family firms, regardless of the cultural environment, often jeopardizes a smooth transition from one generation to the next and can threaten the continuity of the firm.

As we have seen, although the Zhang family did not take an active part in the management of the company, its (minority) stockholdings and its relationship with the accounts office kept its influence alive well into the 1950s. Even today, family influence in corporate business institutions is still prevalent in various cultural contexts, from Thai tycoons reigning over petrochemical conglomerates and defending their family interests to Western high-tech corporations with strong connections to the founders' families.[15] As the case of the Hewlett-Packard corporation has shown recently, if the heirs of the company founders oppose the expansion and diversification plans of the chief executive, family stockholdings are powerful tools for intervention.[16]

In this context Dasheng's case also sheds light on the development of overseas Chinese businesses and their success and failure in contemporary Southeast Asia, particularly in regard to the Asian economic crisis of the late 1990s. As Rajeswary Brown has demonstrated, although Chinese family businesses incorporated and expanded in the postwar period, ownership and control still remained with the family, and the ubiquitous use of holding companies allowed them to expand and diversify their operations.[17] Chinese business groups in Southeast Asia were very successful in Indonesia, Thailand, and Malaysia, before the financial crisis of 1997 exposed their weaknesses in form of staggering indebtedness, financial overextension, and fraudulent speculation. In many conglomerates, this led to the loss of ownership. Brown argues that "family domination and the absence of managerial hierarchies made the Chinese corporation inherently unstable, which in turn destabilized economic growth as a whole."[18] Most significant in comparison with Dasheng's fate is Brown's observation that Chinese conglomerates' approach to diversification led to instability because although diversification was meant to reduce risks, risk was included in the financial liabilities of the enterprise. Dasheng's risky diversification into land-reclamation companies with their high financial liabilities for the cotton mills appears to be an early example of this unhealthy business strategy.

Certainly, as in the case of businesses in China and Southeast Asia today, Dasheng's development as a modern business institution did not occur in a political and socioeconomic vacuum. Since the government and its agencies have always played an important role in China's economic life, we should also consider what role the state played in China's modernization, as exemplified in Dasheng's history. Dasheng can serve as an example of an enterprise in which the government lost its direct financial and managerial influence after 1900 and the director was able to profit from the reforms and new institutions that came into existence to fill the power vacuum left by the retreating state. Institutions like the chamber of commerce helped Zhang Jian to get rid of competitors; company registration with the government brought official acknowledgment; the adoption of limited liability reassured shareholders; and his positions in various local self-government organizations increased his local authority and influence. In this respect, the retreat of the centralized state offered the industrialist the opportunity to be involved in both business and politics. Thus I would argue that in the early twentieth century the centralized state posed much less of an obstacle to private industrial enterprises than in the late nineteenth century.

The phenomenon of the retreating state connects Dasheng with the development of business in contemporary China. As indicated in the Introduction, China's recent economic success owes much to the re-emergence of the corporate economy, from township-village enterprises (TVEs) in what used to be agricultural communes to large financial and industrial trusts in the metropolitan centers.[19] In the 1980s the TVE sector had the highest output share of nonstate industry, and in the 1990s individually owned and other forms of private enterprises attained the highest gross industrial output in the nonstate sector.[20] However, as in the 1920s and 1930s, the performance of regional enterprises varies greatly by geographical location. Today the rural areas in the south and coastal areas in the north and east are doing much better than rural northern China or inland regions, where the budget constraints and severe restrictions of the economic reforms did less to stimulate the performance of enterprises.[21] In Jiangsu, TVEs have been particularly successful in creating economic growth, although the development in the area north of the Yangzi River, including Nantong, is slower than in the southern part of the province.[22]

In China today the regional impact of the Dasheng enterprise is a historical precedent for the regional economic improvements brought about by the TVEs.[23] To be sure, TVEs such as the Yintie Hongfang Tinplate Factory are collectively owned, and Dasheng was organized as a private shareholding company. However, both the TVEs and Dasheng emerged at a time of decreasing government influence. In addition to redefined property rights and newly created incentives, the new role of the local government has created an institutional framework for corporatism, both collective and private, in the wake of the economic reforms.

In Jean Oi's words, local state corporatism or China's new system of financial contracting, which allows local governments to collect and keep tax revenues, is the motor behind local governments' attempts to promote business, especially in the countryside.[24] Special arrangements for contracting and leasing of collective enterprises have de facto created a private management system in those enterprises without formally privatizing ownership.[25] The same could be said of Dasheng and Zhang Jian's private management system without personal private ownership. The recent economic reforms have shifted the control of assets from the central to the local government. In turn, the local government serves as a coordinator of the various component firms and has assumed the function of company headquarters. It thus much resembles a diversified business corporation.[26]

On a more political level, the economic reforms of the 1980s and 1990s have led to a re-evaluation of these new enterprise forms in the collective sector, with the obvious agenda of providing an ideological justification for the introduction of market-oriented economic principles in a socialist system. Although rural TVEs are not required to provide the same social services to their employees as the state-owned enterprises, their economic success creates important and much needed economic and social welfare resources for their communities. Whereas the contributions of these modern regional enterprises to local society are in essence indirect taxation by the state, they also point to the simultaneous "hollowing out" of state power and government influence in contemporary local society, as recently discussed in terms of property rights by Jean Oi and Andrew Walder.[27]

As the TVEs as regional enterprises have assumed the government's responsibilities, the media have eagerly asserted that these new enterprises and their profits represent no threat to the spirit of Chinese socialism. In order to avoid clashes with ideological critiques, these successful businesses and their directors are often presented in terms of patriotism (*aiguozhuyi*).[28] Newspapers and magazine articles focus on the beneficial role played by dynamic directors in public and collectively owned corporate enterprises, who are now labeled progressive "entrepreneurs." According to the foreword to one collection of biographies collected in 1997, these entrepreneurs "are the assistants of socialism and the new force in the development of a market economy" in China.[29]

The great variety of forms of ownership in present-day Chinese enterprises (the *China Statistical Yearbook* for 1996 lists fifteen categories of ownership for nonstate enterprises) has led to great variations in management.[30] Issues of ownership and control as reflected in managerial and financial structures and business customs still need to be clarified and formalized. Complaints by foreign and Chinese businessmen about the lack of accountability and transparency in Chinese enterprises and the surrounding administrative and legal framework will continue. At the same time, the success of regional enterprises, old and new, points to their ability to work effectively in an environment still influenced by personal and local networks and, at least at present, by insecure property rights.

Its rational and efficient corporate appearance to the contrary, the institutionalized mechanisms of control found in Dasheng inherently limited the long-term success of the enterprise. Faced with succession problems and with a deteriorating sociopolitical situation, Dasheng was unable to make the transition to a fully accountable and transparent corporation in the 1930s.

How will regional enterprises in present-day China, who face problems analogous to those Dasheng encountered, perform in the transition to capitalist and private ownership in an era of receding state control? It is a matter of speculation whether a successful collective enterprise will remain collective indefinitely. The transformation of village party secretaries into the local managerial class and local patrons of TVEs is already well recognized.[31] Along the same line, the cases of large, publicly owned industrial enterprises that are under the complete control of the village party secretary and his family show that the interpretation of property rights in contemporary Chinese businesses remains complex and fluid.[32] Thus we need to be careful about using the term "privatization" in reference to China's enterprise reforms, because rural enterprises that are officially collective may in reality be controlled by local political elites and their families.[33] Obviously, in this respect not much has changed between Dasheng's situation in the early twentieth century and Chinese businesses at the beginning of the twenty-first century; Chinese historians who have identified privatization as the most important contribution of what they call the "Dasheng model" (Dasheng *moshi*) have missed the point.[34] For the sake of more accountability and transparency in Chinese business, one hopes that the kinship and social networks of local administrative elites, especially their particularistic and political ties, will in the future be embedded in legally enforced property rights. Whether and when this will happen, only time will tell.

Appendix

Appendix

The tables in this appendix contain the numerical values used to generate Figs. 6.1–6.9. Table A1 corresponds to Fig. 6.1, Table A2 to Fig. 6.2, and so on. All data were extracted from the annual company reports in *DSQXDX*; a blank space indicates that no value was available for the year and category shown.

Table A1
Net Profit and Yarn-Sales Surplus of the Dasheng No. 1 Cotton Mill, 1899–1928
(*taels*)

Year	Net profit	Yarn-sales surplus	Year	Net profit	Yarn-sales surplus
1899	−50,703.75		1914	282,173.76	666,867.59
1900	26,850.79	120,316.79	1915	134,961.98	501,404.25
1901	184,291.13	318,398.85	1916	−97,079.68	623,849.09
1902	187,002.40	409,294.36	1917	661,768.54	1,606,034.56
1903	255,134.21	495,007.11	1918	503,669.78	1,570,802.94
1904	225,124.37	618,462.09	1919	2,514,451.62	3,601,975.19
1905	483,070.47	894,202.03	1920	1,902,007.45	2,992,347.37
1906	400,204.64	840,022.31	1921	691,092.15	2,056,503.26
1907	55,904.73	425,759.26	1922	−396,074.05	996,813.39
1908	158,852.59	525,661.18	1923	−373,080.25	502,279.84
1909	207,383.98	598,840.50	1924	−181,087.93	679,446.65
1910	65,090.68	414,366.25	1925	−241,454.29	1,137,167.52
1911	136,120.56	521,683.91	1926	−100,780.28	566,816.90
1912	261,585.23	627,294.41	1927	133,663.90	
1913	302,291.97	676,614.80	1928	764,258.31	

Table A2
Debts and Interest Payments of the Dasheng No. 1 Cotton Mill, 1900–1926
(*taels*)

Year	Debts	Interest on loans	Year	Debts	Interest on loans
1900	124,910.42	8,656.07	1914	979,384.83	122,095.78
1901	163,619.42	19,057.11	1915	1,833,312.65	136,290.40
1902	165,023.19	33,934.70	1916	1,836,574.55	197,599.72
1903	594,230.06	60,712.65	1917	2,757,621.21	263,018.57
1904	558,397.61	82,164.56	1918	2,545,334.93	348,687.55
1905	651,499.10	81,826.80	1919	2,547,592.42	398,681.36
1906	1,036,131.60	152,489.40	1920	2,986,145.53	445,931.54
1907	1,017,249.02	123,950.11	1921	4,016,602.87	584,770.62
1908	1,178,045.32	105,495.73	1922	6,724,978.00	1,002,745.66
1909	1,503,957.44	107,019.06	1923	7,844,174.00	370,589.59
1910	1,282,150.62	108,185.66	1924	7,943,006.00	467,506.03
1911	861,146.07	101,774.01	1925	9,149,511.00	740,355.75
1912	915,578.70	97,300.99	1926	8,128,247.00	276,401.35
1913	1,129,361.92	99,954.00			

Table A3
Annual Net Profits of the Dasheng No. 1, No. 2, No. 3,
and No. 8 Cotton Mills, 1899–1929
(*taels*)

Year	No. 1 Mill	No. 2 Mill	No. 3 Mill	No. 8 Mill
1899	26,850.79			
1902	184,291.13			
1903	187,002.40			
1904	255,134.21			
1905	225,124.37			
1906	483,070.47			
1907	400,204.64	−108,285.77		
1908	55,904.73	−12,273.19		
1909	158,852.59	40,063.27		
1910	207,383.98	10,234.11		
1911	65,090.68	36,096.21		
1912	136,120.56	180,450.53		
1913	261,585.23	209,939.74		
1914	302,291.97	226,092.30		
1915	282,173.76	94,525.05		
1916	134,961.98	−68,382.43		
1917	−97,079.68	321,270.68		
1918	661,768.54	99,348.08		
1919	503,669.78	1,264,077.15		
1920	2,514,451.62	1,001,644.81		
1921	1,902,007.45	325,864.20	−90,324.24	
1922	691,092.15	−317,134.78	−127,722.72	
1923	−396,074.05	−91,885.15	113,176.38	
1924	−373,080.25	−77,494.20	−98,703.03	
1925	−181,087.93	−82,777.64	131,303.92	
1926	−241,454.29	−5,659.22	103,708.95	24,823.22
1927	−100,780.28	17,570.60	76,833.48	126,182.00
1928	133,663.90	41,141.24	22,661.14	320,151.01
1929	764,258.31	−3,692.38	152,070.95	247,997.59

Table A4
Debts of the Dasheng No. 1, No. 2, No. 3, and No. 8
Cotton Mills, 1900–1929
(*taels*)

Year	No. 1 Mill	No. 2 Mill	No. 3 Mill	No. 8 Mill
1900	124,910.42			
1901	163,619.42			
1902	165,023.19			
1903	594,230.06			
1904	558,397.61			
1905	651,499.10			
1906	1,036,131.60			
1907	1,017,249.02	514,091.60		
1908	1,178,045.32	522,270.06		
1909	1,503,957.44	939,974.75		
1910	1,282,150.62	540,516.21		
1911	861,146.07	195,718.14		
1912	915,578.70	404,779.13		
1913	1,129,361.92	453,773.64		
1914	979,384.83	315,460.36		
1915	1,833,312.65	511,242.37		
1916	1,836,574.55	448,179.53		
1917	2,757,621.21	808,318.82		
1918	2,545,334.93	870,218.22		
1919	2,547,592.42	377,286.35		
1920	2,986,145.53	852,476.87		
1921	4,016,602.87	1,041,752.04	1,120,438.65	
1922	6,724,978.00	1,205,944.00	2,173,966.80	
1923	7,844,174.00	510,845.00	2,347,933.72	
1924	7,943,006.00	411,346.00	2,346,382.60	
1925	9,149,511.00	299,428.00	2,059,677.61	
1926	8,128,247.00	209,504.00	2,116,912.47	1,716,430.21
1927		210,228.00	2,100,562.10	1,564,822.96
1928		158,783.00	2,577,695.88	1,242,945.67
1929		587,016.00	2,666,533.00	1,430,584.34

Table A5
Total Costs, Coal Costs, Wages, and Salaries of the
Dasheng No. 1 Cotton, Mill, 1900–1926
(taels)

Year	Total costs*	Coal costs	Wages	Salaries
1900	108,560.59	22,052.79	36,306.13	9,518.62
1901	258,171.80	54,519.67	69,425.45	11,153.74
1902	277,271.83	59,660.83	68,775.21	11,645.59
1903	383,090.97	73,592.67	100,380.05	15,020.86
1904	512,366.40	107,426.84	125,961.47	14,694.28
1905	524,101.01	105,188.07	129,802.21	14,253.25
1906	648,373.76	137,210.86	140,168.00	15,988.42
1907	560,731.72	106,218.69	114,628.51	16,847.36
1908	529,609.33	98,135.06	116,019.62	21,084.92
1909	588,219.94	122,401.05	127,275.99	23,948.63
1910	554,020.78	111,513.09	118,784.27	23,537.94
1911	534,157.62	111,943.70	108,383.09	26,169.89
1912	531,060.40	105,546.07	121,783.89	25,362.68
1913	557,158.38	107,177.88	128,295.93	25,479.25
1914	621,192.19	114,760.61	147,717.29	28,159.35
1915	621,017.68	107,033.98	134,365.52	29,501.04
1916	890,602.36	166,263.08	182,598.67	38,154.37
1917	1,232,589.53	313,920.22	250,228.96	44,575.71
1918	1,336,087.45	379,286.01	216,627.21	43,685.05
1919	1,663,162.46	480,533.04	284,503.74	50,137.33
1920	1,690,578.33	383,747.82	347,793.79	52,110.31
1921	2,011,928.13	461,189.24	404,200.79	53,085.60
1922	2,288,301.80	430,634.18	358,661.43	58,619.25
1923	1,056,720.45	239,447.93	212,006.90	52,761.16
1924	1,001,499.81	196,933.68	182,392.52	52,262.62
1925	1,730,484.32	325,210.04	402,366.79	67,542.39
1926	698,216.11	171,689.73	230,207.78	32,047.58

*Excluding costs of raw materials.

Table A6
Total Share Capital, Annual Dividends, and Annual Bonuses of the
Dasheng No. 1 Cotton Mill, 1900–1926
(*taels*)

Year	Share capital	Dividend	Bonus
1900	445,100.00	16,876.49	
1901	569,500.00	44,402.71	30,776.69
1902	580,000.00	46,188.86	33,643.37
1903	1,130,000.00	46,400.00	38,280.00
1904	1,130,000.00	90,400.00	20,880.00
1905	1,130,000.00	90,400.00	74,580.00
1906	1,130,000.00	90,400.00	68,615.48
1907	1,130,000.00	90,400.00	7,115.64
1908	1,130,000.00	90,400.00	32,329.31
1909	1,130,000.00	90,400.00	45,252.57
1910	1,130,000.00	90,400.00	9,740.20
1911	1,130,000.00	90,400.00	28,891.59
1912	1,130,000.00	90,400.00	61,881.50
1913	1,130,000.00	90,400.00	73,511.99
1914	1,130,000.00	90,400.00	68,906.79
1915	1,695,000.00	90,400.00	4,876.83
1916	2,000,000.00	160,000.00	
1917	2,000,000.00	160,000.00	165,943.91
1918	2,000,000.00	160,000.00	120,000.00
1919	2,500,000.00	180,000.00	600,000.00
1920	2,500,000.00	200,000.00	488,000.00
1921	2,500,000.00	200,000.00	176,000.00
1922	2,575,050.00	200,000.00	
1923	2,575,050.00		
1924	2,575,050.00		
1925	2,575,050.00		
1926	2,575,050.00		

Table A7
Total Costs and Costs Other Than Interest of the
Dasheng No. 1 Cotton Mill, 1900–1926
(*taels*)

Year	Total costs*	Costs other than interest*	Year	Total costs*	Costs other than interest*
1900	108,560.59	99,904.51	1914	621,192.19	499,069.41
1901	258,171.80	239,114.69	1915	621,017.68	484,727.27
1902	277,271.83	322,378.31	1916	890,602.36	693,002.53
1903	383,090.97	243,337.13	1917	1,232,589.53	969,511.00
1904	512,366.40	430,201.84	1918	1,336,087.45	987,399.90
1905	524,101.01	442,274.20	1919	1,663,162.46	1,264,481.10
1906	648,373.76	495,884.35	1920	1,690,578.33	1,244,647.00
1907	560,731.72	436,781.60	1921	2,011,928.13	1,427,157.50
1908	529,609.33	424,113.60	1922	2,288,301.80	1,285,556.10
1909	588,219.94	481,200.87	1923	1,056,720.45	686,130.90
1910	554,020.78	445,835.12	1924	1,001,499.81	533,993.00
1911	534,157.62	432,383.61	1925	1,730,484.32	991,128.30
1912	531,060.40	433,759.41	1926	698,216.11	412,814.76
1913	557,158.38	457,204.38			

*Excluding costs of raw materials.

Appendix

Table A8
Depreciation and Reserves of the Dasheng
No. 1 Cotton Mill, 1900–1926
(*taels*)

Year	Depreciation	Reserves	Year	Depreciation	Reserves
1900			1914	25,000	16,000
1901		10,000	1915	25,000	2,000
1902		30,000	1916		
1903		40,000	1917	25,000	20,000
1904		27,000	1918	25,000	20,000
1905		100,000	1919	50,000	250,000
1906		80,000	1920	25,000	120,000
1907	25,000	6,000	1921	25,000	40,000
1908	25,000	20,000	1922		
1909	24,000	25,000	1923		
1910	25,000	6,000	1924		
1911	25,000	10,000	1925		
1912	25,000	20,000	1926		
1913	25,000	20,000			

Table A9
Cash Values of Inventories of Yarn and Raw Cotton at the
Dasheng No. 1 Cotton Mill, 1900–1926
(*taels*)

Year	Raw cotton	Ginned cotton and yarn	Yarn and cloth
1900	103,695.24	15,063.13	
1901	427,974.28	20,310.09	
1902	520,990.06	12,549.02	
1903	1,024,498.57	35,821.80	
1904	971,741.90	35,000.00	
1905	974,204.87	41,200.00	
1906	865,509.57	26,500.00	
1907		557,707.22	
1908		691,314.12	
1909		1,169,775.15	
1910		994,706.19	
1911		186,136.49	266,153.81
1912		786,848.66	51,915.46
1913		1,269,889.32	31,011.68
1914		477,206.88	161,995.36
1915		951,204.70	671,029.40
1916		903,099.00	469,554.23
1917		2,112,586.84	408,000.00
1918		1,864,803.20	142,873.00
1919		2,335,691.84	575,909.00
1920		1,645,830.02	1,149,040.00
1921		1,245,345.16	753,032.00
1922		1,907,683.50	136,179.76
1923		1,349,192.07	
1924		1,853,225.52	
1925		2,875,556.17	
1926		1,367,128.30	

Reference Matter

Notes

Introduction

1. See Zhang Jian, *Zhang Jizi jiulu* (hereafter ZJZJL); included in this collection are some official documents and company reports. With the recent boom in "Zhang Jian studies," a new edition of his writings, including his diary, was published by the Nantong Zhang Jian Research Center and the Nantong Municipal Library in 1994; see Zhang Jian yanjiu zhongxin and Nantong shi tushuguan, *Zhang Jian quanji*. Unlike the *Zhang Jizi jiulu*, this is not a facsimile reprint of the 1931 edition but a retypeset version in simplified characters and without the original arrangement in sections (*juan*). For reasons of accuracy, I primarily use the facsimile reprint of Zhang Jian's works. Another volume of published documents, *Zhang Jian cungao*, edited by Yang Liqiang et al., presents a useful collection of Zhang Jian's correspondence with political associates, friends, and family members and contains some information on his business activities.

2. The Nantong Municipal Archives hold the business records of the various Dasheng enterprises; as of 1998, about 3,000 *juan* (files) of material had been processed, with 7,000–8,000 *juan* still waiting to be arranged and catalogued. Apart from documents from the Dasheng cotton mills, a major part of the collection had previously been kept in the Shanghai Municipal Archives, which obtained the materials from Dasheng's Shanghai accounts office after 1949. In the 1960s the Shanghai archives sent them to the Nantong Municipal Archives. According to Mr. Yan Yulong and Mrs. Liu Runhua at the Nantong Municipal Archives, the Shanghai Municipal Archives transferred the files to Nantong in order to save storage space in Shanghai. See Xiao Zhengde, "Dasheng dang'an he Zhang Jian."

3. Nantong shi dang'anguan et al., *Dasheng qiye xitong dang'an xuanbian* (hereafter DSQXDX); Zhang Jizhi xiansheng shiyeshi biancunshu, *Dasheng fangzhi gongsi nianjian (1895–1947)* (hereafter DSFGN).

4. I thank Mr. Liang Zhan and Mr. Zhang Guolin of the Nantong Municipal Library for this information.

5. Nantong Museum (hereafter NTB): E 109/1319, E 110/1320.

Chapter 1

1. Mao Dun, *Ziye*, p. 130. Shuangqiao is a fictional small town somewhere in the hinterland of Shanghai.

2. Ibid., Foreword, p. 2. On the background of the novel, see Zhong Jiasong, *Mao Dun zhuan*, pp. 130–44.

3. Shen Binyi, "Zhuangzhi hui hongtu–rexue jian gutu." In this article in the *Nantong ribao*, Shen, the successful and honored director of the tinplate factory, describes his experiences in running the enterprise. The postscript to the article contains information on Mr. Shen's achievement as a model worker and speaker at activities related to education in patriotism.

4. Zhongguo min(si)ying jingji yanjiuhui, Mishuchu, *Zhongguo minying qiyejia liezhuan*, pp. 23, 67, 91, 108.

5. Zhu Peilian, *Jiangsu sheng ji liushisi xian shi zhilüe*, pp. 168, 171.

6. On the development and image of northern Jiangsu, see Honig, *Creating Chinese Ethnicity*, pp. 20–35; and Finnane, "The Origins of Prejudice." On the more recent economic development, see Fei, "Small Towns in Central Jiangsu."

7. The national newspapers carried frequent reports of Zhang Jian and his industrial and educational projects in Nantong; see, among many others, *Shengjing shibao*, Mar. 6, 1912; and *Dagong bao* (Changsha), Oct. 10, 1917.

8. Fitkin, *The Great River*, pp. 8–9.

9. On regionalism and decentralization, see Goodman and Segal, *China Deconstructs*, and in this volume in particular Dali Yang, "Reform and the Restructuring of Central-Local Relations."

10. See, e.g., Qian Jiang and Tang Keke, "Jianlun Zhang Jian Nantong difang zizhi moshi."

11. For some of the best discussions, see the volume edited by Oi and Walder, *Property Rights and Economic Reform in China*.

12. See, e.g., Ruf, "Collective Enterprise and Property Rights in a Sichuan Village," pp. 36–38.

13. Eastman, *Family, Fields and Ancestors*, p. 170. For a more detailed historical background, see Chapter 2.

14. Eastman, *Family, Fields and Ancestors*, pp. 170–71.

15. Feuerwerker, "Economic Trends in the Late Ch'ing Empire, 1870–1911."

16. Wellington Chan, *Merchants, Mandarins and Modern Enterprise*, pp. 67–76.

17. Du Xuncheng, *Minzu zibenzhuyi yu jiu Zhongguo zhengfu*, pp. 460–70.

18. Faure, *China and Capitalism*, pp. 28–29.

19. See Feuerwerker, *China's Early Industrialization*; Lai, "The Qing State and Merchant Enterprise"; idem, "Lunchuan zhaoshangju jingying guanli wenti"; Zhu Yingui, *Guojia ganyu jingji yu Zhong Ri jindaihua*; Quan Hansheng, *Hanyeping gongsi shilüe*; Zhongguo kexueyuan, Shanghai jingji yanjiusuo, *Hengfeng shachang de fazhan yu gaizao.*

20. Lai, "The Qing State and Merchant Enterprise."

21. Feuerwerker, *China's Early Industrialization*, pp. 161–64.

22. See, e.g., Wellington Chan, "Tradition and Change in the Chinese Business Enterprise"; and Siu-lun Wong, "The Chinese Family Firm."

23. Wellington Chan, *Merchants, Mandarins and Modern Enterprise*, pp. 180–82. The Company Law allowed businesses in the form of partnerships with unlimited or limited liability, joint-stock companies with unlimited or limited liability, and sole proprietorships with unlimited liability to register.

24. Cochran, *Big Business in China*, pp. 56, 100–101.

25. Ibid., pp. 151–52.

26. Shanghai shehui kexueyuan, Jingji yanjiusuo, *Shanghai Yong'an gongsi*, p. 7.

27. Wellington Chan, "The Origins and Early Years of the Wing On Company Group," p. 89; Kubo, "Kindai Chūgoku mengyō no chitai kōzō," pp. 36–38.

28. Choi, "Competition Among Brothers," p. 111.

29. NTD: B 402-111-445.

30. For a useful introduction discussing the key issues in the theory of the firm and summarizing the diverse theoretical approaches, see Casson, *Information and Organization*, pp. 76–116.

31. Brown, "Introduction: Uses and Abuses of Chinese Business History," pp. 2, 12.

32. Braudel, *The Wheels of Commerce*, p. 434.

33. Ibid., pp. 434–43.

34. See Chapter 5 for a detailed discussion of commercial legislation. On the economic consequences of the lack of a company law and the development after its introduction in 1904, see Faure, *China and Capitalism*, pp. 28–53; Kirby, "China Unincorporated"; and Zhu Ying, "Lun Qing mo de jingji fagui."

35. See, e.g., Goodman, *Native Place, City, and Nation.*

36. Weber, *Economy and Society*; see esp. 2: 956–1005, on the development of bureaucratic structures and their importance for the development of the modern capitalist enterprise. For an excellent introduction to Weber's concept of economic sociology, see Swedberg, *Max Weber and the Idea of Economic Sociology*, esp. pp. 39–45.

37. Weber, *Economy and Society*, 1: 52–53, 91, 116–17.

38. Ibid., 2: 957–58.

39. Du Xunzheng, *Zhongguo chuantong lunli yu jindai zibenzhuyi*, pp. 127–33.

40. Ibid., pp. 133, 143–52.

41. Pollard, *The Genesis of Modern Management.*

42. Chandler, *The Visible Hand,* p. 1.

43. For Chandler's eight propositions characterizing modern business enterprise, see ibid., pp. 6–11.

44. The point regarding the lack of any discussion of the government's role in Chandler's work has also been made by Chi-kong Lai in the context of his work on the China Merchants' Steamship Navigation Company; see Lai, "The Emergence of the Modern Corporation in China," pp. 32–35. In *Socializing Capital,* a study of the emergence of the industrial corporation in the United States, William Roy modified Chandler's approach by focusing on the role of the state, the law, and the dynamics of institutional power and their impact on the development of large-scale enterprises in the late nineteenth century.

45. Granovetter, "Business Groups," p. 454.

46. Brown, *Chinese Big Business and the Wealth of Asian Nations;* idem, *Capital and Entrepreneurship in South East Asia;* Gomez, *Chinese Business in Malaysia.*

47. Granovetter points out the need for this approach in "Business Groups," p. 455.

48. Ibid., p. 466. In a vertical configuration, the successive stages of production and distribution are under the control of a single enterprise.

49. Lai, "Enterprise History," pp. 180–81.

50. Some of the historical context explaining the focus on morality and business is provided in Chapter 3.

51. See, e.g., Liu Housheng, *Zhang Jian zhuanji.* Liu was a close friend and associate of Zhang Jian and quotes from conversations with him. See also Zhu Zhiqian, *Zhang Jian de shiye zhuzhang.* Two biographies written in a novelistic style are Xing Ren, *Jindai shiye de kaishan bizu;* and Liu Peilin and Zhang Deyi, *Zhang Jian zhuan.* The numerous fictionalized biographies of Zhang Jian in the form of pamphlets and short articles in local publications in Nantong will not be quoted here in detail.

52. Chu, *Reformer in Modern China.*

53. Ibid., p. 181. Zhang Jian's commitment to Confucian values is the frequent focus of studies by Taiwanese scholars; see, e.g., Lu Baoqian, *Lun Zhang Jian yu Nantong zhi jindaihua,* p. 17.

54. Chu, *Reformer in Modern China,* p. 182.

55. Zhu Xinquan, "Zhang Jian."

56. The first international conference on Zhang Jian, held in Nanjing in August 1987, concerned itself with the problem of the "overall evaluation" of Zhang Jian and the new interpretation of his modernizing activities; see Shuang Mu, "'Zhang Jian guoji xueshu taolunhui'"; Lin Gang, "Shilun Dasheng shachang de shichang jichu"; Yan Xuexi, "Zhang Jian yu Huainan yanken gongsi"; and Wu Yiye, "Zhang Jian yu Nantong 'jindaihua' moshi."

57. Qian Jiang and Tang Keke, "Jianlun Zhang Jian Nantong difang zizhi moshi."

58. On this problem, see Tim Wright, "'The Spiritual Heritage of Chinese Capitalism.'"

59. Xing Ren, *Jindai shiye de kaishan bizu*; Zhong Xiangcai, *Zhongguo jindai minzu qiyejia*, pp. 68–94; Huang Qinggen, "Zhang Jian de kaifang sixiang."

60. Zhang Xuejun, *Shiye zhi meng—Zhang Jian zhuan*. The Zhang Jian Research Center in Nantong (an office housed in the Nantong Library, staffed mainly with retired cadres) is the key institution promoting Zhang Jian's image in the context of Nantong's local socioeconomic development.

61. Mu Changxiao, *Shanghai jushang yanyi*, vol. 2.

62. Zhang Kaiyuan, *Kaituozhe de zuji—Zhang Jian zhuan'gao*. In 2001, Zhang Kaiyuan and Tian Tong published *Zhang Jian yu jindai shehui*, a much expanded biography with a similar approach.

63. Ibid., *zixu*, pp. 3–4. Zhang Kaiyuan's approach to the social environment of "small societies" (*xiao shehui*) is reminiscent of Braudel's concept of society as a "set of sets." As Braudel suggests, intermediate sets with a familiar nature such as economics, politics, culture, are divided into subsets, and so on; society is the collective noun denoting the "set of sets" (Braudel, *The Wheels of Commerce*, pp. 458–61).

64. Qin Shao, "Space, Time, and Politics in Early Twentieth Century Nantong"; idem, "Making Political Culture."

65. Chang Zonghu, *Nantong xiandaihua*.

66. Nakai Hideki, *Chō Ken to Chūgoku kindai kigyō*. This author has written many articles along similar lines over the past twenty years. Nakai's study does not use any new source material nor present a new approach, but it is probably the most complete summary of existing secondary literature on Dasheng and Zhang Jian. Other representative publications by Japanese scholars working on Dasheng and Zhang Jian are Nozawa, "Chūgoku ni okeru kigyōshi kenkyū"; idem, "Riben wenxian zhong de Zhang Jian he Nantong"; and Watanabe, "Zhang Jian de yanye jingying yu yanzheng gaige yundong."

67. Walker, *Chinese Modernity and the Peasant Path*.

68. Ibid., p. 7.

69. Ibid., pp. 130–55.

70. Philip Huang regards the impact of imperialism as the driving force for the involutional growth (i.e., growth without development) of the rural economy in this area during the Republican period. Like Walker, he identifies supply problems in terms of raw materials, the decline in yarn prices, and the negative influence of "extractive" merchants and their capital investments as reasons for the enterprise's difficulties in the early 1920s; see Philip C. C. Huang, *The Peasant Family and Rural Development*, pp. 115–43, esp. pp. 135–36.

71. Dasheng xitong qiyeshi bianxiezu, *Dasheng xitong qiyeshi* (hereafter *Dasheng xitong qiyeshi*). Other studies with an institutional interest are rather piecemeal. Chinese historians such as Lin Jubai (*Jindai Nantong tubu shi*) and Duan Benluo and Shan Qiang ("Dasheng shachang de touzi huanjing") have in their studies examined external factors such as the decline of the Manchurian yarn market or investment strategies that influenced the enterprise's financial performance in the early 1920s. A recent article by Tang Keke and Qian Jiang ("Dasheng shachang de zichan") investigates the structure of Dasheng's assets and profit distribution without paying attention to the internal flow of funds. Japanese historians such as Tomizawa Yoshio ("Ginkōdan sekkanki") or Kanemaru Yūichi ("Chūgoku 'minzoku kōgyō no kōgane jiki'") have started to examine new issues related to Dasheng's business structure and operations, such as the mill operations during the years of financial crisis in the 1920s and the function of the Dasheng subsidiaries within the business complex.

72. This book was the result of a team project initiated by Shanghai's Industrial and Commercial Administrative Bureau in the late 1950s. After being delayed for many years, the project was revived in the 1980s (*Dasheng xitong qiyeshi,* "hou ji," pp. 299–301). The documentation is impressive. Unlike earlier studies, the project entailed to some extent cooperation with the archives and libraries in Nantong. The analysis of documents was enriched by some information gathered from interviews with former employees of the Dasheng enterprise.

73. Ibid., pp. 35–36, 218.

74. The *Dasheng xitong qiyeshi* dedicates only three pages (pp. 122–24) with very general information to the function of the Shanghai accounts office and does not identify its crucial institutional role in Dasheng's financial and managerial structure.

75. See, e.g., Kang Chao, *The Development of Cotton Textile Production in China,* pp. 142–55.

76. Faure, *The Rural Economy of Pre-Liberation China;* Thomas Rawski, *Economic Growth in Prewar China.*

77. Skinner, "Cities and Hierarchy of Local Systems."

78. Pomeranz, *The Making of a Hinterland;* Faure, *The Rural Economy of Pre-Liberation China.*

79. R. Bin Wong, *China Transformed,* pp. 53–70; see also Wu Chengming and Xu Dixin, *Zhongguo zibenzhuyi fazhan shi,* vol. 1; and Brook, "Capitalism and the Writing of Modern History in China."

80. R. Bin Wong, *China Transformed,* p. 69; Pomeranz, *The Great Divergence.*

Chapter 2

1. On the historical background, see Kwang-Ching Liu, "Nineteenth Century China"; Chien-nung Li, *The Political History of China, 1840–1928,* esp. pp. 137–43 on the Sino-Japanese war; and R. Bin Wong, *China Transformed,* pp. 153–58. For data

on the annual income and expenditures of the late Qing government, see Hamashita, *Chūgoku kindai keizaishi kenkyū,* p. 79; and Zhou Yumin, *Wan Qing zaizheng yu shehui bianqian,* pp. 237–41, 315–23.

2. For historical background, see Ichiko, "Political and Institutional Reform, 1901–1911"; and Esherick, *Reform and Revolution in China.*

3. Mary Wright, *The Last Stand of Chinese Conservatism,* pp. 167–70.

4. Feuerwerker, "Economic Trends in the Late Ch'ing Empire"; Chen Zhen and Yao Luo, *Zhongguo jindai gongyeshi ziliao,* 1: 4–5; Eastman, *Family, Fields and Ancestors,* pp. 172–73. For a detailed history of the Jiangnan Arsenal, see Cornet, *Etat et enterprises en Chine.*

5. Mary Wright, *The Last Stand of Chinese Conservatism,* p. 153.

6. On Li Hongzhang's role in the self-strengthening movement, see Kwang-Ching Liu, "Li Hung-chang in Chihli."

7. See Feuerwerker, *China's Early Industrialization;* Lai, "The Qing State and Merchant Enterprise"; and Carlson, *The Kaiping Mines.*

8. For a general introduction, see Wellington Chan, "Government, Merchants and Industry to 1911." On Japan's industrial development, see Hirschmeier, *The Origins of Entrepreneurship in Meiji Japan;* and Smith, *Political Change and Industrial Development in Japan.*

9. Feuerwerker, *China's Early Industrialization;* Guohui Zhang, "The Emergence and Development of China's Modern Capitalist Enterprises."

10. Lai, "Li Hung-chang and Modern Enterprise," p. 238.

11. Wellington Chan, "Government, Merchants and Industry to 1911," pp. 434–35.

12. Quan Hansheng, *Zhongguo jingjishi yanjiu,* 2: 715.

13. Du Xuncheng, *Minzu zibenzhuyi yu jiu Zhongguo zhengfu,* pp. 286–92. All the mills had a starting capital of at least 10,000 yuan.

14. Ibid., pp. 293–304. Many of the weaving mills also listed dyed cloth as part of their business operations. Only five of the 86 new weaving operations established between 1902 and 1916 were under government management.

15. Shao Xunzheng, "Guanyu yangwupai minyong qiye," p. 369.

16. Chia-chien Wang, "Li Hung-chang and the Peiyang Navy." For a short biography of Li Hongzhang, see Hummel, *Eminent Chinese of the Ch'ing Period,* 1: 27–32.

17. Feuerwerker, *China's Early Industrialization,* pp. 210–11; Li Hongzhang, *Li Wenzhong (Hongzhang) quanji,* "zougao," 43.43a–44b.

18. Shao Xunzheng, "Yangwu yundong he Zhongguo zichan jieji fazhan."

19. Li Hongzhang, *Li Wenzhong (Hongzhang) quanji,* "zougao," 78.10b.

20. Ibid., "zougao," 78.10a–12a. In this 1894 draft memorial, Li Hongzhang asked the government to prevent any development beyond 400,000 spindles and 5,000 looms in all of China during the next ten years (78.11b). See also Kang Chao, *The Development of Cotton Textile Production,* p. 111.

21. Yuen-sang Leung, "The Shanghai-Tientsin Connection."

22. The complex changes in politics caused by the fall of Li Hongzhang are beyond the scope of this book. On Zhang Zhidong's political involvement, see Bays, *The Nature of Provincial Political Authority*. For a short biography of Zhang Zhidong, see Hummel, *Eminent Chinese of the Ch'ing Period*, 1: 27–32.

23. On Zhang Zhidong's political ideas, see Wang Ermin, *Wan Qing zhengzhi sixiangshi lun*, pp. 81–100.

24. Kang Chao, *The Development of Cotton Textile Production*, p. 109.

25. Yan Zhongping, *Zhongguo mian fangzhi shigao*, p. 94.

26. Kang Chao, *The Development of Cotton Textile Production*, p. 109. According to the *North China Herald*, May 24, 1895, the old machinery was rented to a Chinese merchant, who paid a fixed rent to the government for it.

27. For financial rewards and official ranks granted to businessmen by the Qing government after 1900, see Wang Jingyu, *Zhongguo jindai gongyeshi ziliao*, 1: 637–47.

28. "The Encouragement of Chinese Enterprise," *North China Herald*, May 15, 1896.

29. Wang Yejian, "Chuantong yu jindai Zhongguo jingji fazhan."

30. See Smith, *Political Change and Industrial Development in Japan*, pp. 36–41. For a general introduction to Japan's industrial and economic development, see Inkster, *Japanese Industrialisation*, pp. 29–93.

31. Smith, *Political Change and Industrial Development in Japan*, pp. 86–100.

32. Feuerwerker, "Industrial Enterprise in Twentieth-Century China," esp. pp. 287–302; Carlson, *The Kaiping Mines*, pp. 105–17.

33. On Jiangnan's economic development in agriculture and manufacture during the Ming and Qing dynasties, see Li Bozhong, *Agricultural Development in Jiangnan*; and idem, *Jiangnan de zaoqi gongyehua*.

34. Tōa Dōbunkai, *Chūgoku shōbetsu zenshi*, chap. 15, appendix "Kōso shō zento." On this 1920 map, a planned railway for northern Jiangsu starts in Haimen city, connects Nantong with Rugao, Dongtai, Yancheng, and Huaiyin city, and ends in Xuzhou, where it would join the northern railway line to Beijing. However, the line never materialized.

35. For a description of Tongzhou and the northern Yangzi Delta during the Ming and Qing dynasties, see Walker, *Chinese Modernity and the Peasant Path*, pp. 52–68, 79–84.

36. Zhu Peilian, *Jiangsu sheng ji liushisi xian shi zhilüe*, p. 168. For the administrative terminology, see Hucker, *A Dictionary of Official Titles in Imperial China*, pp. 160–61, 488; and Brunnert and Hagelstrom, *Present Day Political Organization of China*, pp. 53–54.

37. Shu Zhe, *Tong Yang shi shu jiangyu tushuo*, n.p.

38. Lu Jinyuan, "Nantong diqu chenglu guocheng de tansuo," pp. 21–37.

39. Liu Miao, *Ming Qing yanhai tangdi kaifa yanjiu*, pp. 334–35; Metzger, "The Organizational Capabilities of the Ch'ing State in the Field of Commerce," pp. 41–42. On salt smuggling in the Lianghuai area during the Daoguang period, see Fang Yujin, "Daoguang chunian Lianghuai siyan yanjiu."

40. Wan Guoding et al., *Jiangsu Wujin, Nantong tianfu diaocha baogao*, p. 183.

41. Lu Jinyuan, "Nantong diqu chenglu guocheng de tansuo," pp. 28–33; *North China Herald*, May 7, 1921.

42. Lu Jinyuan, "Nantong diqu chenglu guocheng de tansuo," pp. 32–33.

43. *(Qianlong) Zhili Tongzhou zhi*, 17.18b.

44. Zheng Changgan, *Ming Qing nongmin shangpin jingji*, pp. 210–17.

45. *Chongchuan zhiwen lu*, 11.8a–9a. Chongchuan is another variant of an old name for Nantong, which goes back to the Song dynasty when the area was called Chongzhou.

46. *(Minguo) Nantong xian tuzhi*, 3.17b–19a; Imura, *Zhongguo zhi fangzhiye ji qi chupin*, p. 187.

47. *(Guangxu) Haimen ting tuzhi*, 10.1a–b.

48. *(Jiajing) Haimen xianzhi*, 1.20a; *(Jiajing) Tongzhou zhi*, 1.13a–b. The dye produced from indigo plants is documented as early as the sixteenth century. The proper modern term for the blue-dyed cloth is *lanyin huabu*; it is still sold today as Nantong's traditional fabric.

49. Imura, *Zhongguo zhi fangzhiye ji qi chupin*, p. 187.

50. Zheng Changgan, *Ming Qing nongmin shangpin jingji*, p. 145.

51. Lu Bin, *Chongming pingmin changshi*, pp. 2–3.

52. Imura, *Zhongguo zhi fangzhiye ji qi chupin*, p. 188.

53. Ibid.; see also Zheng Changgan, *Ming Qing nongmin shangpin jingji*, p. 75.

54. Honig, "Native-Place Hierarchy and Labor Market Segmentation"; Finnane, "The Origins of Prejudice." Walker discusses the construction of Tongzhou as a periphery during the Ming and Qing dynasties in *Chinese Modernity and the Peasant Path*, pp. 52–68.

55. Shu Zhe, *Tong Yang shi shu jiangyu tushuo*, n.p.; entry under "Tongzhou zhi xiangli." *Nantong xianshi tu*, 1925. For the urban development and architecture of Nantong in the Republican period, see Chapter 7.

56. *(Minguo) Nantong xian tuzhi*, 14.3b–4b. Another survey listed in this gazetteer for the year 1908 gives the following population figures: 10,233 people for Nantong city (*cheng nei*), 42,483 in the city's suburbs (*xiang*), and 64,109 inhabitants in the villages administratively attached to the city (*fucheng xiang*). Based on the overall similarity of the population figures in the 1908 survey and the 1920 survey for Nantong city, one can assume that the population within Nantong's city walls in 1920 must have been about the same. Numbers are compiled using the data entries in ibid., 1.16a.

57. Ibid., 14.4b; *Ershi nian lai zhi Nantong*, foreword, p. 1; Yin Weihe, *Jiangsu liushi-yi xian zhi*, pp. 53, 111. In 1988, Nantong city had a population of 436,600 people and Nantong county of 1,537,500 people (Nantong shi, Tongjiju, Bianji weiyuanhui, *1949–1988 Nantong jingji gailan*, p. 157).

58. Yin Weihe, *Jiangsu liushiyi xian zhi*, pp. 64, 124, 208.

59. I have calculated the population figures according to data in ibid., pp. 53, 64, 124, 208.

60. *Tong Ru Hai mianye gonghui mianye nianbao*, appendix, pp. 18–24.

61. Lin Jubai, *Jindai Nantong tubu shi*, pp. 58–61.

62. Skinner, "Marketing and Social Structure in Rural China, Part 1," esp. pp. 7–9; idem, "Cities and the Hierarchy of Local Systems."

63. Skinner, "Marketing and Social Structure in Rural China, Part 1," p. 9.

64. Shu Zhe, *Tong Yang shi shu jiangyu tushuo*, n.p., entry under "Tongzhou zhi xiangli."

65. Jiangsu sheng jiaotong shizhi biancun weiyuanhui, *Jiangsu gonglu jiatong shi*, pp. 67–68.

66. Ibid., p. 69.

67. *Chongchuan zhiwen lu*, 11.9a.

68. Tōa Dōbunkai, *Chūgoku shōbetsu zenshi*, pp. 306–7.

69. Ibid., pp. 465–68.

70. Walker, *Chinese Modernity and the Peasant Path*, p. 56.

71. Lin Jubai, *Jindai Nantong tubu shi*, pp. 29–30. Walker's description of Nantong's commercial development and status as periphery in *Chinese Modernity and the Peasant Path* is very much informed by Lin Jubai's detailed study.

72. Lin Jubai, *Jindai Nantong tubu shi*, pp. 42–62.

73. Jiang Zi'an and Cheng Zhouru, "Nantong de huiguan," pp. 27–28. For the terminology of native-place and trading associations, see Goodman, *Native-Place, City, and Nation*, pp. 38–40.

74. *Nantong xianshi tu*, 1925; Xin'an is another name for Huizhou.

75. *Nantong xianshi tu*, 1925; Jiang Zi'an and Cheng Zhouru, "Nantong de huiguan," p. 27.

76. Yan Jinfeng, "Ningbo huiguan"; and idem, "Guangdong huiguan."

77. Tōa dōbunkai, *Zhongguo jingji quanshu*, p. 230. See also Zhang Ziqiang, "Beijing chengnei de Tongzhou huiguan."

78. Finnane, "The Origins of Prejudice," esp. pp. 227–28. Her argument stresses weak local political structures compounded by the presence of a strong state through its administration of water control and the salt monopoly, which prevented merchants from negotiating successfully with the government and its representatives.

79. *Tong Ru Hai mianye gonghui mianye nianbao*, appendix, pp. 18–24; 55 of the shop managers came originally from Nantong, 11 from Rugao, and 9 from Haimen.

80. Ibid. The fact that Nantong city had only six cotton cloth and yarn shops shows that the county seat was not the only commercial center of the cotton trade in the county. Husbandry, especially pig farming, was an important feature of Rugao's economy. By 1918 ten ham factories in the city produced dried meat, which was sold in specialty shops in Nantong and in Taicang in the Jiangnan area (Yu Chi, "Rugao rou lianchang jianshi").

81. Fang Ping et al., "Rucheng Wanhong diandang de jiankuang."

82. Shen Xianrong, "Ji Jingjiang xiaoxue," pp. 33–38. The largest shops in Rugao city, selling wine, cigarettes, and foreign goods, were run by merchants from Anhui, Nantong, Zhenjiang, Rugao, and Shanxi (Song Taowu et al., "Ru cheng jiefang qian 'wu yang, yan jiu' mingdian jilüe").

83. Tōa Dōbunkai, *Chūgoku shōbetsu zenshi*, p. 1221. On the institution of the *qianzhuang*, see McElderry, *Shanghai Old-Style Banks.*

84. Jiangsu sheng jinrong zhi bianjishi, *Jiangsu diandang qianzhuang*, p. 42.

85. NTD: B 401-311-129; see also Tōa dōbunkai, *Chūgoku shōbetsu zenshi*, p. 1221.

86. Tōa dōbunkai, *Chūgoku shōbetsu zenshi*, p. 1221; *Ershi nian lai zhi Nantong*, pt. B, pp. 52–54.

87. *Nantong xianshi tu.*

88. Tōa dōbunkai, *Chūgoku shōbetsu zenshi*, p. 1220.

89. Ge Yuanxun, *Hu you zaji*, pt. B, 4.16a.

90. Honig, "Native-Place Hierarchy and Labor Market Segmentation," pp. 275–77.

91. Li Zishan, "Shanghai laodong zhuangkuang."

92. Zhang Jian initiated the reorganization of the Wusong Commercial Port (Wusong shangbu) in Shanghai in 1921; this aborted effort was designed to serve the increased demands of commercial and passenger transport with wharfs, storehouses, and other facilities (Se Weng [Zhang Jian], "Zhang Jian duban Wusong shangbu zhi xuanyan"). On the socioeconomic and political development of Shanghai in the Republican period, see Bergère, *The Golden Age of the Chinese Bourgeoisie*; and Henriot, *Shanghai, 1927–1937.*

93. Huang Yongxin, "Du Yuesheng dajin Dada lunchuan gongsi jingguo."

94. SHD: Q 117-19-13; Q 117-19-18; Q 117-19-31. As an exception to the rule, Finnane ("The Origins of Prejudice," p. 228) mentions the existence of the Huaiyang gongsuo, a trade association of Subei wine and pig merchants, in Shanghai in the late Qing. As she remarks, this organization is omitted from all the standard listings of trade and merchant associations and thus seems to have been fairly unimportant.

95. Honig, "Native-Place Hierarchy and Labor Market Segmentation," p. 279.

Chapter 3

1. Readers interested in Zhang Jian's early years and non-business-related career should consult Samuel Chu's solid biography, *Reformer in Modern China*. See also Liu Housheng, *Zhang Jian zhuanji*; Nakai, *Chō Ken to Chūgoku kindai kigyō*; and Fujioka, *Chūka minkoku dai'ichi kyōwasei*.

2. Levy (*The Rise of the Modern Chinese Business Class*, pp. 29–34) uses the categories "industrial promoter" and "industrial executive" to describe the generational change in business activities between government officials like Li Hongzhang or Zuo Zongtang and entrepreneurs such as Zhang Jian or Sheng Xuanhuai.

3. In his writings, Zhang Jian described himself as a *Su ren*, a native of Jiangsu (ZJZJL, "Zhengwen lu," 3.15a), or as a *Nantong zhi ren*, a native of Nantong (ibid., "Zizhi lu," 3.6a).

4. *Tongzhou Zhang shi jiapu*, "Ci tu," *juan shou* 1a, 2a–3a; *Zhang shi zongpu*, 18.47a–52b; Zhang Jian, *Nantong Zhang shi Changle zhipu*, *xu* 1a–2a, 23a–26a.

5. *Tongzhou Zhang shi jiapu*, 20.1a–2b.

6. Examples of Zhang Jian's ritual tasks can be found in his diary (*Riji*, vol. 6) for the year 1898 (p. 412), 1904 (p. 531), 1909 (p. 631), and 1923 (p. 801).

7. Interview with Mr. Lu Baoqian, a native of Haimen (b. 1928), in Taibei on August 18, 1996. In an interview in Nantong on March 18, 1995, Mrs. Zhang Rouwu, Zhang Jian's granddaughter, said that she met her grandfather only during ritual ceremonies or at festive occasions like New Year. She remarked that his grandchildren were brought up to be in awe and great respect of their grandfather and were not able to develop a more intimate relationship with him.

8. For a brief biographical sketch, see Boorman, *Biographical Dictionary of Republican China*, 1: 35–38. For a detailed discussion, see Chu, *Reformer in Modern China*; and, esp. on Zhang Jian's childhood, Fujioka, *Chō Ken to Shinkai kakumei*, pp. 441–67.

9. Zhang Jian, *Zhang Se'an xiansheng jiulu lu*, 3.18a–b.

10. Zhu Xinquan, "Zhang Jian," p. 259; Chen Jiayou, "Da shiyejia Zhang Jian," pp. 163–65.

11. Zhang Jian, *Hui shi juan*, entry under "Guangxu Jiawu enke," 1a–7b.

12. Chu, *Reformer in Modern China*, pp. 11–14.

13. Yan Xuexi and Qian Liaoxing, "Xue Nanming, Xue Shouxuan."

14. See, e.g., Qian Jiang and Yang Keke, "Jianlun Zhang Jian Nantong difang zizhi moshi," p. 56; and Nakai, *Chō Ken to Chūgoku kindai kigyō*, pp. 68–72.

15. See, e.g., Zhang Jian, *Zhang Se'an xiansheng jiulu lu*, 3.7b–10b, 11b–12b, 18b–19a.

16. *Tongzhou xingban shiye zhangcheng* (hereafter *TXSZ*), "Dasheng shachang," p. 64.

17. Zhang Zhidong, *Zhang Wenxiang gong quanji*, 42.12a. *Liyuan* (the source of economic/common benefit) was another key term in the debate about China's

economic and political problems in the late nineteenth century. The term connotes concrete economic profits as well as an overall common benefit for the country. For a detailed discussion, see Wang Ermin, *Zhongguo jindai sixiangshi lun*, esp. pp. 333–62.

18. Eastman, *Family, Fields and Ancestors*, pp. 101–3, 133–34. On the relationship between gentry and merchants in Chinese society, see Ma Min, *Guanshang zhi jian*, pp. 64–108.

19. Mann, *Local Merchants and the Chinese Bureaucracy*, pp. 21–23. For a lucid analysis of the roles of gentry, gentry-merchants, and merchants in Zhejiang's elite during the early Republican period, see Schoppa, *Chinese Elites and Political Change*, pp. 59–77.

20. "Kaiban fangsha gongchang," *Tonghai xinbao*, May 2, 1922.

21. Lufrano, *Honorable Merchants*, pp. 23–50.

22. See, e.g., Zhang Jian, *Zhang Se'an xiansheng shiye wenchao*, 2.35b–36a.

23. Ma Min, *Guanshang zhi jian*, pp. 113–21, 182–83.

24. Ibid., pp. 121–25; Hao, *The Comprador in Nineteenth Century China*.

25. Xu Mao, *Zhongguo shi maiban*, pp. 57–83; Feuerwerker, *China's Early Industrialization*.

26. Ichiko, "Political and Institutional Reform, 1901–1911," pp. 388–90.

27. See Bastid, *Educational Reform in Early Twentieth-Century China*, pp. 59–87. Bastid's study examines Zhang Jian's role as an educational reformer and introduces his essays on educational issues.

28. Ibid., p. 63. For example, in 1909 there were 55 educational associations in Jiangsu with 8,593 members. Most members were not professional teachers. It is hard to tell who belonged to the associations, but one would suppose most were in the upper stratum of the literate.

29. Roger Thompson, *China's Local Councils*, p. 5.

30. Fujioka, *Chūka minkoku dai'ichi kyōwasei*, pp. 1–26. On Zheng Xiaoxu's role as an active shareholder in Dasheng, see Chapter 5.

31. Fewsmith, *Party, State, and Local Elites in Republican China*, p. 30.

32. Xu Dingxin and Qian Xiaoming, *Shanghai zongshanghui shi*, p. 37. Western chambers of commerce existed in China before the year 1902.

33. NTD: B 405-III-7. For example, in 1922 Dasheng contributed 1,430 taels to the Nantong Chamber of Commerce.

34. Chu, *Reformer in Modern China*, pp. 66.

35. See Zhongguo di'er lishi dang'anguan and Shen Jiawu, *Zhang Jian nongshang zongzhang*, pp. 1–18.

36. See, e.g., the caricature of Zhang Jian on the front page of *Haijun zhengzhi huabao*, Dec. 13, 1925. I thank Tony Hyder for drawing my attention to this source.

37. Song Xue, *Jinshi banben "Qing shanhu,"* 32b–33b. I thank Maybo Ching for drawing my attention to this source.

38. For detailed accounts of the relationship between Zhang Jian and Zhang Zhidong, see Fan Jizhong, "Zhang Zhidong yu Zhang Jian de jiaowang," pp. 163–69; and Feng Zuyi, "Zhang Zhidong yu Zhang Jian."

39. Zhang Zhidong, *Zhang Wenxiang gong nianpu,* vol. 1, 3.13a; Zhang Jian, *Zhang Se'an shiye wenchao,* "Chengban Tongzhou shachang jielüe," 1.16a.

40. Zhang Jian, *Zhang Se'an shiye wenchao,* 1.16a.

41. Ibid.; *Yingyin chuangban Dasheng shachang ligao.*

42. *Yingyin chuangban Dasheng shachang ligao,* 16a.

43. Zhang Jian, *Zhang Se'an shiye wenchao,* 1.16b.

44. Ibid., 1.16a.

45. ZJZJL, "Shiye lu," 1.14a–16a (two letters to Liu Kunyi from 1899). For a biographical sketch of Liu Kunyi, see Hummel, *Eminent Chinese of the Ch'ing Period,* 1: 523–24.

46. NTD: B 401-III-1, doc.1., handwritten copy of the original contract of purchase from 1893. The purchase of the machinery had been arranged through the two foreign brokerages, Arnhold-Karberg and Diers, in Shanghai.

47. The term *guanshang heban* appears, for example, in company documents from 1899; see TXSZ, "Dasheng shachang," p. 49.

48. Zhang Jian, *Zhang Se'an shiye wenchao,* 1.16a.

49. Feuerwerker, *China's Early Industrialization,* pp. 15–16, 68; Yan Zhongping, *Zhongguo mian fangzhi shigao,* pp. 91–92.

50. See Zhang Jian's letter to Sheng Xuanhuai in Zhang Jian, *Zhang Se'an shiye wenchao,* 1.13b–14a.

51. Quan Hansheng, *Hanyeping gongsi shilüe,* p. 75n6; Feuerwerker, *China's Early Industrialization,* pp. 25, 67–68. Feuerwerker (p. 67) suggests that Sheng Xuanhuai felt obliged to take over the financially weak Hanyang Ironworks from Zhang Zhidong in return for his official protection since Sheng had been accused of corruption and betrayal.

52. Zhang Jian expressed his desperation about the mill's financial problems caused by Sheng Xuanhuai's failure to come up with the promised funds in a letter to Zhang Zhidong (Zhang Jian, *Zhang Se'an shiye wenchao,* 1.13a–b). See also Zhang Jian's plea to Sheng Xuanhuai in ibid., 1.13b–14a. The machinery taken by Sheng Xuanhuai was returned to Dasheng in 1902 and then listed as government capital (*guanji guben*) at a total of 500,000 taels on the company's balance sheet of 1903. (DSQXDX, annual report from 1903, pp. 20–21).

53. DSQXDX, annual report for the year 1900, p. 3.

54. Ibid., report for 1901, p. 7, and report for 1902, p. 15.

55. NTD: B 402-III-1.

56. Lin Jubai, *Jindai Nantong tubu shi,* pp. 42–62.

57. Zhang Jian, *Zhang Se'an shiye wenchao*, "Shen Xiejun zhuan," *juan shou*.19a–b. The exact dates of Shen's birth and death are not known. From Zhang Jian's obituary, which he must have written before 1926, we know that Shen Xiejun was born approximately in 1856.

58. Ibid., *juan shou*.19b.

59. Ibid., 3.9b–10a, quote on 3.9b.

60. Zhang Jian, *Riji*; see, e.g., entries for the year 1896, pp. 377–87.

61. Zhang Jian, *Zhang Se'an shiye wenchao*, "Shen Xiejun zhuan," *juan shou*.19b.

62. Lin Jubai, *Jindai Nantong tubu shi*, pp. 58–60.

63. *DSQXDX*, annual report for 1900 (second half), p. 3, and annual report for 1901, p. 6.

64. NTFB: doc. 182 (1903). On the full restitution of the government's capital in 1903, see note 52 to this chapter.

65. NTFB: doc. 247 (1897); doc. 182 (1903); doc. 183 (1900–1920).

66. NTFB: doc. 193 (1915); doc. 198 (1919).

67. NTFB: doc. 247 (1897); doc. 182 (1903).

68. Feuerwerker, *China's Early Industrialization*, pp. 177–78.

69. NTFB: doc. 105 (1900); doc. 106 (1897).

70. Zhang Jian, *Riji*, 2nd and 19th days, 7th month, 1895, p. 373.

71. Yang Liqiang et al., *Zhang Jian cungao*, "Tonghai kenmu gongsi shuolüe," pp. 554–55.

72. *Ershi nian lai zhi Nantong*, part B, pp. 8–9.

73. *Who's Who in China*, 3d ed. (1925), 2: 7. We know very little about Zhang Cha before he joined his brother's operation; see the biographical entry "Zhang Cha" in *Zhuanji wenxue*, pp. 139–40. The parts of Zhang Cha's diary that have been preserved cover only the period between 1897 and 1899 and have not been published (NTB: D115/129, Zhang Cha, *Jixing*). The second oldest brother, Zhang Mou, died during childhood, the youngest, Zhang Jing, died in 1902 and the oldest, Zhang Yu, in 1914 (Chu, *Reformer in Modern China*, p. 8). I was unable to find further information about their career paths.

74. "Dasheng sanchang chuangban jingguo qingxing baogaoshu" (1921), in *DSQXDX*, pp. 427–29. Zhang Cha personally addressed the shareholders in the first report published in 1921, a task that in the case of the No. 1 and No. 2 mills had always been performed by his brother.

75. Liu Shaotang, *Minguo renwu xiaozhuan*, 4: 139–40.

76. NTFB: doc. 423 (1918).

77. *Who's Who in China*, 2nd ed. (1920), 1: 5–6, and 3d ed. (1925), pp. 7–8; *North China Herald*, May 7, 1921.

78. For Zhang Xiaoruo's biography, see the entry "Zhang Xiaoruo" in *Zhuanji wenxue*, pp. 138–39.

79. See picture in Zhang Xiaoruo, *Shixue ji.*

80. Cochran, *Encountering Chinese Networks*, p. 129.

81. Nantong youyi julebu, *Nantong shiye, jiaotong, cishan fengjin*, pp. 32d, 33.

82. ZJZJL, "Shiye lu," 1.10a.

83. "Dasheng shachang kaiche yiqian zhanglüe," in *DSQXDX*, p. 1.

84. Honeyman, *Origins of Enterprise*, p. 77.

85. NTD: B 401-III-1, doc. 5, original contract of purchase.

86. NTD: B 401-III-1, doc. 1. Paragraph five in the contract concerns the presence of a foreign engineer. His salary of 5,351 taels appears under the expenses of the mill's first profit and loss statement for the years 1896–99 (*DSQXDX*, p. 1).

87. *Rea's Far Eastern Manual*, p. 99 and advertising pages in this volume (n.p.); NTD: B 401-III-1, doc.5; *Dasheng xitong qiyeshi*, pp. 25–26.

88. *Rea's Far Eastern Manual*, p. 99.

89. NTD: B 401-III-13, docs. 2, 3, 4, 5 (1899).

90. Ibid., doc. 19 (1904).

91. See advertising pages in Pearse, *The Cotton Industry of Japan and China*, n.p.

92. NTD: B 401-III-34, 3a–7b.

93. NTD: B 401-III-152, doc. 7 (1921) and doc. 10 (1921).

94. Ibid., doc. 15 (1921) and doc. 29 (1921).

95. Thomas Rawski, *Economic Growth in Prewar China*, p. 105.

96. See Faure, "The Control of Equity in Chinese Firms," p. 62.

97. Ibid., pp. 62–63.

98. Mu Ouchu, "Shachang zuzhifa."

99. Xue Mingjian, *Gongchang sheji ji guanli.*

100. Xiong Yuezhi, *Xixue dongzhe yu wan Qing shehui*, pp. 544–46.

101. NTFB: docs. 215 to 222 (1913–17). For a brief survey of vocational education in China, see Gu Xiaoshui, "Jindai Zhongguo de zhiye jiaoyu."

102. NTFB: doc. 225, contract copy (1917).

103. *Fangzhi zhoukan*, 1932–35.

104. Zhang Jian, *Zhang Se'an shiye wenchao*, 1.16a. The price of the land is not mentioned. The government's initial plan from 1895 budgeted 7,000 taels to purchase land for the factory buildings (*Yingyin chuangban Dasheng shachang ligao*, 12b).

105. NTD: B 401-III-26, doc. 17 (1911), p. 24. Two pieces of land were bought from the Gu family, another two from the Hu family, and one each from the Li and the Chen families. Both taels (silver units of account) and yuan (silver dollars) were used in late imperial and Republican China. Between 1872 and 1932, when the tael was abolished by the central government, 1.0 yuan equaled roughly 0,7 tael.

106. NTD: G 01-III-11, original contract from 1905 and re-registration with the local government in 1914 and 1928.

107. NTD: B 405-III-56, 3a–18b.

108. Ibid., 5a, 27b–30a, 30b–31a.

109. Zhang Jian, *Zhang Se'an shiye wenchao*, 1.16b.

110. Zhang Jian, *Riji*; see, e.g., 23rd day, 2nd month, 1896; 14th day, 10th month, 1896; 21st day, 3rd month, 1897; 17th day, 9th month, 1897; 10th day, 7th month, 1898; 25th day, 1st month, 23rd and 29th days, 3rd month, 1899.

111. Ruppert, *Die Fabrik*, p. 228.

112. Shi Ya, *Lidai fangzhi shi jiexi*, p. 188.

113. Ibid.

114. Ibid., pp. 185–86.

115. Lin Jubai, *Jindai Nantong tubu shi*, pp. 7–10; *Minguo Nantong xian tuzhi*, 5.10b.

116. *Ershi nian lai zhi Nantong*, part B, p. 3.

117. Eng, "Luddism and Labor Protest Among Silk Artisans and Workers."

118. Lin Jubai, *Jindai Nantong tubu shi*, pp. 48, 145–47.

119. Faure, *China and Capitalism*, p. 43.

120. Jiangsu shehui kexueyuan, *Jiangsu shigang ketizu*, *Jiangsu shigang*, 2: 101.

121. Ibid.

Chapter 4

1. The Dasheng No. 1 mill was chosen as the focus for this chapter because of the excellent documentation on it; less information is available for the other mills.

2. Honig, *Sisters and Strangers*; Perry, *Shanghai on Strike*; Hershatter, *Workers in Tianjin*.

3. NTD: B 401-III-2 (1901); B 401-III-13 (1911). When the mill added cotton weaving to spinning, the company's official name was changed to Nantong xian Dasheng fangzhi gongsi (Dasheng cotton spinning and weaving mill of Nantong county) in 1915; see NTD: B 401-III-17 (1915).

4. For a detailed map of Nantong city, see *Nantong xianshi tu*. The Nantong local gazetteer for the Republican period has only a map of Tangjiazha district (*qu*), and Tangjiazha village is one of 45 other villages (*Minguo Nantong xian tuzhi*, p. 11).

5. Min-hsiung Shih, *The Silk Industry in Ch'ing China*, pp. 30–41; Santangelo, "The Imperial Factories of Suzhou," p. 279.

6. The term *gongchang* (using the *chang* meaning "place") originally referred to the workshop in a handicraft industry. Although these characters are used for *factory* (*kōjō*) in Japanese, from the early twentieth century on, the character used for *chang* in *shachang* was used in the term *factory* in Chinese.

7. See, e.g., the detailed map of the Dasheng No. 3 branch mill from the early 1920s, which identifies the workshops in detail, in *Jiangsu Haimen Dasheng di san fangzhi gongsi quantu*.

8. *Ershi nian lai zhi Nantong*, part B, p. 4. The text gives the size as 140 *mu*.

9. On the origin, definition, and usage of the term coolie (*kuli*) in China in the early 1900s, see *Zhongguo jingji quanshu*, pp. 95–96. Carrier, watchman, and rickshaw puller are just some of the occupations classified as coolie labor.

10. On the weighing and inspection of cotton, see *TXSZ*, "Dasheng shachang," pp. 71–72. The porters, however, are not mentioned. Porters and their work in Chinese mills in the early 1940s are documented in photographs in Shanxi sheng zhengxie wenshi ziliao weiyuanhui, *Baoji Shenxin fangzhichang shi* (separately paginated section before the "Introduction").

11. *Jiangsu Tongzhou Dasheng fangsha gufen youxian gongsi zhi tu*. This map is kept in the Nantong Municipal Library.

12. Nantong fangzhishi tulu bianjizu, *Nantong fangzhishi tulu*, photograph on p. 29.

13. The factory map does not show a temple on the compound where workers worshipped, as was the case in the Japanese-owned Kanegafuchi Cotton Mill in Shanghai (also known as the Shanghai Silk Spinning Company's Cotton Mill) or the Shenxin Mill in Wuxi; see Pearse, *The Cotton Industry of Japan and China*, p. 167; and Xu Weiyong and Huang Hanmin, *Rongjia qiye fazhan shi*, p. 118.

14. Photograph in *TXSZ*, no page number.

15. *TXSZ*, photograph in front of the section "Dasheng shachang," n.p.; *Ershi nian lai zhi Nantong*, part B, p. 4; Nantong fangzhishi tulu bianjizu, *Nantong fangzhishi tulu*, p. 35. In 1915 Dasheng No. 1 acquired 400 looms for which new weaving sheds had to be built. We lack precise measurements for the Dasheng No. 1 mill, but in England weaving shed walls were between 14 and 16 feet high. According to English textile manuals, placing the weaving machinery on the ground floor reduced vibration. Top light was considered most suitable for weaving sheds because it provided the steadiest light; see Heylin, *The Cotton Weaver's Handbook*, p. 286. For the terminology of industrial architecture, see Bradley, *The Works*.

16. The workshops in the Dasheng compound and their functions are listed in *TXSZ*, "Dasheng shacheng," pp. 89–96. The carding process, the repeated fluffing and cleaning of the cotton with carding machines, is omitted. For textile terminology, see *Zhongguo dabaike quanshu*, "Fangzhi"; Heylin, *The Cotton Weaver's Handbook*; Watson, *The Principal Articles of Chinese Commerce*; and Honig, *Sisters and Strangers*, pp. 41–56. Also useful is Parker, *Mianbu chang*. In 1915 Oxford University Press published Chinese translations of its series "The Industrial Reader" (original author A. O. Cooke) with volumes on, among other operations, coal mines, cotton mills, woolen mills, and shipyards. In the English original, "The Industrial Reader" is addressed to children; the Chinese version is aimed at technically interested adults but not at professionals like engineers. There seems to have been large demand in China for publications on general technical topics in the 1910s. I thank Peter Foden at Oxford University Press for access to materials on this series.

17. For a detailed description, see *Ershi nian lai zhi Nantong*, part B, pp. 6–7.

18. Mu Xuan and Yan Xuexi, *Dasheng shachang gongren shenghuo*. The 214 interviews were conducted in 1964 and edited in several stages in the 1980s.

19. See, e.g., ibid., pp. 14, 22, 37, 41. *Zuo gong* (for examples, see pp. 20, 41, 64) stood in contrast to working in the fields at home, which was referred to as *zuo tian* (for examples, see pp. 21, 66).

20. Ibid., pp. 24, 79, 96.

21. Nantong fangzhishi tulu bianjizu, *Nantong fangzhishi tulu*, p. 35.

22. *Dasheng xitong qiyeshi*, p. 160; Mu Xuan and Yan Xuexi, *Dasheng shachang gongren*, p. 30.

23. Interview with Li Guangquan in Tangjiazha, Mar. 30, 1995.

24. Mu Xuan and Yan Xuexi, *Dasheng shachang gongren*, p. 17.

25. *TXSZ*, pp. 70–73.

26. Mu Xuan and Yan Xuexi, *Dasheng shachang gongren*, introduction by Mu Xuan, pp. 1–2. The majority of workers interviewed in 1964 were at that time still living in villages surrounding Tangjiazha.

27. Chun Cao, "Tangjia jiegang zhi qutan."

28. NTFB: doc. 332 (1938/39?). Unfortunately, rent books from earlier years are not available in the archives. However, in this rent book the moving-in date is given in many entries and shows that families were living in company housing already in the 1920s and early 1930s.

29. Ibid.

30. Interview with Li Guangquan in Tangjiazha, Mar. 30, 1995. Mr. Li, a retired machinist, still lives in the original Dasheng No. 1 company housing within the compound. He inherited his unit from his elder brother, who had been a mechanic in the mill. One of his daughters is now employed by the mill. The company housing will be handed down to the next generation of the Li family.

31. See, e.g., Xiaobo Lü, "Minor Public Economy."

32. Bian, "Development of Institutions of Social Service"; Yeh, "Republican Origins of the *Danwei*." For further firm-level analysis of pre-1949 labor management institutions informing the socialist *danwei* system, see also Frazier, *The Making of the Chinese Industrial Workplace*.

33. Pearse, *The Cotton Industry of Japan and China*, pp. 91–112; Kidd, *Women Workers in the Japanese Cotton Mills*, pp. 50–59.

34. NTFB: doc. 332 (1938/39?).

35. *TXSZ*, "Dasheng shachang," pp. 65–66.

36. Ibid., p. 75. Interview with Li Guangquan in Tangjiazha, Mar. 30, 1995. Accommodation for engineers was not regulated by Dasheng's company regulations.

37. In photographs Alfred Krupp and his family pose proudly in their garden with the huge iron workshop in the background. Following Krupp's tremendous business success and rise in society, in 1873 the family moved into the palatial residence of the Villa Hügel, surrounded by a spacious park, far away from the industrial noise of the factories (Ruppert, *Die Fabrik*, pp. 101, 107). On Zhang Jian's villa in

Nantong, see Nantong fangzhishi tulu bianjizu, *Nantong fangzhishi tulu*, p. 19; it now houses the collection of the Nantong Museum. Interview with Li Guangquan in Tangjiazha, Mar. 30, 1995.

38. Mu Xuan and Yan Xuexi, *Dasheng shachang gongren*, p. 16. For example, the machinist Wang Jinyuan mistakenly recalled Gao Liqing as director of the factory (*changzhang*) at the time of his entry around 1900. In fact, at that time Gao Liqing was manager of the workshop department (*changgong dongshi*); see Nantong fangzhishi tulu bianjizu, *Nantong fangzhishi tulu*, p. 22. Almost none of the unskilled workers interviewed ever mentioned Zhang Jian as the managing director of the mill.

39. Honig, *Sisters and Strangers*, p. 117–18; see also Tim Wright, "'A Method of Evading Management.'"

40. Honig, *Sisters and Strangers*, p. 117.

41. Mu Xuan and Yan Xuexi, *Dasheng shachang gongren*, for example, pp. 2, 8, 19.

42. NTD: B 401-311-154 (1909–10).

43. As confirmed by the former director of the Nantong Municipal Archives, Yang Wen, and the former director of the Nantong Museum, Mu Xuan, not a single account or notebook with information on unskilled workers' wages in Dasheng exists. This is not unusual: Thomas Winpenny in his study on cotton mills in Lancaster county, Pennsylvania, in the late nineteenth and early twentieth century states in a note on source materials: "Conestoga Steam Mill records did not include payroll information that would have revealed precise job titles and wages paid to specific employees" (*Industrial Progress and Human Welfare*, p. 124).

44. Interview with Li Guangquan in Tangjiazha, Mar. 30, 1995. On working women and their position within the specialized economy of the Ningbo area, see Mann, "Women's Work in the Ningbo Area," esp. pp. 263–69 for an analysis of female factory workers. For a useful description of non-local skilled workers in the factories of Kunming in the late 1940s, see Kuo-Heng Shih, *China Enters the Machine Age*, pp. 18–32.

45. *Dasheng Chongming fenchang shinian shishu*, 4a. In addition, assistant managers from the Chongming factory were required to spend some time at the No. 1 mill to acquire skills necessary for handling textile machinery. After their return to the Chongming factory, they taught the workers there.

46. NTD: B 401-111-152 (1921). The engineer Yang Shizong came to the Dasheng No. 1 Cotton Mill through a foreign brokerage firm, Gaston, Williams and Wigmore, in Shanghai in April 1921.

47. *Nantong xueyuan fangzhike xueyou lu*, pp. 18–19.

48. "Te pin yang gongchengshi," *Tonghai xinbao*, Nov. 23, 1915; NTD: B 401-111-125 (1921).

49. See photograph in the front section of *TXSZ*, "Dasheng shachang," n.p.

50. Chen Shensheng, "Tangjia mishi"; Jiang Binghe, "Nantong Tangjiazhen liangshiye."

51. Shu Zhe, *Tong Yang shishu jiangyu tushuo*, n.p., entry under "Tongzhou zhi xiangli."

52. Dasheng yichang changshi bianjishi, *Dasheng yichang gongren douzhengshi*, pp. 10–11.

53. For the Western context, see E. P. Thompson, "Time, Work-Discipline, and Industrial Capitalism." For an excellent study on time, planning, and discipline in the rural context of Tokugawa and Meiji Japan, see Smith, "Peasant Time and Factory Time in Japan." On time and work in Chinese villages, see Hsiao-tung Fei, *Peasant Life in China*, pp. 144–53.

54. *Ershi nian lai zhi Nantong*, part B, p. 8. The shifts changed at 6:00 A.M. and P.M.

55. Ibid., part B, p. 2.

56. Zhang Jian, *Riji*, p. 402, entry for 28th day, 11th month, 1897. TXSZ, "Dasheng shachang," pp. 65–103. The copy I saw was published in 1910.

57. Altogether six cotton mills, five of them in Shanghai and one in Wuchang, were established under the sponsorship of the Chinese government between 1891 and 1895; see Feuerwerker, *China's Early Industrialization*, pp. 221–22. The Deda Spinning Mill and the Housheng Spinning and Weaving Mill operated under Chinese ownership in Shanghai. For their regulations, see Jiangsu shiye ting, Di san ke, *Jiangsu sheng fangzhiye zhuangkuang*, "neibian," pp. 5–6, and "fubian," pp. 55–72.

58. Kaku, "Management and Labour in German Chemical Companies," p. 210.

59. The Kaiping mines, a *guandu shangban* enterprise under Li Hongzhang's patronage, adopted a set of regulations (*zhangcheng*) as early as 1877. However, they dealt mostly with commercial and general managerial issues and did not address workforce discipline (Zhang Guohui, "Lun Kaiping, Luanzhou meikuang," pp. 55–57; Carlson, *The Kaiping Mines*, pp. 30–34).

60. On the regulations for the Beiyang navy, see Ma Junjie, "Lun Beiyang haijun zhangcheng."

61. For an excellent treatment of the subject, see Narusawa, "The Social Order of Modern Japan."

62. In addition to information contained in the factory regulations, the following analysis of work and life in the Dasheng No. 1 Cotton Mill is supplemented by information from the 214 interviews with former workers in Mu Xuan and Yan Xuexi, *Dasheng shachang gongren*. According to Zhang Jian's diary, night shifts were introduced in the Dasheng No. 1 Cotton Mill in 1900 (Zhang Jian, *Riji*, p. 442, entry for 28th day, 8th month, 1900).

63. TXSZ, "Dasheng shachang," p. 82.

64. Mu Xuan and Yan Xuexi, *Dasheng shachang gongren*, for example, p. 2.

65. Ibid., pp. 13, 75.

66. *TXSZ,* "Dasheng shachang," p. 69.

67. Ibid., p. 75.

68. A comparison of photographs shows that the clock tower must have been built a few years after the mill's founding in 1895. See Nantong fangzhishi tulu bianjizu, *Nantong fangzhishi tulu,* p. 29.

69. Many workers, especially those who did not own a watch, were afraid of being late for work and losing a day's wage; see Mu Xuan and Yan Xuexi, *Dasheng shachang gongren,* p. 39. This was also a familiar phenomenon in English cotton mills in the early nineteenth century. Those who could neither afford a watch nor the services of a "knocker-up" worried about the factory time. Children in particular would often arrive at the mill long before their shift actually began. See Aspin, *Lancashire,* p. 66.

70. Meakin, *Man and Work,* p. 150.

71. *TXSZ,* "Dasheng shachang," p. 89.

72. This regulation was not included in the 1897 factory regulations but was part of the later version for the Dasheng No. 2 Cotton Mill in Chongming; see *TXSZ,* "Dasheng fenchang," p. 48.

73. Ibid.

74. Ibid., p. 86.

75. Parker, *Mianbu chang,* p. 15.

76. For a detailed report of the fire, see *North China Herald,* Oct. 20, 1893. Thereafter the mill, which had been set up with Governor-General Li Hongzhang as official supervisor and Sheng Xuanhuai as merchant-manager, was completely rebuilt and reorganized as the Huasheng Spinning and Weaving Mill (Huasheng fangzhi zongchang). On the history of the mill, see Feuerwerker, *China's Early Industrialization,* pp. 207–25.

77. *TXSZ,* "Dasheng shachang," p. 78.

78. In order to facilitate fire extinguishing, many mills had artificial ponds built in the middle of the factory compound. See, e.g., the map of the Yufeng cotton mill in Zhengzhou (*Huashang shachang lianhehui jikan* 1, no. 4 [July 1920]: 283) or the picture of the cloth mills in Preston in 1920 (Patrick, *Factory Reform,* p. 20). With a reliable water supply from the surrounding canals, this arrangement was not necessary at the Dasheng No. 1 Cotton Mill.

79. *TXSZ,* "Dasheng shachang," pp. 65–66.

80. Ibid., pp. 72, 98–99.

81. Ibid., pp. 65–67.

82. Ibid., p. 67.

83. Ibid., p. 69.

84. Ibid., pp. 68–69.

85. Pollard, *The Genesis of Modern Management,* pp. 193–95, 197.

86. *TXSZ,* "Dasheng fenchang," pp. 3–80.

87. The regulations of the Dasheng No. 2 mill could be considered a model for regulations of other cotton mills. The regulations for the Deda and the Housheng mill in Shanghai in the late 1910s contain in addition exact wage information for each job description. See Jiangsu shiye ting, Di san ke, *Jiangsu sheng fangzhiye zhuangkuang*, appendix, pp. 55–71.

88. See, e.g., *Tonghai xinbao*, Mar. 20 and 22, 1920, and Aug. 23, 1921.

89. Lu Bin, *Chongming pingmin changshi*, pp. 60–61.

90. *TXSZ*, "Dasheng fenchang," p. 49.

91. Mu Xuan and Yan Xuexi, *Dasheng shachang gongren*, pp. 3, 9, 13, 23, 34.

92. Ibid., pp. 8, 19.

93. The gate search was a common feature of cotton mills in China, Chinese- as well as foreign-owned; see Moser, *The Cotton Textile Industry of Far Eastern Countries*, p. 70. Although all the guards at Dasheng were men, cases of harassment of female workers by the guards do not feature prominently in the 214 interviews from 1964. In present-day China, migrant workers in factories are still viewed as potential thieves by the management and urban staff due to their village background and continue to experience strict factory regulations similar to Dasheng's; see Ngai, "Becoming Dagongmei," pp. 5–6; and Ching Kwan Lee, *Gender and the South China Miracle*, pp. 111–13.

94. See, e.g., Honig, *Sisters and Strangers*, p. 148.

95. Mu Xuan and Yan Xuexi, *Dasheng shachang gongren*, p. 9.

96. See, e.g., ibid., pp. 31, 35, 58.

97. Ibid., p. 40. Ling Wenbin's age is given as 16 *sui*.

98. *TXSZ*, "Dasheng shachang," pp. 99–100.

99. Ibid.

100. Ibid., p. 99. As a former machinist in Dasheng, Li Guangquan confirmed the fact that only *waidiren* were employed as company police guards (interview in Tangjiazha, Mar. 30, 1995).

101. Mu Xuan and Yan Xuexi, *Dasheng shachang gongren*, pp. 39–40.

102. Ibid., p. 39.

103. The question of wages in relation to income is discussed in Chesneaux, *The Chinese Labor Movement*.

104. *Dasheng xitong qiyeshi*, p. 24.

105. *Ershi nian lai zhi Nantong*, part B, pp. 5, 8.

106. The Nantong gazetteer notes a population of 51,330 people in 5,253 households for the district of Tangjiazha (Tangjiazha qu) spread over 58 square kilometers. In comparison, the city district of Nantong had a population of 113,793 people in 25,678 households in an area of 118 square kilometers (*Minguo Nantong xian tuzhi*, 1.2b–3a and 1.7b–8a, entry under "Tangjiazha di shiba zhenqu").

107. Numbers for the whole county in ibid., 1.2b–3a.

108. My calculation excludes the 400 members of the administrative staff who lived in company housing or private accommodation and did not commute from the villages on a daily basis.

109. Mu Xuan and Yan Xuexi, *Dasheng shachang gongren*, pp. 41–42, 46–49. Interview with Li Guangquan in Tangjiazha, Mar. 15, 1995.

110. See Dasheng yichang changshi bianjishi, *Dasheng yichang gongren douzheng shi*, pp. 10–11. This report, based on interviews with former workers in 1950, mentions the arrival of 100–200 *waidiren* in Tangjiazha at the opening of the factory in 1899. They came from places such as Wuxi or Ningbo and were described as machinists or experienced textile workers.

111. Qi, "Nantong pingmin shenghuo zhuangkuang." With its strong cottage industry of cloth weaving, the Tongzhou region resembled in its structural development the northwestern part of Lower Austria during the nineteenth and very early twentieth century. In that area home-based cloth weaving as subsidy to farm income was prevalent. Like Nantong, the area became famous for its strong, durable cloth. The second half of the nineteenth century saw the introduction of textile mills, attracting migrant workers from southern Bohemia; see Komlosy, *Industrie Kultur*, pp. 18–21, 26–34, 86–88.

112. All the following data are derived by my own analysis of the interview sample presented in Mu Xuan and Yan Xuexi, *Dasheng shachang gongren*, esp. pp. 201–8.

113. Ibid., pp. 21, 91.

114. All my calculations are based on wages mentioned in the interviews presented in ibid., esp. pp. 187–200. Contemporary sources such as *Ershi nian lai zhi Nantong* from the mid-1920s quote only one average daily wage for male workers (0.25–0.60 yuan) and one for female workers (0.20–0.40 yuan) without any further specification in regard to the job, position, and age.

115. On the boom in the Chinese textile industry and the cotton mill crisis, see Bergère, *The Golden Age of the Chinese Bourgeoisie*, pp. 63–83, 92–98.

116. In the interviews workers always gave their age in *sui*. I count workers under the age of fourteen as child workers.

117. For the examples, see Mu Xuan and Yan Xuexi, *Dasheng shachang gongren*, pp. 190, 193.

118. For examples, see ibid., p. 190.

119. *TXSZ*, "Dasheng shachang," p. 68.

120. Ibid.

121. NTD: B 401-311-154 (1909–10).

122. SHD: Q 193-1-1039.

123. Mu Xuan and Yan Xuexi, *Dasheng shachang gongren*, pp. 4–6.

124. "Jieshaobu xiaoxi," *Huashang shachang lianhehui jikan* 1, no. 1 (Sept. 1919): 267.

125. See, e.g., Mu Xuan and Yan Xuexi, *Dasheng shachang gongren*, pp. 6–7. In this case the worker had entered the factory to work in the reeling room at age twelve. At the age of 30, she was made *gongtou* in the reeling room. The worker used the words *zuo gongtou* (to act as *gongtou*) rather than a term expressing a promotion on the shop floor.

126. Sources like *Ershi nian lai zhi Nantong* from the mid-1920s describe the agricultural situation but do not give price data, whereas land surveys in Nantong county in the 1930s concentrate on the land-reclamation areas and their tenancy problems; see Zhang Huiqun, "Yanken quyu zudian zhidu zhi yanjiu."

127. Zhang Liluan, "Jiangsu Wujin wujia zhi yanjiu," esp. app. 2, pp. 198–214.

128. For discussion of subsistence requirements, see Clark and Haswell, *The Economics of Subsistence Agriculture*, pp. 51, 61. Following Clark's and Haswell's suggestion of a minimum subsistence of between 250 kg and 300 kg of grain per person per year, I chose 285 kg as subsistence average for my calculations. Various other interpretations of minimum subsistence are summarized in Faure, *The Rural Economy of Pre-Liberation China*, p. 227n29. See also Pomeranz, *The Great Divergence*, pp. 319–20.

129. Mu Xuan and Yan Xuexi, *Dasheng shachang gongren*, pp. 14, 23.

130. Thomas Rawski, *Economic Growth in Prewar China*, pp. 301–3. Impressionistic and imprecise average wage data in Jiangsu's industrial handbook for 1933 also suggest generally lower wages for male and female workers in Nantong's textile industry compared to those in Shanghai or Wuxi (Shiyebu, Guoji maoyiju, *Zhongguo shiyezhi*, p. 47).

131. Thomas Rawski, *Economic Growth in Prewar China*, pp. 306–7. Between 1923–25 and 1932, annual farm wages for male laborers in Nantong rose by 7.5 percent, in Chongming by 35.7 percent, and in Haimen by 400 percent (which Rawski correctly discounts as improbably high). Rawski relates the rise in the real value of rural wages in Jiangsu to his argument that rural productivity, incomes, and living standards were on the rise in prewar Republican China and that "wage trends in unskilled nonfarm occupations can be taken as indicators of changes in agricultural productivity" (p. 307).

132. Mu Xuan and Yan Xuexi, *Dasheng shachang gongren*, p. 16.

133. Ibid., p. 69.

134. Ibid., pp. 21, 43.

135. Ibid., p. 37.

136. Fong, *Cotton Industry and Trade in China*, pp. 147–48.

137. Ibid., p. 148.

138. Nantong fangzhishi tulu bianjizu, *Nantong fangzhishi tulu*, p. 35. Unfortunately, the quality of the photograph is so bad that it cannot be reproduced in this book.

139. Mu Xuan and Yan Xuexi, *Dasheng shachang gongren,* pp. 77, 79, 93, 145, 157, 160, 162.

140. Ibid., pp. 12–13.

141. Boot, "How Skilled Were Lancashire Cotton Factory Workers in 1833?"

142. Ibid., p. 289.

143. Mu Xuan and Yan Xuexi, *Dasheng shachang gongren,* pp. 8, 15, 24; quote from p. 8.

144. Clarke, *The Effects of the Factory System,* p. 17; Patrick, *Factory Reform,* p. 45.

145. Fong, *Cotton Industry and Trade in China,* p. 174. For the full text of the 1931 Factory Act, see Porter, *Industrial Reformers in Republican China,* app. 2B, pp. 189–202.

146. Tayler, *Farm and Factory in China,* pp. 98–102; Anderson, *Humanity and Labour,* pp. 128–33; Porter, *Industrial Reformers in Republican China,* pp. 29–72.

147. See Chen Da, "Wo guo gongchangfa de shixing wenti." Despite a prescribed legal minimum age of fourteen years and an eight-hour working day for children, in 1931 children who were nine years old and working the same hours as adults could still be found in the mills. Obviously, the discrepancies between the legal requirements and actual conditions were substantial, and a compromise had to be found. Except for a transitional period of two years between 1931 and 1933, children were not to work ten hours a day or on night shifts. Equally, except for a transitional period of three years, ten-hour night shifts were now thought to be inappropriate for female workers (ibid., p. 425).

148. *Tonghai xinbao,* Mar. 14 and 15, 1928.

149. Mu Xuan and Yan Xuexi, *Dasheng shachang gongren,* pp. 223–24.

150. "Dasheng shachang bei cai gongren naoshi," *Fangzhi zhoukan* 3, no. 21 (1932): 686.

151. *Zhang Jian quanji,* vol. 6, "Seweng ziding nianpu," p. 893, entry for the 12th month, 1922.

152. *Dasheng xitong qiyeshi,* pp. 254–55.

153. Lu Bin, *Chongming pingmin changzhi,* pp. 34–35. Writing in 1925, Lu complained about Chongming's economic backwardness and conceded that the only industrial enterprises with at least some structural organization (in contrast to work done in individual households) were the textile mills. He envisioned industrialization in the form of a local concentration of production and workforce, improvement of the workers' standard of living, knowledge, and organization, as well as a diversification of industrial enterprises in Chongming.

154. Honig, *Sisters and Strangers;* Perry, *Shanghai on Strike.* Hershatter deals with cotton mill workers in the urban context of Tianjin in one chapter of *Workers in Tianjin.*

155. See interviews in Mu Xuan and Yan Xuexi, *Dasheng shachang gongren,* pp. 53, 80, 87, 127.

156. Meng Guilin, "Rijun junguanxia de Dasheng yichang," p. 136.

157. Ibid., pp. 138–39.

158. Wang Minzhi, "Huiyi Tangjia he Tianshenggang jiefang," p. 41.

159. Jiangsu shiye ting, Di san ke, *Jiangsu sheng fangzhiye zhuangkuang*; Fong, *Cotton Industry and Trade in China*.

160. Perry, *Shanghai on Strike*; Hershatter, *Workers in Tianjin*; Cochran, *Big Business in China*.

161. For a comparison with other mills in China in regard to the number of spindles, looms, and workers, see Pearse, *The Cotton Industry of Japan and China*, pp. 154–55.

162. Perry, "Putting Class in Its Place," quotation on p. 10.

163. Perry, *Shanghai on Strike*, pp. 48–64; Hershatter, *Workers in Tianjin*, pp. 144–47; Honig, *Sisters and Strangers*, pp. 56–78.

164. For some urban habits of female mill workers in Shanghai, see Honig, *Sisters and Strangers*, pp. 155, 160–62. The considerable impact of the urban-industrial environment on workers who commuted from villages outside Shanghai to the mills in the Yangshupu area on a daily basis in the late 1920s and the resulting changes in their life-styles and village customs is documented in Lamson, "The Effect of Industrialization."

165. See, e.g., E. P. Thompson, *The Making of the English Working Class*; Katznelson and Zolberg, *Working-Class Formation*; Kiyokawa, "The Transformation of Young Rural Women"; and Taira, "Factory Labour."

166. Kaku, "Management and Labour in German Chemical Companies," p. 210.

167. Tsutsui, *Manufacturing Ideology*, pp. 14–57.

168. Mu Ouchu, himself the manager of several cotton mills and president of the Chinese Cotton Mill Owners' Association in Shanghai, was to my knowledge one of the first to address consciously the problems of mill construction, shop-floor management, and workforce supervision in a professional way; see his "Shachang zuzhifa."

169. NTD: B 405-111-57 (1907).

170. Ibid., 1a–1b.

171. *TXSZ*, "Dasheng shachang," pp. 81–82.

172. Clennell, "Sub-enclosure 8 in no. 7," pp. 43–67, quotation on p. 45.

173. Elsässer, *Soziale Intentionen und Reformen des Robert Owen*, p. 92; Aspin, *Lancashire*, pp. 131–38. Among the second generation of Chinese industrialists, Mu Ouchu, who owned the Housheng and Deda cotton mills in Shanghai and had been trained in America, was one of the first to express concrete concern about his workers. By improving their living conditions, Mu Ouchu envisioned the improvement of society as a whole. For him the factory was "a part of our society" ("Fu Yufeng shachang zongli Mu Ouchu xiansheng kaimu yanshuo ci," *Huashang shachang lianhehui jikan*, no. 4 [1920]: 281–82). The economic historian Fang Xianting (H. D. Fong) started

as an apprentice in the Housheng mill in 1917; Mu Ouchu later sponsored his studies in the United States; see Fong, *Reminiscences of a Chinese Economist at 70*, pp. 3–10.

174. For example, the welfare and educational facilities provided by the Shenxin mills in Wuxi in the 1930s (Xu Weiyong and Huang Hanmin, *Rongjia qiye fazhan shi*, pp. 118–19).

175. *Ershi nian lai zhi Nantong*, pt. B, pp. 145–46.

176. Interview with Li Guangquan in Tangjiazha, Mar. 30, 1995.

Chapter 5

1. See the enterprises listed in *TXSZ*, "Dasheng shachang," pp. 167–71; and in *Ershi nian lai zhi Nantong*, pt. B, pp. 2–55. The second shareholder report (1908) in *TXSZ* lists nineteen affiliated companies; of these, the Yisheng Metal Company and the Dyeing Workshop had already gone out of business.

2. NTFB: doc. 247, share certificate from 1897; doc. 182, share certificate from 1903. Share certificates from the years 1898 to 1903 with the same text are also kept in the Nantong Municipal Archives (NTD: B 402-III-1).

3. *Dagongbao*, Mar. 4, 1905, 2a–b; Mar. 6, 1905, 2a.

4. For the text of this law, see Shangwu yinshuguan bianyisuo, *Da Qing Guangxu xin faling*, "Gongsi lü," 10.3b.

5. NTD: B 402-III-445, 13b.

6. For the biography of Zheng Xiaoxu (courtesy name: Zheng Sukan), see Boorman, *Biographical Dictionary of Republican China*, 1: 271–75. Zheng Xiaoxu is probably most famous for his Manchu loyalism and his refusal to recognize the Republic of China. Between 1925 and 1932 he served as an assistant to the former Xuantong emperor, Puyi.

7. To translate *wufa* as "illegal" here would be beside the point, since there was no company law before 1904 that required registration, and thus a company without official registration was not an illegal operation.

8. NTD: B 402-III-445, 12b.

9. NTFB: doc. 193, share certificate from 1915; doc. 198, share certificate from 1919.

10. *Dagongbao*, Feb. 28, 1905, 2b.

11. NTD: B 401-III-26, doc. 8 (1913), letter from Okura & Co. Bank in Shanghai addressed to Zhang Jian as director of the Chongming Weaving and Spinning Company.

12. NTD: B 402-III-445, 20b.

13. Ibid.

14. Ibid., 9a–12b.

15. Ibid., 12a.

16. Annual company reports for the year 1908 and 1909 in *DSQXDX*, pp. 57, 62.

17. Ibid., p. 206.

18. Shangwu yinshuguan bianyisuo, *Da Qing Guangxu xin faling,* "Gongsi lü."

19. NTD: B 402-III-I. This handwritten record covers the share subscriptions for the period 1898–1903. The business accounts are sometimes identified by the personal name of the owner. The capital increase is documented in the annual reports for 1903 and 1904 in *DSQXDX,* pp. 21, 25.

20. NTD: B 402-III-2.

21. Ibid.; *Nantong bao tekan,* Oct. 29, 1926.

22. NTD: B 402-III-I. The Dunyu *tang* was, for example, an old business account of the Zhang family for land transactions (see Zhang Jian, *Nantong Zhang shi Changle zhipu,* 7a).

23. Faure, *China and Capitalism,* p. 17.

24. See Wellington Chan, *Merchants, Mandarins, and Modern Enterprise,* pp. 36–37. Based on analysis of a court case filed in Hong Kong in 1910, Stephanie Chung ("'Faren' gainian de yizhi," p. 60) points out that neither *tang* nor *hao* were recognized by the law as legal persons (*faren*). Even though this decision was made in the context of a legal system strongly influenced by the West, it confirms the private nature of the *tang, hao,* and *ji* and the legal difficulties in case of litigation.

25. For example, after 1907 the name of the company did not reflect the newly acquired limited liability status, and none of the successive shareholder and company reports or the official company correspondence referred to Dasheng as a *youxian gongsi,* a company with limited liability.

26. NTD: B 402-III-445, 17a–b.

27. For the text of the law, see Shangwu yinshuguan bianyisuo, *Da Qing Guangxu xin faling,* "Gongsi lü," 10.7a–8b.

28. NTD: B 402-III-445, 4a.

29. Dividend payments with passbooks were called *xizhe.* As Ellen Hertz (*The Trading Crowd,* p. 37) points out, even in China today dividends on stocks traded on Shanghai's stock market must be collected in person; checks are not sent through the mail.

30. McElderry, "Shanghai Securities Exchanges: Past and Present," esp. p. 6 and note 1, which gives a partial list of the government securities and government shares traded in 1917.

31. *Shenbao,* Aug. 1920.

32. *DSQXDX,* pp. 18–19, 93–103.

33. Kirby, "China Unincorporated," p. 48.

34. Ibid.

35. Chandler, *The Visible Hand,* pp. 1–3. Although I concentrate on the Dasheng No. 1 Cotton Mill, the branch mills were also organized as multi-unit enterprises under salaried managers.

36. *TXSZ,* "Dasheng shachang," pp. 65–66.

37. Ibid., p. 65.

38. NTD: B 401-311-1, daybook covering the 1st to the 6th month of 1898, 21b. Zhang Jian's travel expenses were recorded in these account books as daily expenses.

39. NTD: B 402-111-445, 14a.

40. Ibid., 11a. The following courtesy names appear often in the documents: Jiang Xishen (Jiang Shuzhen), Gao Qing (Gao Liqing), Shen Xiejun (Shen Jingfu); see also Nantong fangzhishi tulu bianjibu, *Nantong fangzhishi tulu*, p. 22.

41. Lin Jubai, *Jindai Nantong tubu shi*, p. 58.

42. *TXSZ*, "Dasheng shachang," pp. 22–23. Gao Qing and Jiang Xishen invested in Dasheng after the Shanghai promoters had pulled out.

43. Zhang Jian, *Zhang Se'an shiye wenchao*, "Gao jun Liqing muzhi," *juan shou*: 21a–22a.

44. NTD: B 402-111-1, n.p.

45. *TXSZ*, "Dasheng shachang," pp. 65–66, 69–71.

46. For the text of the law, see Shangwu yinshuguan bianyisuo, *Da Qing Guangxu xin faling*, 10.9a.

47. See the annual company reports in *DSQXDX* for the period 1899–1930.

48. See Zhongguo di'er lishi dang'anguan, *Zhang Jian nongshang zongzhang*, "Gongsi tiaoli," pp. 25–56. These company regulations in 251 paragraphs were introduced in January 1914 under Zhang Jian as minister of industry and commerce (*gongshang zongzhang*). For a summary of Chinese company and commercial law, see Xie Zhenmin, *Zhonghua Minguo lifashi*, pp. 976–91. For a detailed discussion of the company law, see Kirby, "China Unincorporated," esp. pp. 49–50.

49. Shangwu yinshuguan bianyisuo, *Da Qing Guangxu xin faling*, 10.9a.

50. Zhongguo di'er lishi dang'anguan, *Zhang Jian nongshang zongzhang*, "Gongsi tiaoli," pp. 46–47.

51. NTD: B 406-111-13.

52. For the introduction of Western-style accounting to China, see Gao Zhiyu, *Zhongguo kuaiji fazhan jianshi*, pp. 84–91. The frequent advertisements for bookkeeping manuals in newspapers and journals from the 1920s on indicate the increasing demand for accounting knowledge (see, e.g., Zuijin zhi wushi nain [Shenbaoguan wushi zhounian jinian], 1922, p. 5 and advertisements without page numbers).

53. NTB: E 123/1334, pp. 6–17, 19–20.

54. NTD: B 401-311-1.

55. NTD: B 401-311-3; B 401-311-30.

56. NTD: B 401-311-35.

57. NTB: E 60/643.

58. Pollard, *The Genesis of Modern Management*, pp. 219–20. See also Edwards and Newell, "The Development of Industrial Cost."

59. Chandler, *The Visible Hand*, pp. 70–71.

60. See Liu Hongsheng, "Wo weishenme zhuzhong chengben kuaiji"; and Xu Yongzuo, "Gailiang Zhongguo kuaiji wenti."

61. NTD: B 401-311-26.

62. *TXSZ*, "Dasheng shachang," pp. 70–71. The fact that most of the extant accounting documents of the Dasheng No. 1 Cotton Mill are marked with the red seal "Shanghai Accounts Office" shows the flow of company records from the factories in Tangjiazha to the financial headquarters in Shanghai.

63. *Ershi nian lai zhi Nantong*, pt. B, pp. 10–38.

64. See, e.g., the annual company reports for Dasheng No. 1 from 1903 and 1905 in *DSQXDX*, pp. 22, 35–36.

65. Ibid., p. 22.

66. Ibid., pp. 35–36. Sometime before 1909 the Fuxin Flour Mill was named Daxing Flour Mill and appears under this name in the accounts.

67. *Ershi nian lai zhi Nantong*, pt. B, pp. 10–17.

68. For this reason, I do not use the term "conglomerate" for Dasheng, since that would require the No. 1 mill to hold the majority of shares in the subsidiaries.

69. "Dasheng shachang di'erci gudong changhui yi'an" (1908), in *TXSZ*, "Dasheng shachang," p. 171.

70. *Ershi nian lai zhi Nantong*, pt. B, pp. 10–17.

71. *TXSZ*, "Dasheng shachang," pp. 167–71.

72. Ibid., pp. 168–69.

73. *Ershi nian lai zhi Nantong*, pt. B, pp. 38–42.

74. Annual report from 1905 in *DSQXDX*, p. 36.

75. *TXSZ*, "Kenmu gongsi," pp. 135, 222.

76. *Tonghai kenmu gongsi disici gudong huiyi'an*. That Dasheng was not an actual shareholder is corroborated by a Tonghai report from 1911 that was not available to me but is quoted in *Dasheng xitong qiyeshi*, p. 47. According to this report, there were 26 shareholders in 1911.

77. Summarized Tonghai company records are available for the period between 1906 and 1909. The Dasheng No. 1 mill provided 21,792 taels in 1906, 12,280 taels in 1907, 25,668 taels in 1908, and 28,043 taels in 1909 (*TXSZ*, "Kenmu gongsi," pp. 135, 159, 189, 222). According to Dasheng's annual accounts, it advanced 20,000 taels to Tonghai in both 1905 and 1906 (*DSQXDX*, pp. 44, 36).

78. NTD: B 402-111-445, 12b–13a.

79. Ibid.

80. Annual company report for 1907 in *DSQXDX*, p. 51.

81. Annual company report for 1906 in ibid., p. 43. The deposits are recorded in a single entry on the balance sheet as "Tonghai ge shiye wanglai" (current accounts with the industrial companies in Tongzhou and Haimen).

82. Ibid., pp. 43, 51.

83. The only document referring to the Industrial Company known to me is a report published by the Nantong Municipal Finance Department in 1953, *Tonghai shiye gongsi baogao shu*, as quoted in *Dasheng xitong qiyeshi*, p. 103. Unfortunately, this document was not available to me.

84. In 1920 Dasheng No. 1 held 171,590 taels as deposits in the Industrial Company; in 1921, 114,870 taels; and in 1922, 100,460 taels (*DSQXDX*, pp. 142, 148, 153). After 1922 no further deposits in the Industrial Company are listed. For further explanation of the overall financial situation in the early 1920s, see Chapter 6.

85. That the Industrial Company never developed into an independent power center within the Dasheng enterprise is corroborated by the fact that it was not attached to the Shanghai office. Indeed, it occupied only one room in the Zisheng Iron Workshop at Tangjiazha (*Dasheng xitong qiyeshi*, p. 102). Matters concerning the Industrial Company were discussed and handled by the head of the Shanghai office and Zhang Jian in their correspondence; see, e.g., NTB: E 109/1319. In short, the Industrial Company did not have a decisive influence on the organizational structure of the Dasheng enterprise as a business group.

86. For further discussion of the special financial function of the Industrial Company, see Chapter 6.

87. The Shanghai office is mentioned only briefly in the regulations concerning the finance department of the Dasheng No. 1 Cotton Mill (*TXSZ*, "Dasheng shachang," p. 70).

88. NTD: B 401-III-9. Unfortunately most of the 93 letters in this file are not dated with a specific year.

89. Ibid., letter no. 6, 7th day, 7th month, probably 1903.

90. Ibid., letter no. 8, 28th day, 9th month, probably 1903.

91. Ibid., letter no. 32, 25th day, 9th month, probably 1905.

92. Ibid., letter no. 33, n.d., probably 1905.

93. NTD: B 401-311-200.

94. NTD: B 401-311-4.

95. Zhu Zhenhua, *Zhongguo jinrong jiushi*, p. 126.

96. Nantong youyi julebu, *Nantong shiye, jiaoyu, cishan fengjing*, p. 32c. Jiujiang Road is south of and parallel to Nanjing Road, where many banks and businesses had offices under the legal protection of the International Settlement.

97. NTD: B 401-311-30. See also Qiu Yunzhang and Yao Lian, "Tonghai kenmu sishi nian," p. 74.

98. NTD: B 403-311-4, p. 6, 17.

99. For example, the Shanghai office held deposits of 188 taels (1906), 5,504 taels (1907), 6,415 taels (1908), and 1,606 taels (1909) in the Tonghai Land Reclamation Company (*TXSZ*, "Kenmu gongsi," pp. 135, 159, 189, 222).

100. NTD: B 405-III-58, pp. 2, 3, 18.

101. *Dasheng xitong qiyeshi*, p. 81.

102. NTD: B 401-311-121.

103. NTD: B 401-311-155 (1909–10). Before 1907, payments to charity and educational projects were recorded in the Dasheng No. 1's annual profit and loss statement as part of the appropriations fund, but not after 1907. Perhaps complaints by the shareholders at the 1907 meeting about the generous donations to the school led to the decision not to list the donations openly.

104. NTD: B 401-111-9, letters nos. 44–47 (probably 1905–6). The Guan *ji* account appears often in connection with transfers of Zhang Jian's private funds and seems to have been one of his many personal business accounts.

105. The *zhangfang* in the silk industry during the Qing period is mentioned, yet without a satisfying explanation of its institutional role, in Min-hsiung Shih, *The Silk Industry in Ch'ing China*, pp. 18–19; and in Wu Chengming and Xu Dixin, *Zhongguo zibenzhuyi de mengya*, pp. 376–82.

106. Min-hsiung Shih, *The Silk Industry in Ch'ing China*, p. 35.

107. Lillian Li, *China's Silk Trade*, pp. 50–61, 52–53. See also Lieu, *The Silk Industry of China*, p. 117.

108. Lillian Li, *China's Silk Trade*, pp. 53–54. Li also convincingly refutes the previous interpretation of the *zhangfang* as an embryonic form of capitalist production according to the "sprouts of capitalism" interpretation (see Wu Chengming and Xu Dixin, *Zhongguo zibenzhuyi de mengya*).

109. Lillian Li, *China's Silk Trade*, p. 54. For her lucid analysis of the debate about the *zhangfang* in the context of comparative putting-out systems and merchant capitalism, see pp. 57–61.

110. Wuhan shi gongshang lianhehui, *Yekaitai lishi ziliao*, n.p.; Rowe, *Hankow: Conflict and Community*, pp. 58, 160. For further examples of the *zhangfang* as a common feature within the business organization of large, multi-branch medicine stores under strong family control, see various company histories in An Guanying et al., *Zhonghua bainian lao yaopu*.

111. Wuhan shi gongshang lianhehui, *Yekaitai lishi ziliao*.

112. Wellington Chan, "The Organizational Structure of the Traditional Chinese Firm"; Gardella, "Squaring Accounts."

113. Wellington Chan, "The Organizational Structure of the Traditional Chinese Firm," pp. 220–21.

114. Ibid., p. 221.

115. See K. Y. Chan, "The Structure of Chinese Business in Republican China."

116. See NTD: B 402-111-1; B 402-111-2. The founding document for the Dasheng No. 3 Cotton Mill in Haimen in 1922 shows that the brothers together owned about 427 shares, or roughly 4 percent of the paid-up share capital (NTD: B 406-111-2, 1a).

117. NTD: B 402-111-2.

118. Hansmann, *The Ownership of Enterprise*, p. 35.

119. *Ershi nian lai zhi Nantong*, pt. B, pp. 52–53.

120. Shen Shu, "Zhangfang xiansheng," p. 227.

121. Ibid.

122. *DSFGN*, pp. 351–54, quotation on p. 353. The obituary says as much about Zhang Jian's management style and the two men's special relationship as it does about Wu Jichen.

123. Liu Housheng, *Zhang Jian zhuanji*, p. 258.

124. Liang Zhan and Guo Qunyi, *Lidai zangshujia cidian*, p. 138.

125. Liu Housheng, *Zhang Jian zhuanji*, p. 258.

126. NTB: E 110/1320, letter to Zhang Jian, 6th day, 6th month, 1923, p. 17 (pagination by the museum archivist).

127. *Nanyang xiongdi yancao gufen*, 20a; Zhongguo renmin yinhang, Shanghai shi fenhang, Jinrong yanjiusuo, *Shanghai shangye chuxu yinhang shiliao*, p. 51.

128. SHD: S 30-1-35, "Yi shilu"; S 30-1-6, "Jishi lu." In 1918 Zhang Jian was elected president of the Chinese Cotton Mill Owners' Association in Shanghai. See also Bush, *The Politics of Cotton Textiles*, pp. 66–73. Zhang Jian's role in the association was rather nominal; Nie Yuntai (1880–1953), the successful director of the Hengfeng Cotton Mill in Shanghai and the vice-president, became the leading figure. According to the documents, most of the meetings were attended by Wu Jichen, who also signed official petitions to the government, for example, asking for a tax exemption on yarn, on behalf of Dasheng.

129. NTB: E110/1320, letter to Zhang Jian, 3rd day, 7th month, 1923, p. 43.

130. Ibid., letter to Zhang Jian, 18th day, 6th month, 1923, p. 26.

131. NTB: E 109/1319, letter to Zhang Xiaoruo, 26th day, 12th month, 1920, p. 85 (pagination by the museum archivist).

132. NTB: E 109/1399, letter dated the 14th day, 1st month, 1920, p. 99 (pagination by the museum archivist).

133. NTD: B 401-311-2.

134. NTB: E 109/1319, letters to Zhang Cha, 24th day, 3rd month, 1921, 1: 200–201; and 7th day, 6th month, 1921, 1: 287.

135. Lin Xi (Gao Zhenbai), "Cong Xianggang de Yuanfahang tanqi"; see also Faure, "The Rice Trade in Hong Kong Before the Second World War."

136. Lin Xi, "Cong Xianggang de Yuanfahang tanqi," vol. 117, pp. 48–49.

137. Ibid., vol. 118, p. 46.

138. Ibid., p. 50.

139. Ibid., p. 47.

140. Ibid.

141. Lu Zhidao and Gu Zhenyu, "Zhang Jian xiansheng er, san shi."

142. *TXSZ*, "Dasheng shachang," pp. 69–70.

143. *Nantong bao tekan*, Oct. 29, 1926, pp. 1–2.

144. Ibid.

145. Ibid. All the measurements were given in *bu*, the local unit for Haimen and Qidong county. One *bu* equals 0.00416 mu or 0.00025 hectare.

146. Interview with Zhang Rouwu in Nantong, Mar. 18, 1995.

147. Liu Shaotang, *Minguo renwu xiaozhuan*, 6: 264; Nantong fangzhishi tulu bianjizu, *Nantong fangzhishi tulu*, p. 19.

148. *Nantong bao tekan*, Oct. 29, 1926, pp. 1–2.

149. *Tonghai xinbao*, Mar. 31, 1928.

150. *Tonghai xinbao*, Apr. 1 and 4, 1928.

151. On warlordism and the political landscape in Republican China, see Sheridan, *China in Disintegration*, pp. 165–67.

152. See Faure, "The Control of Equity in Chinese Firms"; and Choi, "Competition Among Brothers."

153. Zhu Yingui, "Jindai Zhongguo de diyi pi gufenzhi qiye"; idem, "Cong Dasheng shachang kan Zhongguo," quotation on p. 59.

154. On paternalism in Western enterprises, see Ackers and Black, "Paternalist Capitalism."

155. This approach can be found, e.g., in Hamilton and Kao, "The Institutional Foundations of Chinese Business"; and in Redding, "Weak Organizations and Strong Linkages."

156. Hamilton, "The Organizational Foundations," esp. pp. 43 (quotation), 53–54.

157. See, e.g., *Dasheng xitong qiyeshi*, p. 122. The authors mention these reasons as the vital factors in Zhang Jian's ability to stay in control of his enterprises.

158. Hannah, *The Rise of the Corporate Economy*, p. 25. With regard to family businesses in the West, in a comparative study of the British and American textile industry, Mary Rose identifies networks and ties of personal contact as important characteristics of family firms in the first half of the nineteenth century, when "networks, as opposed to more formal integration, were preferred on either side of the Atlantic" (*Firms, Networks and Business Values*, pp. 58–98, quotation on p. 96).

159. "The Future of the Company," *The Economist*, Dec. 22, 2001.

160. "Let 1,000 Casinos Whither," *Far Eastern Economic Review*, Oct. 18, 2001.

161. "Day of the Shareholder," *Far Eastern Economic Review*, Sept. 13, 2001.

Chapter 6

1. Bergère, *The Golden Age of the Chinese Bourgeoisie*, p. 98.

2. Ibid., pp. 92–98.

3. Tang Keke and Qian Jiang, "Dasheng shachang de zichan."

4. I used the original company reports in the Nantong Municipal Archives, but for the reader's convenience, I cite them as they appear in the collection *Dasheng qiye*

xitong dang'an xuanbian (*DSQXDX*), published by the Nantong Municipal Archives and Nanjing University in 1987. The information on Dasheng available to contemporary shareholders and banks consisted of the annual company reports. They are divided into two parts: a verbal statement (*shuolüe*) on the mill's performance for the particular year is followed by a numerical account (*zhanglüe*). This account itself is divided into two parts: the profit-and-loss account (no specific term) and the balance sheet (*pancha shizai*). The profit-and-loss account counts income (*shou*) as profit against loss defined as expenses (*zhi*) with the difference left after subtraction representing the annual profit or loss. After 1900 an additional appropriation account was introduced in which amounts for items designed as extractions (*ti*) were to be set aside for reserves, depreciation costs, and the like. The profit stated at the end of the appropriation account was in fact the retained profit. The balance sheet was divided into two columns, one containing all the liabilities (*cun*) of the company set against one containing all its assets (*zai*). Company liabilities included such items as capital subscribed by shareholders, retained profits, overdraft, and debts, which from the late 1920s on were also referred to as the "debt category" (*fuzhai lei*). Assets included land, buildings, machinery, deposits, and cash and other items; later these were listed under the rubric "property category" (*zichan lei*).

5. Annual company report for 1907, in *DSQXDX*, pp. 47–49. As the company reports show, between 1900 and 1906 as well as between 1922 and 1926, the figure for profits excluded depreciation. The concept of depreciation was not recognized before 1907, and therefore depreciation was indirectly and insufficiently covered by the funds set aside as reserves. *Lijuan*, the commercial transit tax, was deducted directly under expenses; profits as such were not liable to further government taxation.

6. All the statistical data are extracted from Dasheng's annual company reports for the years 1900–1926 in *DSQXDX*. For the exact numbers for each figure, see the Appendix.

7. *Ershi nian lai zhi Nantong*, pt. B, pp. 4–5.

8. *DSQXDX*, pp. 107–11.

9. Information on returns is now considered the most important aspect of the annual shareholder reports of large modern industrial enterprises; see, e.g., Bayer AG, *Bayer Aktionärsbrief*. This report from one of Germany's leading chemical corporations, which has a large contingent of small, private shareholders, focuses on returns, particularly their regional origins, the items that generate them, and their development during the fiscal year. In the Dasheng reports, there is a huge discrepancy between the details on income and those given on expenditures. On average expenditures are split up into twenty-some entries per report, giving, among other things, the amounts paid for salaries, dividends, machinery, and donations, but only four entries describe the sources of income: the amount derived from combined yarn and cloth sales, ginned cotton and waste cotton sales, interests from bank deposits, and

rental income from company housing. The paucity of information on income found in all annual reports until 1926 suggests that shareholders were not interested in information on the company's returns as long as dividends were paid in satisfactory amounts.

10. See, e.g., *DSQXDX*, pp. 2, 5, 9, 13. One must also assume that the price Dasheng paid for raw cotton from the affiliated land-reclamation companies was less than the normal market price. This specific profit would not be apparent in the cotton-purchase yarn-sales lump sum.

11. Annual company report for 1925, in *DSQXDX*, pp. 170–72.

12. Loans taken out by Dasheng were recorded under the entry "various loans" (*diaohui ge kuan*) among the liabilities on the annual balance sheet. Only after 1922 were some of the loans listed separately as mortgages or credits from certain banks next to loans pooled in large lump sums. The labeling of the loans did not follow a uniform pattern, which makes identification of the loan source difficult (see, e.g., *DSQXDX*, pp. 152, 165). Interest on loans appeared under the term "interest payments" (*diaohui li*) among other expenses in the annual profit-and-loss account. What the term might mean in regard to the content hidden in this lump sum is in dispute. I was not able to find further explanation of this item, but I assume that it included interest payments to various creditors such as *qianzhuang*, modern banks, and even private lenders. This opinion is shared by the authors of the *Dasheng xitong qiyeshi* (see p. 151n2).

13. Another problem arises from the fact that the interest payments recorded in the annual reports refer most probably to a loan granted the previous fiscal year; consequently the interest payments and loans recorded in the report for a specific year do not necessarily correspond.

14. Pearse, *The Cotton Industry of Japan and China*, p. 189.

15. Annual company report for 1922 in *DSQXDX*, p. 149.

16. Annual company report for 1909 and 1918, in *DSQXDX*, pp. 65, 126.

17. The Dasheng Auxiliary Branch Mill (also called the No. 8 mill), which was founded in 1926, is not taken into consideration here since its establishment took place under completely new financial and corporate conditions.

18. Annual company reports of the Dasheng No. 3 mill, 1922–29, in *DSQXDX*, pp. 438, 442, 447, 451, 456, 461, 467, 475.

19. *Nantong xian Fuxin mianchang dishijie zhanglüe*, 2a–b, 4b. As with the yarn-sales surplus, the costs for wheat as a raw material were directly deducted from the sales income, and the surplus was then entered under income in the annual profit-and-loss account.

20. *Nantong Guangsheng youchang di shiqijie zhanglüe*, 2a–b. Again, expenditures on cotton seeds as raw material were deducted from the sales income before the lump sum was entered under income in the annual profit-and-loss account.

21. *Nantong Guangsheng zhayou gongsi di ershi'er, ershisan, ershisi zhanglüe*, report for 1924, 1a; report for 1926, 1a.

22. *Nantong xian Zisheng yechang di qi, ba, jiu, shi, sanshi jie shuolüe bing zhanglüe*. The iron-purchase utensil-sales surplus includes the expenses for the raw material, iron, which were deducted from the sales income before the figure was entered under income in the annual profit-and-loss account.

23. Ibid., report for 1934, 2b.

24. Ibid., report for 1911/12, 3b, and for 1914/15, 3b.

25. Ibid., report for 1914/15, 2a.

26. By "total expenses," I mean the total amount listed as annual expenditures in the profit-and-loss account, which, as has been explained, did not include expenditures on raw cotton.

27. The salaries were listed in two categories under expenses in the profit-and-loss accounts: salaries for the senior managers (*shendong gongfei xinshui*), which included the general manager's salary, and salaries of the middle-management (*ge zhishi xinshui*). Salaries for Western engineers were rather exceptional and constituted only a small part of the overall wage and salary bill.

28. See, e.g., NTD: B 401-III-99, doc. 1, receipt for 190 tons of coal delivered by the Chinese Engineering and Mining Company, Shanghai, Aug. 1901; ibid., docs. 4 and 5, receipts for 1,284 and 528 tons of coal delivered by Mitsui bussan kaisha, July 1906; ibid., docs. 7–12, receipts for Ichimura lump coal, dust coal, and small coal from Mitsui bussan, 1907; ibid., docs. 21–27, receipts for Fushun small coal, 1910. On the supply and transportation of coal from various mines in northern China to the Jiangnan area and places along the Yangzi River in the nineteenth century, see Li Bozhong, "Yingguo moshi, Jiangnan daolu," pp. 124–25.

29. Estimate based on data in Liang-lin Hsiao, *China's Foreign Trade Statistics*, pp. 43–44, 93.

30. I took the combined average price of Chinese and imported coal for my estimate. If we assume that Dasheng relied to a greater extent on Chinese coal (as the receipts for coal after 1910 suggest), the decrease in coal amounted to 37 percent.

31. Annual report for 1919, in *DSQXDX*, p. 132.

32. See Chapter 5. Despite the name, the "shares" were thus closer to bonds. The *guanli* was a guaranteed fixed interest rate of 8 percent on the share investment as stated on the share certificate issued by the Dasheng No. 1 Cotton Mill in 1897 (NTFB: doc. 247).

33. The figure of 600,000 taels in the report for 1917 as printed in *DSQXDX* is erroneous. I consider it a misprint since the year before and the year after 1917 annual dividends of 160,000 taels were paid out. Thus the dividend recorded on p. 117 should read *shiliu wan* (160,000) rather than *liushi wan* (600,000).

34. "Dasheng fangzhi gongsi chazhang weiyuanhui baogaoshu" (1924), in *DSQXDX*, p. 181.

35. *TXSZ*, "Dasheng shachang," p. 68. In his regulations, Zhang Jian did not give exact percentages but proposed that the net profits be divided into 13 parts (*gu*), of which ten should go the shareholders as a bonus, two to upper management, and one to middle management. He also explained how the bonus payments should then be further split within the management hierarchy.

36. The value of machinery refers to its value as recorded under fixed assets on the annual balance sheet.

37. NTD: B 402-111-445 (1920), 1b–2b.

38. Bergère, *The Golden Age of the Chinese Bourgeoisie*, p. 93.

39. Mori, *Chūgoku kindai mengyōshi no kenkyū*, esp. chap. 4.

40. Verbal statement in the 1916 annual report in *DSQXDX*, p. 112.

41. NTD: B 401-111-84, doc. 1, prepaid invoice dated Aug. 14, 1919; ibid., doc. 3, receipt dated Nov. 13, 1919.

42. NTD: B 401-111-84, doc. 1; ibid., doc. 5, letter from Chen Guangfu to Wu Jichen, Dec. 9, 1919; ibid., doc. 6, memorandum from the Shanghai Commercial and Savings Bank, June 2, 1920.

43. Tang Keke and Qian Jiang, "Dasheng shachang de zichan," pp. 28–29.

44. On agricultural conditions in Wujin, see Buck, *Chinese Farm Economy*, chap. 6, pp. 175–76, 184, 189.

45. Zhongguo di'er lishi dang'anguan et al., *Zhang Jian nongshang zongzhang renqi*, pp. 326–31.

46. For more details, see Chapter 7.

47. *Tonghai kenmu gongsi disici gudong huiyi'an*, 1a–2a. Zhang Jian held 324 shares, and Zhang Cha 294 shares.

48. *Zhang Jian wei TongTai ge yanken gongsi muji zijin zhi shuomingshu*, pp. 4–5.

49. These large enterprises were fairly representative of many other land-reclamation companies that had started operations in the late 1910s. However, the Tonghai Land Reclamation Company is not even mentioned in a 1933 government survey that claims to list the most prominent land-reclamation companies; see Bureau of Foreign Trade, *China Industrial Handbooks: Kiangsu*, pp. 234–36.

50. For a detailed report, see *Yinhang zhoubao*, no. 392 (1925): 1–9. This group of five land-reclamation companies was generally referred to as the "TongTai yanken wu gongsi."

51. *Zhang Jian wei TongTai ge yanken gongsi muji zijin zhi shuomingshu*.

52. Sun Jiashan, *Subei yanken shi chugao*, pp. 35–37.

53. The figures are extrapolated from surveys quoted in ibid., pp. 80–82.

54. *Yuzhong Dayoujin yanken gongsi wuwu nian diliu jie zhanglüe* (separate pagination), 2a–3b. Since the land-reclamation companies were not producing "products"

as such, I refer to their net income through rent and agricultural stations rather than to a "sales surplus" as in the previous cases for comparison. The shares of the Dayu Land Reclamation Company were listed on the Shanghai stock exchange in 1920, and their prices recorded in the *Shenbao* newspaper; see, e.g., *Shenbao*, May 12, June 12 and 16, 1920.

55. Bureau of Foreign Trade, *China Industrial Handbooks: Kiangsu*, p. 234.

56. *Jiaofu Dalai yanken gongsi chuangli huiyi'an*; Sun Jiashan, *Subei yanken shi chugao*, p. 67.

57. Bureau of Foreign Trade, *China Industrial Handbooks: Kiangsu*, pp. 235–36; *Caoyan Dafeng yanken gongsi chuangli huiyi'an*.

58. *Miaowan Huacheng yanken gongsi zhangcheng*; *Yuzhong Dayoujin yanken gongsi wuwu nian diliu jie zhanglüe*, 1a; *Yinhang zhoubao*, no. 271 (1922): 3–6.

59. Only the 1919 annual report of the Dayu Land Reclamation Company records 520 yuan as "reserves held with associates" (*tongren gongjijin*) among the company's liabilities. However, this sum amounted to only 0.03 percent of Dayu's total assets and is thus negligible (*Zhuogang Dayu yanken gongsi siwei nian disi jie zhanglüe*, 7a).

60. *DSQXDX*, p. 148.

61. Ibid., p. 153.

62. *Yinhang zhoubao*, no. 392 (1925): 1. For biographical information on Zhang Jia'ao, see Boorman, *Biographical Dictionary of Republican China*, 1: 26–30.

63. *Yinhang zhoubao*, no. 392 (1925): 1. I have so far not come across a complete list of the consortium's participating members. All documents are signed by representatives on behalf of the consortium but do not list the banks separately.

64. *Yinhang zhoubao*, no. 392 (1925): 1–9. The contract also stipulated that a second loan of 2 million yuan would be raised at a later stage. To my knowledge, the second loan never materialized. The 3 million yuan were to be redeemed within five years with interest on the loan due every six months (ibid., p. 2). Each of the five land-reclamation companies had to put up three-fifths of its undivided, reclaimed land as collateral (*Yinhang zhoubao*, no. 271 [1922]: 5).

65. *Yinhang zhoubao*, no. 271 (1922): 2.

66. On the historical development of this association, see Bergère, "The Shanghai Bankers' Association, 1915–1927."

67. *Yinhang zhoubao*, no. 271 (1922): 3–4.

68. *Miaowan Huacheng yanken gongsi zhangcheng*, 3b.

69. Ibid., 2a–4a.

70. For example, Wu Jichen held shares in the Tonghai Land Reclamation Company; see *Tonghai yanken gongsi linshi gudong huiyi'an*, 1a.

71. *Miaowan Huacheng yanken gongsi zhangcheng*, 2a, 3a.

72. *Yinhang zhoubao*, no. 392 (1925): 1.

73. *Dasheng xitong qiyeshi*, p. 176.

74. For a detailed description see Mori, *Chūgoku kindai mengyōshi no kenkyū.*

75. Annual report for 1922 in *DSQXDX*, p. 151.

76. "Dasheng fangzhi gongsi chazhang weiyuanhui baogao shu," in *DSQXDX*, p. 180.

77. Annual report for 1921 in *DSQXDX*, p. 146.

78. NTD: B 401-III-125, doc. 12, letter from the Shanghai Bank to the Dasheng Mill, Shanghai office, Apr. 13, 1921; ibid., docs. 64 and 65, letters from Chen Guangfu to Wu Jichen, no date (probably Apr. 1921).

79. See the balance sheet in the annual company report for 1921 in *DSQXDX*, pp. 145–48.

80. See the balance sheet in the annual company report for 1922 in *DSQXDX*, pp. 151–53.

81. Ibid., p. 153.

82. See the balance sheet of the annual company report for 1923 in *DSQXDX*, pp. 164–66.

83. "Chazhang qingce," in *DSQXDX*, pp. 181–226.

84. See the balance sheet in the annual company report for 1924 in *DSQXDX*, pp. 168–70.

85. *DSQXDX*, pp. 181–226.

86. Ibid., p. 212.

87. Ibid., pp. 209–13, 223–24.

88. The auditors' report listed loans to subsidiary and affiliated companies as loans to "various industrial companies" (*ge shiye gongsi*) and as deposits in the current assets (*wanglai*) account. See *DSQXDX*, pp. 210–13.

89. Ibid., pp. 214–21.

90. Ibid.

91. Ibid., p. 219.

92. Ibid., p. 220.

93. NTD: B 405-III-7, 16b.

94. *DSQXDX*, p. 223.

95. Ibid., pp. 212–13.

96. Ibid., p. 213.

97. Ibid., pp. 213–14.

98. Ibid., p. 180.

99. Ibid., p. 181.

100. Zhang Jian tried, unsuccessfully, to raise money on the U.S. and Japanese capital markets in the early 1920s (Zhang Kaiyuan, *Kaituozhe de zuji*, pp. 319–22).

101. Zhongguo renmin yinhang, Shanghai shi fenhang, Jinrong yanjiushi, *Shanghai shangye chuxu yinhang shiliao*, pp. 28, 38. Zhang Jian's investments may seem insignificant, but the bank started with an initial capital of only 50,000 yuan in April 1915.

In advertisements of the Shanghai Bank in 1920 aimed at large industrial customers, both Zhang Jian and Zhang Cha were listed as members of the board (see, e.g., *Huashang shachang lianhehui jikan* 1, no. 3 [1920]: advertisement "Shanghai shangye chuxu yinhang guanggao," n.p.).

102. Zhongguo renmin yinhang, Shanghai shi fenhang, Jinrong yanjiushi, *Shanghai shangye chuxu yinhang shiliao*, pp. 38–39, 51.

103. Zhu Zhenhua, *Zhongguo jinrong jiushi*, p. 126.

104. Zhongguo renmin yinhang, Shanghai shi fenhang, Jinrong yanjiushi, *Shanghai shangye chuxu yinhang shiliao*, pp. 154–55.

105. *Dasheng xitong qiye shi*, pp. 226–27.

106. Ibid.

107. *DSFGN*, p. 341.

108. *DSQXDX*, pp. 179–226.

109. Ibid., p. 152.

110. Zhongguo renmin yinhang, Shanghai shi fenhang, Jinrong yanjiushi, *Jincheng yinhang shiliao*, pp. 406–7.

111. *DSQXDX*, p. 152.

112. See the 1922 annual report for the No. 1 and No. 2 mills in ibid., pp. 148–62, 377–85. Even if the mills valued their machinery as high as possible and we reduce the amount to 3 million taels, the loan arrangement was still relatively risk-free for the banks.

113. Zhongguo renmin yinhang, Shanghai shi fenhang, Jinrong yanjiushi, *Shanghai shangye chuxu yinhang shiliao*, p. 155.

114. Ibid.

115. NTD: B 401-III-26, doc. 19, p. 26; and docs. 14 and 15.

116. Zhongguo renmin yinhang, Shanghai shi fenhang, Jinrong yanjiushi, *Jincheng yinhang shiliao*, pp. 162–63.

117. Ibid., p. 162.

118. Ibid.

119. Ibid., p. 163.

120. Zhongguo renmin yinhang, Shanghai shi fenhang, Jinrong yanjiushi, *Shanghai shangye chuxu yinhang shiliao*, pp. 155, 160. Shen Yanmou, the son of the Dasheng No. 1 mill manager Shen Xiejun, held various positions within the Dasheng business complex. In 1920 he served, for example, as auditor for the Huaihai Bank, managed by Zhang Jian's son, Zhang Xiaoruo (*Huaihai yinhang diyi, di'erjie yingye baogao*).

121. Zhu Zhenhua, *Zhongguo jinrong jiushi*, pp. 127–28.

122. Zhongguo renmin yinhang, Shanghai shi fenhang, Jinrong yanjiusuo, *Jincheng yinhang shiliao*, pp. 413–15.

123. *Yinhang zhoubao*, no. 271 (1922): 4–5; no. 392 (1925): 3.

124. *Yinhang zhoubao*, no. 271 (1922): 5.

125. *DSQXDX*, pp. 165, 169.

126. Zhu Zhenhua, *Zhongguo jinrong jiushi*, p. 126.

127. Ibid., pp. 127–28.

128. See, e.g., the balance sheet from 1923 in *DSQXDX*, p. 164.

129. Zhongguo renmin yinhang, Shanghai shi fenhang, Jinrong yanjiusuo, *Jincheng yinhang shiliao*, p. 162.

130. Ibid.

131. Zhongguo renmin yinhang, Shanghai shi fenhang, Jinrong yanjiusuo, *Shanghai shangye chuxu yinhang shiliao*, p. 154; Xu Xinwu and Huang Hanmin, *Shanghai jindai gongyeshi*, pp. 140–41, 192–95.

132. SHD: Q 195-1-225, pp. 2–3.

133. *Dasheng xitong qiyeshi*, pp. 219–26.

134. See NTB: E 97/920.

135. Zhongguo renmin yinhang, Shanghai shi fenhang, Jinrong yanjiusuo, *Jincheng yinhang shiliao*, pp. 160–61.

136. Totals from numbers quoted in Li Yixiang, *Jindai Zhongguo yinhang yu qiye de guanxi*, pp. 76, 82, 86. The Bank of Communications had invested 11.4 million yuan in mining, textile, and other industrial enterprises by 1937.

137. Thomas Rawski, *Economic Growth in Prewar China*.

138. Bergère, "The Shanghai Bankers' Association, 1915–1927," pp. 26–31.

139. In short, before 1930 the financial affairs and position of the company group as a whole were difficult to judge from its financial statements; see T. A. Lee, "Company Financial Statements."

140. "Fun-House Accounting: The Distorted Numbers at Enron," *New York Times*, Dec. 14, 2001; "Enron Had More Than One Way to Disguise Rapid Rise in Debt," *New York Times*, Feb. 17, 2002.

141. "A Bubble That Enron Insiders and Outsiders Didn't Want to Pop," *New York Times*, Jan. 14, 2002.

Chapter 7

1. See, e.g., Stapleton, *Civilizing Chengdu*; Strand, *Rickshaw Beijing*; Esherick, *Remaking the Chinese City*; Hanchao Lu, *Beyond the Neon Lights*; and Tsin, *Nation, Governance, and Modernity in China*.

2. On the concept of "civilizing" (*wenming*) and the introduction of modern urban planning and city administration in China in the late Qing and early Republican periods, see Stapleton, *Civilizing Chengdu*.

3. Imura, *Zhongguo zhi fangzhi ji qi chupin*, p. 187.

4. *TXSZ*, "Kenmu gongsi," p. 27; Sun Jiashan, *Subei yanken shi chugao*, p. 19; see also Chapter 3 of this book.

5. For a detailed discussion of the New Policies, see Reynolds, *China, 1898–1912*.

6. See Godley, *The Mandarin-Capitalists from Nanyang*, p. 97.

7. For the content of the new legal regulations, see Zhongguo di'er lishi dang'anguan, *Zhang Jian nongshang zongzhang*, pp. 302–31.

8. Amano, "Kōhoku no enkon," table following p. 108. Amano's article is an excellent introduction to the development of the land-reclamation companies along the northern Jiangsu coast. See also Sun Jiashan, *Subei yanken shi chugao*, pp. 35–37.

9. Amano, "Kōhoku no enkon," pp. 89–90 and table following p. 108. See also *Dasheng xitong qiyeshi*, pp. 166–69.

10. *TXSZ*, "Kenmu gongsi," p. 3.

11. Ibid., pp. 27, 116.

12. Wang Shuhuai, "Jiangsu Huainan yanken gongsi," pp. 213–14.

13. *TXSZ*, "Kenmu gongsi," pp. 170–80; see also Wang Shuhuai, "Jiangsu Huainan yanken gongsi," pp. 191–266, esp. the map following p. 266.

14. Zhang Jian, *Zhang Se'an xiansheng jiulu lu*, 3.21b–22b, 22b–23a.

15. *Ershi nian lai zhi Nantong*, pt. B, p. 40.

16. Zhang Jian, *Zhang Se'an xiansheng jiulu lu*, 3.22a–b.

17. See map in Nakai, *Chō Ken to Chūgoku kindai kigyō*, p. 498.

18. The plan and arrangements for the company area are described in detail in "Tonghai kenmu gongsi zhaodian zhangcheng" (1903); reprinted in Yang Liqiang, *Zhang Jian cungao*, pp. 555–59.

19. Yang Gusen, "Kenmu qian shao shuairong shi," pp. 222–26.

20. Ibid., p. 224.

21. Wang Guoding, *Jiangsu Wujin, Nantong tianfu diaocha baogao*, p. 183. The reed was needed to boil the brine. Reed prices must have risen along with the price of coastal land because of the reclamation boom in the mid-1910s.

22. "Tonghai kenmu gongsi zhaodian zhangcheng" in Yang Liqiang, *Zhang Jian cungao*, p. 556.

23. Ibid.

24. Nishizawa, "An Immigrant Community in Northern Jiangsu," p. 31; see also Amano, "Kōhoku no enkon," p. 97.

25. Nishizawa, "An Immigrant Community in Northern Jiangsu," p. 42.

26. The 1935 source by Li Jixin is quoted in Amano, "Kōhoku no enkon," p. 97n10.

27. Qiao Qiming, "Jiangsu Kunshan, Nantong, Anhui Suxian nongtian zhidu," p. 45.

28. Ibid., p. 43.

29. Feng Hefa, *Zhongguo nongcun jingji ziliao*, p. 24. The survey singles out the Zhang family as a large landowner in the county, with more than 10,000 mu of land.

30. Qiao Qiming, "Jiangsu Kunshan, Nantong, Anhui Suxian nongtian zhidu," p. 9.

31. Feng Hefa, *Zhongguo nongcun jingji ziliao*, p. 24. For agricultural conditions in Nantong county, particularly landownership, farm size, and cultivation patterns in the early 1940s, see Minami Manshū tetsudō kabushiki kaisha, Chōsabu, *Kōsō shō, Nantsū ken nōson jittai.*

32. Feng Hefa, *Zhongguo nongcun jingji ziliao*, p. 474.

33. Ibid., p. 392. Of course, some counties in southern Jiangsu such as Kunshan are characterized by high tenancy rates (Qiao Qiming, "Jiangsu Kunshan, Nantong, Anhui Suxian nongtian zhidu," esp. the map and figures opposite p. 1).

34. This survey, which was not available to me, is quoted in Sun Jiashan, *Subei yanken shi chugao*, pp. 48–50.

35. "Tonghai kenmu gongsi zhaodian zhangcheng," in Yang Liqiang, *Zhang Jian chugao*, pp. 556–57.

36. *Ershi nian lai zhi Nantong*, pt. B, p. 40.

37. Qiao Qiming, "Jiangsu Kunshan, Nantong, Anhui Suxian nongtian zhidu," pp. 13–14.

38. Nishizawa, "An Immigrant Community in Northern Jiangsu," pp. 36–38.

39. Zhang Huiqun, "Yanken quyu zudian zhidu zhi yanjiu," pp. 31823, 31829 (editor's pagination).

40. Ibid., pp. 31829–30 (editor's pagination).

41. Qiu Yunzhang and Yao Lian, "Tonghai kenmu sishi nian," esp. p. 66.

42. Zhang Huiqun, "Yanken quyu zudian zhidu zhi yanjiu," p. 31837 (editor's pagination).

43. Qiu Yunzhang and Yao Lian, "Tonghai kenmu sishi nian," pp. 67–68.

44. Ibid., p. 68.

45. Nishizawa, "An Immigrant Community in Northern Jiangsu," p. 38; Qiu Yunzhang and Yao Lian, "Tonghai kenmu sishi nian," p. 64.

46. Qiu Yunzhang and Yao Lian, "Tonghai kenmu sishi nian," pp. 67–68.

47. Zhang Jian, *Yanken gongsi shuili guihua tonggao gudong shu*, p. 2.

48. Qiu Yunzhang and Yao Lian, "Kenmu jishi," esp. p. 40.

49. Ye Xuyuan, "Xingken shi nian."

50. Ibid., pp. 41, 43.

51. Qiu Yunzhang and Yao Lian, "Tonghai kenmu sishi nian," p. 64.

52. Ye Xuyuan, "Xingken shi nian," p. 42.

53. Ibid.

54. Ibid.

55. "Tonghai kenmu gongsi zhaodian zhangcheng," in Yang Liqiang, *Zhang Jian cungao*, pp. 558–59; quotation on p. 558.

56. Ibid.

57. Ibid.

58. Ibid., pp. 558–59.

59. Qiu Yunzhang and Yao Lian, "Kenmu jishi," p. 40.

60. Ibid.

61. Qiu Yunzhang and Yao Lian, "Tonghai kenmu sishi nian," p. 69.

62. Ibid., pp. 69–70.

63. Ibid., p. 64.

64. "Tonghai kenmu gongsi zhaodian zhangcheng," in Yang Liqiang, *Zhang Jian cungao*, p. 558.

65. Wang Shuhuai, "Jiangsu Huainan yanken gongsi," pp. 225–26.

66. Qiao Qiming, "Jiangsu Kunshan, Nantong, Anhui Suxian nongtian zhidu," p. 68. Despite the relatively low number of schools and pupils, according to the survey, Nantong county still outperformed Suxian in Anhui province and Kunshan in southern Jiangsu.

67. "Tonghai kenmu gongsi zhaodian zhangcheng" in Yang Liqiang, *Zhang Jian cungao*, p. 558.

68. Ibid.

69. See, e.g., "Kenmu xiangzhi," 2:35a–43a in Zhang Jian, *Zhang Se'an (Jian) xiansheng shiye wenchao*.

70. Liu Housheng, *Zhang Jian zhuanji*, p. 250.

71. Honig, "Native-Place Hierarchy and Labor Market Segmentation," p. 275.

72. Hanchao Lu, *Beyond the Neon Lights*, p. 75.

73. *Dingxi Suiji yanken gongsi jigu zhangcheng*, 1a.

74. For a definition of the word "modern" and its superimposed Western concept of modernity, see Chapter 1.

75. Fitkin, *The Great River*, p. 8.

76. Qin Shao, "Space, Time, and Politics in Early Twentieth Century Nantong"; idem, "Tempest over Teapots."

77. *Who's Who in China*, 2nd ed., 1: 5.

78. *Nantong xianshi tu*; see also the maps in the front part of *Minguo Nantong xian tuzhi*.

79. TXSZ, "Dasheng shachang," pp. 65–66. In contrast, in the early 1930s the Shenxin Cotton Mills run by the Rong brothers in Wuxi provided a hospital, night school, cinema, and library for their workers (Xu Weiyong and Huang Hanmin, *Rongjia qiye fazhan shi*, p. 118).

80. ZJZJL, "Jiaoyu lu," 1.5b–8b, 12b, and 2.18a–20a.

81. Nantong youyi julebu, *Nantong canguan zhinan*, 2b.

82. *Ershi nian lai zhi Nantong*, pt. A, p. 74.

83. *Tonghai xinbao*, June 24, 1915.

84. See Chapter 4 of this book. For wages in the Dasheng mills, see Mu Xuan and Yan Xuexi, *Dasheng shachang gongren shenghuo*, pp. 186–220; for managers' salaries, see *TXSZ*, "Dasheng shachang," p. 67.

85. *Nantong tushuguan mulu*. Zhang Jian also donated most of the objects for the Nantong museum, which he established in 1905 as the first Chinese museum modeled on Western concepts of museum collections and display (*Nantong bowuyuan pinmu*; Nantong fangzhishi tulu bianjizu, *Nantong fangzhishi tulu*, p. 73).

86. *Ershi nian lai zhi Nantong*, pt. A, pp. 95–96.

87. Nantong youyi julebu, *Nantong canguan zhinan*, 11a. For an excellent analysis of the new schools that emerged during the last years of the Qing dynasty, see Sang Bing, *Wan Qing xuetang*, pp. 139–75, esp. pp. 152–55 on the Nantong Normal School, its students, their numbers, and local origins.

88. Evelyn Rawski, *Education and Popular Literacy*, pp. 62–63.

89. Yu Xutang, "Nantong de miaochan xingxue," p. 138. The Nantong library was established by transforming the Dongyue temple into a library facility (Nantong fangzhishi tulu bianjizu, *Nantong fangzhishi tulu*, p. 74).

90. Nantong youyi julebu, *Nantong canguan zhinan*, 11b.

91. Ibid. On endowments for school lands during the Qing, see Evelyn Rawski, *Education and Popular Literacy*, pp. 66–74.

92. Nantong youyi julebu, *Nantong canguan zhinan*, 12a; *Ershi nian lai zhi Nantong*, pt. B, p. 102.

93. Yu Xutang, "Nantong de miaochan xingxue," p. 140.

94. Ibid.; see also Yu Xutang, "Lang Shan qi fang shimo."

95. Nantong youyi julebu, *Nantong canguan zhinan*, 11b.

96. Shangwu yinshuguan bianyisuo, *Zhongguo lüxing zhinan*, sect. 46, p. 4 (separate pagination).

97. *Ershi nian lai zhi Nantong*, pt. B, pp. 91–102.

98. Li Mingxun et al., *Kaituo yu fazhan*, p. 108.

99. See maps in the front part of the local gazetteer *Minguo Nantong xian tuzhi*.

100. ZJZJL, "Zizhi lu," 2.24a.

101. Foucault, *Discipline and Punish*, esp. pp. 135–69.

102. The fact that school land remained Zhang Jian's private property is obvious from newspaper reports after his death; see *Nantong Bao tekan*, Oct. 29, 1926.

103. Schoppa, *Chinese Elites and Political Change*, pp. 6–7.

104. Ibid., pp. 65–66.

105. *Tong Chong Hai Tai zong shanghui caiwu baogao*.

106. *Tonghai xinbao*, Mar. 29, 1922.

107. *Tong Chong Hai Tai zong shanghui caiwu baogao*, 1a, 2a–2b.

108. Zhang Jian, *Zhang Se'an xiansheng jiulu lu*, 3.13a. At the time, Chongming island was under the administration of Shanghai county; hence Zhang's appeal to the Shanghai chamber.

109. *Tong Ru Hai mianye gonghui mianye nianbao*, p. 3.; see also Imura, *Zhongguo zhi fangzhi ji qi chupin*, p. 188.

110. Ge Mengpu, *Nantong sifa bicun*, pp. 68–69.

111. Shen Xianrong, "Jiefang qian Rugao liren jiaoyuju."

112. *Ershi nian lai zhi Nantong*, pt. B, p. 11.

113. Fan Dangshi, *Fan Bozi wenji*, 6.1a–5a. The scholar Gu Xijue (1848–1917) from Rugao is another example of Zhang Jian's collaboration with members of the local elite who were well connected and supported his political and social agenda (Nanjing shifan daxue, Guwenxian zhengli yanjiusuo, *Jiangsu yiwenzhi*, p. 417).

114. Ling Zhenrong, "Nantong de gudai yu jindai jianzhu."

115. Ibid., pp. 135–36; Fluck et al., *Historic Postcards*, p. 14. The German Club "Concordia" was built in 1907.

116. The family residence of Xu Gengqi, one of Zhang Xiaoruo's friends and business associates, is similar in style to Zhang Jian's residence. Xu's son said in an interview (Nantong, May 15, 1995) that his father wanted to imitate Zhang Jian's life-style and expressed his admiration and aspirations with the proverb *xiaowu jian dawu* (like a small sorcerer in the presence of a great one).

117. Ling Zhenrong, "Nantong de gudai yu jindai jianzhu," p. 136.

118. *Tongzhou zhili zhou zhi*, 3.62a, 66a.

119. Jiang Zi'an and Cheng Zhuoru, "Nantong de huiguan."

120. Zhou Sizhang, "Jiefang qian Ru cheng de shehui cishan jigou."

121. Zhou Sizhang, "Jiefang qian Ru cheng de tongye gongsuo."

122. Lu Bin, *Chongming pingmin changshi*, pp. 29–30.

123. *Tong, Chong, Hai, Tai zong shanghui caiwu baogao; Tongzhou xin yuwatang zhangcheng; Nantong xian nongye xuexiao tiyao.*

124. See, e.g., Nantong youyi julebu, *Nantong canguan zhinan*; or idem, *Nantong shiye, jiaoyu, cishan fengjing.*

125. Nantong youyi julebu, *Nantong shiye, jiaoyu, cishan fengjing.*

126. See, among others, Rankin, *Elite Activism and Political Transformation in China;* Rowe, *Hankow: Commerce and Society in a Chinese City;* and idem, *Hankow: Conflict and Community in a Chinese City.*

127. William Rowe, in his studies of Hankou, has argued for the emergence of organizations and their representatives, in particular among the merchant community, autonomous of the state in late imperial China. Mary Rankin argues in her book on Zhejiang province during the late Qing that gentry and merchants took on new managerial roles in local society independent from the state in an emergent public sphere. Both positions have been contested by Frederic Wakeman, who agrees that the late Qing period definitely saw an expansion of activities outside the government agenda in local society but does not consider the society of late imperial China and its organizations as independent of the state. See Rowe, *Hankow: Commerce and Society in a Chinese City;* idem, *Hankow: Conflict and Community in a Chinese*

City; idem, "The Public Sphere in Modern China"; Rankin, *Elite Activism and Political Transformation in China*; and Wakeman, "The Civil Society and Public Sphere Debate," esp. p. 132.

128. Habermas, "The Public Sphere," quotation on p. 398.

129. *Zuijin zhi wushi nian.*

130. *North China Herald*, May 7, 1921.

131. *North China Herald*, Aug. 28, 1926. In the photograph accompanying the obituary, Zhang Jian wears a traditional Chinese riding jacket. The traditional image probably suited better the article's focus on Zhang Jian's achievements as an eminent scholar, dignitary, and politician.

132. *Tonghai xinbao*, May 18, 1921.

133. *Guanzang zhongwen baozhi mulu*, "Tonghai xinbao," p. 1.

134. *Tonghai xinbao*, Nov. 5 and 23, 1915.

135. *Tonghai xinbao*, Jan. 10, 1915.

136. *Who's Who in China*, 2nd ed., pp. 612–13.

137. Zheng Zeqing, "Zhu Baosan," pp. 138–39.

138. Cochran, *Big Business in China*, p. 66.

139. Ibid.

140. *Gaoming bao*, 1913.

141. Zhou Gaochao, "1910 nian–1949 nian zai Rugao chuban de baokan tonglan."

142. *Gaoming bao*, 1913, no. 6 (5th month): 11.

143. *Tongzhou lishi jiaoke shu*, 11b–12a.

144. Ibid., 12a.

145. *Nantong bao tekan*, Oct. 29, 1926.

146. Ibid.

147. Zhang Kaiyuan, "'Nantong moshi' yu quyu shehui jingji shi yanjiu." In "Zhang Jian yu Nantong 'jindaihua' moshi," Wu Yiye analyzed Nantong's "modernization" model in much the same way in 1989. However, he subtly criticized Nantong as an "exclusive" town under almost monopolistic conditions.

148. Mao Jiaqi et al., *Heng kan cheng ling ce cheng*, pp. 123–38, esp. p. 136.

149. Qin Shao, "Space, Time, and Politics in Early Twentieth Century Nantong"; Walker, *Chinese Modernity and the Peasant Path.*

150. Meng Lin's obituary for Wu Jichen from 1935 in DSFGN, pp. 351–54, quotation on p. 352.

151. Imazeki, "Shina no jitsugyō ōkoku 'Nantsū.'"

152. ZJZJL, "Zizhi lu," 2.9b.

153. Wakeman, "Civil Society in Late Imperial and Modern China." See also note 127 to this chapter.

154. Chung, *Chinese Business Groups in Hong Kong.*

Chapter 8

1. International Anti-Opium Association, *Opium Cultivation and Traffic*, p. 3.

2. Slack, *Opium, State, and Society*, pp. 9–10.

3. On the International Anti-Opium Association and the more successful Chinese efforts for opium suppression by the National Anti-Opium Association (Zhonghua guomin juduhui), see Slack, "The National Anti-Opium Association," esp. pp. 249–51.

4. Slack, *Opium, State, and Society*, pp. 20–21.

5. International Anti-Opium Association, *Opium Cultivation and Traffic*, p. 20.

6. Guo Xuyin, *"Jiu Shanghai" hei shehui*, p. 56; Wakeman, *Policing Shanghai*, p. 120.

7. International Anti-Opium Association, *Opium Cultivation and Traffic*, p. 19.

8. Report of the No. 1 mill shareholders' meeting on May 24, 1919, as quoted in *DSFGN*, p. 154.

9. Slack, *Opium, State, and Society*, pp. 10–11.

10. *Xiangdao zhoubao*, July 21, 1926; quoted in Li Wenzhi and Zhang Youyi, *Zhongguo jindai nongyeshi ziliao*, 2: 621.

11. International Anti-Opium Association, *Opium Cultivation and Traffic*, p. 19.

12. Slack, *Opium, State, and Society*, p. 10.

13. Report of the No. 1 mill shareholders' meeting on May 24, 1919, as quoted in *DSFGN*, p. 154; NTD: G 03-III-15.

14. *Huaihai yinhang diyi, di'erjie yingye baogao*, n.p.

15. NTD: G 03-III-22. This point is also repeated in *Dasheng xitong qiyeshi*, pp. 187–88.

16. NTD: G 03-III-22; *Dasheng xitong qiyeshi*, p. 188.

17. Zhang Kaiyuan (*Kaituozhe de zuji*, p. 329) argues that despite adverse realities Zhang Jian never lost his patriotic aspirations for peace and unity in the country.

18. Letter to Sun Chuanfang, July 16, 1926; reprinted in Yang Liqiang, *Zhang Jian cungao*, p. 524.

19. Chang Zonghu, *Modai zhuangyuan Zhang Jian*, p. 102.

20. Wang Xiaohua, *Beiyang xiaojiang Sun Chuanfang*, pp. 207–14, esp. p. 213.

21. Report of the No. 1 mill shareholders' meeting in November 1935, in *DSFGN*, p. 345.

22. Interview with Mrs. Zhang Rouwu in Nantong, June 7, 1998. The granddaughter became rather flustered when I asked her about the relationship between Wu Jichen and the family, in particular with regard to the family's finances after her father's death, and volunteered no further information on this subject.

23. Zhang Rouwu, "Huiyi wo de fuqin Zhang Xiaoruo." Interview on June 25, 1998. According to Zhang Rouwu, her grandfather was concerned that in Shanghai

his children would adopt the lush life-style of people engaged in commercial activities (*zuo shengyi de ren*) instead of pursuing more scholarly careers.

24. See, e.g., Gersick et al., *Generation to Generation*; and Neubauer and Lank, *The Family Business*.

25. SHSK: R 01-1, docs. 5–7. On the career paths of the many members, mostly male, of the Rong kinship network involved in the family business during the pre- and postwar periods, see Rong Jingben, *Liangxi Rong shi jiazushi*, pp. 62–92.

26. "Zhang Xiaoruo," p. 138.

27. Ibid.; *Who's Who in China*, 2nd ed., 1: 8. Founded as a college for physical education in Brooklyn, New York, in 1886, Arnold College moved to a site adjacent to Yale University in 1892 and merged with the University of Bridgeport in 1953.

28. Some more recent biographical sources refer to Columbia University as the university Zhang Xiaoruo attended in the United States; see, e.g., Chang Zonghu, *Modai zhuangyuan Zhang Jian*, p. 133.

29. Interview with Xu Zhongzheng in Nantong on Apr. 25, 1995. See also *Huaihai yinhang diyi, di'erjie yingye baogao*, n.p., entry under "Nantong zonghang."

30. Nantong xian zizhihui, *Nantong zizhihui baogaoshu*, pt. A, p. 1. The preface to this volume was written by Zhang Jian (ibid., *xu*, pp. 1–3).

31. "Zhang Xiaoruo"; see also Zhang Xiaoruo, *Shixueji*.

32. *Who's Who in China*, 2nd ed., 1: 8.

33. Nantong daxue, *Nantong daxue chengli jiniankan*, p. 41.

34. For the minutes of the board meetings and shareholder reports from 1927 to 1934, see DSFGN, pp. 195–339; for the report of the 1931 meeting, see ibid., pp. 235–39.

35. Wakeman, *Policing Shanghai*, p. 118. Part III of this monograph addresses the issues of organized crime and the role of the Green Gang in Republican Shanghai before the outbreak of the Sino-Japanese war in 1937 in great detail. For an analysis of Shanghai's municipal government during the Nanjing decade, see Henriot, *Shanghai, 1927–1937*. Zhang Rouwu, "Huiyi wo de fuqin Zhang Xiaoruo," p. 105. Unfortunately, this short report by Zhang Xiaoruo's daughter contains no information regarding her father's business dealings in Shanghai but confirms his preference for a modern and sophisticated life-style.

36. "Zhang Xiaoruo," p. 139; Chang Zonghu, *Modai zhuangyuan Zhang Jian*, pp. 172, 182. Since his wife remained with their children in Nantong, Zhang Xiaoruo established a second home in Shanghai with Li Chufu and had a son, Zhang Fanwu, with her.

37. According to Chang Zonghu (*Modai zhuangyuan Zhang Jian*, pp. 184–85), Zhang Xiaoruo's son, Zhang Xuwu, came up with this explanation several decades later.

38. Even suicide was considered as a potential explanation for Zhang Xiaoruo's death; see ibid., p. 183.

39. Interview with Mrs. Zhang Rouwu in Nantong, Mar. 18, 1995.

40. Martin, *The Shanghai Green Gang*, p. 200. On the emergence of Du Yuesheng and his opium racket, see also Wakeman, *Policing Shanghai*, pp. 120–31.

41. See the asset side of the 1906 annual business report of the Dasheng No. 1 mill, in *DSQXDX*, p. 44. Among the investors was the Shanghai entrepreneur Zhu Baosan, one of Zhang Jian's close business associates, who put up 20,000 yuan as share capital and served as one of Dada's managers (Tao Shuimu, *Zhejiang shangbang*, p. 177).

42. Zhang Guorui and Wang Guofan, "Wang Xianglun yu Dada lunbu gongsi," p. 147.

43. *Dasheng xitong qiyeshi*, pp. 66–69.

44. Nantong youyi julebu, *Nantong shiye, jiaoyu, cishan fengjing*, p. 16, separate pagination. A photograph shows the cotton bales stacked up high along the wharf and the storage houses.

45. Xiong Yuezhi, *Lao Shanghai mingren*, p. 242. The Dada wharf stretched out for about half a kilometer along the Huangpu river between present-day Puxidongmen Road and the eastern part of Fuxing Road.

46. *Dasheng xitong qiyeshi*, p. 68. The steamship company's name was changed slightly, to Dada lunchuan gongsi.

47. On the growth of China's steamship transport business between 1927 and 1937, see Zhu Yingui, "1927–1937 nian de Zhongguo lunchuan hangyunye."

48. Martin, *The Shanghai Green Gang*, p. 202; *Dasheng xitong qiyeshi*, pp. 68–69.

49. Du Yuesheng's manipulation of the Dada company is described in detail in Martin, *The Shanghai Green Gang*, pp. 200–206.

50. Ibid., 203–4; *Dasheng xitong qiyeshi*, p. 69.

51. Martin, *The Shanghai Green Gang*, p. 205.

52. *Tonghai xinbao*, Mar. 31, 1928; interview with Mr. Lu Baoqian in Taibei, Aug. 18, 1996. Zhang Xiaoruo is buried with his father in a cemetery on the southern outskirts of Nantong city, the traditional location for burial grounds, but Zhang Cha never received such an honor. When Zhang Cha died in his Shanghai home in 1939, he was buried not in Nantong city with his relatives but in Zhongxiu village. Neither Zhang Cha nor his son was admitted to the family burial grounds, nor have they been incorporated into the recent celebration of the Zhang family's achievements in Nantong.

53. See Fewsmith, *Party, State, and Local Elites*, pp. 118–20.

54. On Zhang Xueliang's rise to power and his relationship with Chiang Kaishek, see Mitter, *The Manchurian Myth*, pp. 20–22, 51–57.

55. For an excellent analysis of the development of the textile market in Dongbei between 1907 and 1931, see Tsukase, "Chūgoku Tōhoku menseihin." On the Chinese

cotton industry in general, see Mori, *Chūgoku kindai mengyōshi no kenkyū*; and Bush, *The Politics of Cotton Textiles*.

56. Shiyebu, Guoji maoyiju, *Zhongguo shiyezhi (Jiangsu sheng)*, pp. 91–92. For a collection of sources on Nantong *tubu* and the Manchurian crisis, see Xu Xinwu, *Jiangnan tubu shi*, pp. 604–63.

57. Lin Jubai, *Jindai Nantong tubu shi*, pp. 114–17.

58. *Dasheng xitong qiyeshi*, p. 233. Dasheng produced very little machine-spun cloth; the inhabitants of Nantong preferred the handwoven *tubu*.

59. Kubo, "Kindai Chūgoku mengyō."

60. Grove, "Chinese Cotton Trade in Comparative Perspective."

61. *Dasheng xitong qiyeshi*, pp. 233–34.

62. Ibid., p. 234; Shiyebu, Guoji maoyiju, *Zhongguo shiyezhi (Jiangsu sheng)*, pp. 30–31.

63. For figures, see *Dasheng xitong qiyeshi*, p. 236, table 3.

64. Lin Zuobo, *Guanwai manyouji*, p. 19.

65. *Dasheng xitong qiyeshi*, p. 234.

66. Business report of the Dasheng No. 2 mill for 1933, in *DSFGN*, p. 291; *Dasheng xitong qiyeshi*, p. 239.

67. *Dasheng xitong qiyeshi*, p. 240. The original source, *Sanchang changyao riji*, was not available to me.

68. Report of shareholders' meeting in Feb. 1933, in *DSFGN*, pp. 274–83, esp. pp. 281–82.

69. *Dasheng xitong qiyeshi*, p. 261.

70. Coble, "Remembering the Anti-Japanese War," pp. 15–16.

71. *DSFGN*, p. 369; *Dasheng xitong qiyeshi*, p. 261.

72. *DSFGN*, pp. 369–70.

73. Coble, "Chinese Capitalists and the Japanese," p. 63. For a detailed discussion of these issues, see Coble, *Chinese Capitalists in Japan's New Order*.

74. Shanghai shehui kexueyuan, Jingji yanjiusuo, *Dalong jiqi chang*, pp. 63–64.

75. *Dasheng xitong qiyeshi*, p. 262.

76. Mu Xuan and Yan Xuexi, *Dasheng shachang gongren shenghuo*.

77. Nantong fangzhishi tulu bianjizu, *Nantong fangzhishi tulu*, pp. 82–85; *Dasheng xitong qiyeshi*, p. 262.

78. *Dasheng xitong qiyeshi*, p. 263; see esp. note 2 on the same page. This particular document was not available to me.

79. Xu Xinwu and Huang Hanmin, *Shanghai jindai gongyeshi*, p. 223.

80. Coble, "Japan's New Order and the Shanghai Capitalists," esp. pp. 140–41.

81. Ibid., quotation on p. 143. Wang Zeren, "Nantong tubu de jingying he fazhan," pp. 186–87. On Japanese development companies, also see Henriot, "War and Economics."

82. Nantong fangzhishi tulu bianjizu, *Nantong fangzhishi tulu*, p. 83.

83. Mu Xuan and Yan Xuexi, *Dasheng shachang gongren shenghuo*.

84. Dasheng yichang changshi bianjishi, *Dasheng yichang gongren douzheng shi*.

85. Meng Guilin, "Rijun junguanxia de Dasheng yichang," p. 137.

86. Ibid.

87. Ibid., p. 138.

88. Mu Xuan and Yan Xuexi, *Dasheng shachang gongren shenghuo*, p. 154.

89. Meng Guilin, "Rijun junguanxia de Dasheng yichang," p. 138.

90. Nantong fangzhishi tulu bianjizu, *Nantong fangzhishi tulu*, p. 86; Mu Xuan and Yan Xuexi, *Dasheng shachang gongren shenghuo*, pp. 149–76. ID cards were already in use in the factories during the 1930s. Former Dasheng worker Li Guangquan gave me the card of his elder brother, Li Guangru, who worked in the No. 1 mill in 1936. The cards contain a black-and-white photograph and record the worker's number, name, age, shift, workshop, occupation, age, and native place.

91. Meng Guilin, "Rijun junguanxia de Dasheng yichang," p. 140.

92. Ibid., pp. 138–40; Mu Xuan and Yan Xuexi, *Dasheng shachang gongren shenghuo*, pp. 149–76.

93. See interviews in Mu Xuan and Yan Xuexi, *Dasheng shachang gongren shenghuo*, esp. p. 99.

94. Ibid., p. 150.

95. On the activities of the Communist party among Dasheng workers, see Chapter 4.

96. See interviews in Mu Xuan and Yan Xuexi, *Dasheng shachang gongren shenghuo*, pp. 80, 83. For offenses by Japanese soldiers, see ibid., pp. 234–41.

97. See, e.g., Yan Yongxiang and Ding Bangjing, "Rijun qinzhan Dingyanzhen."

98. Meng Guilin, "Rijun junguanxia de Dasheng yichang," p. 141. Chen Baochu was executed in 1955 for his collaboration with the Japanese and the Wang Jingwei regime.

99. Business report of the No. 3 mill for 1935, in *DSFGN*, p. 341.

100. Meng Guilin, "Rijun junguanxia de Dasheng yichang," p. 141.

101. The attempt to turn Wuxi into a model district for sericulture in the mid-1930s is an example of centralized economic government policies before the war; see Bell, *One Country, Two Chinas*, pp. 160–70.

102. Henriot, "War and Economics," esp. pp. 14–16, quotation on p. 14.

103. For an excellent analysis of the economic policies and practical arrangements regarding the distribution and trading of cotton goods under the controlled economy, see ibid., pp. 21–26.

104. Meng Guilin, "Rijun junguanxia de Dasheng yichang," p. 141.

105. Ibid.

106. Mu Xuan and Yan Xuexi, *Dasheng shachang gongren shenghuo*, p. 117.

107. Ibid., p. 125.

108. Meng Guilin, "Rijun junguanxia de Dasheng yichang," p. 141.

109. Wang Minzhi, "Huiyi Tangjia he Tianshenggang jiefang," p. 45.

110. Zhang Jingli graduated from Fudan University, Shanghai; see *Guoli Fudan daxue*; and *Nantong shiye gailan*.

111. Zhang Guorui and Wang Guofan, "Wang Xianglun yu Dada lunbu gongsi," p. 148.

112. SHSK: 11-404; Zhang Jingli, "Nantong dasheng fangzhi gongsi de bianqian," p. 27.

113. SHSK: 13-122-388.

114. SHSK: 13-121-388 (2).

115. For example, in 1947, 31 persons with the surname Zhu holding 70 shares each were registered in Shanghai at an address on Henan Road; and 40 persons with the surname Bai with 70 shares each were registered at an address on South Chongqing Road (SHSK: 13-121-388 [2]).

116. *Dasheng xitong qiyeshi*, p. 294.

117. NTD: G 03-111-42, 1951–58.

118. Wang Minzhi, "Huainian dang de shiyou Chen Shiyun nüshi."

119. Zhang Jingli, "Nantong Dasheng fangzhi gongsi de bianqian," p. 27. Although not mentioned in the local histories, one branch of the Zhang family did move to Taiwan, and another went to Hong Kong.

120. Ibid.

121. Ibid., p. 28.

122. Coble, *The Shanghai Capitalists*, pp. 261–69.

123. Coble, "Chinese Capitalists and the Japanese."

124. Xu Weiyong and Huang Hanmin, *Rongjia qiye fazhan shi*, chaps. 5 and 6.

125. Cochran, *Encountering Chinese Networks*, p. 138.

126. Martin, *The Shanghai Green Gang*, pp. 200–201.

127. On the strategic business decisions of the Rong family, see Coble, "Chinese Capitalists and the Japanese," p. 76.

Conclusion

1. See the inset map for the *kaifa qu* in Nantong shi diming bangongshi, *Nantong shiqu tu*. In the 1990s the fast but more expensive hydrofoil service from the Shiliubu dock in Shanghai was the preferred way of traveling to Nantong for businessmen and those with money. This service was terminated in 2001 due to lack of demand. Average commuters and passengers now prefer to go by bus, taxi, or car to Shanghai and other destinations in Jiangsu province. The shift from river to road transport has created a new employment niche in Nantong's local economy. On plans for

railway development in Jiangsu, see also Hook, *Shanghai and the Yangzi Delta*, pp. 102–3.

2. *Nantong sezhi yichang*, p. 1; *Nantong di san mian fangzhi chang*, p. 1.

3. Cochran, *Encountering Chinese Networks*.

4. Ibid., p. 182.

5. See Hamilton, "Organizational Foundations"; Redding, "Weak Organizations and Strong Linkages"; Wong Siu-lun, "Chinese Entrepreneurs and Business Trust"; and other articles in the volume edited by Hamilton, *Business Networks and Economic Development in East and Southeast Asia*.

6. Cochran, *Encountering Chinese Networks*.

7. Ibid., p. 182.

8. Pollard, *The Genesis of Modern Management*, pp. 156–59.

9. Pomeranz, *The Great Divergence*, pp. 182–83, 198–99.

10. Wellington Chan, "Government, Merchants and Industry to 1911," p. 457.

11. Xu Weiyong and Huang Hanmin, *Rongjia qiye fazhan shi*.

12. Ibid., pp. 32–33, 125. See also Cochran, *Encountering Chinese Networks*, pp. 117–46. The Yong'an (Wing On) company founded by the Guo family in Hong Kong in 1907 is another example of a large family business that was registered under English law and continued to exist as a joint-stock limited liability company in 1912. However, the family continued to exert its strong financial control over the company's shareholding structure (Shanghai shehui kexueyuan, Jingji yanjiusuo, *Shanghai Yong'an gongsi*, p. 7).

13. Xu Weiyong and Huang Hanmin, *Rongjia qiye fazhan shi*. For descriptions of factory management and design, see, e.g., Xue Mingjian, *Gongchang sheji ji guanli*, published in 1927.

14. Faure, "The Control of Equity in Chinese firms," pp. 75–77. The Dalong Machine Works, established in Shanghai in 1902, is an example of a family business run in a very autocratic style by its founder, Yan Yutang, who despite the expansion of his business operations never felt the need to register his company (see Shanghai shehui kexueyuan, Jingji yanjiusuo, *Dalong jiqi chang*).

15. "Bankruptcy Struggle at Thai Firm Shows Why Asia Still Lags," *Wall Street Journal*, Feb. 12, 2001. The article discusses the fate of Thai Petrochemical Industries, Inc., and the power of its founder and chairman, Prachai Leophairatana.

16. "H-P Deal's Fate Rests with Skeptical Heirs of Company Founders," *Wall Street Journal*, Nov. 9, 2001; "A Family Struggle, A Company's Fate," *New York Times*, Dec. 2, 2001. In the case of Hewlett-Packard, family-related shareholders hold 17.9 percent of the company's stock.

17. Brown, *Chinese Big Business and the Wealth of Asian Nations*.

18. Ibid, pp. 279–80.

19. On the development and impact of TVEs, see John Wong et al., *China's Rural Entrepreneurs*, esp. pp. 16–51 on the relationship between enterprises and the local government and region. See also Otsuka, *Industrial Reform in China*, pp. 46–50, 221–43.

20. Jefferson and Rawski, "Ownership Change in Chinese Industry," pp. 26–27.

21. Steinfeld, *Forging Reform in China*, pp. 237–41.

22. Fei Xiaotong, *Congshi qiuzhi lu*, pp. 199–201.

23. See, e.g., Qian Jiang and Tang Keke, "Jianlun Zhang Jian Nantong difang zizhi moshi," pp. 55–66.

24. Oi, *Rural China Takes Off*, pp. 11–15.

25. Young, "Ownership and Community Interests in China's Rural Enterprises," pp. 121.

26. Walder, "The County Government as an Industrial Corporation."

27. Walder and Oi, "Property Rights in the Chinese Economy," pp. 17–19.

28. This, for example, is the context in which Shen Binyi is introduced to the newspaper reader.

29. Zhongguo min(si)ying jingji yanjiuhui, Mishuchu, *Zhongguo minying qiyejia liezhuan 1997*, foreword, p. 2.

30. Information from the *China Statistical Yearbook* quoted from Jefferson and Rawski, "Ownership Change in Chinese Industry," p. 24. See also Walder and Oi, "Property Rights in the Chinese Economy"; Steinfeld, *Forging Reform in China*; and Young, "Ownership and Community Interests in China's Rural Enterprises," p. 133.

31. Ruf, "Collective Enterprise and Property Rights in a Sichuan Village."

32. See, e.g., Nan Lin and Chih-Jou Jay Chen, "Local Elites as Officials and Owners."

33. Walder and Oi, "Property Rights in the Chinese Economy," pp. 22–23. On the subversion of property rights, see also Nan Lin and Chih-Jou Jay Chen, "Local Elites as Officials and Owners," pp. 168–70.

34. Chen Zhengping, "Shilun Zhongguo jindai qiye zhidu fazhanshi shang de 'Dasheng' moshi."

Works Cited

Archival Documents

The following abbreviations are used in this section:

NTB   Nantong bowuyuan (Nantong Museum)
NTD   Nantong shih dang'anguan (Nantong Municipal Archives)
NTFB   Nantong fangzhi bowuguan (Nantong Textile Museum)
SHD   Shanghai dang'anguan (Shanghai Municipal Archives)
SHSK   Shanghai shehui kexueyuan, Qiye lishi yanjiusuo (Shanghai Academy of Social Sciences, Research Department for Business History)

NTB: D 115/129. Zhang Cha 張詧. "Jixing" 記行 (Travel report). 1897–99.

NTB: E 60/643. "Ge chang an libai huasha, gongliao bijiao" 各廠按禮拜花紗, 工料比較 (Weekly comparison of cotton, yarn, and materials in each of the factories). 1902.

NTB: E 97/920. "Nantong Jiu'an fangzhi gongsi gaikuang" 南通九安紡織公司 (The situation of the Nantong Jiu'an Textile Company). N.d. (probably early 1920s), n.p.

NTB: E 109/1319. Wu Jichen xin'gao 吳寄塵信稿 (Drafts of letters of Wu Jichen). 1920–21.

NTB: E 110/1320. Wu Jichen xin'gao 吳寄塵信稿 (Drafts of letters of Wu Jichen). 1923–25.

NTB: E 123/1334. "Dasheng fangzhi gongsi kuaiji zhidu." 大生紡織公司會計制度 (Accounting system of the Dasheng Textile Company). 1946.

NTD: B 401-III-1. Contracts of purchase; doc. 1, 1893; doc. 5, 1904.

NTD: B 401-III-2. "Tongzhou Dasheng shachang di'er jie shulüe" 通州大生紗廠第二屆述略 (Second financial statement of the Tongzhou Dasheng Cotton Mill). 1901.

NTD: B 401-III-9. Internal business correspondence. 1898–1909. 93 documents.

NTD: B 401-III-13. "Nantong xian Dasheng shachang di shisan jie shuolüe" 南通縣大生紗廠第十三屆説略 (Thirteenth verbal statement of the Nantong county Dasheng Cotton Mill). 1911.

NTD: B 401-III-17. "Nantong xian Dasheng fangzhi gongsi di shiqi jie shuolüe" 南通縣大生紡織公司第十七屆説略 (Seventeenth verbal statement of the Nantong county Dasheng Textile Company). 1915.

NTD: B 401-III-26. Business contracts; docs. 2, 14, 15, 19, 1912; doc. 17, Dasheng shachang jidi qi liu 大生紗廠機地契六張 (Six land deeds of the Dasheng Cotton Mill), 1911; doc. 8, 1913.

NTD: B 401-III-34. Booklet with business correspondence. 1913–14. Pagination by archivist.

NTD: B 401-III-84. Receipts and invoices, docs. 1, 3, 5, 6. 1919.

NTD: B 401-III-99. Receipts and business correspondence, 1901–19; doc. 1, 1901; docs. 4–5, 1906; docs. 7–12, 1907; docs. 21–27, 1910.

NTD: B 401-III-125. Dasheng Hu shiwusuo 大生滬事務所 (Business correspondence of the Shanghai office), doc. 12, 1921; doc. 15, 1921; docs. 64–65, 1921.

NTD: B 401-III-152. Dasheng Hu shiwusuo 大生滬事務所 (Business correspondence of the Shanghai office), docs. 7, 10, and 29, 1921.

NTD: B 401-311-1. Richao 日抄 (Daybook). 1898–1900.

NTD: B 401-311-2. Ge wanglai 各往來 (Current accounts). 1897–1900.

NTD: B 401-311-3. Caoliu 草流 (Current expenses). 1900.

NTD: B 401-311-4. Songyin huidan 送銀回單 (Receipt book for financial transactions). 1898–1901.

NTD: B 401-311-26. Zongliu 總流 (Main record). 1897–1903.

NTD: B 401-311-30. Neiliu 內流 (Internal transfers). 1903.

NTD: B 401-311-35. Songkuan huidan 送款回單 (Receipt book for cash payments). 1901–3.

NTD: B 401-311-121. Shou fu 收付 (Income and expenditures). 1904–8.

NTD: B 401-311-129. Piaogen ludi 票根錄底 (Copy of the records of stubs). 1906–8.

NTD: B 401-311-154. Ge tongren 各同人 (Affiliated accounts). 1909–10.

NTD: B 401-311-155. Zahu 雜户 (Various accounts). 1909–10.

NTD: B 401-311-200. Gezhuang yuejie 各莊月結 (Monthly records for each business account). 1909–11.

NTD: B 402-III-1. Dasheng diyi fangzhi gongsi laogu, guben dibu 大生第一紡織公司老股, 股本底簿 (Copy of inventory of old shares, Dasheng No. 1 Textile Company). 1898–1903.

NTD: B 402-III-2. Guben cunkuan 股本存款 (Share capital). 1907.

NTD: B 402-III-445. "Tongzhou Dasheng shachang diyici gudong huiyi shilu" 通州大生紗廠第一次股東會議事錄 (Record of the first shareholders' meeting of the Dasheng Cotton Mill), 1907; "Nantong Dasheng fangzhi gongsi Minguo jiu nian gengjia gudong huiyi shilu" 南通大生紡織公司民國九年更甲股東會議事錄 (Record of the shareholders' meeting of the Nantong Dasheng Textile Company in the ninth year of the Republic), 1920; "Dasheng diyi fangzhi gongsi di'ershisi jie gudong huiyi shilu" 大生第一紡織公司第二十四屆股東會議事錄 (Record of the twenty-fourth shareholders' meeting of the Dasheng No. 1 Textile Company). 1923.

NTD: B 403-III-4. Fenhu zhang 分户帳 (Accounts of affiliated companies). 1911.

NTD: B 404-III-13. "Dasheng shachang" contracts and delivery receipts, Docs. 2–5 (1899).

NTD: B 405-III-7. "Chongming di'er fenchang di shiliu jie cunzai xizhang" 崇明第二分廠第十六屆存在細帳 (Sixteenth detailed balance sheet of the liabilities and assets of the Chongming No. 2 branch mill). 1922.

NTD: B 405-III-56. Chongming Dasheng fangzhi gongsi 崇明大生紡織公司, land purchases for the No. 2 mill. 1904–6. Pagination by archivist.

NTD: B 405-III-57. "Chongming Dasheng fenchang diyici gudong huiyi shilu bing zhanglüe" 崇明大生分廠第一次股東會議事錄併帳略 (Record of the first shareholders' meeting and the financial statement of the Dasheng branch mill in Chongming). 1907.

NTD: B 405-III-58. "Er chang diyici zhanglüe" 二廠第一次帳略 (First financial statement of the No. 2 mill). 1904–7.

NTD: B 406-III-2. "Haimen Dasheng disan fangzhi gongsi chuangli huiyi" 海門大生第三紡織公司創立會議 (Meeting for the foundation of the Dasheng No. 3 Mill in Haimen). 1922.

NTD: B 406-III-13. "Dasheng disan fangzhi gongsi: minguo ershi nian zhi ershiyi nian liangge ziran niandu de zhanglüe" 大生第三紡織公司：民國二十年兩個自然年度的帳略 (Dasheng No. 3 Textile Company: two annual numerical statements for the twentieth and twenty-first year of the Republic). 1931–32.

NTD: G 01-III-11. Mai tian qiyüe 賣田契約 (Deed of land sale). 1905.

NTD: G 03-III-15. Huaihai shiye yinhang 淮海事業銀行. Receipts and share certificates, 1920–23.

NTD: G 03-III-22. Huaihai shiye yinhang 淮海事業銀行. Shareholder reports, 1927–37.

NTD: G 03-III-42. Huaihai yinhang qingli qingkuang de biaoce 淮海銀行清理情況的表冊 (Register of the settled accounts of the Huaihai Bank). 1951–58.

NTFB: doc. 105. Xizhe 息摺 (Passbook). 1900.

NTFB: doc. 106. Xizhe 息摺 (Passbook). 1897.

NTFB: doc. 182. Dasheng jiqi fangshachang gupiao 大生機器紡織廠股東 (Share certificate of the Dasheng Machine Textile Mill). 1903.

NTFB: doc. 183. Several share certificates. 1900–1920.

NTFB: doc. 193. Share certificate, 1915.

NTFB: doc. 198. Share certificate, 1919.

NTFB: docs. 215–22. Zhuang Rui 張瑞, "Mianye luncong" 棉業論叢 (Discussion of the cotton business). Handwritten textbooks, 8 vols. 1913–17.

NTFB: doc. 225. Copy of contract. 1917.

NTFB: doc. 247. Dasheng jiqi fangshachang gupiao 大生機器紡紗廠股票 (Share certificate of the Dasheng Machine Textile Mill). 1897.

NTFB: doc. 332. Dasheng yichang gongfang zhuhuce 大生一廠工房住戶冊 (Rent book for company housing at the Dasheng No. 1 Mill). N.d. (probably 1938–39).

NTFB: doc. 423. Nantong fangxiao biye zhengshu 南通紡校畢業證書 (Diploma, Nantong Textile School). 1918.

SHD: Q 117-19-13. Tong Ru Chong Hai Qi wu xian lüe Hu tongxianghui 通如崇海啓五縣略滬同鄉會 (Native-place association for sojourners in Shanghai from the five counties of Nantong, Rugao, Chongming, Haimen and Qidong). 1938–46.

SHD: Q 117-19-18. Tong Ru Chong Hai Qi wu xian lüe Hu tongxianghui 通如崇海啓五縣略滬同鄉會 (Native-place association for sojourners in Shanghai from the five counties of Nantong, Rugao, Chongming, Haimen and Qidong). 1938–39.

SHD: Q 117-19-31. Tong Ru Chong Hai Qi wu xian lüe Hu tongxianghui 通如崇海啓五縣略滬同鄉會 (Native-place association for sojourners in Shanghai from the five counties of Nantong, Rugao, Chongming, Haimen and Qidong). 1924–44.

SHD: Q 193-1-1039. Shenxin fangzhi zonggongsi zhiyuan yangcheng suo: tongxue mingce 申新紡織總公司職員養成所: 同學名冊 (Department for the promotion of employees of the Shenxin Textile Company headquarters: name list). 1928–29.

SHD: Q 195-1-225. Jiekuan hetong 借款合同 (Loan contract). 1931.

SHD: S 30-1-35. Huashang shachang lianhehui. 華商紗廠聯合會 (Chinese Cotton Mill Owners' Association). 1917/18.

SHD: S 30-1-36. Huashang shachang lianhehui 華商紗廠聯合會 (Chinese Cotton Mill Owners' Association). 1919/20.

SHSK: R 01-1. Zonggongsi juan 總公司卷 (Company headquarters [of the Rong family business]), docs. 5–7. Comp. after 1949.

SHSK: 11-404. Nantong Dasheng diyi fangzhi gufen youxian gongsi 南通大生第一紡織股份有限公司 (Nantong Dasheng No. 1 Textile Corporation with Limited Liability). 1946.

SHSK: 13-121-388 (2). Dasheng diyi fangzhi gongsi gudong mingce 大生第一紡織公司股東名冊 (Register of shareholders in the Dasheng No. 1 Textile Company). 1947.

SHSK: 13-122-388. Dasheng diyi fangzhi gongsi dongshi yancha xingming zhudi biao 大生第一紡織公司董事驗查姓名住地表 (Register of names and addresses of shareholders in the Dasheng No. 1 Textile Company). 1947.

Other Sources

Ackers, Peter, and John Black. "Paternalist Capitalism: An Organization Culture in Transition." In *Work and the Enterprise Culture*, ed. Malcolm Cross and Geoff Payne, pp. 30–56. London: Falmer Press, 1991.

Amano Motonosuke 天野元之助. "Kōhoku no enkon kōshi kō" 江北の鹽墾公司考 (Examination of salt and land-reclamation companies in northern Jiangsu). *To-A keizai ronsō* 東亞經濟論叢 3 (Sept. 1942): 85–108.

An Guanying 安冠英 et al. *Zhonghua bainian lao yaopu* 中華百年老藥鋪 (Traditional medicine stores over the past hundred years in China). Beijing: Zhongguo wenshi chubanshe, 1993.

Anderson, Adelaide Mary. *Humanity and Labour in China: An Industrial Visit and Its Sequel, 1923–1926*. London: Student Christian Movement, 1928.

Aspin, C. *Lancashire: The First Industrial Society*. Helmshore, Eng.: Local History Society, 1969.

Bastid, Marianne. *Educational Reform in Early Twentieth-Century China*. Ann Arbor: University of Michigan, Center for Chinese Studies, 1988.

Bayer A.G. *Bayer Aktionärsbrief*. Leverkusen: third quarter 1996, first quarter 1997.

Bays, Daniel H. *The Nature of Provincial Political Authority in Late Ch'ing Times: Chang Chih-tung in Canton, 1884–1889*. Lawrence: University of Kansas, Center for East Asian Studies, 1970.

Bell, Lynda S. *One Industry, Two Chinas: Silk Filatures and Peasant-Family Production in Wuxi County, 1865–1937*. Stanford: Stanford University Press, 1999.

Bergère, Marie-Claire. *The Golden Age of the Chinese Bourgeoisie, 1911–1937*. Cambridge, Eng.: Cambridge University Press, 1989.

———. "The Shanghai Bankers' Association, 1915–1927: Modernization and the Institutionalization of Local Solidarities." In *Shanghai Sojourners*, ed. Frederic Wakeman and Wen-hsin Yeh, pp. 15–34. Berkeley: University of California, Institute of East Asian Studies, 1992.

Bian, Linan. "Development of Institutions of Social Service and Industrial Welfare in State Enterprises in China, 1937–45." Paper presented at the annual meeting of the Association for Asian Studies, Washington D.C., Mar. 1998.

Boorman, Howard L., ed. *Biographical Dictionary of Republican China*. 4 vols. New York: Columbia University Press, 1967–71.

Boot, H. M. "How Skilled Were Lancashire Cotton Factory Workers in 1833?" *Economic History Review* 98, no. 2 (May 1995): 283–303.

Bradley, Betsy Hunter. *The Works: The Industrial Architecture of the United States.* Oxford: Oxford University Press, 1999.

Braudel, Fernand. *The Wheels of Commerce.* London: Collins, 1982.

Brook, Timothy. "Capitalism and the Writing of Modern History in China." In *China and Historical Capitalism: Genealogies of Sinological Knowledge,* ed. Timothy Brook and Gregory Blue, pp. 110–57. Cambridge, Eng.: Cambridge University Press, 1999.

Brown, Rajeswary A. *Capital and Entrepreneurship in South East Asia.* London: Macmillan, 1994.

———. *Chinese Big Business and the Wealth of Asian Nations.* Houndmills/Basingstoke, Eng.: Palgrave, 2000.

———. "Introduction: Uses and Abuses of Chinese Business History and Methodology." In *Chinese Business Enterprise,* ed. idem, 1: 1–14. London: Routledge, 1996.

Brunnert, H. S., and V. V. Hagelstrom. *Present Day Political Organization of China.* 1912. Reprinted—Taipei, 1963.

Buck, John Lossing. *Chinese Farm Economy: A Study of 2865 Farms in Seventeen Localities and Seven Provinces in China.* Chicago: University of Chicago Press, 1930.

Bureau of Foreign Trade, ed. *China Industrial Handbook: Kiangsu.* Shanghai: Ministry of Industry, 1933.

Bush, Richard C. *The Politics of Cotton Textiles in Kuomintang China, 1927–1937.* New York: Garland, 1982.

Caoyan Dafeng yanken gongsi chuangli huiyi'an 草堰大豐鹽墾公司創立會議案 (Record of the meeting to establish the Dafeng Land Reclamation Company) N.p., 1918.

Carlson, Ellsworth C. *The Kaiping Mines (1877–1912).* Cambridge, Mass.: Harvard University, East Asian Research Center, 1971.

Casson, Mark. *Information and Organization: A New Perspective on the Theory of the Firm.* Oxford: Clarendon Press, 1997.

Chan, Kai Yiu. "The Structure of Chinese Business in Republican China: The Case of Liu Hongsheng and His Enterprises, 1920–1937." Ph.D. diss., University of Oxford, 1997.

Chan, Wellington K. K. "Government, Merchants and Industry to 1911." In *The Cambridge History of China,* ed. Denis Twitchett and John K. Fairbank, vol. 11, pt. 2, pp. 416–62. Cambridge, Eng.: Cambridge University Press, 1980.

———. *Merchants, Mandarins and Modern Enterprise in Late Ch'ing China.* Cambridge, Mass.: Harvard University, East Asian Research Center, 1977.

———. "The Organizational Structure of the Traditional Chinese Firm and Its Modern Reform." In *Chinese Business Enterprise*, ed. Rajeswary A. Brown, 1: 216–30. London: Routledge, 1996.

———. "The Origins and Early Years of the Wing On Company Group in Australia, Fiji, Hong Kong and Shanghai: Organisation and Strategy of a New Enterprise." In *Chinese Business Enterprise in Asia*, ed. Rajeswary A. Brown, pp. 80–95. London and New York: Routledge, 1995.

———. "Tradition and Change in the Chinese Business Enterprise: The Family Firm Past and Present." In *Chinese Business History: Interpretive Trends and Priorities for the Future*, ed. Robert Gardella et al., pp. 127–44. Armonk, N.Y.: M. E. Sharpe, 1998.

Chandler, Alfred. *The Visible Hand: The Managerial Revolution in American Business.* Cambridge, Mass.: Harvard University Press, 1977.

Chang Zonghu 常宗虎. *Modai zhuangyuan Zhang Jian jiazu bainianji.* 末代狀元張謇家族百年紀 (Record of one hundred years of the family of Zhang Jian, the last zhuangyuan). Beijing: Zhongguo shehui chubanshe, 2000.

———. *Nantong xiandaihua* 南通現代化, *1895–1938* (Nantong's modernization, 1895–1938). Beijing: Zhongguo shehui kexue chubanshe, 1998.

Chao, Kang. *The Development of Cotton Textile Production in China.* Cambridge, Mass.: Harvard University, East Asian Research Center, 1977.

Chen Da 陳達. "Wo guo gongchang fa de shixing wenti" 我國工廠法的實行問題 (The problem of implementing our country's factory law). *Fangzhi zhoukan* 紡織周刊 1, no. 17 (1931): 424–27.

Chen Jiayou 陳嘉猷. "Da shiyejia Zhang Jian yu Haimen" 大事業家張謇與海門 (The great industrialist Zhang Jian and Haimen). In *Haimen xian wenshi ziliao* 海門縣文史資料, vol. 8 (Zhang Jian), ed. Zhongguo renmin zhengzhi xieshang huiyi 中國人民政治協商會議, pp. 163–90. Haimen: 1989.

Chen Shensheng 陳慎生. "Tangzha mishi" 唐閘米市 (The rice market in Tangzha). *Nantong jingu* 南通今古 (Nantong, past and present), 1991, no. 1: 10–11.

Chen Zhen 陳真 and Yao Luo 姚洛, eds. *Zhongguo jindai gongyeshi ziliao* 中國近代工業史資料 (Material on China's modern industrial history). 2 vols. Beijing: Sanlian shudian, 1957–58. Reprinted—Tokyo: Taian, 1967.

Chen Zhengping 陳爭平. "Shilun Zhongguo jindai qiye zhidu fazhanshi shang de 'Dasheng' moshi" 試論中國近代企業制度發展史上的 "大生" 模式 (Discussion of the "Dasheng" model in terms of the developmental history of the modern Chinese enterprise system). *Zhongguo jingjishi yanjiu* 中國經濟史研究 2001, no. 2: 39–50.

Chesneaux, Jean. *The Chinese Labor Movement, 1919–1927.* Stanford: Stanford University Press, 1968.

Choi, Chi-cheung. "Competition Among Brothers: The Kin Tye Lung Company and Its Associate Companies." In *Chinese Business Enterprise in Asia*, ed. Rajeswary A. Brown, pp. 98–114. London: Routledge, 1995.

Chongchuan zhiwen lu 崇川咫聞錄 (Close records of Chongchuan). 12 *juan*. N.p., 1830.

Chongming Dasheng fenchang diyici gudong huiyi shilu bing zhanglüe 崇明大生分廠第一次股東會議事錄併帳略 (Report and financial statement of the first shareholder meeting of the Dasheng branch mill in Chongming). N.p., 1907.

Chu, Samuel C. *Reformer in Modern China: Chang Chien, 1853–1926*. New York: Columbia University Press, 1965.

Chu, Samuel C., and Kwang-Ching Liu, eds. *Li Hung-Chang and China's Early Modernization*. Armonk, N.Y.: M. E. Sharpe, 1994.

Chun Cao 春草. "Tangzha jiegang zhi qutan" 唐閘街港之趣談 (Interesting talk about the streets and alleys of Tangzha). *Nantong jingu* 南通今古, 1991, no. 3: 36–38.

Chung, Stephanie Po-yin. *Chinese Business Groups in Hong Kong and Political Change in South China, 1900–25*. London: Macmillan; New York: St. Martin's Press, 1998.

———. "'Faren' gainian de yizhi: xifang shangfa zai Zhongguo" 法人概念的移植: 西方商法在中國 (The idea of "legal person": the transplantation of Western commercial law to modern China). *Hong Kong Baptist University Journal of Historical Studies* 1 (1999): 49–69.

Clark, Colin, and Margaret Haswell. *The Economics of Subsistence Agriculture*. London: Macmillan, 1966.

Clarke, Allen. *The Effects of the Factory System*. 1899. Reprinted—Littleborough, Eng.: George Kelsall, 1989.

Clenell, Walter J. "Sub-enclosure 8 in no. 7: Consul Clenell to Sir R. Macleay." In *Papers Respecting Labour Conditions in China*. London: His Majesty's Stationery Office, 1925.

Coase, Ronald H. "The Nature of the Firm." *Economica* 4 (1937): 386–405.

Coble, Parks M. "Chinese Capitalists and the Japanese: Collaboration and Resistance in the Shanghai Area, 1937–45," *Wartime Shanghai*, ed. Wen-Hsin Yeh, pp. 62–85. London and New York: Routledge, 1998.

———. *Chinese Capitalists in Japan's New Order: The Occupied Lower Yangzi, 1937–45*. Berkeley: University of California Press, 2002.

———. "Japan's New Order and the Shanghai Capitalists: Conflict and Collaboration, 1937–1945." In *Chinese Collaboration with Japan, 1932–1945: The Limits of Accommodation*, ed. David P. Barrett and Larry N. Shyu, pp. 135–55. Stanford: Stanford University Press, 2001.

———. "Remembering the Anti-Japanese War: The Making of Patriotic Chinese Capitalists." Paper delivered at the Southwest Regional Conference of the Association for Asian Studies, San Marcos, Texas, Oct. 21, 1999.

———. *The Shanghai Capitalists and the Nationalist Government, 1927–37*. Cambridge, Mass.: Harvard University, Council on East Asian Studies, 1986.

Cochran, Sherman. *Big Business in China: Sino-Foreign Rivalry in the Cigarette Industry, 1890–1930*. Cambridge, Mass.: Harvard University Press, 1980.

———. *Encountering Chinese Networks: Western, Japanese, and Chinese Corporations in China, 1880–1937*. Berkeley: University of California Press, 2000.

Cornet, Christine. *Etat et enterprises en Chine XIXe–XXe siècles: le chantier naval de Jiangnan, 1865–1937*. Paris: Editions Arguments, 1997.

Dagongbao 大公報 (L'Impartial). Tianjin, 1905.

Dasheng Chongming fenchang shinian shishu 大生崇明分廠十年事述 (Report on ten years of the Dasheng branch mill in Chongming). Nantong?, 1917.

Dasheng xitong qiye shi, see Dasheng xitong qiye shi bianxiezu.

Dasheng xitong qiye shi bianxiezu 大生系統企業史編寫組. *Dasheng xitong qiye shi* 大生系統企業史 (Business history of the Dasheng system). Nanjing: Jiangsu Guji Chubanshe, 1990.

Dasheng yichang changshi bianjishi 大生一廠廠史編輯室. *Dasheng yichang gongren douzheng shi* 大生一廠工人斗爭史 (History of the struggle of the workers at Dasheng No. 1). Nantong, 1961.

Dingxi Suiji yanken gongsi jigu zhangcheng 丁溪遂濟鹽墾公司集股章程 (Regulations for attracting share investments in the Suiji Land Reclamation Company at Dingxi). N.p., 1920.

DSFGN (*Dasheng fangzhi gongsi nianjian*), see Zhang Jizhi xiansheng shiyeshi biancunchu.

DSQXDX (*Dasheng qiye xitong dang'an xuanbian*), see Nantong shi dang'anguan et al.

Du Xuncheng 杜恂誠. *Minzu zibenzhuyi yu jiu Zhongguo zhengfu* 民族資本主義與舊中國政府 (Native capitalism and the government of old China). Shanghai: Shanghai shehui kexueyuan chubanshe, 1992.

———. *Zhongguo chuantong lunli yu jindai zibenzhuyi–jianping Weibo "Zhongguo de zongjiao"* 中國傳統倫理與近代資本主義: 兼評韋伯 "中國的宗教" (The ethics of Chinese tradition and modern capitalism; with a criticism of Weber's *The Religion of China*). Shanghai: Shanghai shehui kexueyuan chubanshe, 1998 (1993).

Duan Benluo 段本洛 and Shan Qiang 單強. "Dasheng shachang de touzi huanjing yu duice" 大生紗廠的投資環境與對策 (The investment environment and reactions of the Dasheng cotton mill). *Jianghai xuekan* 江海學刊 1987, no. 6: 34–41.

Eastman, Lloyd E. *Family, Fields and Ancestors: Constancy and Change in China's Social and Economic History, 1550–1949*. Oxford: Oxford University Press, 1989.

Edwards, J. R., and E. Newell. "The Development of Industrial Cost and Management Accounting Before 1850." In *Accounting History: Some British Contributions*, ed. R. H. Parker and B. S. Yamey, pp. 407–33. Oxford: Clarendon Press, 1994.

Elsässer, Markus. *Soziale Intentionen und Reformen des Robert Owen in der Frühzeit der Industrialisierung*. Berlin: Duncker und Humblot, 1984.

Eng, Robert Y. "Luddism and Labor Protest Among Silk Artisans and Workers in Jiangnan and Guangdong, 1860–1930." *Late Imperial China* 11, no. 2 (1990): 63–101.

Ershi nian lai zhi Nantong 二十年來之南通 (Nantong during the past twenty years). Nantong, 1925–26?.

Esherick, Joseph W. *Reform and Revolution in China: The 1911 Revolution in Hunan and Hubei*. Berkeley: University of California Press, 1976.

Esherick, Joseph, ed. *Remaking the Chinese City: Modernity and National Identity, 1900–1950*. Honolulu: University of Hawai'i Press, 2000.

Fan Dangshi 范當世. *Fan Bozi wenji* 范伯子文集 (Fan Bozi). 12 *juan*. N.p., n.d. (1922?).

Fan Jizhong 藩繼忠. "Zhang Zhidong yu Zhang Jian de jiaowang ji wenhua beijing lüelun" 張之洞與張謇的交往及文化背景略論 (A brief discussion of the social interaction between Zhang Zhidong and Zhang Jian and the cultural background). In *Zhang Zhidong yu Zhongguo jindaihua* 張之洞與中國近代化 (Zhang Zhidong and China's modernization), ed. Yuan Shuyi 范書義 and Qin Jincai 秦進才, pp. 162–78. Beijing: Zhonghua shuju, 1999.

Fang Ping 方平 et al. "Rucheng Wanhong diandang de jiankuang" 如城萬鴻典當的簡況 (A brief survey of the Wanhong pawnshop in Rugao city). In *Rugao wenshi ziliao* 如皋文史資料 (Historical materials on Rugao), ed. Zhengxie Rugao xian weiyuanhui 政協如皋縣委員會, 2: 105–7. Rugao: 1986.

Fang Yujin 方裕謹. "Daoguang chunian Lianghuai siyan yanjiu" 道光初年兩淮私鹽研究 (Research on Lianghuai salt smuggling during the first years of the Daoguang period). *Lishi dang'an* 歷史檔案 72, no. 4 (1998): 80–89.

Fangzhi zhoukan 紡織周刊 (Textile weekly), 1932–35.

Faure, David. *China and Capitalism: Business Enterprise in Modern China*. Hong Kong: Hong Kong University of Science and Technology, Division of Humanities, 1994.

———. "The Control of Equity in Chinese Firms Within the Modern Sector from the Late Qing to the Early Republic." In *Chinese Business Enterprise in Asia*, ed. Rajeswary A. Brown, pp. 60–79. London: Routledge, 1995.

———. "The Rice Trade in Hong Kong Before the Second World War." In *Between East and West: Aspects of Social Change and Political Development in Hong Kong*, ed. Elizabeth Sinn, pp. 216–25. Hong Kong: University of Hong Kong, Centre of Asian Studies, 1990.

———. *The Rural Economy of Pre-Liberation China: Trade Expansion and Peasant Live-lihood in Jiangsu and Guangdong, 1870–1937*. Oxford: Oxford University Press, 1989.

Fei Xiaotong (Hsiao-tung Fei) 費孝通. *Congshi qiuzhi lu* 從實求知錄 (Seeking knowledge from reality). Beijing: Beijing daxue chubanshe, 1998.

———. *Peasant Life in China: A Field Study of Country Life in the Yangzte Valley*. London: Kegan Paul, Trench, Trubner & Co., 1947 (1939).

———. "Small Towns in Central Jiangsu." In *Small Towns in China: Functions, Problems and Prospects*, ed. idem et al., pp. 133–70. Beijing: New World Press, 1986.

Feng Hefa 馮和法. *Zhongguo nongcun jingji ziliao* 中國農村經濟資料 (Materials on China's rural economy). Shanghai, 1935.

Feng Zuyi 馮祖貽. "Zhang Zhidong yu Zhang Jian" 張之洞與張謇 (Zhang Zhidong and Zhang Jian). In *Zhang Zhidong yu Zhongguo jindaihua* 張之洞與中國近代化 (Zhang Zhidong and China's modernization), ed. Yuan Shuyi 苑書義 and Qin Jincai 秦進才, pp. 145–61. Beijing: Zhonghua shuju, 1999.

Feuerwerker, Albert. *China's Early Industrialization: Sheng Hsuan-Huai (1844–1916) and Mandarin Enterprise*. New York: Atheneum, 1970 (1958).

———. "Economic Trends in the Late Ch'ing Empire, 1870–1911." In *The Cambridge History of China*, ed. Denis Twitchett and John K. Fairbank, vol. 11, pt. 2, pp. 1–69, Cambridge, Eng.: Cambridge University Press, 1980.

———. "Industrial Enterprise in Twentieth-Century China: The Chee Hsin Cement Co." In *Studies in the Economic History of Late Imperial China: Handicraft, Modern Industry, and the State*, ed. idem, pp. 273–308. Ann Arbor: University of Michigan, Center for Chinese Studies, 1995.

Fewsmith, Joseph. *Party, State, and Local Elites in Republican China: Merchant Organizations and Politics in Shanghai, 1890–1930*. Honolulu: University of Hawai'i Press, 1985.

Finnane, Antonia. "The Origins of Prejudice: The Malintegration of Subei in Late Imperial China." *Comparative Studies in Society and History* 35, no. 2 (Apr. 1993): 211–38.

Fitkin, Gretchen Mae. *The Great River: The Story of a Voyage on the Yangtze Kiang*. Shanghai: Kelly & Walsh, 1922.

Fluck, Hans-R., et al. *Historic Postcards—Historische Ansichtskarten—Shanghai lishi mingxinpian*. Shanghai: Tongji daxue chubanshe, 1993.

Fong, H. D. (Fang Xianting). *Cotton Industry and Trade in China*. Tientsin: Chihli Press, 1932.

———. *Reminiscences of a Chinese Economist at 70*. Singapore: South Seas Society, 1975.

Foucault, Michel. *Discipline and Punish: The Birth of the Prison*. Harmondsworth, Eng.: Penguin Books, 1991 (1977).

Frazier, Mark W. *The Making of the Chinese Industrial Workplace: State, Revolution, and Labor Management.* Cambridge: Cambridge University Press, 2002.

Fujioka Kikuo 藤岡喜久男. *Chō Ken to Shinkai kakumei* 張謇と辛亥革命 (Zhang Jian and the Xinhai revolution). Sapporo: Hokkaido daigaku tosho kankōkai, 1985.

————. *Chūka minkoku dai'ichi kyōwasei to Chō Ken* 中華民國第一共和製と張謇 (The first republican system in the Republic of China and Zhang Jian). Tokyo: Shōbo shōen, 1999.

Gao Zhiyu 高知裕. *Zhongguo kuaiji fazhan jianshi* 中國會計發展簡史 (A brief history of the development of Chinese accounting). (Zhengzhou?): Henan Renmin chubanshe, 1985.

Gaomingbao 臬鳴報 (The Rugao announcer).

Gardella, Robert. "Squaring Accounts: Commercial Bookkeeping Methods and Capitalist Rationalism in Late Qing and Republican China." *Journal of Asian Studies* 51, no. 2 (1992): 317–39.

Gardella, Robert, et al., eds. *Chinese Business History: Interpretive Trends and Priorities for the Future.* Armonk, N.Y.: M. E. Sharpe, 1998.

Ge Mengpu 葛夢樸. *Nantong sifa bicun* 南通司法筆存 (Records of civil law cases in Nantong). Shanghai, 1913.

Ge Yuanxu 葛原序. *Hu you zaji* 滬游雜紀 (Random notes on traveling to Shanghai). 1882. Reprinted—Taibei: Guangwen shuju, 1968.

Gersick, Kelin E., et al. *Generation to Generation: Life Cycles of the Family Business.* Boston: Harvard Business School Press, 1997.

Godley, Michael. *The Mandarin-Capitalists from Nanyang: Overseas Chinese Enterprise in the Modernization of China, 1893–1911.* Cambridge, Eng.: Cambridge University Press, 1981.

Gomez, Edmund Terence. *Chinese Business in Malaysia: Accumulation, Ascendance, Accommodation.* Honolulu: University of Hawai'i Press, 1999.

Goodman, Bryna. *Native Place, City, and Nation: Regional Networks and Identities in Shanghai, 1853–1937.* Berkeley: University of California Press, 1995.

Goodman, David S. G., and Gerald Segal, eds. *China Deconstructs: Politics, Trade and Regionalism.* London and New York: Routledge, 1994.

Granovetter, Mark. "Business Groups." In *The Handbook of Economic Sociology*, ed. Neil J. Smelser and Richard Swedberg, pp. 453–75. Princeton: Princeton University Press, and New York: Russell Sage Foundation, 1994.

Grove, Linda. "Chinese Cotton Trade in Comparative Perspective." Paper presented at the annual meeting of the Association of Asian Studies, Mar. 1999, Washington, D.C.

Gu Xiaoshui 谷小水. "Jindai Zhongguo de zhiye jiaoyu (1866–1927)" 近代中國的職業教育 (Vocational education in modern China, 1866–1927). *Lishi dang'an* 歷史檔案 2 (2000): 93–98.

(Guangxu) Haimen ting tuzhi 光緒海門廳圖志 (Map and gazetteer of Haimen sub-prefecture, Guangxu period). 20 *juan*. N.p., 1900.

Guanzang Zhongwen baozhi mulu 館藏中文報紙目錄, *1872–1982* (Catalog of Chinese newspapers stored in the [Nantong] library, 1872–1982). Nantong: Nantong tushuguan, 1982.

Guo Xuyin 郭緒印. *"Jiu Shanghai" hei shehui* 舊上海黑社會 (The underworld of "old Shanghai"). Shanghai: Shanghai renmin chubanshe, 1997.

Guoli Fudan daxue Nantong tongxuehui huiyuan mingdan 國立復旦大學南通同學會會員名單 (Membership roster of the Nantong Classmates Association of National Fudan University). Nantong, 1947.

Habermas, Jürgen. "The Public Sphere." In *Rethinking Popular Culture: Contemporary Perspectives in Cultural Studies*, ed. Chandra Mukerji and Michael Schudson, pp. 398–404. Berkeley: University of California Press, 1991.

Haijun zhengzhi huabao 海軍政治畫報. 1925.

Hamashita Takeshi 濱下武夫. *Chūgoku kindai keizaishi kenkyū* 中國近代經濟史研究 (Researches on modern Chinese economic history). Tokyo: Tōkyō daigaku, Tōyō bunka kenkyūjo, 1989.

Hamilton, Gary G. "The Organizational Foundations of Western and Chinese Commerce: A Historical and Comparative Analysis." In *Asian Business Networks*, ed. idem, pp. 43–57. Berlin and New York: Walter de Gruyter, 1996.

Hamilton, Gary G., ed. *Business Networks and Economic Development in East and Southeast Asia*. Hong Kong: University of Hong Kong, Centre of Asian Studies, 1991.

Hamilton, Gary G., and Kao Cheng-shu. "The Institutional Foundations of Chinese Business." In *Chinese Business Enterprise*, ed. Rajeswary A. Brown, 1: 188–204. London: Routledge, 1996.

Hannah, Leslie. *The Rise of the Corporate Economy: The British Experience*. Baltimore: Johns Hopkins University Press, 1976.

Hansmann, Henry. *The Ownership of Enterprise*. Cambridge, Mass: Harvard University Press, Belknap Press, 1996.

Hao, Yen-P'ing. *The Comprador in Nineteenth Century China: Bridge Between East and West*. Cambridge, Mass.: Harvard University Press, 1970.

Harrell, Paula. *Sowing the Seeds of Change: Chinese Students, Japanese Teachers, 1895–1905*. Stanford: Stanford University Press, 1992.

Henriot, Christian. *Shanghai, 1927–1937: Municipal Power, Locality and Modernization*. Berkeley: University of California Press, 1993.

———. "War and Economics: The Control of Material Resources in the Lower Yangzi and Shanghai Area Between 1937 and 1945." Paper presented at the annual meeting of the Association of Asian Studies, Apr. 4–7, 2002, Washington D.C.

Hershatter, Gail. *Workers of Tianjin, 1900–1949.* Stanford: Stanford University Press, 1986.

Hertz, Ellen. *The Trading Crowd: An Ethnography of the Shanghai Stock Market.* Cambridge, Eng.: Cambridge University Press, 1998.

Heylin, Henry Brougham. *The Cotton Weaver's Handbook.* London: Charles Griffin, 1923.

Hirschmeier, Johannes. *The Origins of Entrepreneurship in Meiji Japan.* Cambridge, Mass.: Harvard University Press, 1964.

Ho, Ping-ti. *The Ladder of Success in Imperial China: Aspects of Social Mobility, 1368–1911.* New York: Columbia University Press, 1962.

Honeyman, Katrina. *Origins of Enterprise: Business Leadership in the Industrial Revolution.* Manchester, Eng.: Manchester University Press, 1982.

Honig, Emily. *Creating Chinese Ethnicity.* New Haven: Yale University Press, 1992.

———. "Native-Place Hierarchy and Labor Market Segmentation: The Case of Subei People in Shanghai." In *Chinese History in Economic Perspective,* ed. Thomas Rawski and Lillian Li, pp. 271–94. Berkeley: University of California Press, 1992.

———. *Sisters and Strangers: Women in the Shanghai Cotton Mills, 1919–1949.* Stanford: Stanford University Press, 1986.

Hook, Brian. *Shanghai and the Yangzi Delta: A City Reborn.* Hong Kong and Oxford: Oxford University Press, 1998.

Hsiao, Liang-lin. *China's Foreign Trade Statistics, 1864–1949.* Cambridge, Mass.: Harvard University, East Asian Research Center, 1974.

Hua shang shachang lianhehui jikan 華商紗廠聯合會季刊. 1920.

Huaihai yinhang diyi, di'erjie yingye baogao 淮海銀行第一第二屆營業報告 (First and second business reports of the Huaihai Bank). Nantong, 1920.

Huang, Philip C. C. *The Peasant Family and Rural Development in the Yangzi Delta, 1350–1988.* Stanford: Stanford University Press, 1990.

Huang Qinggen 黃清根. "Zhang Jian de kaifang sixiang yu jindai jingshen wenming" 張謇的開放思想與近代精神文明 (The progressive ideas of Zhang Jian and the cultural refinement of the modern spirit). In *Lun Zhang Jian: Zhang Jian guoji xueshu yantaohui lunwenji* 論張謇: 張謇國際學術研討會論文集 (Discussing Zhang Jian: collected essays from the international academic conference on Zhang Jian), ed. Nanjing daxue, Waiguo xuezhe liuxuesheng yanxiubu 南京大學外國學者留學生研修部, pp. 290–302. Nanjing: Jiangsu renmin chubanshe, 1993.

Huang Yongxin 黃永信. "Du Yuesheng dajin Dada lunchuan gongsi jingguo" 杜月笙打進大達輪船公司經過 (Du Yuesheng's takeover of the Dada Steamship Company). In *Jiu Shanghai de banghui* 舊上海的幫會 (The gangs of old Shanghai), ed. Zhongguo renmin zhengzhi xieshang huiyi, Shanghai weiyuanhui 中國人民政治協商會議上海委員會, pp. 284-92. Shanghai: Shanghai renmin chubanshe, 1986.

Hucker, Charles O. *A Dictionary of Official Titles in Imperial China*. Stanford: Stanford University Press, 1985.

Hummel, Arthur W. *Eminent Chinese of the Ch'ing Period*. 2 vols. Washington, D.C.: Government Printing Office, 1943.

Ichiko, Chuzo. "Political and Institutional Reform, 1901–1911." In *The Cambridge History of China*, ed. Denis Twitchett and John K. Fairbank, vol. 11, pt. 2, pp. 375–415. Cambridge, Eng.: Cambridge University Press, 1980.

Imazeki Tempō 今關天彭. "Shina no jitsugyō ōkoku 'Nantsū'" 支那の事業王國南通 (China's industrial kingdom, Nantong). *Pekin shūhō* 北京週報, no. 121 (July 20, 1924): 844–47, 859.

Imura Isao 井村董雄. *Zhongguo zhi fangzhi ji qi chupin* 中國之紡織及其出品 (China's spinning and weaving industry and its products). Trans. Zhou Peilan. Shanghai: Shangwu yinshuguan, 1928.

Inkster, Ian. *Japanese Industrialisation: Historical and Cultural Perspectives*. London and New York: Routledge, 2001.

International Anti-Opium Association. *Opium Cultivation and Traffic in China (An investigation in 1925–1926)*, vol. 6, no. 3. Peking: International Anti-Opium Association, 1926.

Jefferson, Gary H., and Thomas G. Rawski. "Ownership Change in Chinese Industry." In *Enterprise Reform in China: Ownership, Transition, and Performance*, ed. Gary H. Jefferson and Inderjit Singh, pp. 23–42. New York: Oxford University Press for the World Bank, 1999.

(Jiajing) Haimen xianzhi 嘉靖海門縣志 (Gazetteer of Haimen county, Jiajing period). 6 *juan*. N.p., 1536.

(Jiajing) Tongzhou zhi 嘉靖通州志 (Gazetteer of Tongzhou, Jiajing period). 6 *juan*. 1530.

Jiang Binghe 蔣炳和. "Nantong Tangzhazhen liangshiye fazhan jianshi" 南通唐閘鎮糧食業發展簡史 (A short history of the development of the grain trade in Tangzha village in Nantong). In *Nantong wenshi ziliao xuanji* 南通文史資料選集 (Selected materials on the history of Nantong), ed. Jiangsu sheng Nantong shi weiyuanhui 江蘇省南通市委員會 et al., 6: 212–23. Nantong, 1986.

Jiang Zi'an 江子安 and Cheng Zhuoru 程灼如. "Nantong de huiguan" 南通的會館 (Native-place associations in Nantong). *Nantong jingu* 南通今古 1991, no. 6: 27–29.

Jiangsu Haimen Dasheng disan fangzhi gongsi quantu 江蘇海門大生第三紡織公司全圖 (Complete map of the Dasheng No. 3 Textile Company in Haimen, Jiangsu). (Haimen), 1922.

Jiangsu shehui kexueyuan, *Jiangsu shigang* ketizu 江蘇社會科學院江蘇史綱課題組. *Jiangsu shigang* 江蘇史綱 (Historic outline of Jiangsu). 2 vols. (Nanjing): Jiangsu guji chubanshe, 1993.

Jiangsu sheng jiaotong shizhi biancun weiyuanhui 江蘇省交通實質編存委員會. *Jiangsu gonglu jiaotong shi* 江蘇公路交通史 (History of public highways in Jiangsu). Beijing: Renmin jiaotong chubanshe, 1989.

Jiangsu sheng jinrong zhi bianjishi 江蘇省金融之編輯室. *Jiangsu diandang qianzhuang* 江蘇典當錢莊 (Pawnshops and native banks in Jiangsu). Nanjing: Nanjing daxue chubanshe, 1992.

Jiangsu shiye ting, Disan ke 江蘇事業廳第三科. *Jiangsu sheng fangzhiye zhuangkuang* 江蘇省紡織業狀況 (Situation of the textile industry in Jiangsu province). (Nanjing), 1919.

Jiangsu Tongzhou Dasheng fangsha gufen youxian gongsi zhi tu 江蘇通州大生紡紗股份有限公司之圖 (Map of the Dasheng Spinning Company, Inc., in Tongzhou, Jiangsu). (Nantong), 1919(?).

Jiaofu Dalai yanken gongsi chuangli huiyi'an 角富大賫鹽墾公司創立會議案 (Records of the meeting to establish the Dalai land reclamation company at Jiaofu). N.p., 1918.

"Jieshao bu xiaoxi" 介紹部消息 (News [on employment]). *Hua Shang shachang lianhehui jikan* 華商紗廠聯合會季刊 1, no. 1 (Sept. 1919): 267.

Kaku, Sachio. "Management and Labour in German Chemical Companies Before World War One." In *Authority and Control in Modern Industry: Theoretical and Empirical Perspectives*, ed. Paul L. Robertson, pp. 203–20. London and New York: Routledge, 1999.

Kanemaru Yūichi 金丸裕一. "Chūgoku 'minzoku kōgyō no kōgane jiki' to denryoku sangyō" 中國民族工業の黃金時期と電力產業 (China's Golden Age of Native Industry and electrical industries). *Ajia kenkyū* アジア研究 39, no. 4 (1993): 29–84.

Katznelson, Ira, and Aristide R. Zolberg, eds. *Working-Class Formation: Nineteenth-Century Patterns in Western Europe and the United States*. Princeton: Princeton University Press, 1986.

Kidd, Yasue Aoki. *Women Workers in the Japanese Cotton Mills, 1880–1920*. East Asia Papers, no. 20. Ithaca, N.Y.: Cornell University, China-Japan Program, 1978.

Kirby, William C. "China Unincorporated: Company Law and Business Enterprise in Twentieth-Century China." *Journal of Asian Studies* 54, no. 1 (1995): 43–63.

Kiyokawa, Yukihiko. "The Transformation of Young Rural Women into Disciplined Labor Under Competition-Oriented Management." In *The Textile Industry and the Rise of the Japanese Economy*, ed. Michael Smitka, pp. 91–111. New York: Garland Publishing, 1998.

Komlosy, Andrea. *Industrie Kultur: Mühlviertel, Waldviertel, Südböhmen.* Vienna: Deuticke, 1995.

Kubo Tōru 久保亨. "Kindai Chūgoku mengyō no chitai kōzō to keiei ruikei" 近代中國棉業の地帶構造と經營類型 (The regional structure of the modern Chinese cotton industry and similar operational forms). *Tochi seido shigaku* 土地制度史學, no. 113 (1986): 20–39.

Lai, Chi-kong (Li Zhigang 黎志剛). "The Emergence of the Modern Corporation in China." Paper presented at Managing Culture: Chinese Organization in Action, a conference at the Hong Kong University of Science and Technology, Oct. 1995.

————. "Enterprise History: Studies and Archives." In *Chinese Business History: Interpretive Trends and Priorities for the Future,* ed. Robert Gardella et al., pp. 169–88. Armonk, N.Y.: M. E. Sharpe, 1998.

————. "Li Hung-Chang and Modern Enterprise: The China Merchants' Company, 1872–1885." In *Li Hung-chang and China's Early Modernization,* ed. Samuel C. Chu and Kwang Ching-Liu, pp. 216–47. Armonk, N.Y.: M. E. Sharpe, 1994.

————. "Lunchuan zhaoshangju jingying guanli wenti, 1872–1901" 輪船招商局經營管理問題 (Problems of business management in the China Merchants' Steamship Company, 1872–1901). *Zhongyang yanjiuyuan, Jindaishi yanjiusuo jikan* 中央研究院近代史研究所集刊, no. 19 (1990): 67–108.

————. "The Qing State and Merchant Enterprise: The China Merchants' Company, 1872–1902." In *To Achieve Security and Wealth: The Qing Imperial State and the Economy, 1644–1911,* ed. Jane Kate Leonard and John R. Watt, pp. 139–55. Ithaca, N.Y.: Cornell University Press, 1992.

Lamson, H. D. "The Effect of Industrialization upon Village Livelihood." *Chinese Economic Journal* 9, no. 4 (Oct. 1931): 1025–82.

Lee, Ching Kwan. *Gender and the South China Miracle: Two Worlds of Factory Women.* Berkeley: University of California Press, 1998.

Lee, T. A. "Company Financial Statements." In *Business and Businessmen: Studies in Business, Economic and Accounting History,* ed. Sheila Marriner, pp. 237–59. Liverpool: Liverpool University Press, 1978.

Leung, Yuen-sang. "The Shanghai-Tientsin Connection: Li Hung-Chang's Political Control over Shanghai." In *Li Hung-Chang and China's Early Modernization,* ed. Samuel C. Chu and Kwang-Ching Liu, pp. 108–18. Armonk, N.Y.: M. E. Sharpe, 1994.

Levy, Marion J. "The Social Background of Modern Business Development in China." Part I in idem, *The Rise of the Modern Chinese Business Class.* New York: Institute of Pacific Relations, 1949.

Li, Bozhong 李伯重. *Agricultural Development in Jiangnan, 1620–1850.* New York: St. Martin's Press, 1998.

————. *Jiangnan de zaoqi gongyehua, 1550–1850 nian* 江南的早期工業化, 1550–1850 年 (Jiangnan's early industrialization, 1550–1850). Beijing: Shehui kexue wenxian chubanshe, 2000.

————. "Yingguo moshi, Jiangnan daolu yu zibenzhuyi mengya" 英國模式, 江南道路與資本主義萌芽 (The English model, the Jiangnan way, and the sprouts of capitalism). *Lishi yanjiu* 歷史研究 2001, no. 1: 116–26.

Li, Chien-Nung. *The Political History of China, 1840–1928*. Translated and edited by Teng Ssu-yu and Jeremy Ingalls. Princeton: D. Van Nostrand Company, 1956.

Li Hongzhang 李鴻章. *Li Wenzhong (Hongzhang) quanji* 李文忠公鴻章全集 (The complete works of Li Hongzhang). Ed. Wu Rulun 吳汝綸. Nanjing, 1905. Reprinted—Taibei: Wenhai chubanshe, 1980.

Li Kan 李侃. "Quyu shehui jingjishi yanjiu de yiyi ji qi fangfa" 區域社會經濟史研究的意義及其方法 (The significance of research in regional socioeconomic history and its method). *Guangdong shehui kexue* 廣東社會科學 15, no. 1 (1988): 125–27.

Li, Lillian M. *China's Silk Trade: Traditional Industry in the Modern World, 1842–1937*. Cambridge, Mass.: Harvard University, Council on East Asian Studies, 1981.

Li Mingxun 李明勛 et al., eds. *Kaituo yu fazhan* 開拓與發展 (Innovation and development). Nantong: Zhang Jian yanjiu zhongxin, 1993.

Li Wenzhi 李文治 and Zhang Youyi 章有義. *Zhongguo jindai nongyeshi ziliao* 中國近代農業史資料 (Materials on China's modern agrarian history). 4 vols. Beijing: Sanlian shudian, 1957.

Li Yixiang 李一翔. *Jindai Zhongguo yinhang yu qiye de guanxi, 1897–1945* 近代中國銀行與企業的關係 (The relationship between banks and enterprises in modern China, 1897–1945). Taibei: Dongda tushu gongsi, 1997.

Li Zishan 李自善. "Shanghai laodong zhuangkuang" 上海勞動狀況 (Work conditions in Shanghai). *Xin qingnian* 新青年 7, no. 6 (1920): 1–83.

Liang Zhan 梁戰 and Guo Qunyi 郭群一. *Lidai zangshujia cidian* 歷代藏書家辭典 (Dictionary of book collectors in history). Xi'an: Shanxi chubanshe, 1991.

Lieu, D. K. *The Silk Industry of China*. Shanghai: Kelly and Walsh, 1941.

Lin Gang 林剛. "Shilun Dasheng shachang de shichang jichu" 試論大生紗廠的市場基礎 (Discussion of the market foundation of the Dasheng cotton mills). *Lishi yanjiu* 歷史研究 1985, no. 4: 142–54.

————. "Zhang Jian yu Zhongguo tese de zaoyi xiandaihua daolu: dui Huainan yanken shiye de zai fenxi" 張謇與中國特色的早已現代化道路: 對淮南鹽墾事業的再分析 ("Zhang Jian and China's unique path of early modernization: analysis of the land-reclamation business in Huainan). *Zhongguo jingjishi yanjiu* 中國經濟史研究 1997, no. 1: 14–24.

Lin Jubai 林舉百. *Jindai Nantong tubu shi*. 近代南通土布史 (History of native cotton cloth in modern Nantong). Nanjing: Nanjing daxue xuebao bianjibu, 1984.

Lin, Nan, and Chih-Jou Jay Chen. "Local Elites as Officials and Owners: Share-holding and Property Rights in Daqiuzhuang." In *Property Rights and Economic Reform in China*, ed. Jean C. Oi and Andrew G. Walder, pp. 145–70. Stanford: Stanford University Press, 1999.

Lin Xi (Gao Zhenbai 高真白). "Cong Xianggang de Yuanfahang tanqi" 從香港的元發行談起 (Discussion of the Yuanfahang in Xianggang). 4 pts. *Da Cheng* 大成, no. 117 (1983): 47–52; no. 118 (1983): 45–51; no. 119 (1983): 34–39; no. 120 (1983): 46–54.

Lin Zuobo 林左波. *Guanwai manyouji* 關外漫遊記 (Account of leisurely travels outside the pass [i.e., in Manchuria]). N.p., 1931.

Ling Zhenrong 凌振榮. "Nantong de gudai yu jindai jianzhu" 南通的古代與近代建築 (Old and new buildings in Nantong). In *Nantong bowuyuan jianyuan jiushi zhounian jinian wenji* 南通博物苑建苑九十周年紀念文集 (Commemorative essays for the ninetieth anniversary of the Nantong Museum), ed. Xu Zhiya 徐治亞, pp. 123–38. Nantong: 1995.

Liu Hongsheng 劉鴻生. "Wo weishenme zhuzhong chengben kuaiji" 我為什麼注重成本會計 (Why I regard cost accounting as important). *Yinhang zhoubao* 銀行周報 17, no. 14 (1933): 3–8.

———. *Zhang Jian zhuanji* 張謇傳記 (Biography of Zhang Jian). Shanghai: Shanghai shudian, 1985 (1958).

Liu, Kwang-Ching. "Li Hung-chang in Chihli: The Emergence of a Policy, 1870–1875." In *Approaches to Modern Chinese History*, ed. Albert Feuerwerker et al., pp. 68–104. Berkeley: University of California Press, 1967.

———. "Nineteenth Century China: The Disintegration of the Old Order and the Impact of the West." In *China in Crisis*, ed. Ho Ping-ti and Tsou Tang, vol. 1, book one, pp. 93–202. Chicago: University of Chicago Press, 1972.

Liu Miao 劉淼. *Ming Qing yanhai tangdi kaifa yanjiu* 明清沿海蕩地開發研究 (Research on the development of coastal salt production land in the Ming and Qing dynasties). Shantou: Shantou daxue chubanshe, 1996.

Liu Peilin 劉培林 and Zhang Deyi 張德意. *Zhang Jian zhuan* 張謇傳 (Biography of Zhang Jian). Nanjing: Jiangsu wenyi chubanshe, 1992.

Liu Shaotang 劉紹堂, ed. *Minguo renwu xiaozhuan* 民國人物小傳 (Brief biographies of personalities of the Republican period). Taibei: Zhuanji wenxue chubanshe, 1984.

Lu Baoqian 陸寶千. *Lun Zhang Jian yu Nantong zhi jindaihua* 論張謇與南通之近代化 (Discussion of Zhang Jian and the modernization of Nantong). Taibei: Zhongyang yanjiuyuan jindaishi yanjiusuo, 1986.

Lu Bin 陸斌. *Chongming pingmin changshi* 崇明平民常識 (General knowledge about the ordinary people of Chongming). (Chongming): Chongming pingmin jiaoyu cujinhui, 1925.

Lu Hanchao. *Beyond the Neon Lights: Everyday Shanghai in the Early Twentieth Century.* Berkeley: University of California Press, 1999.

Lu Jinyuan 陸金淵. "Nantong diqu chenglu guocheng de tansuo" 南通地區成陸過程的探索 (Exploration of land development in the Nantong region). *Lishi dili* 歷史地理 1983, no. 3 (Nov.): 21–37.

Lu Yangyuan 陸養元. "Lüelun Dasheng qiye yu Rongshi qiye de fazhan tedian" 略論大生企業與榮氏企業的發展 (Discussion of the development of the Dasheng enterprise and the Rong family enterprises). In *Jiangsu shi lunkao* 江蘇史論考 (Analyses of the history of Jiangsu), ed. Jiangsu sheng shelian lishi xuehui 江蘇省社聯歷史學會 et al., pp. 383–97. Nanjing: Jiangsu guji chubanshe, 1989.

Lu Zhidao 陸志道 and Gu Zhenyu 顧振虞. "Zhang Jian xiansheng er, san shi" 張謇先生二三事 (A few things about Mr. Zhang Jian). In *Haimen xian wenshi ziliao* 海門縣文史資料 (Materials on the history and culture of Haimen county), ed. Jiangsu sheng Haimen xian weiyuanhui wenshi ziliao weiyuanhui 江蘇省海門縣委員會文史資料委員會, 8 211–12. Haimen: 1989.

Lü, Xiaobo. "Minor Public Economy: The Revolutionary Origins of the Danwei." In *Danwei: The Changing Chinese Workplace in Historical and Comparative Perspective*, ed. Xiaobo Lü and Elizabeth J. Perry, pp. 21–41. New York: M. E. Sharpe, 1997.

Lufrano, Richard John. *Honorable Merchants: Commerce and Self-Cultivation in Late Imperial China.* Honolulu: University of Hawai'i Press, 1997.

Ma, Bohuang. "Liu Hongsheng's Enterprise Investment and Management." In *The Chinese Economy in the Early Twentieth Century*, ed. Tim Wright, pp. 85–97. New York: St. Martin's Press, 1992.

Ma Junjie 馬駿傑. "Lun 'Beiyang haijun zhangcheng'" 論北洋海軍章程 (Discussion of the "Regulations of the Beiyang Navy"). *Lishi dang'an* 2000, no. 4: 102–9.

Ma Min 馬敏. *Guanshang zhi jian: shehui jubianzhong de jindai shenshang* 官商之間: 社會劇變中的近代紳商 (Between official and merchant: the modern gentry-merchants amid drastic social change). Tianjin: Tianjin renmin chubanshe, 1995.

Mann, Susan. *Local Merchants and the Chinese Bureaucracy, 1750–1950.* Stanford: Stanford University Press, 1987.

———. "Women's Work in the Ningbo Area, 1900–1936." In *Chinese History in Economic Perspective*, ed. Thomas G. Rawski and Lillian M. Li, pp. 243–270. Berkeley: University of California Press, 1992.

Mao Dun 茅盾. *Ziye* 子夜 (Midnight). Beijing: Renmin wenxue chubanshe, 1953.

Mao Jiaqi 茅家琦 et al. *Heng kan cheng ling ce cheng feng: Changjiang xiayou chengshi jindaihua de guiji* 橫看成嶺側成峰: 長江下游城市近代化的軌跡 (From a horizontal point of view it looks like a mountain ridge, from the side it appears to be a peak: tracks of modernization of cities along the lower Yangzi River). Nanjing: Jiangsu renmin chubanshe, 1993.

Martin, Brian G. *The Shanghai Green Gang: Politics and Organized Crime, 1919–1937.* Berkeley: University of California Press, 1996.

McElderry, Andrea L. *Shanghai Old-Style Banks (Ch'ien-chuang), 1800–1935.* Ann Arbor: University of Michigan, Center for Chinese Studies, 1976.

———. "Shanghai Securities Exchanges: Past and Present." Occasional Paper Series, no. 4. Brisbane: University of Queensland, Asian Business History Centre, 2001.

Meakin, David. *Man and Work: Literature and Culture in Industrial Society.* London: Methuen, 1976.

Meng Guilin 孟桂林. "Rijun junguanxia de Dasheng yichang" 日軍軍官下的大生一廠 (The Dasheng no. 1 mill under the Japanese military). In *Nantong wenshi ziliao xuanji* 南通文史資料選集 (Selected materials on the history of Nantong), ed. Zhonguo renmin zhengzhi xieshang huiyi, Jiangsu sheng Nantong shi weiyuanhui 中國人民政治協商會議江蘇省南通市委員會, 5: 134–42. Nantong: 1985.

Metzger, Thomas A. "The Organizational Capabilities of the Ch'ing State in the Field of Commerce: The Liang-huai Salt Monopoly, 1740–1840." In *Economic Organization in Chinese Society*, ed. W. E. Willmott, pp. 9–45. Stanford: Stanford University Press, 1972.

Miaowan Huacheng yanken gufen youxian gongsi zhangcheng 廟灣華成鹽墾股份有限公司章程 (Regulations for inviting share investment of the Huacheng Land Reclamation Company at Miaowan). N.p., 1917.

Milford, Humphrey. Letter to Theodore Leslie, Nov. 13, 1914. Oxford University Press Archive, o/185.

Minami Manshū tetsudō kabushiki kaisha. Chōsabu. Shanhai jimusho chōsashitsu 南滿洲鐵道株式會社調查部上海事務所調查室. *Kōso shō Nantsū ken nōson jittai chōsa hōkokusho* 江蘇省南通縣農村實態調查報告書 (Report on the investigation of conditions in the farm villages of Nantong county, Jiangsu province). Mantetsu Investigation Research Materials, vol. 38. N.p., 1941.

(Minguo) Nantong xian tuzhi 民國南通縣圖志 (Gazetteer with maps of Nantong county from the Republican period). 24 *juan*. 1925?. Reprinted—Nanjing: Jiangsu guji chubanshe, 1991.

Mitter, Rana. *The Manchurian Myth: Nationalism, Resistance, and Collaboration in Modern China.* Berkeley: University of California Press, 2000.

Mori Tokihiko 森時彦. *Chūgoku kindai mengyōshi no kenkyū* 中國近代棉業史の研究 (A study of the history of the modern cotton industry in China). Kyoto: Kyōto daigaku gakujutsu shuppankai, 2001.

Moser, Charles K. *The Cotton Textile Industry of Far Eastern Countries.* Boston: Peppernell Manufacturing Co., 1930.

Mu Changxiao 暮長嘯, ed. *Shanghai jushang yanyi* 上海巨商演義 (Shanghai tycoon legends). 3 vols. Guangzhou: Guangzhou chubanshe, 1998.

Mu Ouchu 穆藕初. "Shachang zuzhifa" 紗廠組織法 (Organization methods of cotton mills). *Hua Shang shachang lianhehui jikan* 華商紗廠聯合會季刊 1, no. 1 (Sept. 1919): 29–44.

Mu Xuan 穆烜 and Yan Xuexi 嚴學熙. *Dasheng shachang gongren shenghuo de diaocha (1899–1949).* 大生紗廠工人生活的調查 (Investigation of the life of workers in the Dasheng spinning mills, 1899–1949). Nanjing: Jiangsu renmin chubanshe, 1994.

Nakai Hideki 中井英基 *Chō Ken to Chūgoku kindai kigyō* 張謇と中國近代企業 (Zhang Jian and modern Chinese enterprise). (Hokkaido): Hokkaido daigaku tosho kankōkai, 1996.

Nanjing daxue, Waiguo xuezhe liuxuesheng yanxiubu 南京大學外國學者留學生研修部, ed. *Lun Zhang Jian: Zhang Jian guoji xueshu yantaohui lunwenji* 論張謇: 張謇國際學術研討會論文集 (Discussing Zhang Jian: collected essays from the international academic conference on Zhang Jian). Nanjing: Jiangsu renmin chubanshe, 1993.

Nanjing shifan daxue, Guwenxian zhengli yanjiusuo 南京師範大學古文獻整理研究所. *Jiangsu yiwenzhi: Nantong juan* 江蘇藝文志: 南通卷 (Bibliography of Jiangsu: Nantong). Nanjing: Jiangsu renmin chubanshe, 1995.

Nantong bao 南通報 (Nantong news). 1926.

Nantong bao tekan 南通報特刊 (Special issue of the *Nantong News*). 29 Oct. 1926.

Nantong bowuyuan pinmu 南通博物苑品目 (Catalog of the Nantong museum). N.p., 1905?.

Nantong daxue 南通大學. *Nantong daxue chengli jiniankan* 南通大學成立紀念刊 (Commemorative volume on the foundation of the Nantong University). (Nantong?), 1928.

Nantong disan mian fangzhi chang 南通第三棉紡織廠 (Nantong No. 3 Cotton Spinning and Weaving Mill). Company prospectus. N.p., n.d. (1993?).

Nantong fangzhishi tulu bianjizu 南通紡織史圖錄編輯組. *Nantong fangzhishi tulu* 南通紡織史圖錄 (Pictorial record of Nantong's textile history). Nanjing: Nanjing daxue chubanshe, 1987.

Nantong Guangsheng youchang dishiqi jie zhanglüe 南通廣生油廠第十七屆帳略 (Seventeenth financial statement of the Guangsheng Oil Mill in Nantong). N.p., 1919.

Nantong Guangsheng zhayou gongsi diershi'er, ershisan, ershisi jie zhanglüe, 1924–26 南通廣生榨油公司第二十二, 二十三, 二十四屆帳略 (Twenty-second, twenty-third, and twenty-fourth financial statements of the Nantong Guangsheng Oil Mill, 1924–26). N.p., 1926.

Nantong ribao 南通日報 (Nantong daily). 1903–8.

Nantong sezhi yichang 南通色織一廠 (Nantong No. 1 Color Weaving Mill). Company brochure. N.p., n.d. (1994?).

Nantong shi dang'anguan 南通市檔案館 et al., eds. *Dasheng qiye xitong dang'an xuanbian* 大生企業系統檔案選編 (Selected archival materials on the Dasheng business complex). Nanjing: Nanjing daxue chubanshe, 1987.

Nantong shi. Diming bangongshi 南通市地名辦公室. *Nantong shiqu tu* 南通市區圖 (Map of Nantong's urban districts). Nantong, 1992.

Nantong shi. Tongjiju. Bianji weiyuanhui 南通市統計局編輯委員會 *1949–1988 Nantong jingji gailan* 南通經濟概覽 (Outline of the economy of Nantong, 1949–1988). Nantong, 1989.

Nantong shiye gailan 南通事業概覽 (Outline of Nantong industries). Nantong, 1947.

Nantong tushuguan mulu 南通圖書館目錄 (Catalog of the Nantong library). N.p., (1912).

Nantong xian Fuxin mianchang dishi jie zhanglüe 南通縣復新麵廠第十屆帳略 (Tenth financial statement of the Fuxin Flour Mill in Nantong). N.p., 1918.

Nantong xian nongye xuexiao tiyao 南通縣農業學校提要 (Summary of the Nantong County Agricultural School). Nantong, 1914.

Nantong xianshi tu 南通縣市圖 (Map of Nantong county seat). Nantong: Hanmolin shuju, 1925.

Nantong xian Zisheng yechang di qi, ba, jiu, shi, shisan jie shuolüe bing zhanglüe 南通縣資生冶廠第七, 八, 九, 十, 十三說略併帳略 (Combined seventh, eight, ninth, tenth, and thirtieth verbal and financial statements of the Zisheng Iron Workshop). N.p., 1936.

Nantong xian zizhihui 南通縣自治會. *Nantong zizhihui baogaoshu* 南通自治會報告書 (Report of the Nantong Self-Government Association). Nantong, 1921.

Nantong xueyuan Fangzhi ke xueyou lu 南通學院紡織科學友錄 (Roster of alumni of the Spinning and Weaving Department of Nantong College). Nantong, 1930.

Nantong youyi julebu 南通友誼俱樂部. *Nantong canguan zhinan* 南通參觀指南 (Guidebook to Nantong). Nantong, 1920.

————. *Nantong shiye, jiaoyu, cishan fengjing* 南通事業, 慈善, 風景 (The industrial, educational, and philanthropical landscape of Nantong). Shanghai: Shanghai shangwu yinshuguan, 1920.

Nanyang xiongdi yancao gufen youxian gongsi kuochong gaizu zhaogu zhangcheng 南洋兄弟煙草股份有限公司擴充改組招股章程 (Regulations of Nanyang Brothers' Tobacco, Inc., on expanding, changing its structure, and attracting investment). N.p., 1919.

Narusawa, Akira. "The Social Order of Modern Japan." In *The Political Economy of Japanese Society*, ed. Banno Junji, 1: 193–236. Oxford: Oxford University Press, 1997.

Neubauer, Fred, and Alden G. Lank. *The Family Business: Its Governance for Sustainability*. New York: Routledge, 1998.

Ngai, Pun. "Becoming *Daogongmei* (Working Girls): The Politics of Identity and Difference in Reform China." *China Journal*, no. 42 (July 1999): 1–18.

Nishizawa, Haruhiko. "An Immigrant Community in Northern Jiangsu: The Dafeng Land Reclamation Company and Farmers from Haimen County." In *Perspectives on Chinese Society: Anthropological Views from Japan*, ed. Suenari Michio et al., pp. 29–47. Canterbury: University of Kent at Canterbury, Centre for Social Anthropology and Computing, 1995.

North China Herald (Shanghai), 1918–26.

Nozawa Yutaka 野澤豐. "Chūgoku ni okeru kigyōshi kenkyū no tokushitsu" 中國における企業史研究の特質 (The characteristics of research on business history in China). In *Chūgoku kankei ronsetsu shiryō* 中國關係論説資料 13, no. 4 (1971): pt. B, pp. 405–31.

———. "Riben wenxian zhong de Zhang Jian he Nantong" 日本文獻中的張謇和南通 (Zhang Jian and Nantong in Japanese documents). In *Lun Zhang Jian: Zhang Jian guoji xueshu yantaohui lunwenji* 論張謇: 張謇國際學術研討會論文集 (Discussing Zhang Jian: collected essays from the international academic conference on Zhang Jian), ed. Nanjing daxue, Waiguo xuezhe liuxuesheng yanxiubu 南京大學外國學者留學生研修部, pp. 146–56. Nanjing: Jiangsu renmin chubanshe, 1993.

Oi, Jean C. *Rural China Takes Off: Institutional Foundations of Economic Reform*. Berkeley: University of California Press, 1999.

Oi, Jean C., and Andrew G. Walder, eds. *Property Rights and Economic Reform in China*. Stanford: Stanford University Press, 1999.

Otsuka, Keijiro et al. *Industrial Reform in China: Past Performance and Future Prospects*. Oxford: Clarendon Press, 1998.

Parker, A. P. *Mianbu chang* 棉布廠 (The cotton mill). Trans. Y. S. Loh (Lu Yongsheng). Shanghai: Oxford University Press, China Agency, 1916.

Patrick, John. *Factory Reform*. Houndmills, Eng.: Macmillan, 1987.

Pearse, Arno S. *The Cotton Industry of Japan and China*. Manchester, Eng.: International Federation of Master Cotton Spinners' & Manufacturers' Association, 1929.

Perry, Elizabeth J. "Putting Class in Its Place: Bases of Worker Identity in East Asia." In *Putting Class in Its Place: Worker Identities in East Asia*, ed. idem, pp. 1–10. Berkeley: University of California, Institute of East Asian Studies, 1996.

———. *Shanghai on Strike: The Politics of Chinese Labor*. Stanford: Stanford University Press, 1993.

Pollard, Sidney. *The Genesis of Modern Management: A Study of the Industrial Revolution in Great Britain*. London: Edward Arnold, 1965.

Pomeranz, Kenneth. *The Great Divergence: China, Europe, and the Making of the Modern World Economy*. Princeton: Princeton University Press, 2000.

————. *The Making of a Hinterland: State, Society, and Economy in Inland North China, 1853–1937*. Berkeley: University of California Press, 1993.

Porter, Robin. *Industrial Reformers in Republican China*. Armonk, N.Y.: M. E. Sharpe, 1994.

Qi Zhi 啓之. "Nantong pingmin shenghuo zhuangkuang" 南通平民生活狀況 (Living conditions of the ordinary people in Nantong). *Jiaoyu yu zhiye* 教育與職業, no. 72 (Feb. 1926): 117–22.

Qian Jiang 錢江 and Tang Keke 湯可可. "Jianlun Zhang Jian Nantong difang zizhi moshi yu Zhongguo jindaihua daolu" 簡論張謇南通地方自治模式與中國近代化道路 (Brief discussion of Zhang Jian's Nantong local self-government model and China's road to modernization). In *Zai lun Zhang Jian* 再論張謇 (On Zhang Jian), ed. Zhang Jian yanjiu zhongxin 張謇研究中心, pp. 55–66. Shanghai: Shanghai shehui kexueyuan chubanshe, 1995.

(Qianlong) Zhili Tongzhou zhi 乾隆直隸通州志 (Gazetteer of Tongzhou independent department, Qianlong period). 22 *juan* N.p., 1755.

Qiao Qiming 喬啓明. "Jiangsu Kunshan, Nantong, Anhui Suxian nongtian zhidu zhi bijao yi ji gailiang nongdian wenti zhi jianyi" 江蘇昆山, 南通, 安徽宿縣農田制度之比較以及改良農佃問題之建議 (Comparison between farming in Kunshan and Nantong, Jiangsu province, and Suxian, Anhui province, and suggestions for improving farmland). *Jinling daxue nonglin congkan* 金陵大學農林叢刊 49, no. 1931 (1926): 1–79.

Qiu Yunzhang 邱雲章 and Yao Lian 姚蓮. "Kenmu jishi" 墾牧記事 (Records of land reclamation). In *Chongchuan wenshi* 崇川文史 (Historical materials on Chongchuan), ed. Zhengxie Nantong shi Chongchuan qu weiyuanhui 政協南通市崇川區委員會, 1: 39–67. Nantong, 1992.

————. "Tonghai kenmu sishi nian" 通海墾牧四十年 (Forty years of land reclamation in Tongzhou and Haimen). In *Nantong yanken shimo* 南通鹽墾始末 (Land reclamation in Nantong from the beginning to the end), ed. Zhengxie Nantong shi wenshi ziliao bianjibu 政協南通市文史資料編輯部, pp. 49–96. Nantong: 1991.

Quan Hansheng 全漢昇. *Hanyeping gongsi shilüe* 漢冶萍公司史略 (Historical outline of the Hanyeping company). Taibei: wenhai chubanshe, 1982.

————. *Zhongguo jingjishi yanjiu* 中國經濟史研究 (Researches on Chinese economic history). 2 vols. Taibei: Xinya yanjiusuo, 1991.

Rankin, Mary Backus. *Elite Activism and Political Transformation in China: Zhejiang Province, 1865–1911*. Stanford: Stanford Univerity Press, 1986.

Rawski, Evelyn Sakakida. *Education and Popular Literacy in Ch'ing China*. Ann Arbor: University of Michigan Press, 1979.

Rawski, Thomas G. *Economic Growth in Prewar China*. Berkeley: University of California Press, 1989.

Rea's Far Eastern Manual (The Industrial Year Book of the Far East). N.p., 1924.

Redding, S. Gordon. "Weak Organizations and Strong Linkages: Managerial Ideology and Chinese Family Business Networks." In *Asian Business Networks*, ed. Gary G. Hamilton, pp. 27–42. Berlin and New York: Walter de Gruyter, 1996.

Reynolds, Douglas R. *China, 1898–1912: The Xinzheng Revolution and Japan*. Cambridge, Mass.: Harvard University, Council on East Asian Studies, 1993.

Rong Jingben 榮敬本 et al. *Liangxi Rong shi jiazu shi* 梁溪榮氏家族史 (Family history of the Rong family from Liangxi). Beijing: Zhongyang bianyi chubanshe, 1995.

Rose, Mary B. *Firms, Networks and Business Values: The British and American Cotton Industries Since 1750*. Cambridge, Eng.: Cambridge University Press, 2000.

Rowe, William T. *Hankow: Commerce and Society in a Chinese City, 1796–1889*. Stanford: Stanford University Press, 1984.

———. *Hankow: Conflict and Community in a Chinese City, 1796–1895*. Stanford: Stanford University Press, 1989.

———. "The Public Sphere in Modern China." *Modern China* 16, no. 3 (July 1990): 309–29.

Roy, William G. *Socializing Capital: The Rise of the Large Industrial Corporation in America*. Princeton: Princeton University Press, 1997.

Ruf, Gregory A. "Collective Enterprise and Property Rights in a Sichuan Village: The Rise and Decline of Managerial Corporatism." In *Property Rights and Economic Reform in China*, ed. Jean C. Oi and Andrew G. Walder, pp. 27–48. Stanford: Stanford University Press, 1999.

Ruppert, Wolfgang. *Die Fabrik: Geschichte von Arbeit und Industrialisierung in Deutschland*. Munich: C. H. Beck, 1983.

Sang Bing 桑兵. *Wan Qing xuetang xuesheng yu shehui bianqian* 晚清學堂學生與社會變遷 (Students in late Qing academies and social transformation). Shanghai: Xuelin chubanshe, 1995.

Santangelo, Paolo. "The Imperial Factories of Suzhou: Limits and Characteristics of State Intervention During the Ming and Qing Dynasties." In *The Scope of State Power in China*, ed. Stuart Schram, pp. 269–94. London: School of Oriental Studies; and Hong Kong: Chinese University Press, 1985.

Schoppa, R. Keith. *Chinese Elites and Political Change: Zhejiang Province in the Early Twentieth Century*. Cambridge, Mass.: Harvard University Press, 1982.

Se Weng 嗇翁 (Zhang Jian 張謇). "Zhang Jian duban Wusong shangbu zhi xuanyan" 張謇督辦吳淞商埠之宣言 (Declaration of Zhang Jian to supervise and manage the Wusong commercial port). *Nantong zazhi* 南通雜志, no. 3 (1921): 1–2.

Shanghai shehui kexueyuan. Jingji yanjiusuo 上海社會科學院經濟研究所. *Dalong jiqi chang de chansheng, fazhan he gaizao* 大隆機器廠的產生, 發展和

改造 (The establishment, development, and transformation of the Dalong Machine Works). Shanghai: Renmin chubanshe, 1980 (1958).

———. *Shanghai Yong'an gongsi de chansheng, fazhan he gaizao* 上海永安公司的產生, 發展和改造 (The establishment, development, and transformation of the Yong'an Company in Shanghai). Shanghai: Renmin chubanshe, 1981.

Shangwu yinshuguan bianyisuo 商務印書館編譯所. *Da Qing Guangxu xin faling* 大清光緒新法令 (New legal regulations of the Guangxu period in the Qing dynasty). 20 *ce*. Shanghai: Shangwu yinshuguan, 1909.

———. *Zhongguo lüxing zhinan* 中國旅行指南 (China travel guide). Shanghai: Shangwu yinshuguan, 1926 (1911).

Shanxi sheng zhengxie wenshi ziliao weiyuanhui 陝西省政協文史資料委員會. *Baoji Shenxin fangzhichang shi* 實雞申新紡織廠史 (History of the Shenxin Textile Mill in Baoji). (Xi'an): Shaanxi Renmin chubanshe, 1992.

Shao, Qin. "Making Political Culture: The Case of Nantong, 1894–1930." Ph.D. diss., Michigan State University, 1994.

———. "Space, Time and Politics in Early Twentieth Century Nantong." *Modern China* 23, no. 1 (Jan. 1997): 99–129.

———. "Tempest Over Teapots: The Vilification of Teahouse Culture in Early Republican China." *Journal of Asian Studies* 57, no. 4 (1998): 1009–41.

Shao Xunzheng 紹循征. "Guanyu yangwupai minyong qiye de xingzhi he daolu: lun guanliao shangban" 關於洋務派民用企業的性質和道路: 論官僚商辦 (The characteristics and ways of civil enterprises founded by the Self-Strengthening Movement: officialdom and merchant management). In *Shao Xunzheng lishi lunwenji* 紹循征歷史論文集 (Collection of Shao Xunzheng's historical essays), ed. Li Kezhen 李課眞, pp. 349–71. Beijing: Beijing daxue chubanshe, 1985.

———. "Yangwu yundong he Zhongguo zichan jieji fazhan de guanxi wenti: cong muji shangren zijin dao guanliao siren qiye" 洋務運動和中國資產階級發展的關係問題: 從募集商人資金到官僚私人企業 (Problems related to the Self-Strengthening Movement and the development of China's bourgeoisie: from raising merchant capital to officialdom and private enterprises). In *Shao Xunzheng lishi lunwenji* 紹循征歷史論文集 (Collection of Shao Xunzheng's historical essays), ed. Li Kezhen 李課眞, pp. 301–22. Beijing: Beijing daxue chubanshe, 1985.

Shen Binyi 沈賓義. "Zhuangzhi hui hongtu-rexue jian gutu" 狀志繪宏圖熱血薦古土 (With strong aspirations design a great plan, with righteous ardor present it to the native land). *Nantong ribao* 南通日報, Nov. 3, 1994.

Shen Shu 沈叔. "Zhangfang xiansheng" 帳房先生 (Mr. Accounts Office). In *Sanbai liushi hang daguan* 三百六十行大觀 (Grand view of 360 trades), ed. idem, p. 227. Shanghai: Shanghai huabao chubanshe, 1997.

Shen Xianrong 沈顯榮. "Jiefang qian Rugao liren jiaoyuju (ke) zhang ji qi huodong qingkuang gaishu" 解放前如皋歷任教育局(科)長及其活動情況概述 (General description of the head of the Education Department in Rugao and his activities before the liberation). In *Rugao wenshi ziliao* 如皋文史資料 (Rugao historical materials), ed. Zhengxie Rugao xian weiyuanhui 政協如皋縣委員會, 2: 31–44. Rugao, 1986.

———. "Ji Jingjiang xiaoxue" 紀京江小學 (Remembering the Jingjiang Primary School). In *Rugao wenshi ziliao* 如皋文史資料 (Rugao historical materials), ed. Zhengxie Rugao xian weiyuanhui 政協如皋縣委員會, 4: 33–38. Rugao, 1989.

Shenbao 申報.

Shengjing bao 盛京報.

Sheridan, James E. *China in Disintegration: The Republican Era in Chinese History, 1912–1949*. New York: Free Press, 1975.

Shi Ya 施亞. *Lidai fangzhi shi jiexi* 歷代紡織詩解析 (Analysis of poetry related to textiles in history). Nantong, 1991.

Shih, Kuo-heng. *China Enters the Machine Age: A Study of Labor in Chinese War Industry*. Cambridge, Mass.: Harvard University Press, 1944.

Shih, Min-hsiung. *The Silk Industry in Ch'ing China*. Trans. E-tu Zen Sun. Ann Arbor: University of Michigan, Center for Chinese Studies, 1976.

Shiyebu. Guoji maoyiju 事業部國際貿易局. *Zhongguo shiyezhi (Jiangsu sheng)* 中國事業志江蘇省 (Industrial Handbook for China: Jiangsu). Shanghai: Shiyebu, Guoji maoyiju, 1933.

Shu Zhe 束哲. *Tong Yang shi shu jiangyu tushuo* 通揚十屬疆域圖説 (Maps and descriptions of ten regions belonging to Tongzhou and Yangzhou). N.p., n.d. (ca. 1905?).

Shuang Mu 霜穆. "Zhang Jian guoji xueshu taolunhui zai Nanjing juxing" 張謇國際學術討論會在南京舉行 (An international academic conference on Zhang Jian held in Nanjing). In *Zhongguo jindai jingji shi yanjiu ziliao* 中國近代經濟史研究資料 (Research materials on modern Chinese economic history), ed. Zhongguo jindai congshu bianweihui 中國近代叢書編委會, 9: 143–49. Shanghai: Shanghai shehui kexueyuan chubanshe, 1989.

Sit, Victor F. S. "Geography and Natural Resources." In *Shanghai and the Yangzi Delta: A City Reborn*, ed. Brian Hook, pp. 74–118. Hong Kong and Oxford: Oxford University Press, 1998.

Skinner, G. William. "Cities and the Hierarchy of Local Systems." In *The City in Late Imperial China*, ed. idem, pp. 275–351. Stanford: Stanford University Press, 1977.

———. "Marketing and Social Structure in Rural China, Part 1." *Journal of Asian Studies* 24, no. 1 (1964): 3–43.

Slack, Edward R., Jr. "The National Anti-Opium Association and the Guomindang State, 1924–1937." In *Opium Regimes: China, Britain, and Japan, 1839–1952*, ed. Timothy Brook and Bob Tadashi Wakabayashi, pp. 248–69. Berkeley: University of California Press, 2000.

————. *Opium, State, and Society: China's Narco-Economy and the Guomindang, 1924–37.* Honolulu: University of Hawai'i Press, 2001.

Smith, Thomas C. "Peasant Time and Factory Time in Japan." In *Native Sources of Japanese Industrialization, 1750–1920*, ed. Thomas C. Smith, pp. 199–235. Berkeley: University of California Press, 1988.

————. *Political Change and Industrial Development in Japan: Government Enterprises, 1868–1880.* Stanford: Stanford University Press, 1968 (1955).

Song Taowu 宋桃吾 et al. "Ru cheng jiefang qian 'wu yang, yan jiu' mingdian jilüe" 如城解放前五洋, 煙酒名店記略 (Remembering famous shops for 'foreign goods, tobacco, and wine' in Rugao city before the liberation). In *Rugao wenshi ziliao* 如皋文史資料 (Rugao historical materials), ed. Zhengxie Rugao xian weiyuanhui 政協如皋縣委員會, 8: 50–58. Rugao, 1994.

Song Xue 松雪. *Jinshi banben "Qing shanhu"* 近事版本青珊瑚 (Present-day edition of the play *The Green Coral*). Hong Kong: Xianggang gonghebao, 1919.

Stapleton, Kristin. *Civilizing Chengdu: Chinese Urban Reform, 1895–1937.* Cambridge, Mass: Harvard University Asia Center, 2000.

Steinfeld, Edward S. *Forging Reform in China: The Fate of State-Owned Industry.* Cambridge, Eng.: Cambridge University Press, 1998.

Strand, David. *Rickshaw Beijing: City People and Politics in the 1920s.* Berkeley: University of California Press, 1989.

Sun Jiashan 孫家山. *Subei yanken shi chugao* 蘇北鹽墾史初稿 (First draft of the history of land reclamation in Subei). Beijing: Nongmin chubanshe, 1984.

Swedberg, Richard. *Max Weber and the Idea of Economic Sociology.* Princeton: Princeton University Press, 1998.

Taira, Koji. "Factory Labour and the Industrial Revolution in Japan." In *The Economic Emergence of Modern Japan*, ed. Kozo Yamamura, pp. 239–93. Cambridge, Eng.: Cambridge University Press, 1997.

Tang Keke 湯可可 and Qian Jiang 錢江. "Dasheng shachang de zichan, yingli he lirun fenpei" 大生紗廠的資產, 盈利和利潤分配 (The assets, surplus, and profit distribution in the Dasheng cotton mill). *Zhongguo jingjishi yanjiu* 中國經濟史研究 1997, no. 1: 25–37.

Tao Shuimu 陶水木. *Zhejiang shangbang yu Shanghai jingji jindaihua yanjiu, 1840–1936* 浙江商幫與上海經濟近代化研究 (Research on Zhejiang's merchant groups and Shanghai's economic modernization, 1840–1936). Shanghai: Sanlian shudian, 2000.

Tayler, J. B. *Farm and Factory in China: Aspects of the Industrial Revolution*. London: Student Christian Movement, 1928.

Thompson, E. P. *The Making of the English Working Class*. Harmondsworth, Eng.: Penguin, 1991 (1963).

———. "Time, Work-Discipline, and Industrial Capitalism." *Past & Present*, no. 38 (Dec. 1967): 56–97.

Thompson, Roger R. *China's Local Councils in the Age of Constitutional Reform, 1898–1911*. Cambridge, Mass.: Harvard University Press, Council on East Asian Studies, 1995.

Tōa dōbunkai 東亞同文會. *Chūgoku shōbetsu zenshi* 中國省別全志 (Complete record of China divided by province). Tokyo: Tōa dōbunkai, 1920.

———. *Zhongguo jingji quanshu* 中國經濟全書 (Complete book on China's economy). Trans. Liu Zupei. (Tokyo): Keizai gakkai, 1910.

Tomizawa Yoshio 富澤芳亞. "Ginkōdan sekkanki no Taishō dai'ichi bōshoku kaisha" 銀行團接管期の大生第一紡織會社 (The Dasheng No. 1 Textile Company under the bank consortium's management). *Shigaku kenkyū* 史學研究, no. 204 (June 1994): 67–94.

Tong Chong Hai Tai zong shanghui caiwu baogao 通崇海泰總商會財務報告 (Financial report of the General Chamber of Commerce for Tongzhou, Chongming, Haimen and Taizhou). N.p. (Nantong?): 1930.

Tonghai kenmu gongsi disici gudong huiyi'an 通海墾牧公司第四次股東會議案 (Record of the fourth shareholders' meeting of the Tonghai Land Reclamation Company). N.p., 1918.

Tonghai kenmu gongsi zhaodian zhangcheng 通海墾牧公司招佃章程 (Regulations of the Tonghai Land Reclamation Company on attracting tenants). In *Zhang Jian cungao* 張謇存稿 (Surviving documents of Zhang Jian), ed. Yang Liqiang 楊立強 et al., pp. 555–59. Shanghai: Shanghai Renmin chubanshe, 1987.

Tonghai xinbao 通海新報 (Tongzhou and Haimen news). 1915–28.

Tonghai yanken gongsi linshi gudong huiyi'an 通海鹽墾公司臨時股東會議案 (Record of the provisional shareholders' meeting of the Tonghai Land Reclamation Company). N.p., 1933.

Tong Ru Hai mianye gonghui mianye nianbao 通如海棉業公會棉業年報 (Annual report on the cotton trade of the Cotton Trade Association of Tongzhou, Rugao, and Haimen). Nantong, 1923.

Tongzhou lishi jiaoke shu 通州歷史教科書 (Tongzhou history textbook). N.p. (Tongzhou?): 1904.

Tongzhou xingban shiye zhangcheng 通州興辦事業章程 (Regulations for establishing industrial enterprises in Tongzhou). N.p. (Nantong?), 1910.

Tongzhou xin yuwatang zhangcheng 通州新育娃堂章程 (Regulations for the new Tongzhou orphanage). Nantong, 1911.

Tongzhou Zhang shi jiapu 通州張氏家譜 (Genealogy of the Zhang family of Tong-zhou). N.p., 1903.

Tongzhou zhili zhou zhi 通州直隸州志 (Gazetteer of Tongzhou independent de-partment). *16 juan.* N.p.: 1875.

Tsin, Michael. *Nation, Governance, and Modernity in China: Canton, 1900–1927.* Stan-ford: Stanford University Press, 1999.

Tsukase Susumu 冢瀬進. "Chūgoku Tōhoku menseihin shijō o meguru Nitchū kankei, 1907–1931" 中國東北綿製品をめぐる日中關係 (Japanese-Chinese relations with regard to the cotton goods market in Northeast China, 1907–1931). *Jinbun ken kiyō* 人文研記要 (Chūō University), 11 (1990): 111–51.

Tsutsui, William M. *Manufacturing Ideology: Scientific Management in Twentieth-Century Japan.* Princeton: Princeton University Press, 1998.

TXSZ, see *Tongzhou xingban shiye zhangcheng*

Wakeman, Frederic, Jr. "The Civil Society and Public Sphere Debate." *Modern China* 19, no. 2 (Apr. 1993): 108–38.

———. "Civil Society in Late Imperial and Modern China." In *China's Quest for Modernization: A Historical Perspective,* ed. idem and Wang Xi, pp. 325–51. Berke-ley: University of California, Institute of East Asian Studies, 1997.

———. *Policing Shanghai, 1927–1937.* Berkeley: University of California Press, 1995.

Walder, Andrew G. " The County Government as an Industrial Corporation." In *Zouping in Transition: The Process of Reform in Rural North China,* ed. Andrew G. Walder, pp. 62–85. Cambridge, Mass.: Harvard University Press, 1998.

Walder, Andrew G., and Jean C. Oi. "Property Rights in the Chinese Economy: Contours of the Process of Change." In *Property Rights and Economic Reform in China,* ed. Jean C. Oi and Andrew G. Walder, pp. 1–24. Stanford: Stanford Uni-versity Press, 1999.

Walker, Kathy Le Mons. *Chinese Modernity and the Peasant Path: Semicolonialism in the Northern Yangzi Delta.* Stanford: Stanford University Press, 1999.

Wan Guoding 萬國鼎 et al. *Jiangsu Wujin, Nantong tianfu diaocha baogao* 江蘇武進南通田賦調查報告 (Survey of land taxation in Wujin and Nantong in Jiangsu). N.p.: 1934. Reprinted as *Minguo shiliao congkan* 民國史料叢刊 (Collec-tion of materials on the Republican period), vol. 14. Taibei: Zhuanji wenxue chubanshe, 1971.

Wang, Chia-chien. "Li Hung-chang and the Peiyang Navy." In *Li Hung-Chang and China's Early Modernization,* ed. Samuel C. Chu and Kwang-Ching Liu, pp. 248–62. Armonk, N.Y.: M. E. Sharpe, 1994.

Wang Ermin 王爾敏. *Wan Qing zhengzhi sixiangshi lun* 晚清政治思想史論 (Dis-cussion of late Qing political thought). Taibei: Taibei shangwu yinshuguan, 1995.

———. *Zhongguo jindai sixiangshi lun* 中國近代思想史論 (Discussion of China's modern intellectual history). Taibei, 1977.

Wang Jingyu 汪敬虞, ed. *Zhongguo jindai gongyeshi zilao* 中國近代工業史資料 (Materials on China's modern industrial history). 2 vols. Beijing: Kexue chubanshe, 1957.

Wang Minzhi 王敏之. "Huainian dang de zhiyou Chen Shiyun nüshi" 懷念黨的 摯友陳石雲女士 (Cherishing the memory of party supporter Mrs. Chen Shiyun). In *Nantong wenshi ziliao xuanji* 南通文史資料選集 (Collection of Nantong historical materials), ed. Zhengxie Nantong shi wenshi ziliao bianjibu 政協 南通市文史資料編輯部, 14: 99–103. Nantong: 1995.

———. "Huiyi Tangzha he Tianshenggang jiefang" 回憶唐閘和天生港解放 (Remembering the liberation of Tangzha and Tianshenggang). In *Nantong wenshi ziliao* 南通文史資料 (Nantong historical materials), ed. Nantong shi weiyuanhui, Wenshi ziliao yanjiu weiyuanhui 南通市委員會文史資料研究委 員會, 9: 41–46. Nantong: 1989.

Wang Shuhuai 王樹槐. "Jiangsu Huainan yanken gongsi de kenzhi shiye, 1901– 1937" 江蘇淮南鹽墾公司的墾殖事業 (Cultivation under land-reclamation companies in Jiangsu and Huainan, 1901–1937). *Zhongyang yanjiuyuan, Jindaishi yanjiusuo jikan* 中央研究院近代史研究所集刊 14 (1985): 191–266.

Wang Xiaohua 王曉華. *Beiyang xiaojiang Sun Chuanfang* 北洋小將孫傳芳 (The fierce and ambitious Beiyang general Sun Chuanfang). Shanghai: Shanghai renmin chubanshe, 2000.

Wang Yejian 王業鍵. "Chuantong yu jindai Zhongguo jingji fazhan" 傳統與近代 中國經濟發展 (Economic development in traditional and modern China). *Si yu yan* 思與言 15, no. 5 (1978): 289–95.

Wang Zeren 汪澤人. "Nantong tubu de jingying he fazhan" 南通土布的經營和 發展 (Production and development of Nantong's local handwoven cotton cloth). In *Nantong jiefang jishi* 南通解放記事 (Record of the liberation of Nantong), ed. Nantong shi wenshi ziliao bianjibu 南通市文史資料編輯部, 9: 183–90. Nantong, 1989.

Watanabe Atsushi 渡邊恆. "Zhang Jian de yanye jingying yu yanzheng gaige yundong" 張謇的鹽業經營與鹽政改革運動 (Zhang Jian's salt business and the movement for reforms in the salt administration). In *Lun Zhang Jian: Zhang Jian guoji xueshu yantaohui lunwenji* 論張謇: 張謇國際學術研討會論文集 (Discussing Zhang Jian: collected essays from the international academic conference on Zhang Jian), ed. Nanjing daxue, Waiguo xuezhe liuxuesheng yanxiubu 南京 大學外國學者留學生研修部, pp. 474–87. Nanjing: Jiangsu renmin chubanshe, 1993.

Watson, Ernest. *The Principal Articles of Chinese Commerce (Import and Export)*. Shanghai: Inspectorate General of Customs, Statistical Department, 1930.

Weber, Max. *Economy and Society (An Outline of Interpretive Sociology)*. 2 vols. Berkeley: University of California Press, 1978.

Wenfeng sezhi 文峰色織 (Wenfeng color weaving). Company newspaper.

Who's Who in China. 2nd ed., 1920; 3rd ed., 1925. Shanghai: Millard's Review, 1925. Reprinted—Hong Kong: Chinese Materials Center, 1982.

Winpenny, Thomas R. *Industrial Progress and Human Welfare: The Rise of the Factory System in 19th Century Lancaster.* Lanham, Md.: University Press of America, 1982.

Wong, John, et al. *China's Rural Entrepreneurs: Ten Case Studies.* Singapore: Times Academic Press, 1995.

Wong, R. Bin. *China Transformed: Historical Change and the Limits of European Experience.* Ithaca, N.Y.: Cornell University Press, 1997.

Wong, Siu-lun. "Chinese Enterpreneurs and Business Trust." In *Business Networks and Economic Development in East and Southeast Asia,* ed. Gary G. Hamilton, pp. 13–29. Hong Kong: University of Hong Kong, Centre of Asian Studies, 1991.

———. "The Chinese Family Firm: A Model." *British Journal of Sociology* 36, no. 1 (Mar. 1985): 58–72.

Wright, Mary Clabaugh. *The Last Stand of Chinese Conservatism: The T'ung-chih Restoration, 1862–1874.* Stanford: Stanford University Press, 1957.

Wright, Tim. "'A Method of Evading Management': Contract Labor in Chinese Coal Mines Before 1937." *Comparative Studies in History and Society* 23, no. 4 (1981): 656–78.

———. "'The Spiritual Heritage of Chinese Capitalism': Recent Trends in the Historiography of Chinese Enterprise Management." In *Using the Past to Serve the Present: Historiography and Politics in Contemporary China,* ed. Jonathan Unger, pp. 205–38. Armonk, N.Y.: M. E. Sharpe, 1993.

Wu Chengming 吳承明 and Xu Dixin 許滌新. *Zhongguo zibenzhuyi fazhan shi* 中國資本主義發展史, vol. 1, *Zhongguo zibenzhuyi de mengya* 中國資本主義的萌芽 (A history of the development of Chinese capitalism: sprouts of Chinese capitalism). Beijing: Renmin chubanshe, 1985.

Wu Yiye 伍貽業. "Zhang Jian yu Nantong 'jindaihua' moshi" 張謇與南通近代化模式 (Zhang Jian and Nantong's "modernization" model). *Lishi yanjiu* 歷史研究 1989, no. 2: 53–67.

Wuhan shi gongshang lianhehui 武漢市工商聯合會. *Yekaitai lishi ziliao* 葉開泰歷史資料 (Material on the history of Yekaitai). *Chugao* 初稿 (first draft). (Wuhan), 1965.

Xiao Zheng 蕭錚, ed. *Minguo ershi nian dai Zhongguo dalu tudi wenti ziliao* 民國二十年代中國大陸土地問題資料 (Materials on land problems on the Chinese mainland during the 1930s). Reprinted—Taibei: Chengwen chubanshe, 1977.

Xiao Zhengde 肖正德. "Dasheng dang'an he Zhang Jian" 大生檔案和張謇 (Dasheng's archives and Zhang Jian). In *Lun Zhang Jian: Zhang Jian guoji xueshu yantaohui lunwenji* 論張謇: 張謇國際學術研討會論文集 (Discussing Zhang Jian: collected essays from the international academic conference on Zhang Jian), ed. Nanjing daxue, Waiguo xuezhe liuxuesheng yanxiubu 南京大學外國學者留學生研修部, pp. 628–35. Nanjing: Jiangsu renmin chubanshe, 1993.

Xie Zhenmin 謝振民. *Zhongguo Minguo lifashi* 中國民國立法史 (History of the legislation in Republican China). Nanjing: Zhengzhong shuju, 1937.

Xing Ren 行人 (pseudonym of Wang Xingren 王行人). *Jindai shiye de kaishan bizu* 近代實業的開山鼻祖 (The origins of modern industry). Shijiazhuang: Hebei Renmin chubanshe, 1995.

Xiong Yuezhi 熊月之. *Xixue dongzhe yu wan Qing shehui* 西學東漸與晚清社會 (The dissemination of Western learning and late Qing society). Shanghai: Shanghai renmin chubanshe, 1994.

Xiong Yuezhi 熊月之 et al. *Lao Shanghai mingren, mingshi, mingwu daguan* 老上海名人, 名事, 名物大觀 (The grand sight of famous people, incidents, and things in old Shanghai). Shanghai: Shanghai renmin chubanshe, 1997.

Xu Dingxin 徐鼎新 and Qian Xiaoming 錢小明. *Shanghai zongshanghui shi* 上海總商會史 (History of the Shanghai General Chamber of Commerce). Shanghai: Shanghai shehui kexueyuan chubanshe, 1992.

Xu Mao 徐矛. *Zhongguo shi maiban* 中國十買辦 (Ten Chinese compradors). Shanghai: Shanghai renmin chubanshe, 1996.

Xu Weiyong 許維雍 and Huang Hanmin 黃漢民. *Rongjia qiye fazhan shi* 榮家企業發展史 (History of the development of the Rong family's enterprises). (Beijing): Renmin chubanshe, 1985.

Xu Xinwu 徐新吾, ed. *Jiangnan tubu shi* 江南土布史 (History of handwoven cotton cloth in Jiangnan). Shanghai: Shanghai shehui kexueyuan chubanshe, 1992.

Xu Xinwu 徐新吾 and Huang Hanmin 黃漢民. *Shanghai jindai gongyeshi* 上海近代工業史 (Shanghai's modern industrial history). Shanghai: Shanghai shehui kexueyuan chubanshe, 1998.

Xu Yongzuo 徐永佐. "Gailiang Zhongguo kuaiji wenti" 改良中國會計問題 (Improving Chinese accounting). In *Zhongguo jingji wenti* 中國經濟問題 (China's economic problems), ed. Zhongguo jingji xueshe 中國經濟學社, pp. 213–30. Shanghai: 1932.

Xue Mingjian 薛明劍. *Gongchang sheji ji guanli* 工廠設計及管理 (Factory design and management). Shanghai: Huaxin shushe, 1927.

Yan Jinfeng 嚴金風. "Ningbo huiguan" 寧波會館 (Ningbo native place association) and "Guangdong huiguan" 廣東會館 (Guangdong native place association). *Nantong jingu* 南通今古 1991, no. 6: 28–29.

Yan Xuexi 嚴學熙. "Zhang Jian yu Huainan yanken gongsi" 張謇與淮南鹽墾公司 (Zhang Jian and the Huainan land reclamation companies). *Lishi yanjiu* 歷史研究 1988, no. 3, pp. 84–97.

Yan Xuexi 嚴學熙 and Qian Liaoxing 錢聊興. "Xue Nanming, Xue Shouxuan" 薛南溟, 薛壽宣 (Xue Nanming and Xue Shouxuan). In *Zhongguo jindai qiye de kaituozhe* 中國近代企業的開拓者 (Initiators of modern Chinese enterprises), ed. Kong Lingren 孔令仁 et al., 2: 597–609. Ji'nan: Shandong renmin chubanshe, 1991.

Yan Yongxiang 嚴永祥 and Ding Bangjing 丁邦敬. "Rijun qinzhan Dingyanzhen yu Fengshixiang renmin de kang Ri douzheng" 日軍侵佔丁堰鎮與馮石鄉人民的抗日鬥爭 (The anti-Japanese struggle of people in the town of Dingyan and the village of Fengshi during the Japanese occupation). In *Rugao wenshi ziliao* 如皋文史資料 (Materials on the history of Rugao), ed. Zhongguo renmin zhengzhi xieshang huiyi, Jiangsu sheng Rugao xian weiyuanhui 中國人民政治協商會議江蘇省如皋縣委員會, 3: 66–84. Rugao, 1987.

Yan Zhongping 嚴中平. *Zhongguo mian fangzhi shigao* 中國棉紡織史稿 (Draft history of Chinese cotton spinning and weaving). Beijing: Kexue chubanshe, 1963 (1955).

Yang, Dali. "Reform and the Restructuring of Central-Local Relations." In *China Deconstructs: Politics, Trade and Regionalism*, ed. David S. G. Goodman and Gerald Segal, pp. 59–98. London and New York: Routledge, 1994.

Yang Gusen 楊谷森. "Kenmu qian shao shuairong shi: Haifuzhen shilu" 墾牧前哨衰榮史:海復鎮實錄 (The history of failure and success in land reclamation: the records of Haifuzhen village). In *Nantong mingzhen fengjinglu* 南通名鎮風景錄 (Record of the scenery of famous villages in Nantong), ed. Nantong shi zhengxie wenshi bianjibu 南通市政協文史編輯部. Nantong: Jia'en chubanshe, 1993.

Yang Liqiang 楊立強 et al., eds. *Zhang Jian cungao* 張謇存稿 (Surviving documents of Zhang Jian). Shanghai: Shanghai renmin chubanshe, 1987.

Ye Xuyuan 葉胥原. "Xing ken shi nian" 行墾十年 (Ten years of land reclamation). In *Nantong yanken shimo* 南通鹽墾始末 (Land reclamation in Nantong from beginning to end), ed. Zhengxie Nantong shi wenshi ziliao bianjibu 政協南通市文史編輯部, pp. 41–48. Nantong, 1991

Yeh, Wen-hsin. "Republican Origins of the *Danwei*: The Case of Shanghai's Bank of China." In *Danwei: The Changing Chinese Workplace in Historical and Comparative Perspective*, ed. Xiaobo Lü and Elizabeth J. Perry, pp. 60–88. New York: M. E. Sharpe, 1997.

Yin Weihe 殷惟和. *Jiangsu liushiyi xian zhi* 江蘇六十一縣志 (Gazetteer for the 61 counties of Jiangsu). Shanghai: Shangwu yinshuguan, 1935.

Yingyin chuangban Dasheng shachang binggao ji zhaogu zhangcheng yuanben 影印創辦大生紗廠稟稿暨招股章程原本 (Original document of the draft for the establishment of the business of the Dasheng mill and the regulations for raising funds). N.p., 1895.

Young, Susan. "Ownership and Community Interests in China's Rural Enterprises." In *Reconstructing Twentieth-Century China: State Control, Civil Society, and National*

Identity, ed. Kjeld Erik Brodsgaard and David Strand, pp. 113–36. Oxford: Clarendon Press, 1998.

Yu Chi 于赤. "Rugao rou lianchang jianshi" 如皋肉聯廠簡史 (A brief history of the Rugao meat factories). In *Rugao wenshi ziliao* 如皋文史資料 (Rugao historical materials), ed. Zhongguo renmin zhengzhi xieshang huiyi, Jiangsu sheng Rugao xian weiyuanhui 中國人民政治協商會議江蘇省如皋縣委員會, 2: 98–104. Rugao, 1986.

Yu Xutang 余續堂. "Lang Shan qi fang shimo" 狼山七房始末 (The seven mansions on Wolf Hill from beginning to end). In *Chongchuan wenshi* 崇川文史 (Historical materials on Chongchuan), ed. Zhengxie Nantong shi Chongchuan qu weiyuanhui 政協南通市崇川區委員會, pp. 174–81. Nantong, 1992.

———. "Nantong de miaochan xingxue he sengban jiaoyu" 南通的廟產興學和僧辦教育 (The promotion of learning through Nantong's temples and monastic education). In *Chongchuan wenshi* 崇川文史 Historical materials on Chongchuan), ed. Zhengxie Nantong shi Chongchuan qu weiyuanhui 政協南通市崇川區委員會, pp. 137–42. Nantong: 1992.

Yuzhong Dayoujin yanken gongsi wuwu nian diliu jie zhanglüe 餘中大有晉鹽墾公司戊午年第六屆帳略 (Sixth financial statement of the Dayoujin Land Reclamation Company at Yuzhong). N.p., 1918.

"Zhang Cha" 張察. *Zhuanji wenxue* 傳記文學 42, no. 4 (1983): 138–40.

Zhang, Guohui 張國輝. "The Emergence and Development of China's Modern Capitalist Enterprises." In *China's Quest for Modernization: A Historical Perspective*, ed. Frederic Wakeman, Jr., and Wang Xi, pp. 234–49. Berkeley: University of California, Institute of East Asian Studies, 1997.

———. "Lun Kaiping, Luanzhou meikuang de chuangjian, fazhan he lishi jieju" 論開平，灤州煤礦的創建，發展和歷史結局 (Discussion of the establishment, development, and historical outcome of the Kaiping and Luanzhou mines). In *Jindai Zhongguo* 近代中國, ed. Ding Richu 丁日出, 3: 54–76. Shanghai: Shanghai shehui kexueyuan chubanshe, 1993.

Zhang Guorui 張國瑞 and Wang Guofan 汪國番. "Wang Xianglun yu Dada lunbu gongsi" 汪湘綸與大達輪步公司 (Wang Xianglun and the Dada Steamship Company). In *Nantong wenshi ziliao xuanji* 南通文史資料選集 (Selected historical materials on Nantong), ed. Nantong shi weiyuanhui, Wenshi ziliao yanjiu weiyuanhui 南通市委員會文史資料研究委員會, 7: 143–50. Nantong, 1987.

Zhang Huiqun 張惠群. "Yanken quyu zudian zhidu zhi yanjiu" 鹽墾區域租佃制之研究 (Research on the tenant system in the reclamation area). In *Minguo ershi niandai Zhongguo dalu tudi wenti ziliao* 民國二十年代中國大陸土地問題資料 (Materials on land problems on the Chinese mainland during the 1930s), ed. Xiao Zheng 蕭錚, 61: 31785–952. Reprinted—Taibei: Chengwen chubanshe, 1977.

Zhang Jian 張謇. *Hui shi juan* 會試卷 (Paper for the metropolitan examination). N.p., n.d. (ca. 1895–96).

————. *Nantong Zhang shi Changle zhipu* 南通張氏常樂支譜 (Genealogy of the Changle branch of the Zhang family in Nantong). 1921.

————. *Riji* 日記 (Diary). In *Zhang Jian quanji* 張謇全集 (Complete works of Zhang Jian), ed. Zhang Jian yanjiu zhongxin 張謇研究中心 and Nantong shi tushuguan 南通市圖書館, vol. 6. Nanjing: Jiangsu guji chubanshe, 1994.

————. *Yanken gongsi shuili guihua tonggao gudong shu* 鹽墾公司水例規劃通告股東書 (Report to shareholders on the irrigation plans of the land-reclamation companies). N.p., 1923.

————. *Zhang Jizi jiulu* 張季子九錄 (The nine records of Zhang Jizhi). Ed. Zhang Xiaoruo 張孝若. 7 vols. 1931. Reprinted—Taibei: Wenhai chubanshe, 1980.

————. *Zhang Se'an (Jian) xiansheng shiye wenchao* 張嗇俺先生實業文鈔 (Mister Zhang Jian's writings on industrial enterprises). Ed. Cao Wenlin 曹文麟. Taibei: Wenhai chubanshe, 1980 (1948).

————. *Zhang Se'an xiansheng jiulu lu* 張嗇俺先生九錄錄 (Abstract of the nine records of Zhang Jizhi). Ed. Gu Gongyi 顧公毅 10 *juan*. Nantong: Hanmolin yinshuju, 1947.

Zhang Jian cungao, see Yang Liqiang et al.

Zhang Jian quanji, see Zhang Jian yanjiu zhongxin and Nantong tushuguan

Zhang Jian wei Tong Tai ge yanken gongsi muji zijin zhi shuomingshu 張謇爲通泰各鹽墾公司募集資金之説明書 (Explanation by Zhang Jian on the raising of funds for all land-reclamation companies in Tongzhou and Taizhou). N.p., n.d. (1924?).

Zhang Jian yanjiu zhongxin 張謇研究中心 and Nantong shi tushuguan 南通市圖書館, eds. *Zhang Jian quanji* 張謇全集 (Complete works of Zhang Jian). 7 vols. Nanjing: Jiangsu guji chubanshe, 1994.

Zhang Jingli 張敬禮. "Nantong Dasheng fangzhi gongsi de bianqian" 南通大生紡織公司的變遷 (The transformation of the Dasheng No. 1 Textile Company in Nantong). In *Nantong jiefang jishi* (Record of the liberation of Nantong) 南通解放紀實, ed. Nantong shi wenshi ziliao bianjibu 南通市文史資料編輯部, 9: 26–31. Nantong: 1989.

Zhang Jizhi xiansheng shiyeshi biancunchu 張季直先生實業史編存處, ed. *Dasheng fangzhi gongsi nianjian, 1895–1947* 大生紡織公司年鑒 (Yearbook of the Dasheng textile companies, 1895–1947). Nanjing: Jiangsu renmin chubanshe, 1998.

Zhang Kaiyuan 張開沅. *Kaituozhe de zuji—Zhang Jian zhuan'gao* 開拓者的足跡—張謇傳稿 (Footprints of the innovator—biography of Zhang Jian). Beijing: Zhonghua shuju, 1986.

———. "Nantong moshi' yu quyu shehui jingjishi yanjiu" 南通模式與區域社會經濟史研究 (The "Nantong model" and research on regional socioeconomic history). *Guangdong shehui kexue* 廣東社會科學 1988, vol. 15, no. 1, pp. 128–130.

———. "Zhang Jian" 張謇. In *Zhongguo jindai qiye de kaituozhe* 中國近代企業的開拓者 (Initiators of China's modern enterprises), ed. Kong Lingren 孔令仁 et al., 1: 470–85. Ji'nan: Shandong renmin chubanshe, 1991.

Zhang Kaiyuan 張開沅 and Tian Tong 田彤. *Zhang Jian yu jindai shehui* 張謇與近代社會 (Zhang Jian and modern society). Wuhan: Huazhong shifan daxue chubanshe, 2001.

Zhang Liluan 張儷鸞. "Jiangsu Wujin wujia zhi yanjiu" 江蘇武進物價之研究 (Research on prices in Wujin, Jiangsu"). *Jinling xuebao* 金陵學報 3, no. 1 (May 1933): 158–216.

Zhang Rouwu 張柔武. "Huiyi wo de fuqin Zhang Xiaoruo" 回憶我的父親張孝若 (Remembering my father, Zhang Xiaoruo). In *Nantong wenshi ziliao xuanji* 南通文史資料選集 (Collected historical materials on Nantong), ed. Zhengxie Nantong shi wenshi bianjibu 政協南通市文史編輯部, 14: 104–7. Nantong, 1995.

Zhang shi zongpu 張氏宗譜 (Genealogy of the Zhang family). 1899.

Zhang Xiaoruo 張孝若. *Shixue ji* 史學集 (Collection of the learning of a scholar). N.p., n.d. (1919?).

"Zhang Xiaoruo" 張孝若. In *Zhuanji wenxue* 傳記文學 42, no. 4 (1983): 138–39.

Zhang Xuejun 張學君. *Shiye zhi meng: Zhang Jian zhuan* 實業之夢: 張謇夢 (Dreaming of industry: a biography of Zhang Jian). Chengdu: Sichuan renmin chubanshe, 1995.

Zhang Zhidong 張之洞. *Zhang Wenxiang gong nianpu* 張文襄公年譜 (Chronological biography of Zhang Zhidong). 2 vols. Beijing: Tianhua yinshuguan, 1939.

———. *Zhang Wenxiang gong quanji* 張文襄公全集 (Complete works of Zhang Zhidong). Taibei: Wenhai chubanshe, 1970.

Zhang Ziqiang 張自強. "Beijing chengnei de Tongzhou huiguan" 北京城內的通州會館 (The Tongzhou *huiguan* in the city of Beijing). *Nantong jingu* 南通今古 1991, no. 5: 41.

Zheng Changgan 鄭昌淦. *Ming Qing nongmin shangpin jingji* 明清農民商品經濟 (The agricultural commodities economy in the Ming and Qing). Beijing: Renmin chubanshe, 1989.

Zheng Zeqing 鄭澤青. "Zhu Baosan" 朱葆三 (Zhu Baosan). In *Zhongguo shi maiban* 中國十買辦 (Ten Chinese compradors), ed. Xu Mao 徐矛, pp. 113–39. Shanghai: Shanghai renmin chubanshe, 1996.

Zhong Jiasong 鐘佳松. *Mao Dun zhuan* 茅盾傳 (Biography of Mao Dun). Beijing: Dongfang chubanshe, 1996.

Zhong Xiangcai 鐘祥財. *Zhongguo jindai minzu qiyejia jingji sixiang shi* 中國近代民族企業家經濟思想史 (The economic thinking of modern Chinese entrepreneurs). Shanghai: Shanghai shehui kexueyuan chubanshe, 1992.

Zhongguo dabaike quanshu: fangzhi 中國大百科全書：紡織 (Encyclopaedia of China: textiles). Beijing: Zhongguo dabaike quanshu chubanshe, 1992.

Zhongguo di'er lishi dang'anguan 中國第二歷史檔案館 and Shen Jiawu 沈家五, eds. *Zhang Jian nongshang zongzhang renqi jingji ziliao xuanbian* 張謇農商總長任期經濟資料選編 (Selection materials on economics from Zhang Jian's tenure as minister of agriculture and commerce). Nanjing: Nanjing daxue chubanshe, 1987.

Zhongguo jingji quanshu 中國經濟全書 (Complete book on the Chinese economy). Tokyo, 1908.

Zhongguo kexueyuan. Shanghai jingji yanjiusuo 中國科學院上海經濟研究所. *Hengfeng shachang de fazhan yu gaizao* 恆豐紗廠的發展與改造 (The development and transformation of the Hengfeng spinning mills). Shanghai: Renmin chubanshe, 1959 (1958).

Zhongguo min(si)ying jingji yanjiuhui. Mishuchu 中國民(私)營經濟研究會秘書處. *Zhongguo minying qiyejia liezhuan, 1997* 中國民營企業家列傳 (Biographies of Chinese entrepreneurs with private operations in 1997). Beijing: Jingji guanli chubanshe, 1998.

Zhongguo renmin yinhang. Shanghai shi fenhang. Jinrong yanjiushi 中國人民銀行上海市分行金融研究室. *Jincheng yinhang shiliao* 金城銀行史料 (Historical materials on the Jincheng Bank). Shanghai: Shanghai renmin chubanshe, 1983.

———. *Shanghai shangye chuxu yinhang shiliao* 上海商業儲蓄銀行史料 (Historical material on the Shanghai Commercial and Savings Bank). Shanghai: Shanghai renmin chubanshe, 1990.

Zhou Gaochao 周高潮. "1910 nian–1949 nian zai Rugao chuban de baokan tonglan" 1910 年–1949 年在如皋出版的報刊通覽 (Survey of newspapers and journals published in Rugao between 1910 and 1949). In *Rugao wenshi ziliao* 如皋文史資料 (Rugao historical materials), ed. Zhengxie Rugao xian weiyuanhui 政協如皋縣委員會, 4: 1–21. Rugao, 1989.

Zhou Sizhang 周思璋. "Jiefang qian Ru cheng de shehui cishan jigou" 解放前如城的社會慈善機構 (Charitable organizations in Rugao city before the liberation). In *Rugao wenshi ziliao* 如皋文史資料 (Historical materials on Rugao), ed. Zhengxie Rugao shi weiyuanhui 政協如皋縣委員會, 6: 44–52. Rugao, 1991.

———. "Jiefang qian Ru cheng de tongye gongsuo" 解放前如城的同業工所 (Professional organizations in Rugao city before the liberation). In *Rugao wenshi ziliao* 如皋文史資料 (Rugao historical materials), ed. Zhengxie Rugao xian weiyuanhui 政協如皋縣委員會, 4: 96–99. Rugao, 1989.

Zhou Yumin 周育民. *Wan Qing caizheng yu shehui bianqian* 晚清財政與社會變遷 (Fiscal policies of the late Qing and social transformation). Shanghai: Shanghai renmin chubanshe, 2000.

Zhu Peilian 朱培連, comp. *Jiangsu sheng ji liushisi xian shi zhilüe* 江蘇省及六十四縣市志略 (Historical gazetteer of Jiangsu province and its 64 counties). Taibei: Guoshiguan, 1987.

Zhu Xinquan 朱信泉. "Zhang Jian" 張謇. In *Minguo renwu zhuan* 民國人物傳 (Biographies of notable people of the Republican era), ed. Li Xin 李新 and Sun Sibai 孫思白, 1: 259–65. Beijing: Zhonghua Shuju, 1978.

Zhu Ying 朱英. "Lun Qing mo de jingji fagui" 論清末的經濟法規 (Economic regulations at the end of the Qing dynasty). *Lishi yanjiu* 歷史研究 1993, no. 5: 92–109.

Zhu Yingui 朱隱貴. "Cong Dasheng shachang kan Zhongguo zaoqi gufenzhi qiye de tedian" 從大生紗廠看中國早期股份製企業的特點 (A review of the characteristics of China's early incorporated enterprises based on the Dasheng cotton mills). *Zhongguo jingjishi yanjiu* 中國經濟史研究 63, no. 3 (2001): 49–59.

———. *Guojia ganyu jingji yu Zhong Ri jindaihua* 國家干預經濟與中日近代化 (The interfering state in the economy and the modernization of China and Japan). Beijing: Dongfang chubanshe, 1994.

———. "Jindai Zhongguo de diyi pi gufenzhi qiye" 近代中國的第一批股份製企業 (The first group of shareholding enterprises in modern China). *Lishi yanjiu* 歷史研究 2001, no. 5: 19–29.

———. "1927–1937 nian de Zhongguo lunchuan hangyunye" 1927–1937 年的中國輪船航運業 (China's steamship transportation sector, 1927–37). *Zhongguo jingjishi yanjiu* 中國經濟史研究 57, no. 1 (Mar. 2000): 37–54.

Zhu Zhenhua 朱鎮華. *Zhongguo jinrong jiushi* 中國金融舊事 (Financial matters in old China). Beijing: Zhongguo guoji guangbo chubanshe, 1991.

Zhu Zhiqian 朱志騫. *Zhang Jian de shiye zhuzhang* 張謇的實業主張 (Zhang Jian's views on industry). Taibei: Jiaxin shuini gongsi wenhua jijinhui, 1972.

Zhuogang Dayu yanken gongsi siwei nian disijie zhanglüe 拙港大預鹽墾公司巳未年第四屆帳略 (The fourth financial statement, 1919, of the Dayu Land Reclamation Company at Zhuogang). N.p., 1919.

ZJZJL, see Zhang Jian. *Zhang Jizhi jiulu.*

Zuijin zhi wushi nian (Shenbaoguan wushi zhounian jinian) 最近之五十年(申報館五十周年記念) (The past fifty years [Commemorating the fiftieth anniversary of the Shenbao press]). Shanghai, 1922.

Character List

Entries are alphabetized letter by letter, ignoring word and syllable breaks, with the exception of personal names, which are ordered first by the surname and then by the given name.

Aiyiji 艾益吉

bang 幫
bangdong 幫董
baogongzhi 包工制
baoshenzhi 包身制
Beiyang haijun zhangcheng 北洋海軍章程
Beiyang Lanzhou guankuang youxian gongsi 北洋蘭州官礦有限公司
bieshu 別墅
bu 步
buzhuang 布莊

chang 廠
changgong dongshi 廠工董事
Changle 常樂
changyue 廠約
changzhang 廠長
Changzhou 常州
chazhangyuan 查帳員
Chen Chunquan 陳春泉
Chen Guangfu 陳光甫

Chen San 陳三
Chen Shiyun 陳石雲
Chen Weiyong 陳維鏞
chengbao chang 成包廠
chengbao jingying 承包經營
chengnei 城内
Chongming 崇明
chongzi 蟲子
churu zongzhang 出入總帳
cuishou gekuan 催收各款
cun 存
cusha chang 粗紗廠

Dada lunbu gongsi 大達輪埠公司
Dada matou 大達碼頭
Dafeng 大豐
Dagang 大綱
Dalai 大賚
Dalong 大隆
Dalu 大陸
Dantu 丹徒
danwei 單位
dao 道
daode 道德

daotai 道臺

Dasheng 大生

Dasheng fangzhi gongsi 大生紡織
　公司

Dasheng gufen youxian gongsi
　大生股份有限公司

Dasheng matou 大生碼頭

Dasheng mingxia 大生名下

Dasheng shachang 大生紗廠

Dayoujin 大有晉

Dayu 大裕

Deji 得記

diandang 典當

dianyue 佃約

diaohui gekuan 調匯各款

diaohui li 調匯利

difang 地方

difang zizhi 地方自治

Doitsujin shoyū zaisan 德人所有
　財產

Dongbei 東北

dong gongfang 東公房

dongshi 董事

dongshiju 董事局

Du Yuesheng 杜月笙

Dun ji 敦記

Dunyu tang 敦裕堂

fahuan 發還

Fan Dangshi 藩當世

Fan Fen 樊芬

Fan Xuqing 樊序卿

faqiren 發起人

faren 法人

fatuan 法團

fenhu 分戶

fucheng xiang 附城鄉

Fuxin 復新

fuzhai lei 付債類

Gao An 高安

Gao Manhua 高滿華

Gao Qing 高清

Gao Shunqin 高舜琴

Gao Zhenbai 高眞白

gehu qiankuan 各戶錢款

ge shiye gongsi 各實業公司

gexiang diankuan 各項墊款

ge zhishi xinshui 各執事薪水

gong 工

gongchang (factory; Japanese: *kōjō*)
　工場

gongchang (workshop) 工廠

gongfang 工房

gongguo 公過

gongji 公積

Gong ji 公記

gongkuan 公款

gongren 工人

gong shou 公手

gongsi 公司

Gongsi lü 公司律

gongsi zhi jisuan 公司之計算

gongsuo 公所

gongtou 工頭

gongyi cishan diankuan 公益慈善
　墊款

gu 股

guan 官

guanban 官辦

guandu shangban 官督商辦

Guangjiao si 廣教寺

guangong zhishi 管工執事

Guangsheng 廣生

Guan ji 貫記

guanji 官機

guanji guanli 官機官利

guanjigu chengben 官機股成本

guanli 官利

guanshang heban 官商合辦
guanxi 關係
guanzhuang 關莊
gudao 孤島
gudong hu 股東户
gufen 股份
gufen youxian gongsi 股份有限
　公司
Guo Xun 郭勳
gupiao 股票

Haifuzhen 海復鎮
Haimen 海門
hang 行
hanjian 漢奸
Hanlin 翰林
Hanlin yuan xiuzhuan 翰林院
　修撰
Hanmolin 翰墨林
Hanyeping 漢冶萍
hao 號
Haohe 濠河
Heng ji 恆記
hezuo 合作
Hou Sheng 厚生
Hu Shi 胡適
huabu hang 花布行
Huacheng 華成
huahong 花紅
Huaibei 淮北
Huaihai 淮海
Huaihai shiye yinhang 淮海實業
　銀行
Huang Jinrong 黃金榮
Huashang shachang lianhehui 華商
　紗廠聯合會
Huasheng 華盛
huayi 花衣
huazhan 花棧
Hubei zhiguanju 湖北織官局

Huguang 湖廣
huiguan 會館
huikuan 匯款
Huizhou 徽州
hutoupai 虎頭派
Hu zongzhangfang 滬總帳房

ji 記
Jian Zhaonan 簡照南
Jiang Xishen 蔣錫紳
Jiangbei xingye gongsi 江北興業
　公司
Jiangnan 江南
Jiangnan zhizaoju 江南制造局
jianhua chang 揀花廠
jianjie 間接
ji chengben 機成本
jiemeihui 姐妹會
Ji gong 記公
jigong 機工
jijiao 雞腳
jin chang 進廠
Jincheng 金城
Jingjiang 靖江
jingli dongshi 經理董事
jinhua chusha heyu 進花出紗
　核餘
jinrong huodong jiguan 金融活動
　機關
Jinsha 金沙
jinshi 進士
Jiulong 久隆
jizhang 記帳
ju 局
juan 卷
juren 舉人
Juru tang 具孺堂

kaifa qu 開發區
Kaiping meikuang 開平煤礦

kuaiji 會計

Laiyuan 賚源
lanbu 藍布
Langshan 狼山
lanyin huabu 藍印花布
laodong mofan 勞動模範
laoshu 老鼠
li 利
Li Guangquan 李廣泉
Li Hongzhang 李鴻章
Li Jisheng 李濟生
Li Shengbo 李昇伯
Liang Qichao 梁啓超
lianggong 良工
Liangjiang 兩江
lijin 厘金
lijuan 厘捐
Lin Lansheng 林藍生
lingong 臨工
Liu Guixing 劉桂馨
Liu Hongsheng 劉鴻生
Liu Housheng 劉厚生
Liu Kunyi 劉坤一
Liu Yishan 劉一山
liyuan 利原
Lu Jingwei 陸景魏
Lunchuan zhaoshangju 輪船招
　商局
Lüsi 呂四

Ma Yinchu 馬寅初
maiban 買辦
Mao Dun 茅盾
maoyi qingxing jielüe 貿易情形
　節略
matou 碼頭
Meng Luochuan 孟洛川
mianye gonghui 棉業公會
minsheng 民生

miqie 密切
mofan 模範
mu 畝
Mu Ouchu 穆藕初
Muchou tang 慕疇堂
mufu 幕府

namowen 拿麼溫
Nantong 南通
Nantong fangzhi zhuanmen xuexiao
　南通紡織專門學校
Nantong moshi 南通模式
Nantong ren 南通人
Nantong xian 南通縣
Nantong xian Dasheng shachang
　南通縣大生紗廠
Nantong youyi julebu 南通友誼俱
　樂部
Nanyang 南洋
neiliu 內流
Nie Qigui 聶緝槼
Nie Yuntai 聶雲臺
Ningbo 寧波
nonghui 農會
nügong 女工

Pan Huamao 潘華茂
pancha shizai 盤查實在
pifasuo 批發所
Pingchao 平潮
pingmin 平民

Qianfo si 千佛寺
qianzhuang 錢莊
Qidong 啓東
Qing bang 青幫
qinghua chang 清花廠
Qixin yanghui gongsi 啓新洋灰
　公司
qiyejia 企業家

qu 區
quan zhi shi 勸之事

riyeban sishi 日夜班司事
Rong 榮
Rong Zongjing 榮宗敬
Rugao 如皋
Ruifuxiang 瑞蚨祥
Ruo ji 若記

sanfang you qian, sifang you ming
　三房有錢, 四房有名
Sanxin gongsi 三鑫公司
Sha Yuanbing 沙元炳
shachang 紗廠
shadi 沙地
shahua jiaohuanchu 沙花交換處
shamin 沙民
shang 商
shangban 商辦
shang bu 商部
Shanghai jiqi zhibuju 上海機器織
　布局
Shanghai shangwu yinshuguan
　上海商務印書館
Shanghai shangye chuxu yinhang
　上海商業儲蓄銀行
shanghui 商會
Shanxi shangwu zongju 山西商務
　總局
shazhan 紗棧
shazhuang 紗莊
shen 紳
Shen Binyi 沈賓義
Shen Jingfu 沈敬夫
Shen Shou 沈壽
Shen Xiejun 沈燮均
Shen Yanmou 沈燕謀
shendong gongfei xinshui 紳董公
　費薪水

sheng 昇
Sheng Xuanhuai 盛宣懷
shenshang 紳商
Shenxin 申新
shi 市
Shigang 石港
shitou 事頭
shitou fang 事頭房
shiye gongsi 實業公司
shiyejia 實業家
shou 收
shouhua chu 收花處
shuilong 水龍
Shun ji 順記
shuolüe 説略
sige xiandaihua 四個現代化
si gongzi 四公子
siguo 私過
songyin huidan 送銀回單
Subei 蘇北
sui 歲
Sui ji 遂記
Sun Chuanfang 孫傳芳
suozhang 所長
sushe 宿舍

tang 堂
Tangjiazha 唐家閘
ti 堤
Tianhou 天后
Tianshenggang 天生港
tiao 條
ti jingli 堤經理
tonggong 童工
Tonghai 通海
Tonghai ge shiye wanglai 通海各
　實業往來
Tonghai kenmu gongsi zhaodian
　zhangcheng 通海墾牧公司招
　佃章程

Tonghai shiye gongsi 通海實業公司
Tongli 通利
tongren gongjijin 同人公積金
Tongrentai 同仁泰
Tongsui 通遂
Tongxing 通興
Tongyang 通揚
tongzhi jingji 統制經濟
Tongzhou 通州
Tongzhou Dasheng shachang 通州大生紗廠
Tongzhou zhili zhou 通州直隸州
touban sishi 頭班司事
tubu 土布
tuchan tuxiao 土產土銷
tuhao lieshen 土豪劣紳
Tui ji 退記
turen 土人

waidiren 外地人
waisha 外沙
wanglai 往來
Wu Changqing 吳長慶
Wu gong ji 吳公記
Wu Jichen 吳寄塵
Wu Youchun 吳又春
wufa 無法
Wujin 武進
Wusong 吳淞

xian 縣
xiangzhen qiye 鄉鎮企業
xianzhi 縣知
xiaogong 小工
Xiao ji 孝記
xiao shehui 小社會
xiaowu jian dawu 小巫見大巫
xieli 協理
xi gongfang 西工房

Xin'an gongshan tang 新安公善堂
xingming 姓名
xin gongfang 新工房
xing zhi shi 刑之事
xinzheng 新政
xisha chang 細紗廠
xitong 系統
xizhe 息折
Xu Gengqi 徐賡起
Xu Jingren 徐靜仁
Xu Jingweng 徐靜翁
Xu Xianglin 徐翔林
Xu Zhongzheng 徐仲鉦
Xue Nanming 薛南溟
xuehui 學會
Xujin ji 許金記
xunding 巡丁

yahua chang 軋花廠
yanglou 洋樓
yangshi 洋式
Yanye 鹽業
yaosha chang 搖紗廠
Ye 業
Yekaitai 葉開泰
yi Hua zhi Hua 以華制華
yichang 一廠
yinqian zongzhangfang 銀錢總帳房
Yintie Hongfang 印鐵烘防
yintuan 銀團
Yisheng 頤生
yizhan yangzhan 以戰養戰
yizhuang 意莊
yizu 議租
Yong'an (Wing On) 永安
Yongfeng 永豐
yongyuan heban 永遠合辦
Yongzhong 永中
youxian gongsi 有限公司

yuan 元
Yuan Shikai 袁世凱
Yuanfahang 元發行
Yubei lixian gonghui 預備立憲公
　會
Yuchigang 魚池港
Yudesheng 裕德盛
Yu ji 裕記
Yun Zuqi 惲祖祁
Yuyuan 裕元

zahu 雜戶
zai 在
zanji qiankuan 暫記錢款
zaomin 灶民
zhahua chang 扎花廠
Zhang Bishi 張弼士
Zhang Cha 張察
Zhang Chen 張忱
Zhang gong shou 張公手
Zhang Jian 張謇
Zhang Jingli 張敬禮
Zhang Jizhi 張季直
Zhang Liang 張梁
Zhang Pengnian 張彭年
Zhang Rouwu 張柔武
Zhang Se'an 張嗇安
Zhang Seweng 張嗇翁
Zhang Wu 張吳
Zhang Xiaolin 張曉林
Zhang Xiaoruo 張孝若
Zhang Xiaoxu 張孝胥
Zhang Xu 張徐
Zhang Zhidong 張之洞

zhangcheng 章程
zhangfang 帳房
zhangfang xiansheng 帳房先生
zhanglüe 帳略
zhejiu 折舊
zhen 鎮
Zhenjiang 鎮江
zhi 支
zhijie 直接
Zhili 直隸
zhishi 執事
zhiyuan 職員
Zhongfu 中孚
Zhongnan 中南
Zhongxiu 鐘秀
Zhongyi 中一
Zhou Xuexi 周學熙
Zhu 褚
Zhu Chou 朱籌
zhuangyuan 狀元
zhuangyuan zibenjia 狀元資本家
zichan lei 資產類
Zisheng 資生
Ziye 子夜
zong banshichu 總辦事處
zong shanghui 總商會
zongli 總理
zonglu 總錄
Zunsu tang 尊素堂
zuo gong 做工
zuo gongtou 做工頭
zuo shengyi de ren 做生意的人
zuo tian 做田
Zuo zhuan 左傳

Index

Harvard East Asian Monographs

(* out-of-print)

Harvard East Asian Monographs

Harvard East Asian Monographs

Harvard East Asian Monographs

Harvard East Asian Monographs

Harvard East Asian Monographs

Harvard East Asian Monographs

Harvard East Asian Monographs

Harvard East Asian Monographs